THE WORLD ENCYCLOPEDIA OF
FLAGS

THE WORLD ENCYCLOPEDIA OF
FLAGS

The definitive guide to international flags, banners, standards and ensigns

ALFRED ZNAMIEROWSKI

LORENZ BOOKS

First published in 1999 by Lorenz Books

LORENZ BOOKS are available for bulk purchase for sales promotion and for premium use.
For details, write or call the sales director, Lorenz Books, 27 West 20th Street, New York, NY 10011; (800) 354-9657

ISBN 0 7548 0167 5

Publisher: Joanna Lorenz
Project Editor: Debra Mayhew
Designer: Michael Morey
Flag artwork: Alfred Znamierowski
Map artwork: Mike Taylor

Printed and bound in Italy

1 3 5 7 9 10 8 6 4 2

Author's Acknowledgements

The author wishes to dedicate this book to the memory of his late teacher and friend Dr Ottfried Neubecker,
and to extend thanks for encouragement, help and support to Beata Gierblinska (Warsaw),
Whitney Smith (Winchester, Massachussetts), Roman Klimes (Bonn) and Jacek Skorupski (Warsaw).

Publisher's Acknowledgements

The publishers would like to thank: The Flag Design Center, Warsaw, for use of images from the archive;
Judy Cox; John Clarke; and Dr Lawrie Wright of Queen Mary and Westfield College, University of London.

The publisher wouldalso like to thank the following for kindly supplying photographs for this book: page 24 *b* Bruno Barbey at Magnum;
page 33 *br* Beata Gierblinska; page 40 *br* Miroslaw Stelmach; page 41 *m* NASA; page 43 *tl* Chad Ehlers and Tony Stone Images,
tr Ron Sherman and Tony Stone Images; page 45 *tr* Ron Sherman and Tony Stone Images; page 47 *m* Raghu Rai and Magnum;
page 50 *b* Hulton Getty; page 97 *b* National Geographic Society; page 231 *tl tm m* (3 artworks) Der Flggenkurier (Achim);
page 233 *br* Instytut Wzornictwa Przemyslowego (Warsaw); page 235 *tr* Alex Majoli and Magnum, *bl* James Nachtwey and Magnum,
br Robert Van Der Hilst and Tony Stone Images; page 248 *bl* A. Hornak and Westminster Abbey; page 249 *tr* Bruno Barbey and Magnum.

Every effort has been made to obtain permission to reproduce copyright material, but there may be cases where we have
been unable to trace a copyright holder. The publisher will be happy to correct any omissions in future printings.

All opinions expressed in this book are those of the author.

◆ **HALF TITLE PAGE**
The Presidential flag of Gabon, since 1961.

◆ **FRONTISPIECE**
Armorial banners of Bavaria, Brunswick and
Saxony carried in the triumphal procession
of the Emporer of Germany Maximilian I at
the beginning of the 16th century.

◆ **TITLE PAGE**
A member of the pan-African flag family:
the national flag of Zaire from 1971–1997.

◆ **OPPOSITE PAGE**
A member of the Muslim crescent flag
family: the national flag of South Arabia
from 1959–1967.

CONTENTS

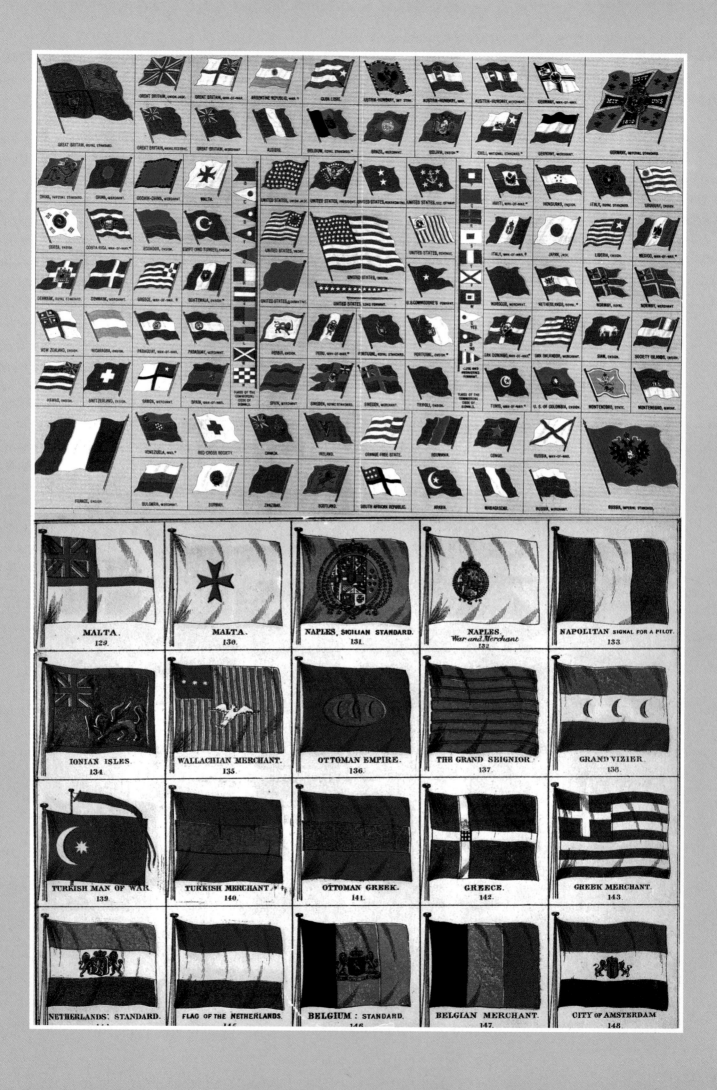

MALTA.
129.

MALTA.
130.

NAPLES, SICILIAN STANDARD.
131.

NAPLES.
War and Merchant
132.

NAPOLITAN SIGNAL FOR A PILOT.
133.

IONIAN ISLES.
134.

WALLACHIAN MERCHANT.
135.

OTTOMAN EMPIRE.
136.

THE GRAND SEIGNIOR
137.

GRAND VIZIER
138.

TURKISH MAN OF WAR.
139.

TURKISH MERCHANT.
140.

OTTOMAN GREEK.
141.

GREECE.
142.

GREEK MERCHANT.
143.

NETHERLANDS: STANDARD.

FLAG OF THE NETHERLANDS.

BELGIUM : STANDARD.

BELGIAN MERCHANT.
147.

CITY OF AMSTERDAM
148.

Flags Through the Ages

The fascinating story of flags is closely interwoven with historical events, reflecting the aspirations and lives of people over many centuries. The eagle-topped standards of the Roman legions, the flame-edged flag of Genghis Khan and the heraldic banners carried by medieval knights in tournament are all part of a continuing development that has led to the flags we know today. Changes in society can be seen in the representations of flags in early maps, books and art, many of which are very decorative. Modern flags show how the revolutions of the 19th century abolished the old order of monarchy, replacing the traditional heraldic flags with simple symbolic designs that carried a very different political and ideological message.

In a useful reference section the physical characteristics of flags are described in detail, followed by the various types of flag, flag usage and etiquette, each with its own separate glossary for ease of reference. A discussion of the flags of emperors, sovereigns and presidents and of government is followed by chapters on military signs from battle banners to war ensigns, including the flags of the armed services. A final, important chapter on flag families shows how the flags of a few countries have influenced those of the rest of the world.

In some flags an emblem such as the Muslim crescent or Scandinavian cross shows that it belongs to a particular "flag family". Kinship within flag families sometimes reaches across the world, indicating that these countries are somehow connected even if physical ties such as colonies no longer exist.

◆ **OPPOSITE ABOVE**
Various types of flags and ensigns as well as royal standards, distinguishing flags, jacks and pennants are represented on this American chart, published by F.E. Wright in 1896.

◆ **OPPOSITE BELOW**
Among flags presented on this plate from Colton's *Delineation of Flags of All Nations* (1862) are royal standards of Naples, the Netherlands and Belgium, the civil ensigns of Turkey and Greece introduced at the end of the 18th century, and the flag of the Ionian Islands under British rule (1817–1864).

The Origin and Development of Flags

Symbols are sacred things, and one of the chief that every man holds dear is the national flag. Deep down in our nature is the strong emotion that swells the heart and brings the tear and makes us follow the flag and die round it rather than let it fall into the hands of an enemy. This is no new emotion, no growth of a few generations, but an inheritance from the ages before history began.

W.J. GORDON, *FLAGS OF THE WORLD*, LONDON, 1915

The origin of flags lies in our remote prehistoric past. When people started to form large groups to live and hunt together, they appointed a leader to rule them and settle disputes. As a mark of office the leader wore a ceremonial head-dress and held a long decorated staff, rod or spear, topped with an ornament or emblem. The staff was also used as a visible sign to rally around, or to point out the direction of a march or attack. This proto-flag is known as a vexilloid.

Later in China, a different tradition developed when silk was invented. This strong, light fabric was ideal for making banners, which were much easier to carry than vexilloids and are easier to see from a distance. From China the use of fabric flags spread to Mongolia, India and Persia, and finally they arrived in Rome and the rest of Europe.

The first vexilloids and flags were military and ceremonial signs. But by the 12th century they began to serve as a way of identifying rulers and their domains, and nationality at sea. During the next two centuries cities and guilds adopted their own flags, and the 17th century saw the introduction of standardized regimental colours, war ensigns, jacks and the house flags of the trading companies. The first national flags on land appeared in the last quarter of the 18th century, as did the flags of yacht clubs. During the 19th and 20th centuries a host of other flags also appeared: flags of government agencies and officials; provincial flags; rank flags in all branches of the armed forces; and flags of schools, universities, scientific institutions, organizations, political parties, trades unions and guerrilla movements. There are also flags of nationalities and ethnic groups, flags of business corporations and sporting clubs, and occasionally flags for fun. It seems that you have no identity unless you have a flag.

◆ **ABOVE**
Standard of West Egypt, found on the sarcophagus of Khons-mose (c.1000 BC).

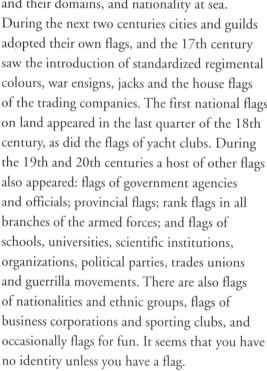

◆ **ABOVE**
Detail of the palette of Narmer, 3000 BC. The palette is in the Egyptian Museum in Cairo.

◆ **BELOW LEFT**
Detail of the Osiris' misteria stela (2000 BC).

◆ **BELOW**
Standard of the Two Falcons *nome*.

Vexilloids

The original vexilloids were made of wood, feathers and the horns, tails, hooves and skins of animals. Later ornaments or emblems on top of the staff were made of carved and painted wood or metal. We know this from the well-documented Aztec vexilloids, and those of societies that 100 years ago still lived in Stone Age conditions. The characteristic feature of the Aztec vexilloids was extensive use of green quetzal feathers, metals such as gold, silver and copper, and precious stones. The vexilloids still used today by tribes in New Guinea are ancient Melanesian; the way they are made and their symbolism reveal no influence from other cultures. They consist mostly of wood, dried grass and feathers, with emblems of painted wood, feathers and pieces of cloth.

The oldest known vexilloids appear on Egyptian pottery of the Gerzean period (3400 BC) and on the reverse of the King Narmer palette (3000 BC). They were the signs of *nomes*, the provinces of pre-dynastic Egypt. The *nomes* were named after things or animals (Two Falcons, Sceptre, Ibis, Double Feather, and so on), which were depicted as highly stylized emblems on the vexilloids. Some provincial vexilloids displayed the emblems of local gods. They were made of wood, and the emblems were painted.

There is very little evidence of Assyrian, Babylonian and Persian vexilloids, although the oldest vexilloid still in existence was carried in Persia 5000 years ago. It has a metal staff, with a finial in the form of an eagle, and a square metal "flag" covered with reliefs. Two primitive vexilloids appear on a stela of Naramsin, King of Babylonia (*c.*3000 BC). At Alacahöyük, in north-central Turkey, archaeologists have found Hittite standards dating from *c.*2400–2200 BC. The metal emblems show a stag, a stag with two bulls and a sun disc.

The Romans copied the use of vexilloids as well as the eagle emblem from Persia. The military standard (*signum*) of the Roman legions consisted of a lance with a silver-plated shaft, topped with a crosspiece carrying figures of various beasts. The most important was an eagle

◆ ABOVE
Standard of the Double Feather *nome*.

◆ ABOVE
Dragon standard from *Psalterium Aureum* (9th century).

◆ BELOW
Vexilloids: *(left to right)* Assyrian, Roman, Aztec, Mongolian, Japanese.

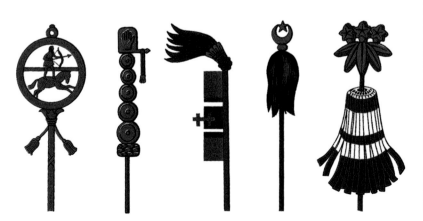

(*aquila*). Attached to the shaft were several metal rings in the form of a laurel wreath, and medallions with the eagle of Jupiter or with portraits of the emperor and members of the imperial house. According to Pliny the Elder:

Gaius Marius in his second consulship (103 BC) assigned the eagle exclusively to the Roman legions. Before that period it had only held the first rank, there being four others as well – the wolf, the minotaur, the horse and the wild boar – each of which preceded a single division.

Popular in the Roman Army from the 2nd century was the *draco* (dragon flag), borrowed from the Parthians or Sarmatians, who used this kind of flag several centuries earlier. A hollow bronze dragon's head sat at the top of the staff with a serpent-shaped silk windsock attached. When the wind blew it moved like a serpent and a device in its head made a whistling noise.

The dragon flag was used in Britain during the Dark Ages, and in the 6th century was adopted by the Saxon conquerors. It was borne in front of the armies of the Anglo-Saxons and Normans at least until the 12th century.

The Mongols also had an instantly recognizable vexilloid consisting of a staff topped with a metal ball or spear, with a horse's tail attached to it. These spread quickly among the Turkish people; in the Turkish Army they became the sign of a commander and in the 17th and 18th centuries they were carried before the commanders-in-chief of the Polish Army.

EARLY FLAGS

Long before flags appeared in Europe they had been used in China. Written sources even mention the flag of the Yellow Emperor, a mythological ancestor of the Chinese. The oldest iconographic information on the shape and function of flags in China dates from about 1500 BC. A bamboo staff was topped with a metal trident, to which were attached small rings holding tassels made of horses' tails. The number of narrow ribbons attached to the outer edge denoted the social rank of the flag-bearer, ranging from twelve for the Emperor down to just one for a functionary of the lowest rank. A long, wide, swallow-tailed ribbon was attached to make it into a signal for battle.

The Chinese, who first made cloth out of silk, were the first to make flags out of fabric and attach them sideways to the staff to form a banner. The hierarchy of Chinese society was reflected in a large number of different types of flag for use by the emperor, nobility, commanders of the imperial army, and governors of the provinces and counties. The most common flag symbols were a dragon, tiger, hawk, turtle and snake. The emperor had five chariots, each flying a different flag in yellow, blue, red, white and black. In the course of history the shape of Chinese flags changed to square or triangular with "flammules" (flame-shaped edges), but the hierarchy reflected in the number of flags was maintained. For example, in the 19th century there were nine classes of mandarins and the army used some 50 different flags; there were also special flags for eleven ranks of envoys.

After the Mongols under Kublai Khan conquered China in 1279 they also began to use triangular flags with flammules, mounted sideways on a staff that was topped with the Chinese trident. The Mongols added flames to the trident and attached horses' tails to its base. This was the shape of the flag of Genghis Khan, which carried an image of a gerfalcon (gyrfalcon) and had nine yaks' tails attached to the nine flammules.

The earliest accounts of a flag in Europe are those of Greek writers, who mention a purple flag as the sign of the admiral's ship in the Athenian navy at the end of the 5th century BC. Two Samnite flags from 330 BC appear on frescoes from Paestum (now in the National Museum in Naples), which are the oldest known illustrations of flags in Europe. In the same museum there is a huge mosaic from Pompeii, depicting Alexander the Great defeating the Persians. It shows a Persian standard, an almost square piece of cloth hanging from a crossbar fastened underneath the spear-top of the lance; the bottom edge of the cloth is fringed. According to sketches made when the mosaic was discovered in 1831, the red field carried an image of a golden cock, the Zoroastrian symbol known as *parodash*.

A flag of exactly the same shape and mounted on the staff in the same way was adopted by the Romans for their cavalry and named *vexillum*.

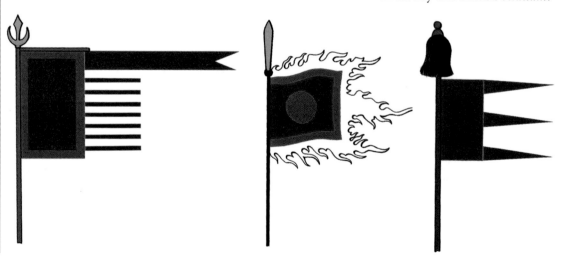

♦ **FAR LEFT**
Reconstruction of the earliest Chinese banner.

♦ **MIDDLE LEFT**
Flag of Kublai Khan's armada, (13th century).

♦ **LEFT**
Mongol banner (c.1310).

The cloth was red, sometimes carrying the name
of the unit, an emblem or a portrait of the
emperor. There was a heavy fringe on the
bottom edge, and the cloth was fastened so that
it always looked draped.

Another similar flag was the *labarum* adopted
by Constantine the Great after his victory over
his rival Maxentius in AD 312, won in the name
of the Christian cross. The purple cloth carried
the gold monogram of Christ, formed of the

first two letters of the Greek word for Christ,
ΧΡΙΣΤΟΣ. The shaft was encased in beaten
gold, and bore medallions with the portraits
of Constantine and his two sons. It seems that
there were two forms of *labarum*; the other one
displayed Christ's monogram at the top of the
staff and the portraits appeared on the cloth.

In the 6th century the Byzantine army
replaced the Roman *vexillum* with a square or
rectangular banner, with one or two triangular
tongues extending from the top edge. In the
8th century they spread to Hungary and Central
Europe. Also in the 8th century the Arabs began
to use triangular flags that were plain black or
white. Later they increased the range of colours
and the flags carried religious inscriptions and
geometric ornaments (because of the religious
ban on representational art).

One of the oldest flags in Europe was not
a flag at all. It was the blue cape of St Martin,
found in his grave by Clovis I of France (who
reigned AD 481–511) and adopted as his banner.
It was later carried in battle by French kings.
In peacetime the cape was kept in a specially
built oratory, which became known as a "chapel"
(from the Latin word *cappa*). Another non-flag
was the royal standard of the Persians, which
for several hundred years until the Muslim
conquest in the 7th century was a blacksmith's
leather apron.

The very beginning of the 9th century saw
the introduction of a new form of flag, the
gonfanon. It is first seen in a mosaic that Pope

Leo III (AD *c*.750–816) had placed in the Triclinium of the Lateran Palace in Rome in about AD 800. On the right-hand side the mosaic shows Christ handing the keys of the Church to Pope Sylvester and a flag to Constantine, while on the left St Peter presents a cloak to Pope Leo and a flag to Charlemagne. The mosaic commemorates the crowning of Charlemagne as emperor, when he received from the Patriarch of Jerusalem the keys of that city and a flag. The original mosaic has not survived but contemporary sources tell us that the green field of the gonfanon was sprinkled with gold and bore six concentric rings of red, black and gold. This event started a tradition of ceremonial presentations of flags by ecclesiastical authorities to rulers or leaders of expeditions approved by the Church. Emperors also ceremonially handed flags to their subjects. The

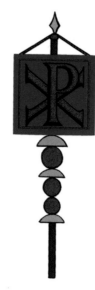

♦ ABOVE
Labarum of Constantine the Great.

form of the gonfanon was for several centuries reserved for rulers, but after the 11th century it prevailed in the army and from the 12th to the 14th centuries was used by cities.

From the late 8th century, northern European waters were the realm of the Vikings, whose longships sailed as far as Greenland and North America. They raided coastal towns and villages in Britain and France, sometimes settling and intermarrying with the local people. They were the first Europeans to use flags at sea, mounted on vertical staffs. The flags were triangular, with a slightly rounded outer edge; those mounted on the high bows of ships were probably vanes. A gilded vane dating from the 11th century, in the Historika Museet in Stockholm, has several holes along the curved edge to which rings with tassels could be attached to make the exact shape of the Viking flag. The Vikings had various flags, but the most important seems to have been the raven flag. Both the flag and the raven on its own also appear on Northumbrian coins of the first half of the 10th century.

The Bayeux Tapestry, made in about 1077, contains more than 70 embroidered scenes of the Norman Conquest of England in 1066. It illustrates a very similar flag to the Viking flag, carried immediately behind the Duke of Normandy, William the Conqueror and shows that by that time flags were already being made of cloth. Among the many banners depicted, most of the Norman ones bear a cross, which in pre-heraldic times was the main emblem used by both the military and seamen. More banners with the sign of the cross appeared during the First Crusade (1096–9). One is shown on the seal of Bohemund III, Prince of Antioch. The oldest known account of flags with crosses, the *Gesta Regis Henrici Secundi* by Benedict Abbas, tells us that on 13 January 1188 the Kings of England and France (together with their men) received a white and red cross respectively, while the Count of Flanders received a green cross. We do not know whether these banners were used exclusively on land or also at sea.

EARLY EUROPEAN FLAGS

PENNANT FROM AN IVORY PANEL MADE IN THE CIRCLE OF CHARLES THE BALD (AD *c*.840).

GONFANON FROM THE WESTMINSTER PSALTER (12TH CENTURY).

PENNANT FROM THE BAYEAUX TAPESTRY (AD *c*.1077).

GONFANON OF THE MILITIA OF VERONA (12TH CENTURY).

From the 9th to the 12th centuries merchant ships on the North Sea and the Baltic Sea carried a metal gridcross, a symbol of the king's protection, at the top of the mast. From at least the 12th century the same symbol, in the form of a staff topped with a cross, was used on land, mainly by princes and cities in the territories dependent on the German Empire. A second symbol of the king's protection also appeared in the 12th century: a gonfanon without any emblems, attached to a spear or to a staff topped with a cross. This is the *vexillo roseum imperiali* or the *Blutbanner* (blood banner), a red banner presented by the emperor to princes and counts. The *Blutbanner* gave them the right of judicial power over life and death in their domains, and imposed the obligation to contribute men for the imperial army. The *Blutbanner* was awarded also to the cities that became free imperial cities in the 12th and 13th centuries, and to the freed peasants of Schwyz in 1240.

At the beginning of the 13th century merchant ships in northern Europe began to fasten single-coloured gonfanons to the mast, topped with a cross. Those of the Hanseatic cities and of Denmark were red; the English gonfanon was presumably white, later to carry the red cross of St George. In the second half of the 13th century port cities began to differentiate their flags either by dividing them into different coloured areas or by adding simple emblems, the most common of which was the Christian cross. New flags in banner form were placed at the stern, while the mast still carried the single-coloured gonfanons, later replaced by pennants or banners. The oldest is the plain red flag of Hamburg; the date of its adoption is not known, but it was in use from at least the middle of the 13th century. A little later Riga and Lübeck adopted their flags, followed by Stralsund, Elbing, Danzig, Bremen and Rostock in the 14th century, and Königsberg, Wismar and Stettin in the 15th century.

The oldest flag on record in the Mediterranean region is that of Genoa; the earliest illustration, dated 1113, shows it as

FLAGS OF PORT CITIES OF NORTHERN EUROPE

HAMBURG · RIGA · LÜBECK · STRALSUND

ELBING · DANZIG · BREMEN

ROSTOCK · KÖNIGSBERG · WISMAR · STETTIN

◆ **ABOVE**
Raven flag
(9th century).

white with a red cross. Pisa received the red imperial banner in 1162. Both flags are much older than those of England or Hamburg, which they resemble. Even in the 13th century, when all of these flags were in existence, merchant vessels did not travel very long distances so it was impossible for an English ship to meet a vessel from Genoa or a vessel from Pisa to meet a ship from Hamburg, so the flags could not be confused. Nevertheless Pisa later added a distinctive white cross to its red flag, and the red flag of Hamburg was given a white shield with a red castle (since 1751 the white castle has been located directly on the red background).

In the 14th century the flags of Savoy and Denmark were also identical, but the Danish ships did not venture as far as the Mediterranean. When, 400 years later, they did sail there they adopted especially for that purpose the Danish merchant flag, which had a white square in the centre carrying the royal cipher.

THE AGE OF CHIVALRY

The invention of a helmet to cover and protect the face of a warrior, and thus hide his identity, was one reason why it became necessary to develop signs of identification. The other reason was the widespread use of the cross by all armed forces in Western Europe. The similarity between the banners of friend and foe could cause major misunderstandings on the battlefield.

The basic rules of heraldry were adopted during the Second Crusade (1147–9) and the returning knights took them back to their countries. In the Middle East they had seen the traditional stylization of natural and mythological beasts, and they decided that simple figures on contrasting backgrounds would make excellent signs of identification. The shield was the ideal background. The number of heraldic tinctures was limited to seven: five colours (red, blue, green, black and purple) and two metals (gold and silver). To achieve the best possible identification from a distance the rule of alternation was adopted, which forbade putting colour on colour or metal on metal. A "fimbriation", or border, of metal was used to separate adjacent areas of two colours. The only pre-heraldic device incorporated into the arms was the Christian cross, and to distinguish the crosses that appeared in many arms a great number of different shapes were invented. Other popular heraldic emblems included the lion, eagle, griffin, horse, fleur-de-lis, rose and various weapons.

The invention of heraldry not only helped to distinguish flags denoting ducal, princely or civic domains, but also led to a rapid growth in personal flags. As well as a coat of arms, each qualified person carried an armorial banner, which now became the principal kind of flag. It was either square or much wider than it was long, and sizes varied according to the rank of its owner. According to one medieval source, the banner of an emperor should be 1.8 m (2 yd) square, that of a king 1.5 m (5 ft) square, that of a prince or duke 1.2 m (4 ft) square, and that of an earl, marquis, viscount or baron 90 cm (3 ft) square.

The personal heraldic badges of rulers, unrelated to their coats of arms, appeared on their standards, banners and the flags of their retainers. The most famous ones still remembered are the white and red roses of York and Lancaster, the white boar of Richard III, the salamander of Francis I, the porcupine of Louis XII and the radiant sun of Louis XIV.

A distinct type of armorial flag, designed to indicate the rallying point or headquarters of the arms-bearer, or "armiger", was the standard. It was a long, tapering flag with a rounded swallow-tail, and it bore the livery colours arranged horizontally. The hoist carried either the national mark (for example, the cross of St George, the cross of St Andrew or the cross of Burgundy) or a coat of arms in the form of an armorial banner. Next appeared the heraldic badge of the arms-bearer with his motto, and then another badge or crest, and around the edge was a border of pieces in the livery colour.

◆ BELOW
Banners of Swiss troops, 15th century.

CIVIC BANNERS IN THE 14TH CENTURY

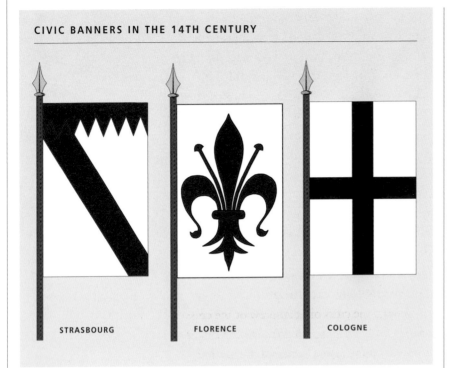

STRASBOURG   FLORENCE   COLOGNE

Only the arms-bearer could carry his banner or standard, so three other types of flag were used by his retainers: the guidon, pennon and badge-flag. The guidon was a simpler version of the standard. It was also tapered but was shorter with a descate outer edge (see *Flag Design*), bore the national device on the inner edge and had one badge on the livery colours. It was used on horseback, and was a precursor of the cavalry guidon. The pennon was a swallow-tailed flag carried on a mounted warrior's lance. In most cases it bore the badge on a background in the livery colours. The badge-flag was a rectangular flag with the background divided in the livery colours, bearing the heraldic badge or badges.

From the beginning of the heraldic period arms were also adopted and used by ecclesiastics and military orders such as the Knights Templar, the Knights of St John of Jerusalem, great Spanish and Portuguese orders and the Teutonic Knights. The arms and armorial banners of bishops and the abbots of monasteries did not represent them but the orders they temporarily represented; they were also signs of their domains. The rise of the guilds and universities also contributed to the increase in the use of arms and armorial banners as they began to

obtain charters from the crown and were granted arms. An even greater impact was created by the steady growth in the number of towns that adopted arms. Civic armorial banners became the real national flags for the burghers, as the symbols of their rights and privileges.

Not all banners in the Age of Chivalry were armorial. There was also extensive use of Christian symbols in non-heraldic form, including representations of the Holy Trinity, the Holy Ghost, the vernicle (veronica) and scenes of the Crucifixion. As well as banners with symbols of the saints, such as the cross of St George or the lion of St Mark, there were banners displaying the painted figures of saints with their attributes. The most popular were St Peter with his keys, St Andrew with a diagonal cross, St George (mounted) slaying the dragon, St Michael overcoming the Devil, St Paul with a book and sword, and St Catherine with the wheel. The lion of St Mark became the emblem of the Republic of Venice in the pre-heraldic period, the eagle of St John was adopted by the monarchs of Spain, St Peter's keys became the emblem of the papacy, and St Andrew's cross was adopted as the national symbol of Scotland and, in a slightly different form, by Burgundy and later by Spain. Banners with the figures of saints or the Virgin Mary were used until the 17th century as military signs, and also as the ceremonial banners of towns.

♦ **FAR RIGHT**
Italian *portolano*, 1544.

Even before the heraldic age, as early as the 11th century, peculiar vehicles called *carroccio* appeared in northern Italy which were designed to carry huge civic flags. In France *carrocci* appeared a century later, and German versions by the 13th century. They were the centre of all civic festivities and served as a rallying point during battle. The most ceremonial were made of fine wood, inlaid with gold, silver and ivory. According to the *Chronicle of Charlemagne* in the late 9th century, the Saracens used a *carroccio* "which eight oxen bore, upon which their red flag was elevated". From other sources we know that a *carroccio* appeared on the battlefield at the Battle of the Standard near Northallerton, Yorkshire, in 1138: indeed, the battle was named after it. In this the English displayed not only the banners of their patron saints, but also the consecrated Host. In 1191, during a battle with the Saracens near Acre, the banner of Richard I was flown from a *carroccio*. An eye-witness described the vehicle:

It consists, then, of a very long beam, like the mast of a ship, placed upon four wheels in a frame very solidly fastened together and bound with iron, so that it seems incapable of yielding either to sword, axe or fire. Affixed to the very top of this, the royal flag, commonly called banner, flies in the wind.

He explains that "because it stands fast as a sign to all the people, it is called the Standard". In the Battle of Bouvines in 1214 the *carroccio* of Emperor Otto IV was topped by a golden eagle. In the 12th and 13th centuries *carrocci* were in general use in the armies of western Europe and the transference of its original Italian name was completed in the 13th century.

Displays of banners were not limited to the battlefield. Tournaments were enormously popular from the 13th to the 16th centuries. Announced by heralds in many countries, they were an opportunity for knights from all parts of Europe to meet and exhibit their proficiency in handling a horse and weapons. During the

tournament the heralds presented the personal coats of arms of the participants.

The main sources of information about medieval flags are coins and medals, grants of arms, illustrations in chronicles, mosaics and paintings in numerous churches. Especially valuable are some of the armorial rolls. The oldest is the *Zürcher Wappenrolle* (1340), which presents 28 flags of German, Austrian and Bohemian cities and bishoprics; the flags of Strasbourg and Cologne illustrated are taken from this document. The flag of Florence is taken from illustrations in the *Cronaca del Sercambi* (end of the 14th century).

Important information about flags used at sea from the 14th to the 16th centuries can be gleaned from *portolanos*. These are navigational charts depicting coastlines and ports, some rivers and mountain ranges, and flags and coats of arms. Often the flags are very small and their design simplified, but the *portolanos* still contain valuable data. These and the manuscript of a Franciscan friar, a native of Spain, are the oldest sources depicting the flags of North Africa and the Middle East. The manuscript, written and illuminated in about 1350, has a long Spanish title that translates into English as the *Book of the Knowledge of All the Kingdoms, Countries, and Lordships that there are in the World and of the Ensigns and Arms of Each Country and Lordship; also of the Kings and Lords Who Govern Them.* Although the friar claimed to have visited all the places he described, from Spain to China and

◆ **ABOVE LEFT**
Banner of Brandenburg, wood engraving from the *Arms Book of Master IK*, 16th century.

◆ **ABOVE RIGHT**
Banner of Chur, wood engraving by Conrad Schmidt, first half of the 16th century.

◆ **ABOVE**
Banner of Brandenburg from *Banderia Prutenorum*, 1448.

EARLY JAPANESE FLAGS

SASHIMONO

TWO VARIATIONS OF NOBORI

from Norway to Egypt, some of his accounts are not very reliable; nevertheless the text has great value as the earliest account of flags of all nations, with illustrations of nearly 100 flags.

The first authoritative vexillological work was by the Polish historian Jan Dlugosz in 1448. Entitled *Banderia Prutenorum*, it contains detailed descriptions and measurements, as well as large and exact colour illustrations, of all 56 banners captured by the Polish-Lithuanian troops at Tannenberg in 1410.

From the end of the 15th century, banners were often depicted on stained-glass panels, mainly the Swiss *Standesscheiben*. In later centuries woodcarvings in numerous books show banner-bearers with banners of various domains and cities. Especially valuable are a print with representations of the Julius Banners, published in 1513 in Zürich; the *Arms Book of Master IK* (1545), with 144 banners of the cities and territories of the Holy Roman Empire; and the woodcarvings of Conrad Schmidt.

Although the use of symbols was universal among civilized communities, it is only in Europe and Japan that comprehensive heraldic systems developed. The Japanese *mons* are the equivalent of the heraldic badge rather than the heraldic figure. They do not appear on a shield, but in other respects they play the same role as the arms in Europe. The *mon* is a hereditary symbol, and since the 17th century there has been a legal requirement of registration. Like arms, the *mon* is used on banners, armour and the clothes of the retainers of great lords. It decorates castles, carriages, lanterns and the belongings of the individual and his family. *Mons* are usually symmetrical, simple and stylized representations of flowers (mallow, apricot, wisteria), birds (crane, wild goose) or everyday objects (fan, arrow, hatchet) or geometric designs. The banners used in Japan since the Middle Ages differed from both the Chinese and European ones. They were attached to the staff in the same way as Chinese banners but the shape of the cloth was different, the width being several times greater than the length. The *mon* was often repeated several times on the banner. These banners, like the much smaller *sashimono* banners, were fastened into a socket attached to the back of a cuirass, a piece of chest armour. Modern Japanese banners are rectangular, with the *mon* in the centre. Recently the *mons* have come to represent not only families but also cities and provinces.

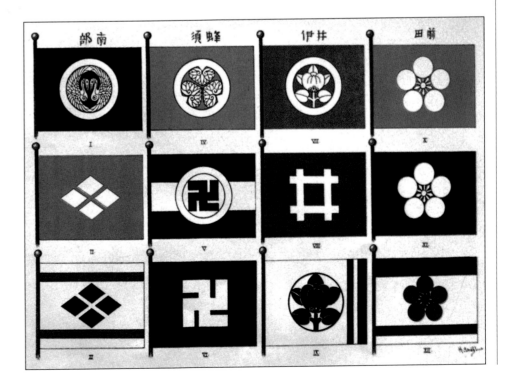

◆ **RIGHT**
Mons appear on flags of all Japanese and noble families, as we see on this plate from *Herold*, 1909.

MODERN FLAGS

In the 16th century the general use of armorial banners ended. Although the monarchs of a few countries such as Great Britain retained their armorial banners, most of the royal flags displayed at sea after this date were single-coloured and bore the whole achievement of arms, i.e. with helmets, mantlings, crests, supporters, collars of orders and mottoes.

The first modern flag was the Dutch revolutionary *Prinsenvlag*, composed of simple stripes instead of heraldic devices, followed by the flags created after the revolutions in America and France. The design of these newly created flags reflected the idea that, with the abolition of monarchy, the heraldic system of identification was also rejected. The colours and designs acquired symbolic meaning and flags began to carry ideological and political messages. Flags were based on simple shapes and in most cases only very simple emblems were used. The most popular emblem was the five-pointed star, a symbol of liberty and independence.

This trend has survived to the present day. Even when thousands and even tens of thousands of flags exist at the same time, it is possible to create quite simple yet very distinctive designs. Some recent, but now obsolete, flags are illustrated below. At the time that the Chinese flag was adopted, consisting only of simple stripes, there were many other striped flags, especially in Europe. Nevertheless, since they were bicolours or tricolours, the Chinese flag with its five colours was still very distinctive. The flag of Malaya had different colours and bore the tiger badge. The flag of Manchukuo displayed the same colours as the earlier Chinese flag, but because of the canton it was distinctively different. The thin stripes in the flag of South Vietnam were the only device of this kind among all the world's flags, and the emblems on the flags of Lesotho and Surinam were also very distinctive. The flag of Congo for most of the time was the only flag to display a large star in its centre.

The best insight into the development of modern flags is provided by numerous charts and albums. The first collections of flags used at sea are in Dutch manuscripts of 1667 and 1669, and in a manuscript from 1670 ascribed to J. Moutton of France. The first English collections of flags for use at sea appeared in the notebook of William Downman (1685) and in *Insignia Navalia*, a manuscript by Lieutenant John Graydon dated 1686. The most thorough flag book of this period was *Nieuwe Hollandse Scheeps-bouw* by Carl Allard, published in Amsterdam in 1694 and reprinted several times; it was also extensively copied by other authors. The best were Cornelius Dankerts, who produced the first flag chart *c.*1700 entitled

MODERN FLAGS

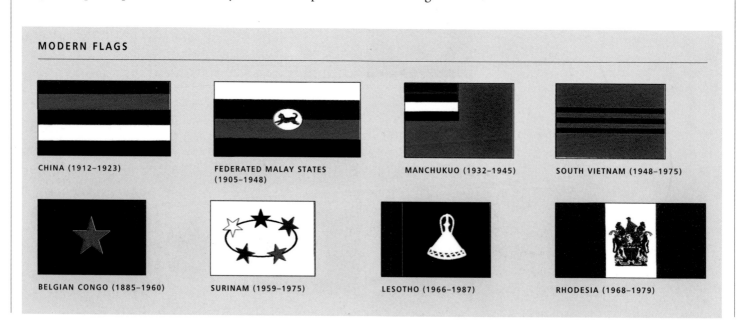

CHINA (1912–1923)

FEDERATED MALAY STATES (1905–1948)

MANCHUKUO (1932–1945)

SOUTH VIETNAM (1948–1975)

BELGIAN CONGO (1885–1960)

SURINAM (1959–1975)

LESOTHO (1966–1987)

RHODESIA (1968–1979)

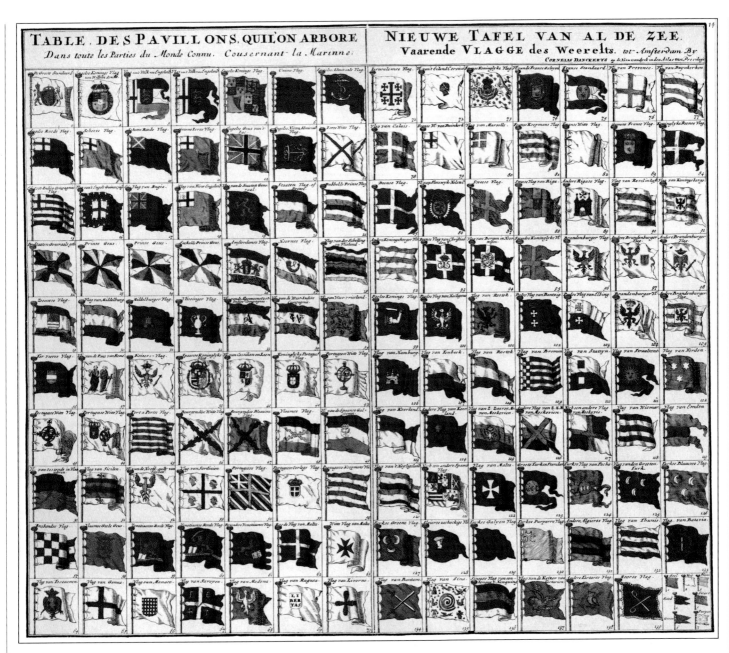

◆ ABOVE
Dutch flag chart by
C. Dankerts (c.1700).

◆ RIGHT
Page from the book by
Jaques van den Kiebom,
*La Connaissance des Pavillons
ou Bannières, que la Plûspart
des Nations Arborent en
Mer, 1737.*

*Table des Pavillons quil'on arbore dans toute les
Parties du Monde Connu, Consernant la Marinne*,
and Jaques van den Kiebom, who in 1737
published the book *La Connaissance des Pavillons
ou Bannières, que la Plûspart des Nations Arborent
en Mer*. In the 19th century most charts were
folded in handbooks. The best are *Plates
Descriptive of the Maritime Flags of all Nations*,
published by J.W. Norie in 1819, and *Three
Hundred and Six Illustrations of the Maritime
Flags of all Nations*, originally compiled by
J.W. Norie and considerably augmented by
J.S. Hobbs in 1848. The first official handbook
on flags was compiled by Captain Le Gras and
published in 1858 by the Secretary of State for
the French Imperial Navy under the title *Album
des Pavillons, Guidons, Flammes, de toutes les*

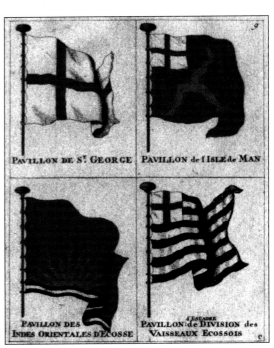

◆ LEFT
A fragment of the French flag chart from *Tableau des Pavillons que la Plûspart des Nations Arborent à la Mer*, 1756.

Puissances Maritimes. Ten years later the American Bureau of Navigation published the album *Flags of Maritime Nations from the Most Authentic Sources*. In 1874 George Hounsell with the approval of the British Admiralty produced *Flags and Signals of All Nations*, and in 1905 the German Admiralty followed suit with the *Flaggenbuch*, the best flag book of all. Although the French and British naval authorities published several updated versions, even after World War II, they never approached the perfection of the *Flaggenbuch*, edited by Ottfried Neubecker and published in 1939.

Since the late 19th century manufacturers of cigarettes, tea and chocolate have made a real contribution to the popularization of national flags and ensigns throughout the world. In the United States, Great Britain, Germany, the Netherlands and other countries cards or pieces of silk with pictures of various flags have been added to cigarette or cigar packets, boxes of tea and wrappers for sweets. Collectors could send for an album with additional information and, although some of the pictures were inaccurate, they were still of great documentary value. Worth mentioning are the sets produced in the 1900s by Players in Great Britain and the German sets produced in about 1930 by

◆ OPPOSITE PAGE
◆ TOP
Two pages from the book by J.W. Norie and augmented by J.S. Hobbs, 1848.

◆ BOTTOM LEFT
Plate from the album J.H. Colton's *Delineation of the Flags of all Nations*, 1862.

◆ BOTTOM RIGHT
Plate VIII from *Flags of All Nations* presented by J. & G. Stewart, Old Vatted Scotch Whiskey Merchants, Edinburgh, 1897.

◆ RIGHT
Page from the album *Pavillons des Puissances Maritimes*, 1819.

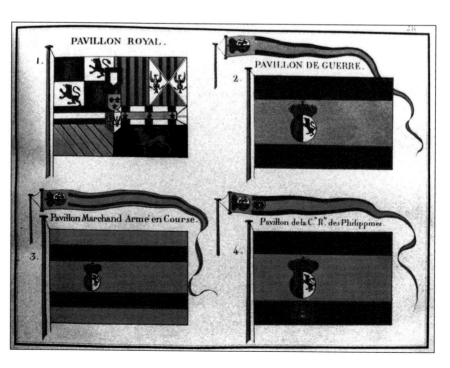

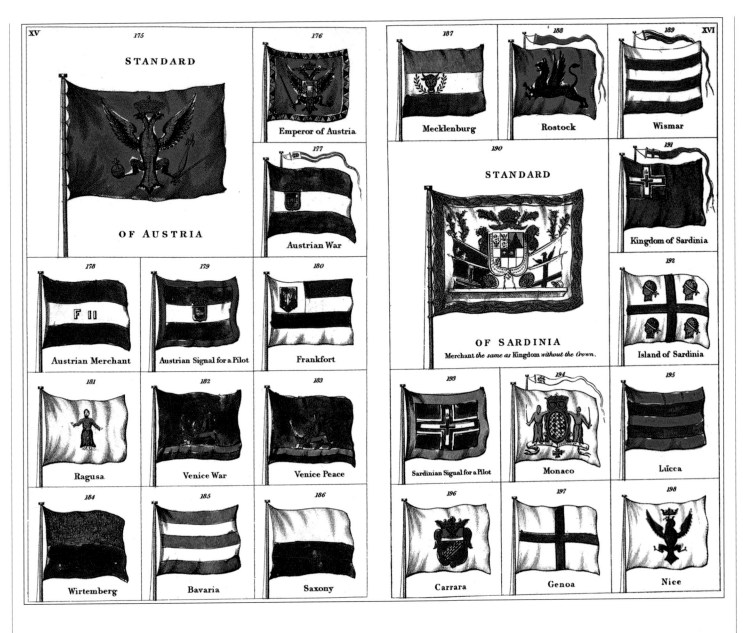

XV	175		176			XVI

STANDARD

OF AUSTRIA

Emperor of Austria.

Austrian War

178	179	180

Austrian Merchant

Austrian Signal for a Pilot

Frankfort

181	182	183

Ragusa

Venice War

Venice Peace

184	185	186

Wirtemberg

Bavaria

Saxony

187	188	189

Mecklenburg

Rostock

Wismar

190

STANDARD

OF SARDINIA

Merchant *the same as Kingdom without the Crown.*

191

Kingdom of Sardinia

192

Island of Sardinia

193	194	195

Sardinian Signal for a Pilot

Monaco

Lucca

196	197	198

Carrara

Genoa

Nice

AMERICAN PRESIDENT.
3

UNITED STATES OF AMERICA
STANDARD & PENDANT.

AMERICAN JACK.
4

AMERICAN ADMIRAL.
5

COLTON'S
FLAGS
OF ALL NATIONS
PUBLISHED BY J.H.COLTON. 172, WILLIAM STREET,
NEW YORK.
1

AMERICAN REVENUE.
7

AMERICAN COMMODORE'S PENNANT.
6

U.S. QUARANTINE.
8

U.S. SIGNAL FOR PILOT.
9

MEXICAN.
10

CENTRAL AMERICA.
11

GUATEMALA.
12

Turkey Ensign & Merchant 49	Roumania Royal Standard 50	Roumania Merchant 51
Servia Royal Standard 52	Servia Merchant 53	Montenegro Prince Standard 54
Bulgaria Merchant 55	Greece Royal Standard 56	Greece Merchant 57
Persia Royal Standard 58	Persia Merchant 59	Siam Royal Standard 60

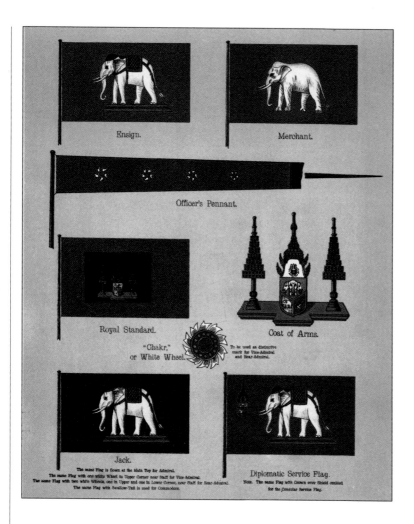

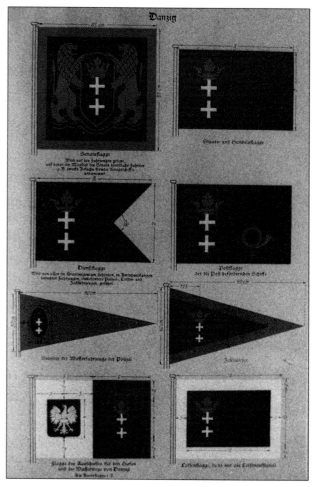

Bulgaria Cigarettes (*Flaggen der Welt*) and Massary Cigarettes (*Wer nent die Länder, kennt die Fahnen?*). Particularly valuable are the card sets edited by O. Neubecker, the foremost German flag authority, *Länder, Wappen und Nationalfarben* and *Flaggen der Welt*. The set produced by Sultan cigarettes from Dresden to celebrate Germany's hosting of the 1936 Olympic Games in Berlin contains flawless

information, and is also a real gem in the art of printing; it was produced in consultation with Karl Fachinger, the forerunner of vexillology. The pictures and information contained in two albums of cigarette cards, edited by O. Neubecker and published in 1950 under the title *Die Welt im bunten Flaggenbild*, are so accurate that these books deserve to be among the leading sources of vexillological knowledge.

In the 20th century several dozen general books on flags have been published, a few of which have made major contributions to vexillology (see Bibliography). These are *Die Flagge* by Vice-Admiral R. Siegel, 1912; a special edition of the National Geographic Magazine, *Flags of the World*, 1917; *Fahnen und Flaggen* by O. Neubecker, 1939; *The Flag Book* by Preben Kannik (in Danish 1956; in English 1957), with several subsequent editions prepared by Christian Fogd Pedersen, the foremost Scandinavian vexillologue; and the comprehensive *Flags Through the Ages and Across the World* by Whitney Smith, 1975.

In 1962 Whitney Smith established the Flag Research Center in Massachusetts, USA, which was the first professional vexillological institute in the world. He coined the word "vexillology", which is now a generally accepted term and used in many languages. Since October 1961 he has published *The Flag Bulletin*, the most authoritative journal on vexillology. Together with O. Neubecker, Louis Mühlemann and Klaes Sierksma, Smith organized the first international vexillological congress in 1965 and established the International Federation of Vexillological Associations (FIAV). The current membership of FIAV comprises 39 vexillological associations and institutions from 24 countries in all six continents. Most publish newsletters, of which the most important are the Swiss *Vexilla Helvetica*, the Italian *Vexilla Italica*, the Belgian *Vexilla Belgica*, the Czech *Vexilologie*, the Spanish *Banderas*, the South African *SAVA Newsletter*, the American *Raven*, the German *Der Flaggenkurier* and the Ukrainian *Znak*. *The Flag Bulletin* and the publications of these vexillological associations have contributed to the tremendous recent increase in vexillological knowledge.

◆ **RIGHT (TOP ROW)**
The Flag of the governor general of India (19th century–1950) and the flag of the governor-general of Canada (1921–1957) are a small part of the flag collection produced by the *Massary Zigarettenfabrik* in Berlin.
(*bottom row*)
Lübeck. Flags of the government vessels at sea (1921–1935). Produced by the *Massary Zigarettenfabrik* in Berlin.

◆ **BELOW**
(*left to right*)
National flag of Cambodia under French protectorate; presidential standard of Brazil (1907–1968), and Presidential Standard of China (1928–1949, and since 1949 Taiwan). Such beautiful and error-free renderings were possible owing to the collaboration with Ottfried Neubecker, the foremost German heraldist and vexillologist.

BRITISCHES REICH
FLAGGE DES GENERAL-GOUVERNEURS VON INDIEN
Serie 76 (1—130) Bild 33

BRITISCHES REICH
FLAGGE DES GENERAL-GOUVERNEURS VON KANADA
Serie 76 (1—130) Bild 40

DEUTSCHES REICH
FREIE UND HANSESTADT LÜBECK
STAATSFLAGGE FÜR STAATS-FAHRZEUGE D. BINNENSCHIFFFAHRT
(ältere Flagge)
Serie 2 (1—40) Bild 29

DEUTSCHES REICH
LÜBECK
DIENSTFLAGGE FÜR STAATSFAHRZEUGE DER SEESCHIFFAHRT
Serie 2 (1—40) Bild 30

Kambodja
(französisches Protektorat)
Nationalflagge

Brasilien
Präsidentenflagge

China
Flagge des Präsidenten

All About Flags

A flag may be defined as a piece of pliable material, attached at one end so as to move freely in the wind, serving as a sign or a decoration. This word is now common to the nations of north-western Europe (Danish and Norse Flag, *Swedish* Flagg, *German* Flagge, *Dutch* Vlag), *but it does not appear to have come into use in this particular meaning until the 16th century, and the etymology of it is obscure. Perhaps the most satisfactory of the derivations hitherto put forward is that of Professor Skeat, who derives it from the Middle English* flakken *to fly, one of a number of similar onomatopoeic words suggestive of the sound of something flapping in the wind. Its first appearance with a meaning coming within the above definition is a specific term denoting a rectangular piece of material attached by one vertical edge, flown at the masthead of a ship, as a symbol of nationality or leadership. Before the 17th century there was no generic term in the English language that covered the various forms – banners, ensigns, streamers, pendants, etc. – that are now generally included under the term "flag".*

W.G. PERRIN, *BRITISH FLAGS*, CAMBRIDGE 1922

Precise terminology is needed to describe the various characteristics of a flag: its shape, proportions, design and colours. There are many different types of flag, made of different materials and with various accessories. Even hoisting a flag can be done in various ways. In what follows it is assumed that the flag is hoisted on a vertical staff and is flying to the right of the staff. This is termed the obverse, the main side of the flag. In most cases the reverse is a mirror image of the obverse but some flags – mainly military colours – have different obverse and reverse and are really two flags sewn back to back.

The usage of flags has changed radically over the centuries, but some flag customs and etiquette, for example flying a flag at half-mast, have become part of everyday consciousness. Understanding the symbolic language of national flags is particularly important in diplomatic contexts, and on many occasions in recent history serious conflicts have arisen through ignorance or misunderstanding.

◆ **LEFT**
A huge Tunisian flag is displayed in Marseilles, France, during the 1998 World Cup.

FLAG DESIGN

The first characteristic of a flag is its shape. Most ensigns and national flags are rectangular. Some ensigns are swallow-tailed or double swallow-tailed, two national flags are square and one consists of two triangles. Most yacht flags are triangular or swallow-tailed, and the flags used by the army and navy are much more diversified.

The second characteristic of a flag is its proportions, i.e. the ratio of the width to the length. The width is measured along the hoist,

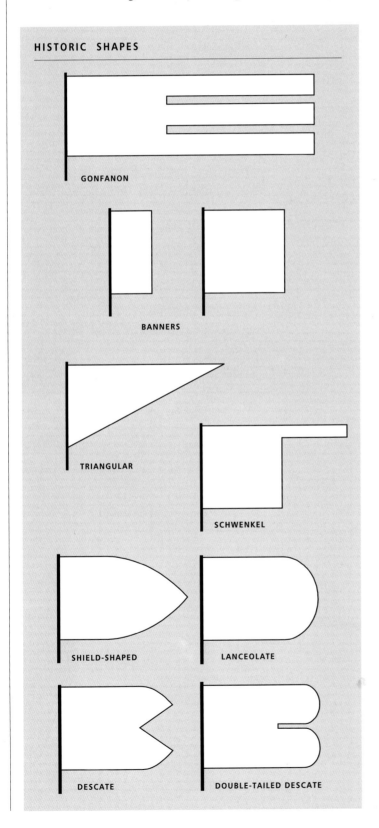

HISTORIC SHAPES

GONFANON

BANNERS

TRIANGULAR

SCHWENKEL

SHIELD-SHAPED

LANCEOLATE

DESCATE

DOUBLE-TAILED DESCATE

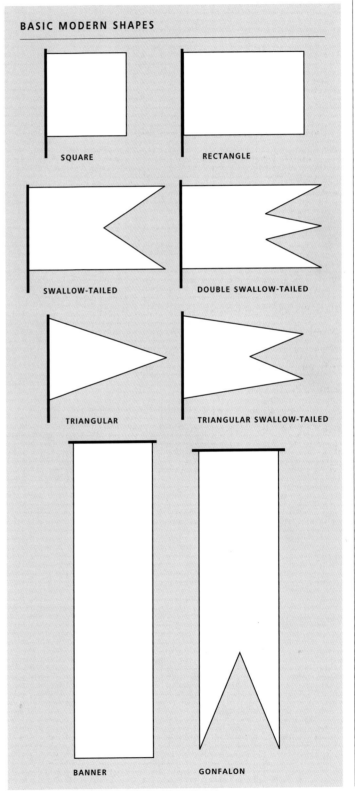

BASIC MODERN SHAPES

SQUARE

RECTANGLE

SWALLOW-TAILED

DOUBLE SWALLOW-TAILED

TRIANGULAR

TRIANGULAR SWALLOW-TAILED

BANNER

GONFALON

so it is the vertical measurement of a flag that is displayed horizontally and a horizontal measurement of a flag that is designed to hang vertically. The length is measured from the hoist to the fly end of a flag, and in triangular and swallow-tailed flags it is measured from the hoist to the apex of a triangle. For the sake of uniformity, organizers of international conferences and sports events usually adopt the same proportions for flags that are displayed together, although this can lead to distortion of the elements of the design. The correct way to present national flags on such occasions, and in flag charts and book illustrations, is to make all the hoists the same width and to retain the official proportions. In this arrangement, only the length of the flags will vary.

The third characteristic of a flag is its design. The terms for the basic parts of a flag are the "hoist" (first half), the "fly" (second half), "top"

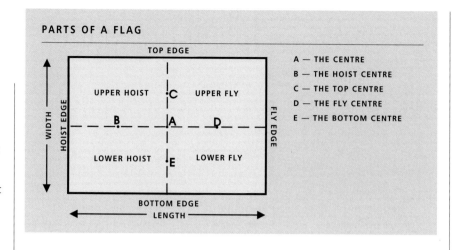

PARTS OF A FLAG

A — THE CENTRE
B — THE HOIST CENTRE
C — THE TOP CENTRE
D — THE FLY CENTRE
E — THE BOTTOM CENTRE

(upper half) and "bottom" (lower half). In addition, there are terms for all the edges and particular points on the "field" (the whole area of the flag). In Europe many flags are historic armorial banners and therefore need to be described in heraldic terms; other flags display the coat of arms on a single-colour field. However, most flags have modern designs based on simple divisions of the field and/or display "simple charges" (simple figures).

Division of the field by horizontal or vertical lines results in horizontal or vertical stripes; dividing the field diagonally creates "bends". If these are of equal width, only their number is given in the flag's description. But if a design consists of stripes or bends of unequal size, the proportionate width must be quoted. For example, the description of the flag of Thailand is five horizontal stripes, 1:1:2:1:1, which means that the middle stripe is twice as wide as each of the outer stripes.

To divide the field into four parts a cross, or "saltire", is used. When the field is divided quarterly, the parts are called "quarters" and their colours are given in the following order: upper hoist, upper fly, lower hoist and lower fly. The colours of the triangles resulting from a division by saltire are given clockwise, beginning with the triangle based on the hoist.

The pieces of a chequered field are called "checks". The description of the field is given as follows: "checky a x b", where "a" is the number of checks in a horizontal line and "b" is their number in a vertical line. The field can also be divided with "gyrons"; there are normally eight or twelve. Their colours are given in a clockwise direction, beginning with the one

BASIC DIVISIONS

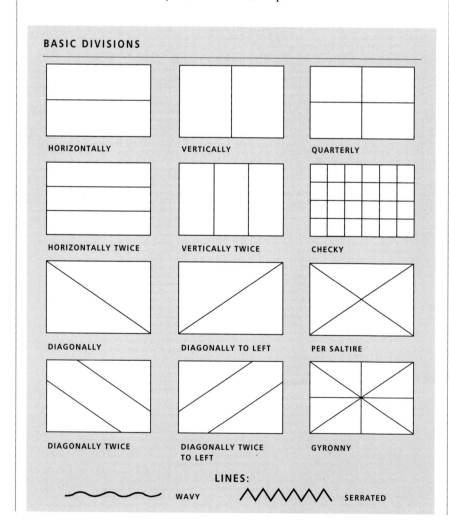

HORIZONTALLY   VERTICALLY   QUARTERLY

HORIZONTALLY TWICE   VERTICALLY TWICE   CHECKY

DIAGONALLY   DIAGONALLY TO LEFT   PER SALTIRE

DIAGONALLY TWICE   DIAGONALLY TWICE TO LEFT   GYRONNY

LINES:

WAVY   SERRATED

BASIC CHARGES

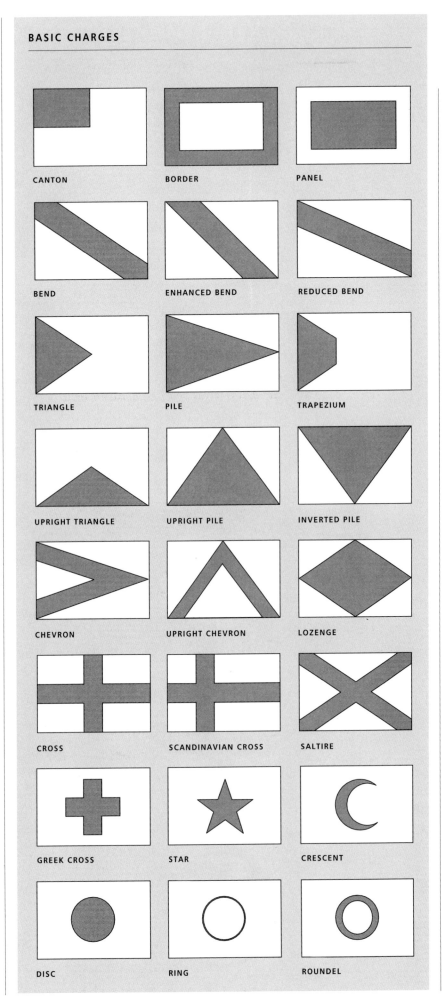

CANTON BORDER PANEL

BEND ENHANCED BEND REDUCED BEND

TRIANGLE PILE TRAPEZIUM

UPRIGHT TRIANGLE UPRIGHT PILE INVERTED PILE

CHEVRON UPRIGHT CHEVRON LOZENGE

CROSS SCANDINAVIAN CROSS SALTIRE

GREEK CROSS STAR CRESCENT

DISC RING ROUNDEL

whose longer edge coincides with the horizontal line dividing the hoist in half.

In most flag designs the division lines are straight, but in the design of some national, provincial and civic flags wavy and serrated lines are used. In heraldry there are more than a dozen other decorative lines of partition, which can be seen on armorial banners.

Most modern flags display charges, the most popular being cantons (squares or oblongs), stars, bends (diagonal stripes), crosses, triangles and piles (wedges). Charges such as a cross or bend are sometimes "fimbriated", i.e. edged with narrow stripes. Other charges such as a canton, pile or lozenge often carry another charge such as stars, a badge or other device. In medieval times the most widespread charges were crosses, lions, eagles and fleurs-de-lis, and today the most popular charge is a star. Before the American Revolution the stars that occasionally appeared on flags were heraldic stars with six or eight points. Since 1777, five-pointed stars have been used almost exclusively, and they currently appear on more than 50 national flags.

When a charge appears in a horizontal mirror position it is described as being "reversed". A charge pointing to the top of the flag is "upright" and one pointing to the bottom is "inverted". The width or diameter of charges is always quoted as a proportion of the width of the flag. The exceptions are a normal canton, a normal triangle and a pile. A normal canton covers the entire area of the upper hoist; if its dimensions are different, its proportion of the width of the flag is given. The apex of a normal triangle reaches the centre of the field; if the triangle reaches another point, it is specifically described by quoting the height of the triangle as a proportion of the width of the flag.

The next, very important, characteristic of a flag is its colour. Single colours or colour combinations are the main way a flag conveys its symbolic meaning. They may imply a political or religious ideology, symbolize national traditions or geographical features or, as in many European flags, display livery colours, i.e. heraldic tinctures that do not convey any symbolic meaning. There are seven heraldic tinctures, two "metals" and five "colours". The metals are gold (or) and silver (argent), represented on flags by yellow and white. The colours are red (gules), blue (azure), green (vert), black (sable) and purple (purpure). In Britain the livery colours are usually the first "metal" and the first "colour" mentioned in the "blazon" (a herald's description of a coat of arms), but in continental Europe the livery colours may be all the tinctures (three or four) of a coat of arms.

To simplify the description of livery colours, the International Federation of Vexillological Associations has adopted the following code:

R = red, O = orange, Y = yellow, V = green, B = blue, P = purple, N = black, W = white, Au = gold, Ag = silver, M = brown, G = grey.

There are also symbols for lighter and darker shades of colours:

– light, – – very light, + dark, ++ very dark

This code helps to give a rough idea about flag colours, but it is insufficient to describe specific shades such as United Nations blue, Kenya red, Qatar maroon or olive green.

Other basic rules of flag description are able to describe accurately only the simpler flags. To know the exact design and colouring of a particular flag, the reliable source of information is either the official government specification or a specification prepared by one of a few professional vexillologists. Such a specification should contain a large colour illustration of the flag together with enlarged details, accompanied by a description of the type of flag, dates of usage, proportions and exact colours given in the Pantone Matching System or CMYK (cyan, magenta, yellow, black), as used by printers and modern computer systems. Two examples are given here, the specification of the German fleet admiral made in the 1930s by the navy department in Berlin, and one of hundreds of flag specifications prepared by the Flag Design Center.

◆ **BELOW LEFT**
Flag of the German fleet admiral with construction details. Print of the German Admiralty, 1939.

◆ **BELOW**
Flag specification for the state flag of Germany (1935–1945) produced by the Flag Design Center.

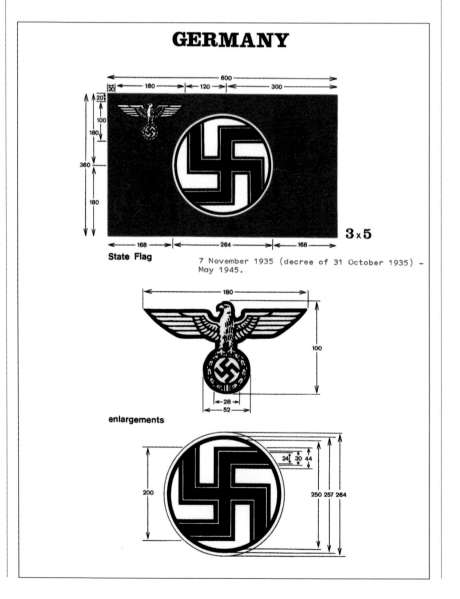

GERMANY

3×5

State Flag

7 November 1935 (decree of 31 October 1935) – May 1945.

enlargements

A good flag design should be simple, yet distinctive and meaningful. As a medium of communication a flag must be easily recognizable. The divisions should be chosen not only for aesthetic value but also to enhance the flag's symbolic meaning. The emblems need to be large and as simple as possible, and should be placed in the most important parts of the field, such as the canton or centre of the flag. Light colours should be placed next to darker ones; no more than three colours should be used. Flags are employed as alternatives to written messages so should not bear any lettering or numbers. The reason, as in heraldry, is a practical one: colours and symbols are easier to "read" when a flag is seen from a distance or fluttering. It is also not a good idea to add a hatchment of arms or an armorial shield because the details would not be clear. The only effective way to make a coat of arms into a flag is as an armorial banner.

FLAG DESIGN GLOSSARY

Armorial banner A flag whose field consists of the field and charges of a coat of arms. In Great Britain the banner is square or rectangular (proportions 1:2), in Europe it is almost exclusively square

Badge A heraldic emblem, different from the coat of arms (it does not employ a shield)

Bicolour A flag with the field divided horizontally (horizontal bicolour), vertically (vertical bicolour) or diagonally (diagonal bicolour) into two equal parts in two different colours

Border A wide band surrounding a field of different colour

Breadth see Width

Canton The area of the upper hoist corner of a flag; also a square or rectangular field covering that area

Charge Any object placed on the field of a flag. The most common are charges that are based on a simple division of the field with straight lines. Frequently used charges are the star, cross, crescent, disc, fleur–de–lis and sun. Unlike the badge, the charge is not used separately

Checky A field bearing squares of alternating colours

Counterchanged Having two colours alternating on each side of a line drawn through a flag or arms

Crest An armorial figure attached to the helmet above the shield of a coat of arms. Sometimes used alone as a badge

Cross A charge in the form of a cross concentric with the field, its arms extending to the edges of the flag. See also Greek Cross, Scandinavian Cross

Deface To add a badge or crest to a flag

Disc A circular device of a single colour used as a charge

Ensign-banner A rectangular flag with a field and fringe of livery colours of a coat of arms, charged with the full achievement of the arms

Field The whole area of a flag

Fimbriation A very narrow border of a simple geometric charge, usually in a contrast colour

Flammule A flame–shaped edge to a flag, often used in the past in the Far East

Fly The second half of the flag, the opposite end to the staff

Greek Cross A charge in the form of a cross with arms of equal length

Gyronny Divided into eight or twelve triangles whose apexes meet at the centre of the field

Hoist The half of a flag nearest the staff

Length The dimension of a flag measured from the heading or sleeve to the end of the fly; the opposite of Width

Livery colours The principal colours of a coat of arms. On a flag usually the first metal (gold or silver, i.e. yellow or white) is positioned above the first colour (red, blue, green, black or purple)

Obverse The more important, front side of a flag. It is the side to the observer's right from the staff; the opposite of reverse

Proportions The ratio of the width to the length of a flag. The proportions of a square flag are 1:1, a flag twice as long as it is wide is 1:2. The proportions of charges are always given in relation to the width of the flag

Quarterly Divided in four equal parts in a crosswise fashion

Reverse The less important side of a flag. It is the side to the observer's left from the staff; the opposite of obverse

Roundel A circular emblem of nationality employed on military aircraft and air force flags, usually consisting of concentric rings of national colours

Saltire A diagonal cross whose arms extend to the edges of a flag. Known also as a St Andrew's Cross

Scandinavian Cross A Latin cross positioned on the field of a flag horizontally, with the vertical arms in the hoist portion of the flag

Serrated A jagged division line or edge

Swallow-tailed A flag with a triangular section cut out from the fly end

Tricolour A flag whose field is divided horizontally (called a horizontal tricolour), vertically (vertical tricolour) or diagonally (diagonal tricolour) into three parts in three different colours

Triple swallow-tailed A flag with two symmetrical triangular sections cut out from the fly end

Union mark A symbol expressing the political unification of two territories, used in the canton of other flags. The most widespread is the British Union Jack

Width The measurement of a flag along its hoist; the opposite of length. In Commonwealth countries the British term "breadth" is used

TYPES OF FLAGS

"Flag" is an all-embracing general term used for a piece of fabric or other flexible material of distinctive design and coloration as a symbol of the identity of a nation, territory, office, corporation, organization, and so on. There are many types of flag, with different functions and usage as well as design and shape.

FLAG FUNCTION, USAGE AND SHAPE

The types of flags according to function are:
air force flag, armed forces flags, civil air flag, civil ensign, civil flag, colour, command pennant, commission pennant, courtesy flag, distinguishing flag, fanion, guidon, house flag, national ensign, national flag, naval reserve ensign, parley flag, pennon, pilot flag, rank flag, service ensign, signal flag, state ensign, state flag, war ensign;

The types of flags according to usage are:
banner, bannerol, car flag, courtesy flag, drum-banner, indoor flag, jack, lance pennon, outdoor flag, parade flag, parley flag, pipe-banner, table flag, trumpet-banner;

The types of flags according to shape are:
broad pennant, burgee, gonfalon, gonfanon, pennant, schwenkel, standard.

FLAG TYPES GLOSSARY

Air force flag A special flag for use at a military airport

Armed forces flags Special flags for each part of the armed forces (army, navy, air force, marines). They are used to mark military garrisons and quarters, and during parades and ceremonies of a particular armed force

Banner (i) General term referring to a square or rectangular flag fastened to a staff or attached to a crossbar, having an armorial or other elaborate design and made of costly material, often hand-painted and/or embroidered. Unless the word is used figuratively, it is necessary to use a more specific term such as armorial banner, royal banner, civic banner, church banner, corporate banner, ensign banner, drum-banner, pipe-banner, trumpet-banner etc
(ii) Any flag designed to hang vertically from a crossbar, with the design arranged accordingly. It is also called a hanging flag

BANNER OF RHINELAND-PALATINE IN GERMANY

Bannerol A small square flag charged with a single quartering of a deceased person and carried at his or her funeral; now obsolete

Battle honour A mark added to a colour or to a flag of a branch of the armed forces to show its military service

Broad pennant A tapering descate or swallow-tailed flag, mostly used by navies as the flag of the head of state. In British and American naval and yachting usage, it is the rank flag of a commodore

Burgee A small distinguishing flag of a club or individual yachtsman, usually either triangular or tapering swallow-tailed. Flown from the main mast, or from the bows in the case of a powerboat

BROAD PENNANT OF THE EMPEROR OF GERMANY

Car flag Any flag flown from a car. Usually the flag of a head of state or government official, i.e. a rank flag or distinguishing flag. In most cases, it is displayed from a staff mounted on the right front fender. In the past it was on a staff clamped to a radiator cap

Civil air flag A flag for use at civil airports and landing fields

Civil ensign A flag designating national identity, flown on commercial or pleasure vessels. Formerly called a merchant flag

Civil flag A flag designating national identity, flown by private citizens on land

Club pennant A triangular flag to be hung vertically, usually charged with the emblem and livery colours of a sporting club

Cockade A rosette originally worn in a hat as a military badge, usually in livery or national colours. Since the 18th century also worn by civilians as an expression of revolutionary or patriotic feelings. In many European countries the first regulations pertaining to national colours related to the cockade, and later the colours of the cockade translated directly into a bicolour or tricolour flag

Colour Flag of a military unit (regiment, battalion or company). It usually has different designs on the obverse and reverse, and is fringed and attached to the staff

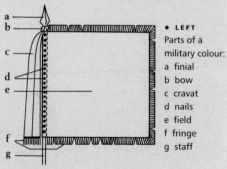

◆ LEFT
Parts of a military colour:
a finial
b bow
c cravat
d nails
e field
f fringe
g staff

Command pennant A flag identifying the commander of a particular navy formation (flotilla, squadron, group etc) or an individual ship. Usually triangular or tapering swallow–tailed

Commission pennant A very long, narrow flag (of proportions 1:15–1:50 or more), flown on a warship to indicate its commissioned status. If the ship's commander is of the rank of commodore or higher, the commission pennant is replaced by a rank flag. The term *Masthead pennant* is synonymous

COMMISSION PENNANT OF SAUDI ARABIA

Courtesy flag The civil ensign of a country being visited by a merchant vessel or yacht of a different nationality. Usually flown from the foremast or yardarm. It is hoisted on entering a foreign port

Desk flag See *Table flag*

DESK OR TABLE
FLAG, SLOVAKIA

Distinguishing flag A flag identifying a branch of government, military or naval service, or an official. In the latter case it denotes his or her office, authority, rank or command, and indicates his or her presence in a vessel, vehicle or place

Drum-banner A small flag decorating a parade drum. Used by a military, civic or other brass band parading in uniform or historic costume

Eagle (i) A vexilloid with a representation of an eagle on the top of the staff;
(ii) The name of the French colour during the Napoleonic era;

Ensign (i) A flag used to indicate the nationality of civil, government and naval vessels. Flown by ships at or near the stern. The term should always be preceded by an explanatory name (war ensign, civil ensign etc);
(ii) In the United States, the lowest commissioned officer in the navy;
(iii) In the 17th and 18th centuries, the usual term for a military colour and the colour–bearer

False colours An ensign worn by a ship not entitled to it

Fan A semi–circular patriotic decoration made of national flags or fabric in livery colours

Fanion (i) A small bicolour used for marking a position in surveying;
(ii) A small pennon in the regimental colours that is used on military vehicles for marker purposes

Flag This term most frequently refers to the rectangular flag used mainly on land by nations, government institutions, agencies and officials, provinces, cities, commercial firms, corporations, organizations, and so on

Flag of convenience The civil ensign of a country with low taxation and without stringent maritime regulations. The term applies to a ship whose owner is not a citizen of that country, but who registers the vessel there to avoid high taxes and in order to hire cheap labour

Gonfalon A long flag with a square or triangular tail, displayed from a crossbar. It originated in medieval Italy (a gonfaloniero was the person who carried such a flag), and is still used there by cities and communes. In other European countries it is used mainly by parishes and various associations

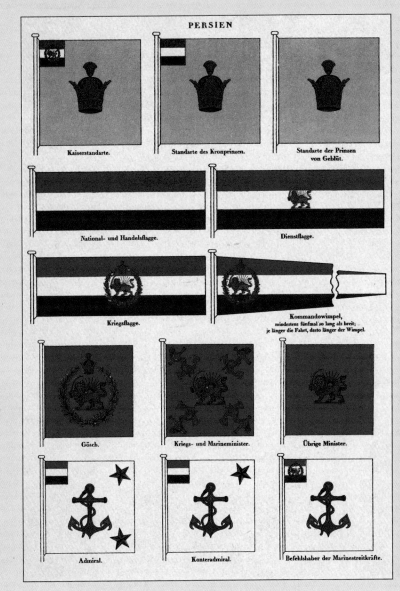

◆ LEFT Distinguishing flags of Persia 1933–1958: (*top row*) imperial standard, crown prince's standard, prince's standard; (*2nd and 3rd flag in the 4th row*) ministers of defence or navy, other ministers; (*5th row*) admiral, rear admiral, Commander of the navy.

Gonfanon Large lance flag with a square or rectangular field, and two to five squared long tails. The term derives from the Norse *gunn-fane*, which means a "war flag". In pre-heraldic and medieval times it was the flag of a ruler for carrying on horseback

Government flag see *State flag*

Guidon A small military flag, usually swallow-tailed or with a fly descate or cloven-descate, serving as a guide to troops. In Great Britain it was originally charged with the Union Flag in the hoist, and the badge and livery colours in the fly. Later guidons were charged with the arms

Hanging flag see *Banner*

Homeward-bound pennant United

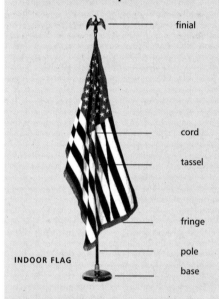

- finial
- cord
- tassel
- fringe
- pole
- base

INDOOR FLAG

States term for the *paying-off pennant*

House flag The flag of a commercial firm flown at sea, and from its headquarters or branches on land

Indoor flag A flag made expressly for use in offices. It is made of more expensive fabric and the charge is often embroidered. It also differs from an outdoor flag by having a fringe, and it has a sleeve instead of the heading

Jack A small flag flown from a special jack-staff set in the bow of a warship. Usually hoisted when a warship is in harbour or lying in the roadstead. It may be a diminutive of the national flag, or of historic or other special design

LANCE PENNON
(JORDANIAN)

Jolly Roger Popular term for a black flag with a design in white referring to death. Modern flags show a skull and crossbones. The term was coined in the early 18th century for a flag used by pirates

Lance pennon A small flag, usually triangular or swallow-tailed, attached to the end of a lance

Masthead pennant see *Commission pennant*

Merchant flag see *Civil ensign*

Mourning ribbon Long black ribbon tied in a bow and attached to the staff just above the flag as a sign of mourning. An alternative to half–masting the flag

National flag (i) A flag of a nation-state, or formerly independent state, or of a non-independent national group that has its own government;
(ii) In the case of an independent state, a flag and ensign used by the government authorities, general public and the navy

Naval ensign see *War ensign*

Naval reserve ensign A flag used as a civil ensign on merchant vessels commanded by retired naval officers

OCCASIONAL FLAG – FLAG OF THE BICENTENNIAL OF THE AMERICAN REVOLUTION (1976).

Occasional flag A flag made for a particular occasion, such as an anniversary, holiday or international congress

Outdoor flag A flag made of stronger fabric with enforced edges and corners,

suitable for hoisting on flagstaffs and able to endure strong winds and inclement weather for a long period

Parade flag A flag to be carried outdoors by a marcher, usually made in the same way as an indoor flag

Parley flag A plain white flag displayed by combatants to request a ceasefire and to indicate the desire to negotiate terms of surrender

Paying-off pennant A commission pennant of a vessel returning home after a long period of service. It has up to 75 m (82 yd) of extra material added to the length

Pendant see *Pennant*

Pennant This is a general term for flags that are tapering, triangular or swallow-tailed in shape, originally flown from a crossbar and in modern times also flown from a vertical staff. Pennants differ from flags mainly in shape, size and manner of display. They originated at sea and some are used in this way (*Broad pennant, Commission pennant, Burgee*). There are, however, many more types of pennants for use on land, mainly as award and souvenir flags of corporate bodies and of sports, fraternal and other organizations

Pennon In medieval times a small personal flag of the arms-bearer below the rank of knight-banneret, intended for use on a lance borne by a mounted warrior. A pennon bore the arms in such a way that they were upright when the lance was in a horizontal position. In Britain since Tudor times pennons have consisted of the livery colours charged with a badge

Pilot flag A flag flown by a vessel requiring or carrying a pilot. Some countries have a special flag for this purpose, but in many others the "G" of the International Code of Signals is used

grommet

appliquéd eagle

heading

hem

sewn chevrons

hem

◆ RIGHT
OUTDOOR
FLAG: FLAG
OF THE
FLAG DESIGN
CENTER

Pinsil Scottish triangular flag of proportions 4:9 with a fringe of the livery colours, charged with the crest and a strap badge in the hoist, and a plant badge in the fly. Used as a rallying point by a clan captain in the absence of the clan chief

Pipe-banner A small banner attached to the drone pipes of bagpipes. Military pipe-banners are two-sided, the obverse being charged with the regimental badge and the reverse with the company commander's arms

Quarantine flag A yellow flag flown by a ship that has not yet received medical clearance on arrival. It is the request for a certificate of good health

Rank flag A distinguishing flag indicating the rank of the officer of the navy (commodore to fleet admiral), army or air force (generals)

Regimental colour see *Colour*

Schwenkel A rectangular or triangular tail extending from the upper fly corner of a flag, or a strip along the top edge of a flag, with a dependent tail. Common in medieval

FLAG OF ZÜRICH WITH SCHWENKEL, 15TH CENTURY

Europe, now obsolete. The term is also means a whole flag with a schwenkel

Service ensign An ensign designated to identify a vessel, providing a particular service for customs, mail, fishery inspection, lighthouse service, environmental protection, and so on

Signal flag A flag used to transmit messages, especially at sea. The most widely used are the flags of the International Code of Signals

TRADITIONAL DESIGN OF AN ENGLISH HERALDIC STANDARD

Standard (i) A vexilloid used by the army; (ii) A long, tapering descate flag of heraldic design. Size varied according to the person's rank i.e. the length ranged from 7.3 m (8 yd) for the King to 3.5 m (4 yd) for a knight; (iii) A rectangular flag of heraldic design which is not an armorial banner; (iv) A flag of a head of state

State ensign A flag designating national identity, flown on non-military vessels in government service. Also called a *Government ensign*

State flag A flag designating national identity, used by government authorities and institutions on land. Also called a *Government flag*

Streamer (i) A long ribbon attached to the staff, which is used mainly in the form of battle honours; (ii) A long, narrow pennant used until the 17th century as a decoration on vessels

Table flag A small flag hanging vertically from a crossbar or attached to the staff with a stand. Used during international conferences and document signing ceremonies, or on a desk

Trumpet banner A small flag to decorate a ceremonial trumpet, usually a proper armorial banner. Used by a military, civic or other brass band parading in uniform or historic costume

Vane (i) A small metal flag set to swivel on a rod, mainly to indicate wind-direction. Usually attached to a steeple or roof; (ii) A short pennant used in the 17th and 18th centuries by merchant and naval vessels at each mast where no proper pennant was flying

Vexilloid This serves the same purpose as a flag but differs from it in appearance. It consists of a wooden or metal staff topped by an emblem made of animal bones, feathers, hide, wood or metal

Vexillum A square piece of cloth fastened to a crossbar, the standard of the Roman cavalry

War ensign The naval flag of a nation, also called a naval ensign. Carried by warships at or near the stern

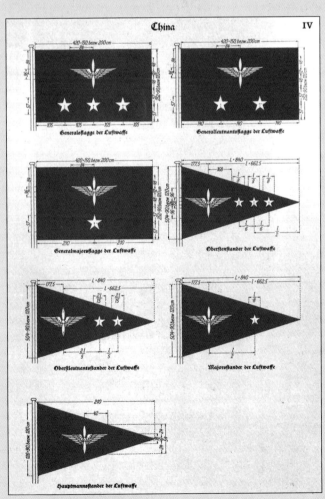

RANK FLAGS OF THE CHINESE AIR FORCE, PLATE FROM THE FLAGGENBUCH, BERLIN 1939

TRUMPET BANNER WITH THE ARMS OF FLORENCE CARRIED BY TRUMPETERS IN HISTORIC COSTUMES IN A PARADE PROCEEDING AN HISTORICAL SOCCER GAME

MATERIALS AND TECHNIQUES

The earliest flags were usually made of wool or silk. By the 13th century, the banners of rulers and the military were made of silk taffeta, and after the 15th century of silk damask. From the early Middle Ages these silk fabrics were decorated with colourful designs created using appliqué, gold leaf, chain stitch or flat stitch, or a combination of these techniques. From the 14th to the 16th centuries the ornamentation became more elaborate, featuring emblems of painted leather, delicate embroidery and pearls. From the end of the 16th century through to the 19th century most flags were painted and/or embroidered. The seams of ceremonial banners were often trimmed with silver or gold cord; the cantons or fields were adorned with relief embroidery and decorated with pearls and small gold spangles. The finest examples of craftsmanship are the so-called Julius banners, the war flags presented by Pope Julius II to the Swiss in 1512 as a token of appreciation for the Protectors of the Liberty of the Church.

◆ ABOVE
Relief embroidery has been used on the canton of the Julius banner of Basel (1512).

◆ LEFT
Large parts of the Madonna with Child, as well as the canton and letters on the border, are painted with gold leaf on the Julius banner of Schwyz (1512).

◆ LEFT
An example of a printed flag
is the civic flag of the city of
Lubin in Poland.

More general purpose flags, used by the army on land and by merchant or war vessels at sea, were made of cheaper fabrics, mostly rough or fine linen. Sendal was another popular fabric. From the 17th to the 19th centuries most ensigns were made of bunting and the emblems were painted or appliquéd on to it.

Only in recent years have fabrics been developed that can fulfil the numerous requirements of outdoor flags. The fabric has to give the flag a lustrous appearance at the same time as superb wearing strength, and it must also be washable, fire-resistant, mildew-resistant and mothproof. The flag should be light and able to fly well, even in rain, and both the fabric and the durable, fast colours must be able to resist high winds, intense sun, dirt and air pollution. Ideal fabrics for this have proved to be heavyweight, two-ply polyester or fabrics made of 25 per cent wool and 75 per cent nylon.

The designs on flags for outdoor use are normally sewn together; simple charges are appliquéd on, intricate ones are dyed and sewn. When many flags of the same design are required, they are dyed in large silkscreen workshops equipped with rows of tables 30–50 m (33–55 yd) in length. The chemical dyes, identical to those used in textile mills, are applied one colour at a time and penetrate the fibres so well that it is almost impossible to tell which side of the fabric is the reverse. Some flag emblems are larger than the silkscreen tables, so they have to be hand-painted using special paint. To assemble the flags, pieces of fabric in different colours are joined together with double

seams using colour-matched thread. The top and bottom hems are made with two rows of stitching, while the fly-end hem has four rows of lock stitching with back-stitch reinforcement. Sometimes there are also several diagonal rows of stitching in the fly corners. The hoist is usually inserted and sewn into a heavy white canvas heading, either with grommets or with the rope sewn in. In Japan, instead of the heading, triangular pieces of canvas are used to reinforce the hoist corners.

The fabrics used for colours and for indoor and parade flags need to be particularly lustrous, with a surface suitable for embroidery. Embroidery is ideal for intricate multicoloured

◆ BELOW
Hand-painted seal of Idaho
for a flag of 6 m (6½ yd) hoist.

◆ **BELOW**
Detail of modern embroidery
with silver metal thread.

designs, and in recent years more and more flag manufacturers are using computer–aided embroidery machines. In the United States the stars of the national flag are embroidered on huge machines that are capable of producing hundreds of star fields simultaneously.

Large flag manufacturers have well-organized production lines, which begin at the art department where paper patterns of flag designs are prepared and stored. In a sewn flag, the relevant pattern is sent to the cutting department, which provides the sewing department with pieces of fabric in the exact sizes and colours needed. Once the pieces of fabric have been stitched together, the emblems are applied on top. Simple pre-cut emblems such as stars, fleurs-de-lis, crescents and crosses are pasted on and large emblems are then reinforced by stitching around the edges. In the finishing department the heading and grommets are added to outdoor flags, and indoor and parade flags are fitted with tabs and fringes.

MATERIALS GLOSSARY

Bunting A traditional all-wool fabric used for making flags from the 17th century to the present day

Calico A plain-woven cotton fabric of Indian origin. Used in the 17th and 18th centuries in Europe for some flags

Cotton A fabric made from the seed fibres of a variety of cotton plants native to most sub-tropical countries. Flag manufacturers use mercerized cotton because of its greater strength and lustre, and modern finishing processes make it resistant to stains, water and mildew. Widely used to make relatively inexpensive outdoor flags

Damask A patterned material, originally made of silk, which originated in the Middle East and was introduced to Europe by the Crusaders in the 11th century. Single damask has one set of warp and weft threads, and can be woven in one or two colours; double damask has a greater number of weft threads

Linen A cloth woven from flax, a plant of the family *Linaceae*. Flax is the oldest textile fibre, used in Anatolia for making clothes in the early Neolithic period, around 8000 BC

Nylon A synthetic plastic material manufactured since the late 1930s as a fibre from long-chain polyamides. Resistant to wear, heat and chemicals. Nylon taffeta is used to manufacture indoor and parade flags and heavyweight nylon is used for outdoor flags

Polyester A material manufactured from Terylene (Dacron) fibres, for which the basis is a long-chain polyester made from organic chemicals (ethylene glycol and terephthalic acid). Very durable, elastic, non-combustible and resistant to chemicals and micro-organisms, but prolonged exposure to even minimal sunlight affects colours

Rayon An artificial silk material, woven from fibres produced from the plant substance cellulose since the end of the 19th century. Used mainly to manufacture smaller dyed flags, 10 x 15 cm to 60 x 90 cm (4 x 6 in to 24 x 36 in). Heavy Bemberg rayon is used for the most luxurious indoor and parade flags

Sendal A fabric with a linen warp and silk weft. Used in northern Europe since the 13th century. It is suitable for painted heraldic banners

Silk A lightweight fabric woven from the filament of cocoons produced by the caterpillars of a few moth species belonging to the genus *Bombyx*. Relatively strong with a smooth, lustrous surface. Silkweaving originated in China in 2600 BC, and was known in Egypt from at least 1000 BC, and since the 12th century in Italy

Taffeta A plain-weave fabric, made of silk or nylon fibres, in which the warp and weft threads are evenly interlaced. Fine with a lustrous surface. Used mainly for indoor and parade flags, and colours

FLAG PARTS AND ACCESSORIES

Most of the accessories on flags for outdoor use constitute part of the design; the two that do not are the canvas heading and the hoist rope or grommets.

Indoor flags have various devices to attach the flag to the staff. These differ from country to country. The most popular device is a sleeve, which in Europe is fastened to the staff with special decorative nails. These nails bear engraved emblems with the names of the institutions or individuals who founded the flag or colour. In the United States of America the sleeve has leather tabs at each end, which attach to screwheads protruding from the staff. In Japan, instead of a sleeve, there are two or three leather triangles with eyelets that enable the flag to be fastened to the staff with decorative tasselled cords. Indoor flags will often also feature a fringe, a decorative tasselled cord and a cravat or the ribbons of an order.

◆ **LEFT**
Japanese flag for indoor or ceremonial use.

◆ **BELOW LEFT**
Heading with a hoist rope, ring and clip. Jack of Saudi Arabia (since 1981).

◆ **BELOW RIGHT**
Heading with a hoist rope and becket. Polish jack (1919–1945 and 1959–1993).

FLAG ACCESSORIES GLOSSARY

Cord A decorative, flexible string or rope made from several twisted strands. When attached to a ferrule, it has tassels and is tied in the middle. Used also to finish the edges of a flag. Usually of gold or silver thread, or in national livery colours

Cravat A wide ribbon attached to a staff below the finial, used as a distinction or as a mark of honour with a military colour or flag. Usually in national livery colours and richly decorated

Ferrule A metal ring at the top end of the staff, just below the finial

Finial An ornament on the top of the staff. Usually made of metal in the form of a spearhead, armorial crest or other three-dimensional figure

Fringe A decoration made of twisted thread or metal (gold or silver). Usually attached to the edges of the flag on the three free sides. Appropriate for indoor flags, parade flags and car flags

Grommet A metal eyelet reinforcing a hole near both ends of the heading, through

FINIAL OF THE FRENCH COLOUR OF THE 2ND REPUBLIC (1848–1851)

which clips are attached to a halyard pass

Heading A piece of canvas into which the hoist edge of a flag is sewn. To facilitate hoisting, it may have a rope sewn in or grommets fastened near the upper and lower edge

Sleeve A tube of material along the hoist of a flag through which the staff is passed. Used mainly for a colour or an indoor or parade flag

Staff A cylindrical piece of wood to which the flag is fastened. The staff of a colour is usually made of two pieces connected with a metal tube. See also *Finial; Crossbar, Flagpole, Gaff (Hardware Glossary)*

Tab A small piece of leather sewn inside the sleeve near both ends. When fastened to a screwhead protruding from the staff, it prevents the flag from slipping on the staff

Tassel A tuft of loosely hanging twisted threads or metal hanging from a cord attached to the staff. Used with a colour, or other ceremonial or decorative flag. Without a cord, tassels are also used at the points of a triangular or tailed flag hung vertically

FLAG HARDWARE

It would not be possible to display a flag without a few pieces of specially designed hardware. Beckets and toggles, rings and snaps, grommets and Inglefield clips all allow a flag to be fastened to the rope. Flagpoles make it possible to fly a flag at the desired height whilst flag belts enable someone to carry a heavy parade flag or colour more easily.

There are several ways of fastening a flag to a flagpole. In Europe a rope is sewn into the heading and attached to the halyard with a becket and toggle. Some flags, especially those for use at sea, have looped clips and Inglefield clips instead of beckets and toggles. In the United States brass grommets are inserted on each end of the heading, and the halyard is furnished with clips that attach to the grommets. In Japan the hoist edges are reinforced with triangles of heavy canvas with ribbons, which attach the flag to clips on the halyard.

A flagpole consists of a pole made of glass fibre, aluminium, steel or wood, with a truck on the top. Above the truck is a cap in the form of a disc, ball, eagle or other figure. The bottom part of the flagpole is embedded in a ground socket in a concrete foundation, or permanently welded to a base made of heavy cast aluminium. The halyard passes through a pulley in the truck and is secured to a cleat on the lower part of the flagpole. To prevent malicious damage or theft of flags, modern flagpoles are fitted with an internal halyard system and an access door with a lock. Older flagpoles can be modified with the addition of halyard covers and cleat-cover lock boxes. In cities, outrigger staffs or vertical flagpoles are usually set into a wall. They are constructed in a similar way to flagpoles, but the lower part is mounted in a metal base fastened with anchor bolts through the wall. Much smaller and lighter outrigger staffs are used by private home-owners who are well served by buying an inexpensive kit containing a sectional aluminium staff about 2 m (6 ft) long and a steel mounting bracket with screws.

FLAG HARDWARE GLOSSARY

Becket A loop at the end of a hoist rope that fastens to a toggle at the end of the halyard, making it easier to bend on a flag

Case A narrow sack to protect a parade flag in inclement weather, or to store it when not in use

Cleat A metal device with two arms, attached to the lower part of a flagstaff, to which the halyards are made fast

Crossbar A rod bearing a flag (usually a pennant, banner or gonfalon), attached directly or by a rope to a staff. The crossbar usually passes through the sleeve. Parts of the sleeve can be cut out to reveal parts of the crossbar

CLEAT

Flagpole A pole made of wood, metal or glass fibre on which a flag may be hoisted. It may be upright or projecting at an angle from a wall. Sometimes an upright flagpole is fitted with a yardarm or gaff to increase the number of flags that may be hoisted.

This practice is found mainly at naval establishments ashore

Flagstaff see *Flagpole*

Frame A wood or metal device designed to hold the top edge of a flag

Gaff A spar from which a flag is hoisted. It is set diagonally on the aft side of a mast. A flag is attached to a halyard passing through the outer end of the gaff. An ensign is flown from the gaff of the mizzen mast, or of the main mast in a two-masted ship

Halyard The rope to which a flag is bent in order to be hoisted

Inglefield clips Interlocking metal clips used to attach a flag securely to the halyard. Their quick-release mechanism makes it possible to bend on a flag easily

Mast A long, upright post of timber or metal set up on a ship or on a building

Staff see *Flagpole*

Tangle rod A metal device attached to a staff projecting at an angle from a wall,

which clasps a flag and prevents it from wrapping around the staff

Toggle A device at the end of a rope sewn into the heading, consisting of an oval-shaped wooden or plastic crosspiece that fastens to a becket at the end of the halyard, making it easier to bend on a flag

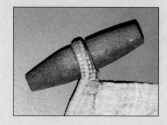

TOGGLE

Truck A circular metal cap fixed on the head of a flagpole below the finial. It contains a pulley over which the halyard passes

Yardarm A bar attached horizontally to a mast of a ship or to a flagpole on shore to increase the number of flags that may be hoisted, attached to separate halyards

USAGE AND CUSTOM: ON LAND

From time immemorial flags and banners were used to distinguish bodies of troops and to serve as rallying points when they needed to regroup or retreat. In the Middle Ages the number of banners carried into battle was imposing. There were royal banners, banners of provinces, cities and guilds, and banners of knights who were able to raise their own troops. At Buironfosse, where in 1339 the French and English Armies did not dare to stage battle, the French forces displayed 220 banners and 560 pennons, while the English had 74 banners and 230 pennons. In the battle of Tannenberg in 1410, the 56 banners unfurled by the Teutonic knights and the 91 banners by the Polish–Lithuanian forces were mainly the emblems of cities and provinces. Banners like these continued to be used on the battlefield until the 16th century, when European countries began to build standing armies based on permanent groupings of troops in legions and regiments.

After this date banners began to lose their heraldic character and by the beginning of the 17th century most of them displayed instead painted representations of patron saints or allegorical figures. Gradually all countries began to follow the example set by the French in 1597 and developed consistent designs for their infantry colours and cavalry standards. Military colours served their purpose on the battlefield until the end of the 19th century, when modern warfare made the function of colours in battle obsolete. (Several instances of troops displaying their colours were still reported even in World War II.) Today military colours are displayed only during military or state ceremonies.

In the Middle Ages banners were not only used in battle, however. In peacetime they were proudly displayed on the towers of castles and city halls, carried in triumphal marches and processions, and exhibited during all manner of festivities. The whole life of a banner was closely connected with the local church; every battle banner was consecrated in the church, was kept there in peacetime and was deposited there when it could no longer serve its purpose. Most

of the banners used on the battlefield in the Middle Ages served later to identify states, provinces, cities and guilds, and to this day many cities in Central Europe and Italy use the same flags as in medieval times.

Until the 19th century, the use of flags on land was limited and only a few countries had a national flag. The radical changes in the world that led to the revolutions in Europe of 1848 gave birth to the idea of the nation-state and from then on, in many sovereign countries, the civil ensign became the national flag.

In the same way that the coat of arms had been the sign identified with the ruler and the state, so the national flag was from the beginning a symbol with which people could identify. The concept of a national flag as a symbol of the people rather than the state became prevalent, and in many cases the flag was introduced by leaders of independence movements, revolutionaries or students and was only later officially adopted by government. The case of the British Union Jack, which to this day has never officially been declared to be the national flag, is proof that for the people of a

◆ **ABOVE**
Armorial banners of Bavaria, Brunswick and Saxony carried in the triumphal procession of the Emperor of Germany Maximilian I at the beginning of the 16th century.

◆ LEFT
British recruitment poster,
World War I.

◆ RIGHT
American patriotic postcard,
World War I.

◆ ABOVE
British match label.

country legislative action is less important than their feelings. Almost everywhere in the world the national flag is not just a piece of bunting but something so close to people's hearts that they will risk their lives for it. Under foreign occupation, to display the national flag has often been an offence punishable by death, yet there have always been people defiantly hoisting their flag as a strong message that says, "This is our country, we are here to stay and we shall overcome!"

Awareness that the flag is a powerful symbol has induced totalitarian and oppressive regimes to de-legalize the flags of their opponents and to persecute those who defy the ban. In Spain, for example, it was illegal under Franco's regime to display the Basque flag. In answer to this, the Basque separatists hoisted a booby-

trapped flag that would blow up when the police tried to remove it. Israeli authorities have for decades harshly persecuted Palestinians caught with the flag of Palestine, and in the Soviet Union people could be sent to a concentration camp for publicly displaying the national flag of Lithuania, Armenia or any other nation that had been forcibly incorporated into the Soviet Union.

To sustain patriotic feelings during the Civil War in the United States, both sides published postcards of the national and Confederate flags, featuring allegorical figures of Liberty. In most of the countries involved in World War I, patriotic cards and posters displayed the national flag and the flags of the Allies. The message was clear: we fight for our country and have foreign friends on our side.

◆ LEFT
Flag mutilated during a street
demonstration.

◆ RIGHT
Flag burning in Warsaw,
1998. Photo courtesy of
Miroslaw Stelmach.

A common form of protest against the actions of a foreign country is to publicly burn its national flag. Left-wing students in France burnt the German flag as a protest against the arrest of Red Brigade terrorists. In many countries in the West, refugees from countries subjugated by the Soviet Union have burnt the Soviet flag, and under the regime of Ayatollah Khomeini the Iranians burnt United States flags. Workers belonging to the Polish "Solidarity" trade unions burnt the European Union flag out of fear that they would lose their jobs if Poland joined the EEC.

A traditional custom involving the national flag is to symbolically plant it in places that are discovered or conquered. The British have taken the Union Jack to all parts of the world. Roald Amundsen in 1911 planted the Norwegian flag at the South Pole, and in 1953 Edmund Hillary and Sherpa Tenzing Norgay placed the flags of New Zealand and Nepal on top of Mount Everest. The United States flag was carried to the North Pole in 1909 by Robert E. Peary, and in 1969 Neil Armstrong and Edwin E. Aldrin took it to the moon.

The political changes and development of international contacts in the 20th century have had a great impact on the development of all kinds of flags. In 1900 there were 49 sovereign countries and by 1998 their number had grown to more than 200. Many of these new countries adopted not only a national flag but also

numerous government services flags, as well as ensigns and other flags for use at sea. Tens of thousands of new flags have been adopted by political parties, trade unions, firms and corporations, youth movements, universities, schools, and yacht and sporting clubs. Occasional flags are designed for anniversaries such as the bicentennials of the American and French Revolutions, and for Olympic Games and international congresses. In some countries there are also flags for special occasions such as Christmas, Easter, Hallowe'en, birthdays or the birth of a baby.

In most countries the daily display of flags is limited to the flags of the head of state, national and state flags, flags of government agencies and officers, flags of certain companies and the flags of political parties, but in some countries flags are almost everywhere. Probably the most flag-filled nation is Switzerland. There, at least three flags (national, that of the canton and that of the commune or town) are displayed together and

the larger streets in the cities are decorated with the national flag and the flags of all the cantons. National, provincial and civic flags, mostly in banner form, are permanently displayed in Germany. In the United States and Scandinavian countries the national flag is displayed not only by the authorities and public bodies, but also by a large part of the population in front of private houses. Throughout the world national flags are displayed on state holidays, and it is inconceivable to have street parades or demonstrations without a large number of flags. Hundreds of national or club flags are waved in stadiums and sports arenas by ardent fans, and in the 1990s the custom of painting the colours and design of the national flag on to the body developed.

The steadily increasing use of flags has been augmented by countless international meetings, conferences and sporting events. The national

◆ **ABOVE**
Three flags from a match label set: Ethiopia (1941–1975); United States (1959); Laos (1952–1975).

◆ **LEFT**
This poster, produced in 1991 by Konstantin Geraymovich, was an expression of indignation of the Russian artist at the Soviet military intervention in the capital of Lithuania. The other two dates are those of Soviet invasions of Hungary (1956) and Czechoslovakia (1968).

◆ **RIGHT**
Flags used to great effect on a poster promoting the Marshall Plan, produced in 1950.

flags of member-countries are permanently displayed at the headquarters of international organizations throughout the world, for example the United Nations in New York and the Commonwealth Institute in London.

The national flag as the visual symbol of a nation is so deeply engrained in modern consciousness that the media often show a flag as a symbol of a nation rather than just its name. Advertisers use pictures of national flags to suggest the international scope of their business, and large hotels eager to attract international clientele often display many different national flags. Most countries issue postage stamps to honour and promote their national flags. One of the first sets of stamps to illustrate flags in

colour was the famous American set of thirteen flags for the "Over-run Countries", issued in 1943–4. The largest series of 160 national flags was published by the United Nations in 1980–89. Sets of matchbox labels with national flags have been issued in Australia, Germany, Hungary, Spain and the former Yugoslavia. Flags also appear on lapel pins, ties and belt buckles, and on souvenir articles such as keyrings, T-shirts, mugs, umbrellas and playing cards.

USAGE AND CUSTOM: AT SEA

The first flags identifying nationality were used at sea. The oldest international legal obligation on record for ships to display flags as identification was agreed by King Edward I of England and Guy, Count of Flanders, in 1297. It explicitly compelled merchant ships to "carry in their ensigns or flags the arms of their own ports certifying their belonging to the said ports". From the beginning of the 13th century England claimed sovereignty over the seas and demanded that all ships belonging to other countries should salute the English ships by lowering their topsails, and later also by striking the flag. Captains who refused to do so were regarded as enemies and their ships and cargo forfeited. Foreign ships submitted because England insisted only on a salute and levied no duties on ships passing through the English Channel. The practice became obsolete in 1805, but the custom of saluting a foreign vessel remains to this day. Merchant ships salute each other by dipping the ensign as an act of courtesy; warships do not dip to each other, but if a merchant vessel dips to them they reply.

For a long time the national ensigns of the main maritime powers served as passports for merchant ships sailing to Turkey, North Africa, China and India. Under a treaty made by King Henry VI of France and Sultan Ahmed of the Turkish Empire, from 1604 to 1675 ships of all nations could visit the Turkish ports and trade there only "under the authorization and security of the Banner of France". The situation changed in 1675 when a British–Turkish capitulation treaty reserved the right to free trade in Turkey for the "English nation and the English Merchants and all other nations or Merchants who are or shall come under the banner and protection of England". Similar provisions concerning the protection of ships and citizens and/or free trade were included in treaties made between France and the Turkish vassal states in North Africa: Morocco (1682), Tripoli (1685) and Tunis (1685). Another example is Austria's peace treaties with Morocco and Turkey (1783–5). One of the purposes of these and subsequent treaties was to protect commercial shipping from pirates.

As well as the national ensign there were, and still are, many other flags for use on ships. The oldest is the jack, flown from the bow. Currently private ships display the civil ensign or service ensign on the stern, the house flag on the foremast and (in Britain) the jack on the bow. On sailing ships the civil ensign is often displayed from a halyard attached to the mizzen mast. Yachts fly the civil ensign on the stern and the club burgee or private flag on the mast. On war ships the war ensign is flown on the stern and the jack on the bow; on the main mast either the commission pennant or a command flag, with the rank flag below, is flown.

◆ **BELOW**
Flags on a warship.

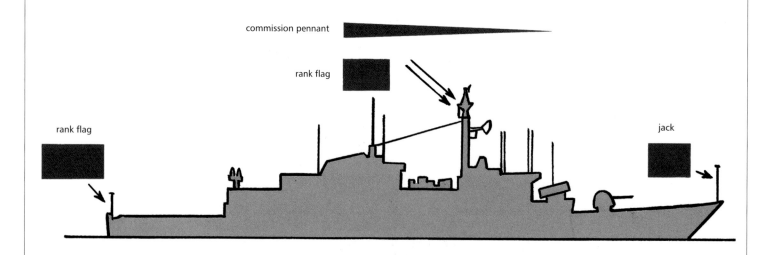

commission pennant

rank flag

rank flag

jack

FLAG ETIQUETTE

There are no international regulations governing flag etiquette but the rules adopted by many countries have so much in common that it is possible to formulate general guidelines. They are slightly different for a flag displayed inside a country and for one at an international forum. The general rule in both cases is that all flags hoisted as a group should be the same width and should be hoisted on separate flagpoles, or separate halyards in the case of a flagpole with a yardarm. The practice of hoisting two or more flags on the same halyard is not correct.

In most countries the following rules are observed for hoisting flags inside the country:

◆ The flag should be displayed in the open from sunrise to sunset, but it should not be displayed on days when the weather is inclement. It may be displayed at night providing that it is well illuminated.

◆ The flag should be hoisted briskly and lowered ceremoniously.

◆ The flag should always be used in a dignified manner. It should never touch the ground, the floor or water. It should never be carried flat or horizontally, but always aloft and free. It should never be used as a table or seat cover, or as drapery of any sort. It should never be used as a receptacle for receiving, holding, carrying or delivering anything.

◆ The national flag should not be displayed in a position inferior to any other flag. The national flag takes precedence over all other flags. When flown with the flags of other sovereign nations, all flags should be flown on separate flagpoles of the same size. The flags should be of the same size or the same width, and should be flown at the same height. The other national flags should be displayed in alphabetical order according to the official language of the country.

◆ When there are two flags displayed, the national flag should be on the left of the observer, facing the staff. The same rule should be observed when the national flag is crossed with another flag; its staff should be in front of the staff of another flag; see diagram overleaf.

◆ In a line of three flags, the national flag should be positioned in the centre; see diagram overleaf.

◆ In a line of four flags, the national flag should be the first to appear on the observer's left; see diagram overleaf.

◆ In a line of five or more flags, two national flags should be used, one at each end of the line, see diagram overleaf.

◆ In a semi-circle, the national flag should be in the centre; see diagram overleaf.

◆ In an enclosed circle, the national flag should be positioned and centred immediately opposite the main entrance to a building or arena; see diagram overleaf.

◆ The order of flags hoisted together depends on the place of each particular flag in the following hierarchy: (a) national flag, (b) regional or provincial flag, (c) county, parish or commune flag, (d) civic flag, (e) service flag (e.g. police, fire brigade), (f) other flags (university, school, commercial firm, sports club etc).

◆ When the national flag is carried in a procession it should always be aloft and free. In a single line the national flag must always lead. If carried in line abreast with one other flag, it should be on the right-hand end of the line facing the direction of movement; if carried with two or more other flags, it should either be in the centre, or two national flags should be displayed, one at each end of the line.

◆ **ABOVE**
A huge flag carried flat looks good from above, but since its design is not visible to the spectators standing on the ground it is not correct flag etiquette. In this example, the event is a 4th July parade in Georgia, USA.

ETIQUETTE

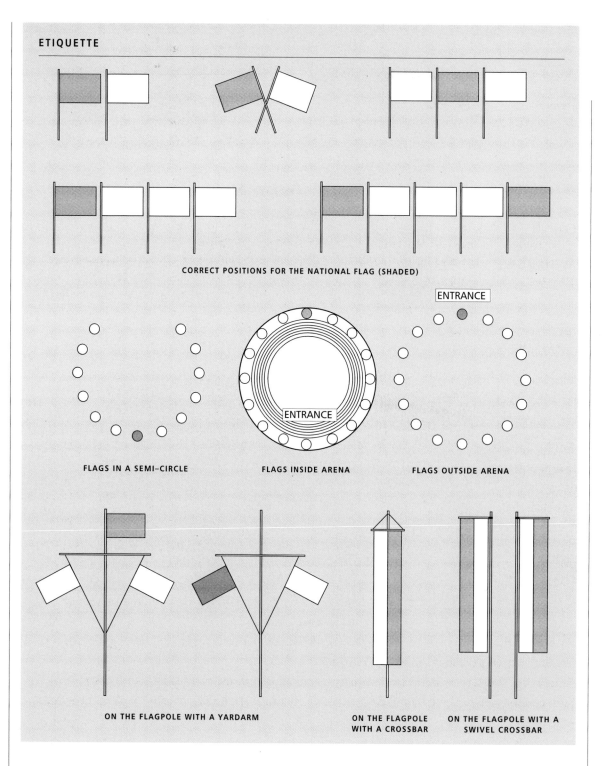

CORRECT POSITIONS FOR THE NATIONAL FLAG (SHADED)

FLAGS IN A SEMI–CIRCLE   ENTRANCE   FLAGS INSIDE ARENA   ENTRANCE   FLAGS OUTSIDE ARENA

ON THE FLAGPOLE WITH A YARDARM   ON THE FLAGPOLE WITH A CROSSBAR   ON THE FLAGPOLE WITH A SWIVEL CROSSBAR

♦ The correct position of the national flag displayed on a flagpole fitted with a yardarm is illustrated above.

♦ When a flag is displayed over the middle of a street, it should be suspended vertically, with its top edge to the north in an east–west street or to the east in a north–south street.

♦ When a flag is displayed vertically on a flagpole with a crossbar, the upper edge of the flag is to be on the observer's left; see above.

♦ When a flag is displayed vertically on a flagpole with a swivel crossbar, the upper edge of the flag should face the flagpole; see illustration above.

♦ When a flag is displayed from a staff on a speaker's platform, it should be on the speaker's right as he faces the audience.

♦ When used to cover a coffin, a flag should be placed so that the hoist is at the head and the top edge is over the left shoulder.

♦ As a sign of mourning the flags on flagpoles are half-masted. A black ribbon is attached to flags hoisted on short outrigger staffs, and a black cravat to military parade flags.

FLAG ETIQUETTE GLOSSARY

Bend on a flag To fasten a flag to halyards in order to hoist it

Break out a flag To unfurl a flag that has been rolled and tied in such a way that a sharp tug on the halyard will cause it to open out

Consecration The dedication ceremony of a colour or other flag

Desecration Disrespectful treatment of a flag such as burning it in public, defacing it with inappropriate inscriptions or emblems, mutilating it, trampling it or throwing it on the floor or ground. Punishable in most countries of the world

Dip a flag The custom of lowering a flag briefly and temporarily in salute. A sign of respect used to honour the national anthem, an important person or another vessel

Drape a flag The custom of attaching a black cravat to a staff as a sign of mourning

Dress ship To decorate a vessel with flags for a holiday or special occasion. Until the 20th century all flags in the ship's store were raised on every available halyard but now only signal flags are displayed

Flag officer A naval officer entitled to use a rank flag, usually above the rank of captain

Fold a flag A ceremony performed after a flag is taken down from a flagpole or removed from a coffin it has covered. The flag is folded lengthwise three times in such a way that the upper hoist part is on the outside. A series of triangular folds follows, beginning at the fly, until the flag resembles a cocked hat with only part of the hoist still visible

Half-mast To fly a flag at a point much below its normal position, usually as a sign of mourning. The flag should be first hoisted to the peak for an instant then lowered to the half-mast position. It should be raised again to the peak before it is lowered for the day

Honour a flag Whenever a military unit or civil organization is awarded, the order ribbons are ceremoniously attached to the staff of the colour or banner. The head of state or his deputy personally presents the award at a ceremony held in the presence of the military unit or a representative of the organization

Lay up colours To deposit old colours ceremoniously in a church or museum

Pall flag A flag laid over a coffin, hearse or tomb. This is used mainly at government and military funerals. It is removed from the coffin before it is lowered into the grave

Salute the flag Flags are saluted when being hoisted, lowered or passed in a parade review. Civilians stand at attention, men remove their headgear and military personnel place the right hand to the head in a prescribed salute

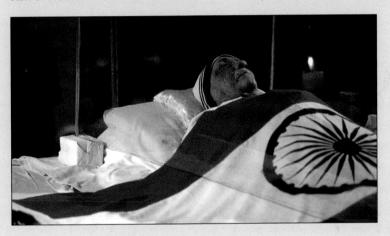

◆ **LEFT**
Pall flag - Mother Theresa lying in state with the Indian national flag laid over her body, 1997.

◆ When a flag is no longer in a suitable condition to be used it should be destroyed in a dignified way by burning it privately. At the headquarters of international organizations and at international conferences or sports events, national flags should be arranged in alphabetical order, either in the official language of the host country or in English. National flags hoisted together should be the same width. When the flagpoles form an enclosed circle the order of flags should be clockwise, with the first flag positioned opposite the main entrance.

Flags are designed in such a way that they should be displayed in a horizontal position. There are, however, at least two circumstances when flags are displayed vertically: on a table (see *Types of Flags: Table flag*), and when they are positioned against a wall. In other circumstances vertical is an unsatisfactory way to display

flags because coats of arms or emblems may lose their upright position. Indeed, at least four countries, namely Brazil, Pakistan, Saudi Arabia and Sri Lanka, explicitly forbid vertical display of their national flags. However, Liechtenstein, Slovakia and Slovenia have special designs for displaying their national flags in a vertical position, and Germany and Austria both have a custom of turning coats of arms upright in state flags that are hanging vertically. The general rule to be observed when a flag is displayed vertically is that the upper edge of the flag should be to the observer's left (the observer will see the reverse of the flag). The only exceptions are the flags of Liechtenstein, Slovakia and Slovenia, which should be displayed in accordance with their official

FLAG CONFLICTS

The knowledge of flags and flag etiquette is a very important part of diplomatic protocol, unfortunately not always observed correctly. For example, the Iranian delegation to a European country almost abandoned talks because the hosts placed on their table the flag of Iran used by the overthrown Shah regime. An incorrect vertical display of some flags can cause serious consternation because the Polish flag becomes the flag of Monaco or Indonesia, the Dutch flag becomes that of Yugoslavia, the Russian flag changes into the Serbian flag and the civil flag of Ethiopia becomes that of Bolivia.

One of the first recorded incidents happened in September 1916 when King Vajiravudh (Rama VI) of Siam was visiting areas devastated by floods. All the towns and villages he visited were decorated with the national flag, red with a white elephant, but one was flying upside down. The sight of the elephant lying on its back shocked the King to such an extent that he decided to adopt a new flag with a simple design of red and white stripes that was incapable of being flown upside down.

Serious and long-lasting conflicts have been provoked by changing the national flag. The longest was the *Flaggenstreit* (flag conflict) in Germany after World War I. The struggle was between those who wanted to restore the

tricolour of 1848 and those who wanted to keep the flag designed by Bismarck in 1867, so it was a conflict between the adherents of two ideologies. The black, red and yellow were perceived as the colours of the democratic republic, and of unity, law and freedom, whereas the black–white–red tricolour, combining the colours of Prussia (black and white) and Brandenburg (red and white), was a reminder of the glorious days of the empire dominated by the militant Prussia. The situation was so tense that the republican government decided on a compromise. The flag of 1848 was restored as

♦ LEFT
The national flag of Siam (Thailand) (until 1916).

♦ LEFT
The national flag and civil ensign of Siam (Thailand) (1916–1917).

♦ BELOW
(left to right)
German national flag and civil ensign (1848–1866); German national flag and civil ensign (1867–1919); German civil ensign (1919–1933); German civil ensign (1933–1935).

the national flag, but all flags for use at sea (civil ensign, state ensign, war ensign, jack) remained black–white–red, with the addition of the national colours in the canton. When Adolf Hitler came to power in 1933 the German flags were changed again. The black–white–red tricolour was reinstated as the national flag but it could be displayed only together with the

Hakenkreuzflagge of the Nazi Party. Two years later the *Hakenkreuzflagge* became the national flag and civil ensign, and the base for all other ensigns and flags of the Third Reich.

Similar, but less intense, conflicts occurred between supporters of the Union Jack and the proponents of a new national flag in South Africa in the 1920s, and in Canada in the 1960s. Currently there is conflict in Russia between the pro-democratic forces and the communists who want to restore the Soviet flag. In Belarus patriots are demonstrating under the

with the Olympic rings in white. Then, after Taiwan was denied its seat in the United Nations, the International Olympic Committee denied it the right to use its national flag at the Olympics and demanded that a special flag be designed for the Chinese–Taiwan Olympic team; it was carried for the first time at the 1984 Olympic Games. The flag is white with the national emblem and Olympic rings within a stylised five-petalled flower shape. For political reasons, the national flag of South Africa was also banned and the South African team was

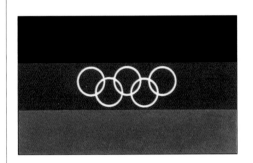

◆ **ABOVE LEFT**
All-German Olympic flag (1959–1968).

◆ **ABOVE CENTRE**
The Taiwan Olympic Flag (since 1984).

◆ **ABOVE RIGHT**
The flag of the South African team carried at the Summer Olympic games in Barcelona, Spain (1992).

historic flag against the president, who has decreed a flag similar to that used when Belarus was a Soviet republic.

In the 1990s flag conflicts were clearly visible during street demonstrations in Russia and Germany. In Russia the democrats march under the national flag, the communists under the Soviet flags and the Soviet war ensign, the monarchists under the black–gold–white tricolour or the national flag with the imperial eagle added, and the militant nationalists under the current war ensign. In Germany the militant neo-Nazis carry the imperial war ensign or flags of the *Freie Arbeitspartei*.

On the international scene, there have been several incidents at the Olympic Games. The first involved teams from both West and East Germany who were compelled to use the All-German Olympic flag (*Gesamtdeutsche Olympiaflagge*), the German flag defaced

compelled to use a special flag at the Olympic Games of 1992. At the same Olympics the teams from Bosnia and Herzegovina, Serbia and member-countries of the Commonwealth of Independent Countries were disqualified from holding any flags.

The latest flag conflict began in 1991 when Macedonia broke its ties with Yugoslavia and proclaimed an independent republic. As one of Greece's provinces is also named Macedonia, Greece began to contest the new country's right to this name. The Greek protests intensified in 1992 when Macedonia adopted a flag with the Star of Vergina, associated with King Philip II of Macedon and his son, Alexander III the Great (356–323 BC). Because a similar flag is used in Greek Macedonia, the Greek Prime Minister denounced the flag of Macedonia as a clear provocation. Because of the objections raised by Greece, Macedonia was admitted to the United Nations in April 1993 under the name "The Former Yugoslav Republic of Macedonia" and was denied the right to have its flag flown at the UN headquarters in New York, a move unprecedented in UN history.

◆ **BELOW**
The national flag of Macedonia (1992–1995).

Emperors, Sovereigns and Presidents

In the Middle Ages and much later in some countries, the state flag was the personal heraldic standard of the ruler. He was the state, and when his subjects went to battle or sailed the seas they flew his flag.

G.A. HAYES-MCCOY, *A HISTORY OF IRISH FLAGS*, BOSTON, 1979.

In the Middle Ages the ruler was regarded as the embodiment of the state, and for many centuries his banner was synonymous with the national flag. It marked his castle (or his tent in a military camp), was carried into battle and was flown on the masthead of his ships. Before the dawn of heraldry the personal flag of a ruler was plain red, showing that it was the flag of the emperor (*vexillo roseum imperiali*) or of someone with the right to govern in his name. Sometimes the red field of the emperor's flag was charged with a white cross as a sign that he had taken part in a crusade.

Diversification of these flags began in the second half of the 12th century when heraldic devices were introduced, and until the 15th century all of the flags of Europe's rulers were armorial banners. Most sovereigns continued to use armorial banners until the late 19th century, but in the 15th century the monarchs of southern Europe began to use unicolour royal flags, usually a white field carrying the royal coat of arms. At the end of the 17th century Scandinavian monarchs defaced their war ensigns with white panels bearing the whole arms, and a few further modifications have taken place during the last two centuries. These basic designs have served as the models for almost all the royal and presidential banners and flags in use throughout the world even to this day.

◆ **LEFT**
The presidential and national flags decorate the car which carries the president in the motorcade, travelling through Dallas a few moments before John F. Kennedy, 35th President of the United States, was shot.

MEDIEVAL EUROPE

In the course of the century from 1195 to 1295, most European rulers adopted coats of arms and armorial banners bearing one of the two most important heraldic figures: the lion, the king of the beasts, or the eagle, the king of heaven. There was the imperial black eagle, the three golden lions of England, the red lion of Scotland, the white lion of Bohemia, the black lion of Flanders, the purple lion of Leon, the three blue lions of Denmark, the lion with an axe of Norway and the white eagle of Poland.

In the Mediterranean region the King of Portugal in 1185 adopted a complex coat of arms displaying four blue shields forming a cross on a silver field, each shield charged with five white dots arranged in a saltire (diagonal cross).

♦ **LEFT**
Royal banners in 1300.

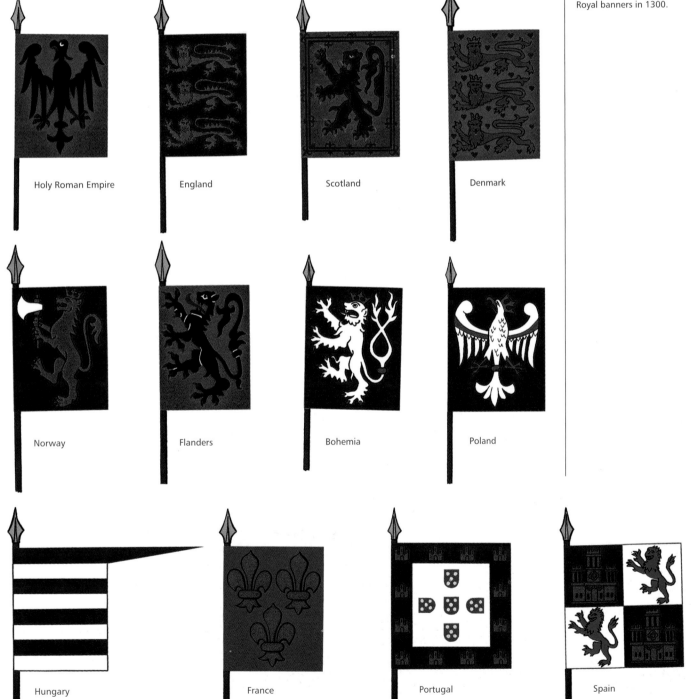

Holy Roman Empire

England

Scotland

Denmark

Norway

Flanders

Bohemia

Poland

Hungary

France

Portugal

Spain

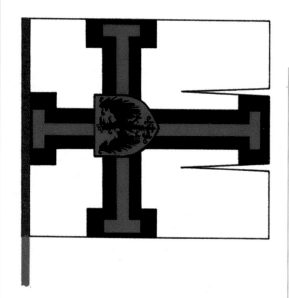

◆ ABOVE
(clockwise from top left)
Grand Master of the Teutonic
Order; England (1405–1603);
Hungary (1387–1437).

The shields symbolize the five Moorish kings defeated by the Portuguese and the five dots refer to the five wounds of Christ. After the final annexation of Algarve and the wedding of the King to Beatriz of Castile, a red border charged with golden castles was added to the arms. The other three kingdoms on the Iberian Peninsula had quite simple arms. The arms of Castile were the canting arms, a golden castle on red; those of Aragon were four red pallets on red; and those of Navarre were a gold chain arranged per cross, per saltire and in orle (as a border), with an emerald at the centre, all on red. From 1230 to 1479 the Spanish coat of arms was quarterly Castile and León. The arms of Sicily were per saltire Aragon and Hohenstaufen (black eagle on white). The royal coat of arms of France was golden fleurs-de-lis on a blue field; until the end of the 14th century their number was not limited, thereafter it was reduced to three.

Although it was not a kingdom, one of the most important states of the medieval period was the domain of the Teutonic Order. The white banner of the Grand Master of the Order was charged with a yellow and black cross, with the arms of the Holy Roman Empire in the centre.

As we saw in the example of Spain, already by the 13th century a king ruling over more than one domain incorporated their arms in his coat of arms and on his banner. Where there were two territories, this was done by either quartering or impaling the shield. In the case of quartering, the first arms appeared in the first and fourth quarter, and the second arms in the second and third quarter. The arms impaled had the shield divided per pale (vertically), as in the arms of Hungary under the rule of the Anjou dynasty (1387–1437), which displayed the Hungarian arms and the arms of France. In time the number of shield divisions grew to accommodate the arms of the extra territories, but even so at the ruler's funeral the separate banners of all of his domains were carried as well as his state banner.

THE MODERN WORLD

An example of a quite complex armorial banner is that of Burgundy, which reunified in the 14th century and for more than 100 years was one of the richest countries of Europe. It extended its possessions northwards to Flanders, Brabant and Holland, but in the 1470s was torn apart by Austria and France. The banner of Burgundy is quarterly the arms of Burgundy Modern (first and fourth quarters), Burgundy Ancient impaling Brabant (second quarter) and Burgundy Ancient impaling Limburg (third quarter), and displays the arms of Flanders on an inescutcheon.

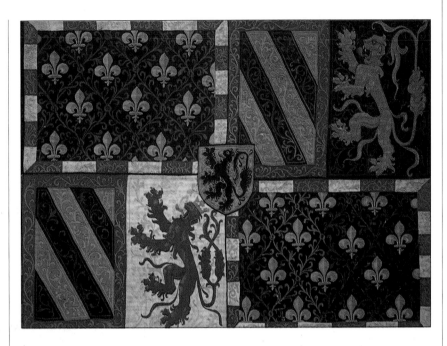

◆ **ABOVE**
Great Britain (1714–1801).

The expansion of the domains of other rulers was similarly reflected in their arms and banners. In 1438 Rudolf I of Habsburg was chosen to rule the Holy Roman Empire and Austria was established as his family's principal duchy. The imperial eagle was therefore ensigned in 1493 with the escutcheon of the arms of Austria, and from 1508 to 1519 the arms of Austria were impaled with those of Burgundy. Later the crowned eagle with a sword and a sceptre in its claws appeared on the imperial banner without the inescutcheon. In 1479 the kings of Spain augmented the arms of León and Castile with

the arms of Aragon and Sicily; the arms of Granada were added in 1492, and the arms of Austria, Burgundy Modern, Burgundy Ancient, Brabant, Flanders and Tyrol in 1504. Since 1603 the British royal banner has displayed the arms of England together with those of Scotland and the Irish harp, and since 1714 also the arms of Hanover.

At the end of the 15th century the diversification of the personal flags of European rulers began. The armorial banner still usually

◆ **ABOVE**
Banner of Burgundy.

◆ **BELOW**
Banner of the Duke of Brunswick-Lüneburg (1914–1918).

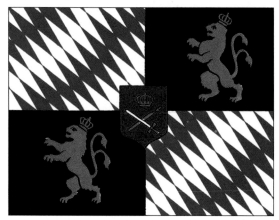

rulers for use at sea. The fields of these flags were white, the only exceptions being the yellow field of the imperial flags of Austria and Russia. Some later royal flags displayed the whole state arms on a red field.

In the 18th century Prussia emerged as one of the most powerful countries in Europe. Its arms had evolved from those of East Prussia, which was created by the secularization of the powerful

prevailed on land, but the Catholic monarchs of Spain introduced a white flag with the arms in the centre, designed for use at sea. In a few countries this kind of flag became the alternative personal flag of the ruler on land and thus the second model of the personal flag for heads of state came into being.

In the late 17th and 18th centuries the second model was adopted by most European

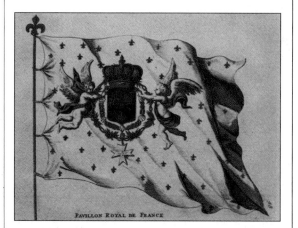

PAVILLON ROYAL DE FRANCE

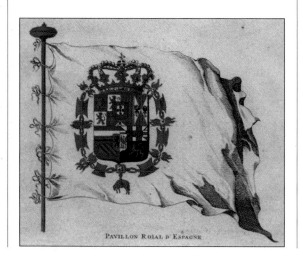

PAVILLON ROIAL D'ESPAGNE

PAVILLON ROIAL DE PORTUGAL.

◆ **RIGHT**
Austria (German emperor),
standard of the Emperor.

◆ **FAR RIGHT**
Tuscany, royal flag
(17th to 18th century).

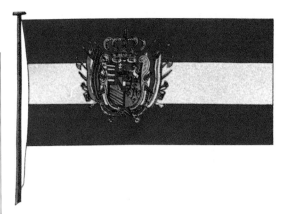

◆ **FAR RIGHT**
Russia, standard of the
emperor (18th century).

◆ **BELOW**
Spanish royal standard
(1833–1868 and 1875–1931).

Teutonic Order. In 1525 the Grand Master of
the Teutonic Order had sworn allegiance to
King Sigismund the Old of Poland and had
received from him a white banner defaced with
the new arms of East Prussia: a black eagle with
the royal crown on its neck,
and the royal cipher "S" on its breast. In 1569
the cipher was replaced by the "SA" of the
Polish King Sigismund August, and later it

combined the letters of the Polish kings and the
Prussian princes (VG for Vladislaus-Georgius
and JCF for Johannes Casimirus-Frederick). In
1618 East Prussia came under the direct control
of the electors of Brandenburg and the eagle was
ensigned with their crown. When the kingdom
of Prussia was proclaimed in 1713 the crown
was replaced with the royal one and the cipher
changed to "FR" (*Fredericus Rex*).

The other country to attain the position of a
world power at this time was Russia, which at
the beginning of the 18th century was
modernized by Peter the Great. He introduced
the yellow imperial banner with a representation
of the state arms in the centre. The arms had
been adopted by Ivan III after his marriage to
Sophia Paleologue, a niece of the last Byzantine
emperor, and were those of Byzantium – a
golden double-headed eagle on a red field. In
the 16th century this was defaced with the arms
of Moscow (St George slaying the dragon) and
at the end of the 17th century the colour of the
eagle was changed to black and the field to gold.

In some countries until the end of the 18th
century the ruler had at least two different flags
and in many countries there was no special flag

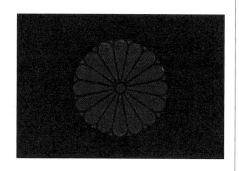

♦ **ABOVE LEFT**
Royal flag of the Netherlands
(1815–1840).

♦ **ABOVE CENTRE**
Royal flag of Afghanistan
(1930–1973).

♦ **ABOVE RIGHT**
Imperial flag of Japan since
the second half of the
19th century.

for the head of state. But in the 19th century the rulers and presidents of all countries began to adopt their flags.

The first presidential flag in the world followed the second model. It was a blue flag with the state arms of the United States in the centre, used on naval ships since the first half of the 19th century and made official in 1882. As commander-in-chief of the army, the President of the United States used a different flag on land. This was also blue with many white stars within its angles and a large crimson

war ensign introduced in 1690 by Denmark. This had a white square placed in the centre, charged at first with the royal cipher and later with the whole achievement of the royal arms. This model became standard in Scandinavia and was later copied by many other countries.

The third model was adopted by Napoleon I, who in 1804 placed the state arms in gold in the centre of the French *Tricolore*, on which golden bees were scattered. This flag was again in use from 1852 to 1970, and since 1871 the French presidents have placed their ciphers in the centre. The first to add an additional device (the cross of Lorraine) was Charles de Gaulle. From 1974 to 1995 the French presidential flag was charged with the presidential emblem instead of a cipher.

♦ **ABOVE**
Royal flag of Poland (1605).
Personal flag of King
Sigismund III.

♦ **FAR RIGHT ABOVE**
Flag of the Duke of Anhalt
(1815–1918).

♦ **FAR RIGHT BELOW**
Presidential flag of Germany
(1919–1921).

star in the centre, heavily outlined in white and defaced with the state coat of arms.

A variation of the second model was the field striped in the livery colours and/or swallow-tailed. Such, for example, were the Polish royal flags of the three kings from the Vasa dynasty (1587–1668).

The third model appeared next. The arms are displayed in the centre of a national flag or war ensign. The first of such flags was the was the

FRENCH PRESIDENTIAL FLAGS

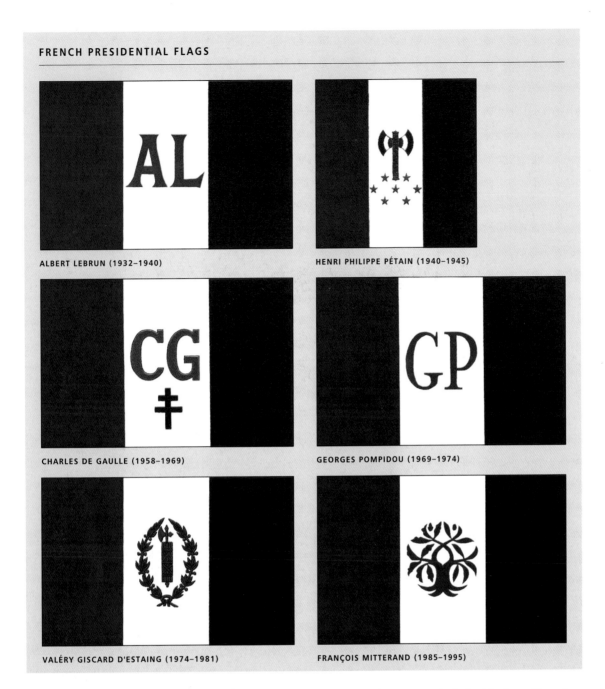

ALBERT LEBRUN (1932–1940)

HENRI PHILIPPE PÉTAIN (1940–1945)

CHARLES DE GAULLE (1958–1969)

GEORGES POMPIDOU (1969–1974)

VALÉRY GISCARD D'ESTAING (1974–1981)

FRANÇOIS MITTERAND (1985–1995)

The first major modification of the second model of the flag of a head of state was accomplished in 1828 when Austria changed the design of its imperial banner. A border in livery colours composed of white, red, yellow and black triangles was added to the yellow square field and the state arms were placed in the centre. This design was copied by Brunswick (1831–84), Bavaria and several other countries after World War I so it may be considered to be the fourth model.

Elaborate personal flags were introduced in 1844 in Prussia for the king, the queen and the crown prince and, although slightly modified in 1858 and 1889, they survived until 1918. Three elements of the design – the cross, the arms encircled with the collar of an order and the emblems in the corners – influenced not only the imperial flags of Germany but also the flags of other rulers. A very similar flag with a cross and three crowns in each corner was adopted by the grand duke of Oldeburg. The flag of the grand duke of Baden had a cross but the emblems in the corners were omitted. The royal flag of Italy, adopted in 1880, followed the Prussian design to some extent. The arms were placed in the centre of a square field and encircled with the collar of the Order of the Annunciation, and in each corner appeared a representation of the royal crown. Thus the fifth model of a royal or presidential flag was established.

FLAGS OF RULERS AND PRESIDENTS FOLLOWING THE AUSTRIAN DESIGN

EMPEROR OF AUSTRIA (1828–1894)

EMPEROR OF AUSTRIA – HUNGARY (1894–1915)

KING OF BULGARIA (1908–1918)

KING OF BULGARIA (1918–1947)

PRESIDENT OF CZECHOSLOVAKIA (1920–1939
AND 1945–1960)

PRESIDENT OF POLAND (1928–1945)

CHIEF OF THE HUNGARIAN STATE (1938–1945)

KING OF ROMANIA (1938–1947)

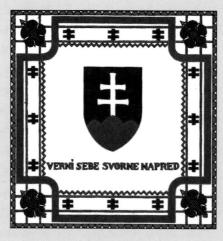

PRESIDENT OF SLOVAKIA (1939–1945)

CHIEF OF STATE OF CROATIA (1941–1945)

◆ **RIGHT**
King of Prussia's
standard
(1889–1918). Drawing
by Hugo S. Ströhl.

◆ **FAR RIGHT**
Crown prince of
Prussia's standard
(1889–1918).

◆ **BELOW RIGHT**
Empress of Prussia's
standard (1889–1918).

◆ **BELOW**
German imperial flags:
(first row) 1871–1890: emperor's standard, empress' standard,
crown prince's standard; (second row) 1890–1918: emperor's
standard, empress' standard, crown prince's standard.

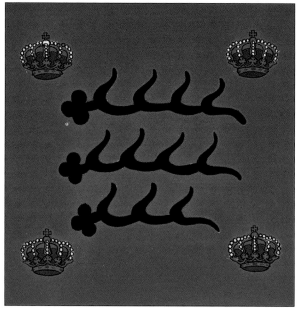

◆ **ABOVE**
Flag of the King of Italy
(1880–1946).

◆ **RIGHT**
Flag of the German chief
of state (Adolf Hitler)
(1935–1945).

◆ **TOP**
Flag of the king of Württemberg
(1884–1918).

◆ **ABOVE**
Egypt, royal naval flag (1923–1952).

◆ **LEFT**
Presidential flag of the United States
(1888–1945).

Tunis combined emblems from the Turkish
military flags with stripes in colours
characteristic of the flags of North Africa. The
King of Siam chose a blue field with a red
border, charged with a combination of the
attributes of his royal and military authority
and the coat of arms.

In some countries, including Prussia and
Germany, there were separate flags for the ruler's
wife and for the crown prince. Some monarchies
also had flags for the queen mother and other

When in 1916 the President of the United
States decided to have just one flag for use both
on land and at sea, he added a white star to each
corner of his naval flag. This inspired several
countries in Latin America and the Philippines
to adopt similar flags. The American presidential
flag was modified again in 1945, the four stars
in the corners being replaced by a ring of
48 white stars (one for each state) encircling the
coat of arms. The number of stars was increased
to 49 in 1959 (for Alaska), and to 50 in 1960

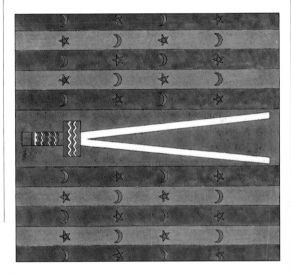

members of the royal family. In the last quarter
of the 19th century, for example, Russia had
five flags and five broad pennants for the
members of the imperial family: Empress,
crown prince, crown princess, grand duke,
grand duchess.

(for Hawaii). The only country that has
followed suit is the Philippines.

The models established in Europe for the
flags of heads of state were widely copied in the
Americas and partly in Africa and Asia. Some
rulers, however, adopted flags of a quite different
design. The King of Annam followed the
pattern of the Chinese flags, while the Bey of

CURRENT PRESIDENTIAL AND ROYAL FLAGS

Contemporary presidential and royal flags are presented in this section in chronological order according to the appearance of each model of flag. The oldest model, the armorial banner, has been used as a personal flag without interruption only by the rulers of Great Britain. Since 1837 the British royal banner has been quarterly England (first and fourth quarters), Scotland (second quarter) and Ireland (third quarter). There are separate armorial banners for the Duke of Edinburgh, the Queen Mother, the Prince of Wales, Princess Margaret and the other members of the Royal Family. The last of these, identical to the royal banner with a border of ermine, made history when it covered the coffin of Princess Diana.

Queen Elizabeth II also has special royal banners when she visits her ex-dominions such as Canada, Australia, New Zealand and Jamaica, or other monarchies of which she is the head of state. If she is visiting a country for which no special banner has been designed, she uses her personal flag which is a blue fringed field with the initial "E" in gold and ensigned with the royal crown, all within a chaplet of golden roses. This flag was used for the first time during the Queen's visit to India in 1961.

Remarkably, armorial banners are used as the flags of heads of state not only in European countries with a long heraldic tradition, such as Norway and Ireland, but in countries where this

◆ ABOVE
Royal banner of Great Britain (since 1837).

tradition is quite recent or non-existent. The oldest example is the royal banner of Tonga, introduced in 1862; another is the royal banner of Thailand, adopted in 1917, which displays the mythical Garuda, the bird of the god Vishnu. The banners of the presidents of Gabon and Guyana are fairly recent; the first was designed by Louis Mühlemann, the famous Swiss heraldist and vexillologist, the second by the College of Arms in London.

The largest group of current royal and presidential flags has a unicolour field charged with the arms or emblem, and in a few cases

◆ LEFT
Royal flag of Tonga (since 1862).

◆ LEFT
Royal flag of Norway (since 1905).

◆ FAR LEFT
Personal flag of Queen Elizabeth II.

◆ **RIGHT**
Presidential flag of Ireland
(since 1945).

◆ **FAR RIGHT**
Royal flag of Thailand
(since 1917).

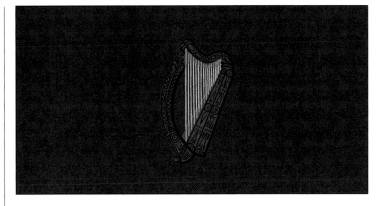

◆ **RIGHT**
Presidential flag of Gabon
(since 1960).

◆ **FAR RIGHT**
Presidential flag of Guyana
(since 1970).

◆ **BELOW LEFT**
Presidential flag of Uruguay
(since 1908).

◆ **BELOW CENTRE**
Presidential flag of Argentina
(since 1916).

◆ **BELOW RIGHT**
Presidential flag of Malta
(since 1988).

displaying another device such as the party emblem (Kenya) or an inscription (Bangladesh, Kazakhstan, Malawi). The colour of the field is usually one of the colours of the national flag. Several presidential flags displaying the arms in the centre of a unicoloured field have a border of one to three colours. In the Czech Republic the border is patterned on the Austrian version.

There are several ways to deface a national flag with the arms or a presidential emblem.

They are usually positioned in the centre of the flag but sometimes appear in the upper hoist (Egypt, Finland, Morocco, Turkey), centre hoist (Eritrea, Namibia), top centre (Kuwait, Swaziland) or lower hoist (Saudi Arabia). In a few cases the emblem replaces the one on the national flag (Eritrea, Maldives, Pakistan).

The fifth, and last, model survived mainly in countries that copied the American flag. For example, the presidential flag of Cuba has

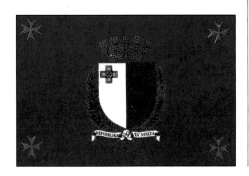

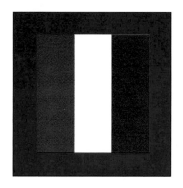

been modified to display six stars instead of four, and in the Peruvian flag the stars have been replaced by yellow suns.

These five models inspired the designs of almost all the flags adopted before World War II. Another model was added when the French colonies gained independence. This is the simplest model, a square and fringed variant of the national flag, used in some former French colonies south of the Sahara, and in Tunisia and Syria.

Several flags of heads of state defy classification. Their designs combine features of the first and fourth models (Slovakia), the second, fourth and fifth (Sri Lanka) or the third

and fourth (Liechtenstein). The presidential flag of India looks heraldic but instead of heraldic figures it displays: the whole state arms (first quarter); an elephant symbolizing patience and strength (second quarter); scales representing justice and thrift (third quarter); a vase of lotus flowers representing prosperity and wealth (fourth quarter). The royal flag of the Netherlands is the only flag to have a cross as

◆ **ABOVE**
(left to right)
Presidential flag of Israel (since 1948); presidential flag of Germany (since 1950); presidential flag of Italy (since 1990); presidential flag of Slovenia (since 1995).

◆ **LEFT**
Presidential flag of the Czech Republic (since 1993).

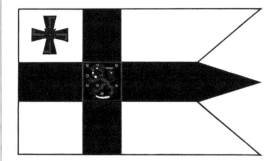

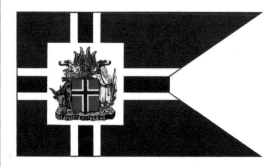

◆ **FAR LEFT TOP**
Presidential flag of Iceland (since 1944).

◆ **FAR LEFT CENTRE**
Presidential flag of Finland (since 1978).

◆ **FAR LEFT BOTTOM**
Royal flag of Denmark (since 1972).

◆ **LEFT**
Presidential flag of Russia (since 1994).

◆ **LEFT**
Presidential flag of the
United States (since 1960).

◆ **RIGHT**
Royal flag of the Netherlands
(since 1908).

◆ **LEFT**
Presidential flag of Ghana
(since 1960).

◆ **BELOW LEFT TOP**
Presidential flag of South
Korea (since 1967).

◆ **BELOW LEFT CENTRE**
Presidential flag of India
(since 1950).

◆ **BELOW LEFT BOTTOM**
Royal flag of Jordan
(since 1928).

an additional charge. Around the arms is a ribbon with the insignia of the most distinguished Dutch military decoration, the Order of William.

Many countries do not have a special flag for the head of state, including the sixteen monarchies under Queen Elizabeth II of Great Britain. Some one-party countries do not have presidential flags for political reasons and a few simply do not see the need for a special flag.

THE BASIC MODELS OF CURRENT HEAD OF STATE FLAGS

An armorial banner is used in:
GABON, GREAT BRITAIN, GUYANA, IRELAND, NORWAY, THAILAND, TONGA.

A unicolour flag defaced with the arms or an emblem is used in:
BANGLADESH, BOTSWANA, BRAZIL, BRUNEI, DOMINICA, GREECE, INDONESIA, JAPAN, KAZAKHSTAN, KENYA, KOREA, LUXEMBOURG, MALAWI, MALAYSIA, MONACO, MOZAMBIQUE, PHILIPPINES, PORTUGAL, SINGAPORE, SPAIN, TRINIDAD AND TOBAGO, UNITED STATES, URUGUAY, ZAMBIA.

A national flag or ensign defaced with the arms or an emblem is used in:
AUSTRIA, BELARUS, CHILE, DENMARK, EGYPT, ERITREA, FINLAND, FRANCE, ICELAND, KUWAIT, MALDIVES, MOROCCO, PAKISTAN, RUSSIA, SAUDI ARABIA,

SENEGAL, SEYCHELLES, SUDAN, SURINAM, SWAZILAND, SWEDEN, TURKEY.

A flag with a border and defaced with the arms or emblem is used in:
CZECH REPUBLIC, GERMANY, ISRAEL, ITALY, NEPAL, SLOVENIA, TAIWAN, TANZANIA.

A flag defaced with the state or royal arms and with an emblem repeated in all four corners or sides is used in:
ARGENTINA, BELGIUM, CUBA, LIBERIA, MALTA, THE NETHERLANDS, PARAGUAY, PERU, VENEZUELA.

The heads of state of the following countries have flags that do not conform to any of the models described: CROATIA, DOMINICAN REPUBLIC, INDIA, JORDAN, LIECHTENSTEIN, NAMIBIA, SLOVAKIA, SRI LANKA, UGANDA.

Government Flags

As well as a national flag, over 20 nations also have a state flag for use by government authorities. In five Scandinavian countries the state flag is a swallow-tailed or triple swallow-tailed version of the national flag. The state flags of other countries are their national flags but with the addition of the state arms in the centre.

The United States has one flag for all purposes, but the federal government and military authorities use it only in the official proportions of 10:19, making it the de facto state flag. The same flag in different proportions (2:3, 3:5 and 5:8) is the national flag for other uses, including use by the general public. There are no international regulations pertaining to the use of foreign flags in a country hosting an international conference or officials from a foreign country. Normally state flags should

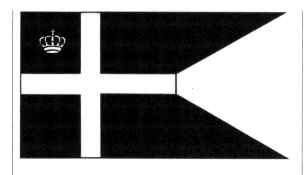

◆ **LEFT**
Denmark, state ensign
(since 1907).

◆ **LEFT**
Iceland, state flag and ensign
(since 1918).

be used but there are exceptions to this rule. At the United Nations headquarters in New York, although some countries (Austria, Denmark, Finland, Germany, Iceland, Monaco, Norway and Sweden) have both state and national flags, they choose to be represented by their national flag.

◆ **FAR LEFT TOP**
Germany, state flag
(1893–1918).

◆ **FAR LEFT BOTTOM**
Germany, state ensign
(1893–1918).

◆ **BELOW**
Mecklenburg, state flag
(1900–1918).

GOVERNMENT DEPARTMENTS AND AGENCIES

The United States is the only country with special flags for all its government departments, and some government agencies. They are displayed at, or on, the buildings of the departments and in the offices of high-ranking officials. The oldest is the flag of the National Aeronautics and Space Administration (NASA), introduced in 1960. Other countries have only a few departmental flags: Russia instituted a flag for its Finance Ministry in 1902, and Denmark adopted a flag for its Naval Ministry in 1916.

Many countries have flags for members of the government. The idea of distinguishing important members of the imperial or royal household with flags probably originated in highly hierarchical societies such as China, Russia and Prussia. From China the custom spread to several countries in South-east Asia such as Kelantan, one of the member-states of Malaysia. In the 1930s Kelantan had seven flags for the members of the royal family and the titled members of the royal dynasty, nine for members of the government and eight for the chiefs of districts.

◆ LEFT
Hesse, state flag (1902–1918).

◆ LEFT
US Department of Treasury (since 1963).

◆ BELOW
Flags of Kelantan.

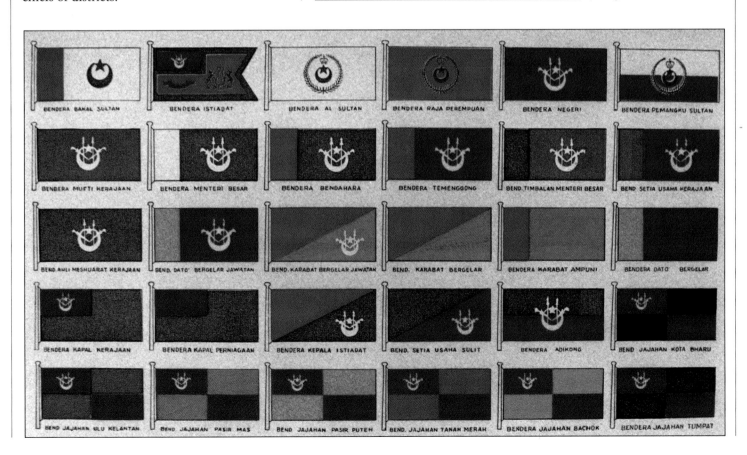

◆ LEFT
Car flags of the officials of
the Bavarian Government:
(*from far left to right*) prime
minister, minister of state,
chief of the state secretariat.

In monarchies, and also in some countries with a republican government, there were (and in a few instances still are) flags for the prime minister. In the past the prime ministers of Italy, Greece and South Africa had their own distinctive flags. Countries that still have a flag for the prime minister include Portugal, Spain, Japan, the Maldives, Thailand, the Bahamas, Barbados, Jamaica, Surinam, and Trinidad and Tobago. In most of Germany there are different flags for the members of the local government (prime minister, ministers, state secretaries, senators and council members).

In countries where government officials have their own flags, the most common examples are flags of the navy and defence (or war) ministers. These were first seen in Russia in 1827 and 1893 respectively, and since then more than 20 countries, mainly in Europe and the Americas, have adopted separate flags for their ministers. Portugal, the United States and Chile have separate flags for their defence minister and their navy minister. Spain, Austria, Thailand, Chile and Ecuador have a separate flag that can be used by other cabinet ministers.

◆ BELOW
Ministers' flags:
(*clockwise from top left*)
The Italian prime minister,
Benito Mussolini (1927–
1944); prime minister of
the Bahamas (since 1973);
Russian navy minister (1827–
1918); German defence
minister (1935–1945);
Spanish navy minister.

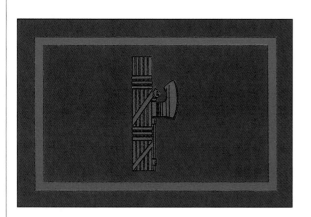 

◆ **RIGHT**

Flags of ministers in the United States:
(*from left to right*) Secretary of State, under Secretary of State; secretary of war, assistant secretary of war; secretary of treasury, under secretary of treasury; assistant secretary of treasury, attorney general. Plate from the *Flaggenbuch*, 1939.

◆ **BELOW**

Current flags of Ministers of Defence: (*from top to bottom right*) Great Britain, France, The Netherlands, Italy, Slovenia, Saudi Arabia.

Vereinigte Staaten von Amerika

II

Flagge des Staatsekretärs (Außenminister)

Flagge des Unterstaatssekretärs

Flagge des Kriegssekretärs

Flagge des Hilfskriegssekretärs

Flagge des Schatzsekretärs

Flagge des Unterschatzsekretärs

Flagge des Hilfsschatzsekretärs

Flagge des Generalstaatsanwalts

The most complete set of flags for government officials, as well as departments, is in the United States, where in all departments there are separate flags for the secretary, under-secretary and assistant secretary. The heads of

The Danish flag is the war ensign with a white crown in the canton; the government vessels of Fiji display the national flag with the field changed to dark blue. The field of the government vessels' flags in India and Sri Lanka

many government agencies and services also have their own distinguishing flags. The first to possess his own flag was the secretary of the navy in 1866, followed by the secretary of war in 1897.

In many countries government-owned vessels and vessels that provide services for the government do not fly the civil ensign. In New Zealand and Peru they hoist the national flag but in Argentina, the Dominican Republic, Ecuador, Haiti and Venezuela they hoist the state flag. Denmark, Belgium and some Commonwealth countries have special flags for government service vessels.

is also dark blue, with the national flag in the canton and an emblem in the fly which consists of a golden anchor and two crossed golden anchors, respectively. A few countries also have ensigns for vessels providing specialized services such as fishery control or lighthouse services.

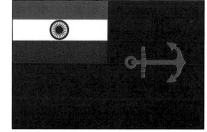

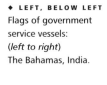

GOVERNORS AND ENVOYS

The colonies of European powers were at first administrated by the trade companies such as the East India Company, but in the 19th century this role was taken over by governors who acted as the representatives of the crown or government. Their flags followed the pattern of the national flag (Germany, the Netherlands, Spain, Belgium); displayed the national flag in the canton (France); or were charged with the state arms (Italy, Portugal).

Since 1891 the Italians had had a flag for their governors and in the 1930s they adopted a different one for the viceroy of Ethiopia which was white with a blue border, the state arms in the centre and yellow fasces in the corners. Portugal had three flags for its governors, all of which displayed the same emblem of the state arms on the cross of the Order of Christ. The flag of the Portuguese governor-

Governor of Belgian Congo.

general is illustrated; the flag of the governor had two vertical green stripes instead of horizontal ones; the flag of the governor of a district had one horizontal stripe.

Great Britain introduced two different flags for the representatives of the king or queen in its dominions and colonies. The flag of the governor-general of a dominion is dark blue, with the royal crest in the centre and the name of the dominion in a scroll beneath. A governor or lieutenant-governor uses the Union flag with a badge on a white disc surrounded by a garland of laurel superimposed on the centre of the flag. The last flag remains unchanged to this day but some of the governor-generals' flags have been diversified by the addition of local emblems such as a maple leaf (Canada), a whale's tooth (Fiji) and a two-headed frigate bird (Solomon Islands). In Canada the lieutenant-governors of the provinces have flags, of which only the flag of the lieutenant-governor of Nova Scotia follows the British pattern, with a garland of

Governor of German colonies.

Governor-general of Dutch colonies.

Governor of the Italian colonies.

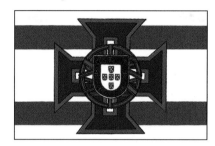

Governor-general of Portuguese colonies.

Governor of French West Africa.

Governor of Surinam.

Governor-general of Australia (1902–1936).

Governor-general of Pakistan.

Governor-general of South East Asia.

Governor-general of the West Indies.

Governor-general of the Union of South Africa.

Governor-general of the Federation of Rhodesia and Nyasaland.

◆ **ABOVE**
Historic flags of governors.

Governor-general of Canada.

Governor-general of Fiji.

Governor-general of Solomon Islands.

Lieutenant-governor of Nova Scotia.

Lieutenant-governor of Quebec.

Lieutenant-governor of British Columbia.

Governor-general of Gibraltar.

Administrator of the French Southern and
Antarctic Territory.

◆ ABOVE
Current flags of governors.

maple instead of laurel. The flags of other
lieutenant-governors (except that of Quebec)
have the same design as that of the lieutenant-
governor of British Colombia.

A few countries have special flags for their
diplomatic representatives. The first were
introduced in Russia in 1833 for the ambassador
or envoy extraordinary, consul-general, consul
and chargé d'affaires or resident. The flag of the
ambassador was in the form of the Russian jack,
with the small imperial arms in the white
canton. The national flag with the war ensign
in the canton, served as the flag of the consul-
general, and the flag of the consul was a
swallow-tailed version of the consul-general flag.
The flag of the chargé d'affaires or resident was
white, with the war ensign in the canton. The

designs of these flags were changed in 1870,
and again in 1896. Not many countries followed
suit but among them were China, Italy and
Thailand, which adopted their diplomatic flags
at the end of the 19th century. In the 20th
century the United States introduced a flag for
consuls and flags for envoys were also
introduced by Iran (the ambassador's flag and
the flag of the envoy extraordinary), Egypt,
Spain, Colombia and Mexico (the flag of the
Diplomatic Corps and the Consular Corps).

Great Britain has two flags for its diplomats.
The flag of an ambassador is the Union flag
with the royal arms on a disc encircled by a
garland of laurel superimposed in the centre.
The consul's flag is identical except that it
displays the royal crown instead of the arms.

POST, CUSTOMS AND COASTGUARD FLAGS

The first flag for customs vessels was introduced by Denmark in 1778. It was a specially marked Danish war ensign and was flown by vessels when hailing other ships in the course of duty. In 1793 Denmark adopted a similar flag for mail-carrying ships. At the end of the 18th century two other countries, Spain in 1793 and the United States in 1799, adopted flags for their customs vessels. It was prescribed that the American Revenue ensign, as it was called, would be used by cutters and boats employed in the service of the Revenue and would be "always displayed over the custom-houses of the United States, and over the buildings appertaining to the Treasury Department of the United States". The ensign, which underwent some minor alterations, is still in use today at sea.

Flags for both post and customs services were introduced by Great Britain in the early 19th

♦ **BELOW**
Current customs flags:
from (*left to right*) Denmark,
Great Britain, Russia,
Turkey, China, United States,
Mexico, Ukraine.

century; by Russia in 1849 (post) and 1858 (customs); Prussia in 1863; and Norway in 1898. In this century both post and customs flags were adopted by the other Scandinavian countries, as well as by Thailand and Mexico. Currently customs flags are also used in Spain, Russia, Turkey, Brazil, China and Tonga.

France, the United States, Poland and a few other countries use a distinctive post flag. In some countries there are two post flags of different designs; one is flown from the post office's buildings, the other is flown from mail-carrying vessels.

In most countries the responsibility to guard territorial waters and fight against smugglers belongs to the navy and, indeed, it is the only task of the naval forces of most countries in the Caribbean, Africa and Oceania. In some countries, however, guarding the coastline is the

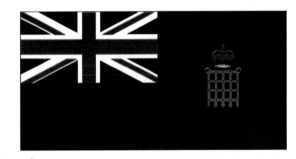

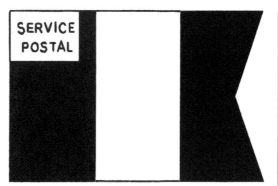

♦ LEFT
Post flags:
(*top row*) Norway (since 1898), France (since 1933), (*second row*) Denmark (since 1939), Free City of Danzig (1922–1945) (*third row, far left only*) Germany (1950–1995).

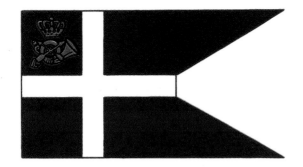

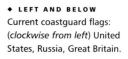

♦ LEFT AND BELOW
Current coastguard flags:
(*clockwise from left*) United States, Russia, Great Britain.

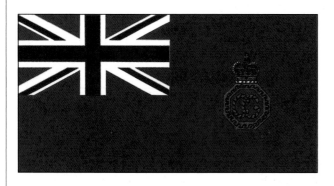

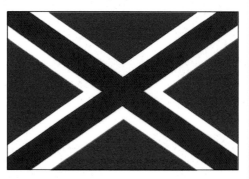

duty of a special force, the coastguard, which is not actually a part of the navy. The United States Coastguard has the longest-standing traditions. Their ensign was based on the revenue ensign flown on ships of the Revenue Cutter Service. The name "coastguard" was first used in 1915 when the Revenue Cutter Service merged with the Life-saving Service. The current United States Coastguard ensign was introduced in 1966 and a similar one with six vertical stripes was soon adopted by Haiti. Other countries that currently use a distinctive coastguard flag include Great Britain, Poland, Russia and Yugoslavia.

POLICE FLAGS

Only a few countries have police flags displayed at police stations or elsewhere outdoors. Generally they are of two types: a ceremonial flag made of expensive fabric with embroidered police badges, designed for the interior of the building, or a flag that resembles a military colour. In some countries there is also a distinguishing flag for police commandants, used both as a decoration of office and as a car flag.

The same devices appear regularly on police flags. A flaming grenade is an emblem that Napoleon I granted to his élite troops as a battle honour and it is now used as a police emblem in France, Belgium, the Netherlands and Italy. Another device is a silver (white) star with five to nine points made of different-length rays which is found on police emblems on all continents but mainly in Great Britain and Commonwealth countries, the United States and Germany. Police flags are flown on police stations in Great Britain, Turkey, Finland, Israel and Japan.

In France there is no police flag. The organization of the police resembles that of the military so there are regimental and battalion

◆ BELOW
Police flags: (*clockwise from top left*) Finland, Turkey, Bermuda (central emblem), Brabant, *Gendarmerie mobile* standard (France).

standards, in the same design as military colours. The units of the Gendarmerie Mobile and Gendarmerie Départementale have standards with their names in semi-circles above and below a flaming grenade, and the reverse bears a shield with the regional arms or the arms of the legion. Belgium also does not have a police flag but it has a flag for the commandant of gendarmerie, the commandants of the six regions, the commandants of the Mobile Legion and the Royal School of Gendarmerie. These are used in offices and as a car flags.

The Royal Canadian Mounted Police (RCMP) adopted its flag in 1991, together with flags for its divisions in all provinces and territories. All of them have a red field with a blue canton bordered with yellow and defaced with the badge of the RCMP. The flags of the divisions have an emblem in the lower hoist displaying the most characteristic figure from the arms of the province or territory.

In some countries there is a specialized harbour police. Its vessels fly distinctive ensigns, which generally consist of the national or war ensign charged with the police badge.

Military Signs

The flag epitomizes for an army the high principles for which it strives in battle ... It keeps men's motives lofty even in mortal combat, making them forgetful of personal gain and of personal revenge, but eager for personal sacrifice in the cause of country they serve.

GILBERT GROSVENOR, *SPECIAL EDITION OF THE NATIONAL GEOGRAPHIC MAGAZINE*
"FLAGS OF THE WORLD", WASHINGTON, 1917.

We shall probably never know when and where vexilloids were first used in battle, but it is safe to guess that large groups of early warriors had signs to rally around and to follow. The oldest surviving vexilloids, from Egypt, follow definite patterns, suggesting that they had evolved from earlier models.

From earliest times a vexilloid or flag carried in battle had a semi-sacred quality. In the Middle Ages and subsequent centuries a new flag was consecrated before a battle and blessed by priests, and after the campaign it was kept in a local church. Mercenaries, and later the soldiers of standing armies, took a holy oath to defend their "colour" to the death. At the time of the crusades, banners with a cross prevailed, but soon armorial banners and pennons, standards and guidons were introduced. Many troops used banners with religious motifs, such as painted figures of the Virgin Mary and Child or various saints.

By the 16th century the banners carried by infantry had reached enormous dimensions, and in the cavalry a large swallow-tailed pennon was the most common form of flag. In the first half of the 17th century regiments began to wear uniforms, and the flags of both infantry and cavalry were therefore in the same colours. Military banners in France, Spain and England acquired marks of national identification: a white cross, the cross of Burgundy and the cross of St George, respectively.

Regulations adopted in the 18th century prescribed both the design and the number of colours in a regiment, and from then on the colour consisted of a staff with a finial and a flag. These three parts were inseparable and had to be treated as a simple unit; sometimes saving just the colour's finial from a battlefield saved the honour of the unit. Standardization gradually occurred in most countries, and more colours acquired national characters. The armed forces of many countries also adopted a wide range of other flags to distinguish the branches of the armed forces and the ranks of their commanders.

◆ **LEFT**
Banner of the Republic of Venice (15th century).

BATTLE BANNERS

In the Middle Ages five types of flag were used on a battlefield. Three of them (banner, pennon and pencel) bore the owners' arms, the other two (standard and guidon) were in the livery colours with badges. Most important was the banner representing the troops of the king, prince, duke, earl, baron or bishop, and the banners of the military orders. Royal banners are described in the chapter *Emperors, Sovereigns and Presidents*, but the flag of the Teutonic Order and some territorial flags are illustrated here. The pennon was the personal flag of a knight bachelor responsible for smaller formations of men. The pencel, or *pennoncelle*, was the personal flag of a knight, carried on a lance. The standard and the guidon were used by the infantry and cavalry, respectively, to identify bodies of troops within an army

♦ **BELOW**
Territorial flags in the 14th century: *(from left to right)* Teutonic Order; Silesia; Pomerania; Bishopric of Warmia.

The 16th century witnessed an entirely new way of conducting warfare. In some countries, mainly the German states, mercenaries replaced troops in a province or country. The ruler contracted an experienced soldier to raise and lead a regiment of infantry and provided arms and flags for each company, with up to ten flags for the whole regiment. The design of these banners was usually based on multiple divisions of the field (horizontal, vertical, diagonal and combinations of these) and simple charges such as bend, cross or saltire and narrow wavy triangles. The banners were called *Landknechtsfahnen*, after the German word *Landknecht* (foot-soldier). The banners of these regiments became more elaborate in the 17th century, and regiments fighting on the Protestant side often displayed flags that insulted the

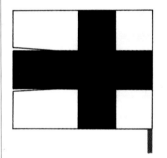

In contrast with the earlier simplicity, the armorial banners of the 15th century were made of costly materials decorated with rich embroidery. Heraldic figures became very ornate and battle banners with religious motifs gradually became more numerous, the most popular being the Virgin Mary and Child or Christ on the Cross. Spain, Austria and Bavaria used a border on their colours, which was not seen on the colours of Protestant countries. The custom of using religious motifs on military flags survived into the 20th century. The Virgin Mary appeared on Austrian colours until 1938; Christ's Passion was depicted on many Russian colours in the 19th century; St Andrew and his cross appeared on the Serbian colours carried in World War I and St George slaying the dragon was painted on the colours of the Greek Army.

♦ **BELOW**
(top) Bavarian infantry (17th century); *(bottom)* Polish cavalry (17th century).

Catholic Church and the clergy, or scenes from fables such as a bear with lambs or a fox with hens. Both sides began to use propaganda slogans and allegorical emblems such as the Roman goddesses Fortuna and Justice, an arm in armour emerging from a cloud, or a lion trampling a fallen warrior.

At the beginning of the 17th century the standing armies established permanent units divided into a regular number of companies, with a clear division between infantry and cavalry. Banners reached enormous sizes, exceeding the men's height. During the Thirty Years War (1618–1648) the company under the command of the colonel adopted a different-coloured flag to the other companies in the regiment. In most countries white was chosen for the field of the colonel's flag.

STANDARDIZATION OF COLOURS

Regimentation and standardization began early in the 17th century. The infantry regiments were divided into three wings, each with a distinctive flag. They began to display the colours of the uniforms, the wings being distinguished only by different heraldic badges or symbols. In some countries the colours bore national symbols such as the cross of St George or the cross of Burgundy, in which case they revealed country, regiment and battalion at a glance. A century later the number of wings was reduced to two and so there were only two colours. The first was generally called the "king's or sovereign's colour" and was a symbol of allegiance and service to monarch and country. It was borne by the first battalion, originally the colonel's battalion, and was therefore referred to as the "colonel's colour". The second was known as the "battalion colour" ("regimental colour" in Great Britain and the United States) and represented the honour and traditions of the regiment and the soldier's duty to the regiment.

The first national symbol to appear on military flags was the red cross of Burgundy, introduced in 1516 as the main device of the flags of the Spanish infantry. Under a decree of 1707, each battalion had three colours, and the 1st Battalion carried the colonel's colour, white, with the cross of Burgundy and badges between

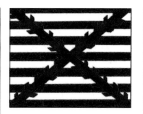

♦ **ABOVE**
Spanish colours: (*from the top*) Regimental infantry banner (1550); colonel's infantry colour (1707); regimental infantry colour (1775); colonel's infantry colour (1802–1931).

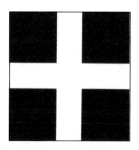

♦ **ABOVE AND LEFT**
French colours: (*above*) Regiment of Picardy (1597); (*left*) infantry colour (1812).

its arms. The regimental colours had fields in the regiment's facing colours or in the principal colour of the coat of arms from the place where the regiment was formed; a badge and the name of the unit were in the centre. In the late 16th century the fields of some flags became multicoloured, borders were added, and some fields and borders displayed very intricate designs. A decree of 1728 introduced a new model of the colonel's colour and provided each battalion with two colours: the 1st Battalion having the colonel's colour and one battalion colour, both white. The battalion colour had the cross of Burgundy with a badge at each end, while the colonel's colour displayed the royal arms with the Order of the Golden Fleece and the provincial arms in each corner. On the reverse the arms were placed on the cross of Burgundy with the provincial arms at each end, and were supported by two red lions. In 1808 the number of colours was reduced to one per battalion: the 1st Battalion used the king's colour in the same design as the previous colonel's colour, and the battalion colour remained unchanged.

The next to standardize their battle flags were the French in 1597. The flags were square, with a width exceeding 180 cm (6 ft). They were divided by a white cross and the four parts of the field displayed the regimental colours. The first four permanent regiments were assigned the following colours: red (Picardy), green (Champagne), gold (Navarre) and black (Piedmont). The colours of the other regiments had fields in two or three colours. Borders and simple devices (squares, fleurs-de-lis, crowns) or mottoes were added, but the basic design survived until 1794. In 1804 Napoleon I introduced the famous "eagles", named after the finial in the form of an eagle of ancient Rome. The plinth on which the eagle stood bore metal numerals indicating the regiment to which the colour belonged. The design was changed in 1812, and again in 1815. The French pattern of colours was adopted by Italy, and in the 20th century by many countries in Europe and elsewhere.

◆ **ABOVE**
Prussian colours (*from left to right*) Infantry colour (1701–1729); infantry colour (late 18th century).

The first colours of the Prussian infantry, introduced in 1701, had a central oval emblem containing the Prussian eagle encircled by a wreath and ensigned with the royal crown, with the royal ciphers in the corners. There were two flags for each battalion. The first flag of the 1st Battalion was called the *Leibfahne*, the second the *Regimentsfahne*. The 2nd battalion had two *Regimentsfahnen* in the same design but with the colours interchanged. The *Leibfahne* had the centre in the regiment's colour and the field in the same colour as the centre of the *Regimentsfahne*. In 1729 a cross was added to the field, which was either wavy or straight. The Prussian design was followed by Baden, Brunswick and Hesse during the Napoleonic Wars, and by Saxony (1735–1810), Russia (1800–57), Bavaria (1841–1918) and Poland (1919).

The first standardization of Russian military flags was carried out in 1712, when the infantry and dragoon regiments obtained flags in the same design. Usually the fields were unicolours, some with simple divisions or charges such as a cross or saltire. The regimental emblem appeared in the upper hoist, with the heraldic charge of the province or town after which the regiment was named. In 1727 the colonel's

◆ **RIGHT**
German colours in 1910. Plate from the *Fahnen und Standartenträger*.

Bild: 7
Fahne vom I. Bataillon des 8. thür. Infanterie-Rgts. Nr. 153 Sachsen-Altenburg 1910

Bild: 8
Fahne vom I. Bataillon des 7. thür. Infanterie-Rgts. Nr. 96 Reuß j. L. 1910

Bild: 9
Fahne vom III. Bataillon des 7. thür. Infanterie-Rgts. Nr. 96 Schwarzburg-Rudolstadt 1910

Bild: 10
Fahne vom anhaltschen Infanterie-Rgt. Nr. 93, 1910

Bild: 11
Fahne vom braunschweig. Infanterie-Rgt. Nr. 92, 1910

Bild: 12
Fahne vom großherzogl.-oldenburg. Infanterie-Rgt. Nr. 91, 1910

colour in both the infantry and cavalry attained national character. It was white, with a large representation of the imperial arms, and the company and squadron flags had fields in the regiment's facing colour, with a border of triangles. The emblem was the crowned imperial cipher encircled by a wreath, underneath which was a scroll with the regiment's name. Each infantry regiment received a colonel's colour and six company colours, and each dragoon regiment received a colonel's colour and eight squadron guidons. Under Catherine the Great the design of the Russian colours gradually changed until in 1800 it was nearly identical to that of Prussia. Further minimal changes took place in 1803 and 1813. After 1813 the colours of the line infantry were green with white corners; the colours of the guard infantry had the same design, but with yellow fields and corners in different colours.

The first detailed regulations governing the design of British colours were issued in 1747 and reduced the number of flags to two per battalion of the line infantry. The first was the King's colour, i.e. the Union flag with the regimental badge in the centre. Badges recalling service overseas were the green dragon (China), the sphinx (Egypt), the tiger (Bengal) and the

elephant (India), and each badge was encircled by a wreath of roses (England) and thistles (Scotland). The other flag was the regimental colour, usually in the regimental facing colour with a small Union flag in the canton and the same badges as on the king's colour. In 1801 the Irish cross of St Patrick was added to the Union flag and the shamrock to the wreath.

The common element of the colours of Swiss regiments in foreign services were the "flammes", long wavy triangles radiating in all directions from the centre to the edges of the field. They were mostly in the livery colours of the regimental owners or commanders. This design was created at the end of the 17th century as the ordnance flag of regiments in service to the king of France and it was later introduced by other Swiss troops in service in the Netherlands, Spain, Venice, England and Naples.

In 1796 the United States Army introduced colours for the infantry. The national colour was blue with a representation of the national arms (in many artistic variations) in gold, and a golden scroll with the name of the regiment; the regimental colours were white or yellow. Very similar colours were used by the cavalry until 1895. In 1841 the infantry were given entirely different colours resembling the national flag.

◆ **ABOVE**
Austrian colours:
(*left*) Regimental colour (1806–1815);
(*right*) infantry colour (1915–1918).

◆ **FAR LEFT**
Battalion colour of the Cisalpine Republic.

◆ **LEFT**
Polish legion in Lombardy. Colour of the 1st Battalion of Riflemen.

appeared in the centre of the company's colour and in the upper hoist of the king's colour. In the kingdom of Hanover, where the same custom applied, the provincial arms were placed in the corners of the military colours. Similarily, the colours of the Spanish infantry bore the provincial arms in all four corners, and the arms of the province encircled by a wreath was the central device for the Finnish colours during World War II.

◆ **ABOVE AND LEFT**
(*clockwise from far left*)
Colours of Swiss troops in foreign services: Spain, France, Great Britain, Holy See.

◆ **ABOVE**
Colours of the United States: (*left to right*) Infantry colour (1841 model); artillery regimental colour (Civil War period); first cavalry division (Civil War period).

The arrangement of the stars on the new colours varied considerably, as did their colour (white, yellow or gold) and number of points. During the Civil War the Southern armies' battle flag and colours were based on the national flag's design, with inscriptions identifying the regiment and places of victorious battles.

As well as the national symbol, many of the colours used by different armies also carry symbols of the province of the regiment's origin. In Sweden, where regiments were named after provinces, the arms of the province

◆ **LEFT**
Battle flag of the Confederacy States of America (1861–1865).

BATTLE HONOURS

In ancient Rome the military standards, or vexilloids, of the bravest troops were augmented with battle honours, in the form of crowns, wreaths, medals or rings attached to the staff. In modern times there have been several methods of distinguishing a military colour with battle honours: an inscription sewn or painted on the field; a ring attached to the staff; a streamer with metal plates or with embroidered or painted inscriptions; or the order, or other decoration, pinned to the flag or the cravat.

In modern times, the custom first developed in the Prussian Army at the beginning of the 18th century. The awards took the form of a ribbon with a small metal plate, tied to the top of the staff. In 1785 three regiments of the Army of Hanover received the first honours in the form of golden embroidered inscriptions.

In the French Army the first battle honours were added to the colours in 1791. After 1808 the honours were restricted to major victories where Napoleon commanded in person: Ulm, Austerlitz, Jena, Eylau, Friedland, Eckmühl, Essling and Wagram, Marengo and Moscowa (Moscow). In Britain the practice of naming the places of great victories on the colours themselves was sanctioned in 1811. After 1844 the addition of battle honours was allowed only for the regimental colour. The most often awarded honours were for the Battle of Waterloo and the Peninsula war.

In the United States Army awards were inscribed on flags long before the first regulation

allowed this in 1862. During the Civil War the first battle honour appeared in the form of streamers with inscriptions. This practice was supported by many, both military and civilians, who believed that nothing should be allowed to mar the stripes of the national flag. This sentiment grew and in 1890 the United States Army decided to use awards in the form of silver rings or bands only, and in 1920 they were replaced with streamers. The Marine Corps followed suit in 1939, the Air Force in 1956, the Coastguard in 1968 and the Navy in 1971. Today the honours earned by a unit are displayed as streamers attached to the staff of the unit's battle and organizational colour. There are fewer than ten award streamers (commendations and presidential citations) but over 100 campaign streamers.

FLAGS OF ARMED FORCES

Many flags have been designed since World War II for use at ceremonies and parades as well as inside offices or headquarters buildings. At least three countries have a special flag for their armed forces as a whole. The flag of the British Joint Services, introduced in 1964, is composed of three vertical stripes of dark blue (the Royal Navy), red (the Army) and light blue (the Royal Air Force). In the centre is a black emblem: a foul anchor for the Navy, two swords for the Army and an eagle for the Air Force. A similar emblem designed for the Canadian armed forces in 1968 is blue on the white field of the Canadian forces ensign, which also serves as the naval jack. China has a flag for use by its Army, Navy and Air Force. It resembles the national flag but instead

◆ **ABOVE LEFT**
Canadian forces ensign.

◆ **ABOVE RIGHT**
Chinese armed forces flag.

◆ **RIGHT**
Poland: (*from top to bottom*)
Branches of the armed forces since 1993: Army, Navy, Air Force.

◆ **ABOVE AND RIGHT**
United States: (*clockwise from top left*)
Army (since 1956); Navy (since 1959); Marine Corps (since 1956); Air Force (since 1952); Coastguard (since 1964).

of stars has stylized characters for "8" and "1" to commemorate the date of the foundation of the People's Liberation Army, 1 August 1928.

A few countries have flags for each branch of the armed forces. The United States and South Korea also have a flag for their Marine Corps, and the United States has a fifth flag for its Coastguard. In 1962 the United States Army field flag was introduced. It is the same design as the army flag with an ultramarine blue field, the army emblem (without the Roman numerals) in white and a white scroll inscribed in scarlet. Others authorized to use this flag include separate brigades such as divisions, numbered commands,

Israel: (*from left to right*) Army, Navy, Air Force.

general officer commands, headquarters of the United States Army garrisons, missions, recruiting main stations and the regional headquarters of the Reserve Officers' Training Corps.

A set of flags for the Polish armed forces was introduced in 1993; their main characteristic was uniform shape and colour. The fields are defaced with representations of the metal cap badges of each branch of the armed forces. The flags of the three branches of the armed forces in Israel have either the national flag in the canton or the flag design on the field. They also have distinctive finials in the same shape as the emblem on the particular flag.

The first army flag was probably the Chinese one, introduced in 1911. Great Britain also chose red for the background of its army flag, adopted in 1938, with the royal crest on two crossed swords. A similar flag was adopted for the Army of Independent India. The army flags of Colombia and Indonesia have a unicoloured field defaced with the army emblem, and the army flags of Japan and Taiwan are variations of the national flag. In other countries the army uses the national flag with an emblem in the centre (Thailand) or in the upper hoist (such as the two crossed sabres of Egypt or the army emblem of Kuwait).

◆ RIGHT AND BELOW
Army flags: (*from left to right*) China (1911–1928), Great Britain, India, Jordan, Japan, Taiwan, South Korea.

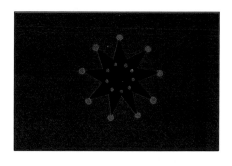

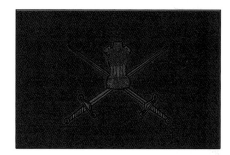

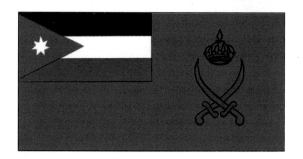

AIR FORCE FLAGS

Air force flags are flown on land at airfields and where units are stationed. They are also hoisted on a small staff over an aircraft when VIPs are embarking or disembarking.

The first flag for use by the aeronautic division of the army was introduced in Russia at the end of the 19th century. It was similar to many flags used by the navy, a white field with the jack in the canton but with the centre of the fly defaced with the aeronautical emblem in red. The British Air Force flag, introduced in 1918, was patterned on the navy ensigns but with light blue for the field. This colour and the design of the British Air Force flag have been adopted by many countries.

Many countries adopted air force flags with the light blue field but without the canton. Zambia has a roundel in the centre, while Japan, South Korea, Taiwan, Indonesia,

◆ **BELOW**
Air force flags:
(from left to right)
United Kingdom, Colombia, India, Sri Lanka, Malaysia, Belgium, Taiwan, Poland.

the Philippines and Colombia have the air force emblem in the centre. Belgium positioned the air force emblem in the upper hoist and the roundel in the centre, and Kuwait positioned the emblem in the centre and the roundel in the upper hoist. The air force flag of the Netherlands is blue with an orange pile charged with the Military Order of William. The design of the Israeli Air Force's flag resembles the national flag but the shield of David is solid. The flag of the Australian Air Force is a light blue version of the national flag, with the roundel in the lower hoist.

The fields of the air force flags of Spain, Poland and Thailand consist of the national flag. The air force emblem appears in the centre of the top stripe (Spain) or in the centre (Thailand). The Spanish flag also displays the state arms in the centre.

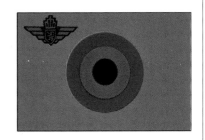

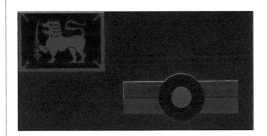

AIR FORCE FLAGS OF THE BRITISH MODEL

The air force flags of the following countries have a light blue field, a canton with the national flag and the air force roundel in the fly:
CANADA, COLOMBIA, EGYPT, GHANA, GREAT BRITAIN, INDIA, JORDAN, KENYA, MALAYSIA, MYANMAR, NEW ZEALAND, OMAN, PAKISTAN, SAUDI ARABIA, SINGAPORE, SRI LANKA, SUDAN.

DISTINGUISHING FLAGS

In most republican countries the head of state is also the commander-in-chief of the armed forces, so there are no special flags for the commander-in-chief. In monarchies such flags are also very rare, although Sweden has such a flag. In some countries there are separate flags for the commanders-in-chief of the army and navy.

Distinguishing flags of chiefs of staff are more common. In Great Britain and Italy the chiefs of the defence staffs have flags, as do the chiefs of

the general staff or the chiefs of the staff of the army and/or the air force in many other countries.

The largest set of these flags is in the United States, where the armed forces use many distinguishing flags. For example, the Army's own flags are adjutant general, chief of the army reserve, judge advocate general, chief of chaplains, chief of the national guard bureau, chief of engineers, surgeon general and inspector general.

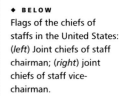

◆ **ABOVE, LEFT AND BELOW**
Flags of chiefs of staff: Great Britain, chief of defence staff; France, chief of general staff; Italy, chief of defence staff.

◆ **FAR LEFT**
The flag of the commander-in-chief of the armed forces, Sweden.

◆ **BELOW**
Flags of the chiefs of staffs in the United States: (*left*) Joint chiefs of staff chairman; (*right*) joint chiefs of staff vice-chairman.

The rank flags of the United States Army correspond with those of the Navy, but the Army uses red for the field colour.

There are also rank flags for the National Guard, blue with the crest of the individual State Army National Guard. The lieutenant-general's flag has three white stars, one on each side of the crest and one above the crest. Two other flags have the crest in the centre of the field: the flag of the major general has one star on each side of the crest; the brigadier general's flag has one star above the crest.

◆ **ABOVE AND RIGHT**
Rank flags in the United States Army: (*clockwise from far left*) General of the army, general, lieutenant general, major general, brigadier general.

   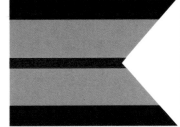

◆ **ABOVE**
Rank flags in the British Royal Air Force: (*from left to right*) Marshal, air marshal, air vice-marshal, air commodore.

◆ **RIGHT**
Flag of the lieutenant general of the National Guard in New Mexico.

Naval Ensigns and Flags

At sea, flags became a necessity from the first time a ship ventured out of its home waters. Wherever men have sailed on the oceans their flags have indicated their nationality and allegiance and the ship without a flag has justly been recognized in international law as a pirate.

WHITNEY SMITH, *THE FLAGBOOK OF THE UNITED STATES*, NEW YORK, 1970

The main flag on a ship of war is the war ensign, which identifies its nationality; the jack has a similar function to this. Rank flags and commission pennants indicate the rank of the ship's commander.

For centuries most flags were designed for use at sea rather than on land. The first markings of ownership and nationality were emblems (and later coats of arms) painted on a ship's sails; shields attached along the gunwales served a similar function. When flags were gradually introduced in the 12th and the 13th centuries they became an indispensable means of

identifying the nationality and function of a ship, and the rank of its commander.

Until the 13th century naval activity was local and temporary. All ships were armed to some degree but there was no distinction between merchant and naval ships. To denote nationality, most ships flew the flag of their home port. The first national flags used by ships seem to have been the English cross of St George and the Danish *dannebrog* in northern Europe; the Genoese cross of St George and the Venetian lion of St Mark in the Mediterranean region.

◆ **BELOW**
(from left to right) English red ensign (1653–1801); English white ensign (1653–1702); English blue ensign (1653–1801); English white ensign (1702–1801); Denmark (since 1625).

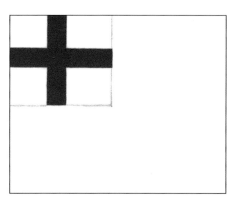

WAR ENSIGNS THROUGH HISTORY

The first navy, equipped with well-armed fighting ships, was organized in England in the first half of the 16th century. Under Elizabeth I (1558–1603) it developed into a major defence force and later played a decisive role in the extension of the British Empire. In Elizabethan times each English ship of war

◆ **BELOW**
(*from left to right*)
Sweden (1663–1815 and since 1906); Sweden (1844–1905); Sweden (1815–1844).

flew a different striped ensign, but the device common to all of them was the cross of St George in the canton. The stripes, mostly horizontal, varied in number (from five to eleven) and colouring (red, white; green, white; red, white, blue; red, green, red, blue, and so on). In 1625 the British Navy was divided into three squadrons, each of which was given an ensign in a different colour. Red was assigned to the centre, commanded by the admiral of the fleet; blue to the van, commanded by the vice-admiral, and white to the rear, commanded by the rear-admiral. This division was abolished in 1864, leaving only the white war ensign. The blue ensign became the ensign of the Royal Naval Reserve and could also be used by the officers of the Reserve when they commanded a private vessel. Currently, the criteria for warrants to wear the blue ensign, laid down in the Queen's Regulations of 1983, are:

The officer commanding a ship other than a fishing vessel must be an officer on the Retired or Emergency Lists of the Royal Navy or a Commonwealth Navy, or an officer on the Active or Retired Lists of any branch of the Reserves of such navies. If the rank held on one of these Lists by the officer commanding the ship is below that of Commander, at least one other officer in the ship's company must be an officer on one of the Lists mentioned.

◆ **RIGHT**
Sardinia (1815–1848).

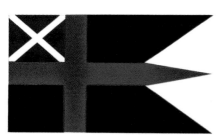

◆ **RIGHT**
France (1790–1794).

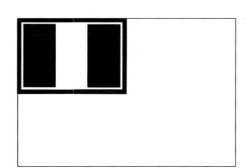

◆ **RIGHT**
Confederate States of America (1863–1865).

The design of the British ensigns with the Union Jack in the canton had a great impact on the war ensigns of many other European countries. France adopted a similar ensign in 1790, adding a canton displaying the jack in republican colours to the white field of the ensign used in times of monarchy. The next

countries to follow suit were Sweden and Sardinia in 1815, and in 1844 the Swedish jack was changed to display the colours of the flags of Sweden and Norway. The jack, in a square form, was used in the canton of the white war ensign of the Confederate States of America.

Prussia (1819–1850).

Germany (1867–1892).

Germany (1892–1903).

Germany (1903–1919).

Spain (1785–1931).

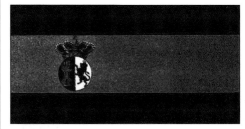

Austria (1787–1915).

Russia (c.1700–1918 and since 1992).

Soviet Union (1924–1935).

EARLY AMERICAN WAR ENSIGNS

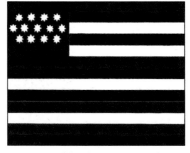

War ensign of the ship *Serapis* (1779).

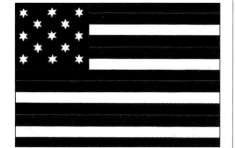

Ensign from the Lotter flag chart (1793).

War ensign from the Scotti flag chart (1796).

Ensign from a Swedish flag chart (1805).

In the 18th and 19th centuries another popular model for a war ensign was the Dutch ensign, with horizontal stripes. In 1701 Prussia introduced a plain white ensign charged with the small arms and the Iran cross. The Spanish ensign, adapted in 1785, displayed livery colours defaced with the state arms. The stripes of the Austrian war ensign, adopted in 1787, were of the same width, charged with the crowned shield of the historic arms.

The united Germany settled on a design combining a Scandinavian cross with a jack in the canton and a small state arms displayed on a white disc in the centre of the cross. There were minor subsequent changes to this design.

The American war ensign was presumably intended to be identical to the national flag but most of the actual ensigns show the stripes in three colours, which conform to the descriptions given by American diplomats in response to questions from European governments. Replying to the kingdom of Naples, Benjamin Franklin and John Adams wrote, "the flag of the United States of America consists of thirteen stripes, alternately red, white and blue". American ensigns with stripes in these three colours are depicted in many British, German, French, Italian and Swedish almanacs, and in flag charts dating from the late 18th and early 19th centuries. It seems that ensigns with three colours of stripes and those with red and white stripes were in use simultaneously. Paintings of ships in John Paul Jones's squadron by a Dutch artist show the ensign of *Serapis* with blue, red and white stripes and the ensign of *Alliance* with red and white stripes.

One of the oldest war ensigns still in existence today is the Russian one, adopted in about 1700 by Peter the Great for his navy, which displays a blue St Andrew's cross on a white field. As in Great Britain, this ensign was assigned to the centre, commanded by the admiral of the fleet; blue and red ensigns with a blue saltire in a white canton were assigned to the van and the rear respectively. Since 1865 the sole war ensign has been the white one.

WORLD WAR II

Among the major nations taking part in World War II only Italy, Japan, the United States, Great Britain and France used the same war ensign that they had used during World War I, which had ended some 21 years earlier. Similarly, most of the ensigns used in World War II are now obsolete; the war ensigns of Japan, Great Britain and France are the only exceptions. Indeed, France's ensign has remained the same since 1853, Great Britain's since 1864 and Japan's since 1889. The war ensign of Poland has now

Germany (1937–1945).

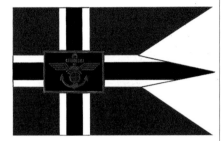

Italy (1848–1945).

Japan (since 1889).

The Norwegian Hirdmarinen.

Croatia (1941–1945).

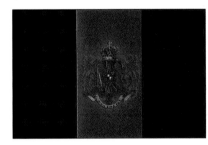

Romania (1921–1948).

Bulgaria (1928–1947).

only slightly different arms to the World War II version, and the ensign of the United States now has two more stars in the canton. The war ensign of China did not change, but it is now used by Taiwan.

Two war ensigns were also used on land. The war ensign of Nazi Germany was also the flag of the armed forces, and the ensign of the United States was traditionally both the national flag and the ensign.

The Norwegian Hirdmarinen, illustrated here, which was formed by the Quisling regime in 1942 was intended mainly to train recruits for the German Navy.

◆ ABOVE
War ensigns of the Axis countries.

◆ BELOW
War ensigns of the Allied countries.

Poland (1928–1945).

United Kingdom (since 1864).

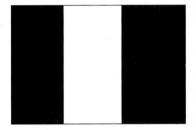

France (since 1853).

United States (1912–1959).

Egypt (1923–1958).

Soviet Union (1935–1992).

CURRENT WAR ENSIGNS

Most of the countries that became independent after World War II adopted national flags for general use on land and at sea, i.e. the national flag also served as the war ensign. Almost all of the countries that have adopted distinctive war ensigns were part of the British Empire and most of them followed the example of the British white ensign. The war ensigns of the Bahamas, Ghana, India, Jamaica, Nigeria and the Solomon Islands are white with the red cross of St George and a national flag in the canton. The war ensigns of Bangladesh, Kenya, Malaysia and Singapore are white with the national flag in the canton and in some a badge in the fly, while the ensigns of Australia, Fiji and New Zealand are variations of the national flag and have a white field. Two other war ensigns,

those of Tonga and Ukraine, are clearly based on the British white ensign.

Fewer than 40 countries of the world have war ensigns that differ from their national flags, and in several other cases the war ensign has the same design as the national flag but in different proportions. The ensigns of Grenada, Guyana, Pakistan, and Trinidad and Tobago have overall proportions 1:2 and each stripe of the French has a different width (90, 99 and 111 units when the width of the ensign is 200 units).

The ensigns of the Scandinavian countries, Germany, Poland and Estonia are swallow-tailed and triple swallow-tailed, following the custom that evolved centuries ago in the Baltic Sea region. The Finnish ensign was adopted in 1918 and the current pattern was introduced in 1978,

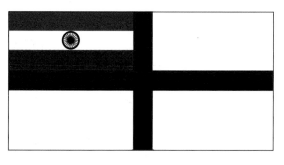

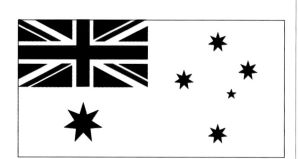

◆ **FAR LEFT**
India (since 1950).

◆ **LEFT**
Tonga (since 1985).

◆ **FAR LEFT**
Ukraine (since 1997).

◆ **LEFT**
Australia (since 1967).

◆ **FAR LEFT**
New Zealand (since 1968).

◆ **LEFT**
Malaysia (since 1968).

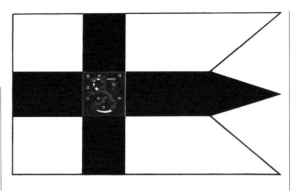

when the shape of the arms and the shade of blue were changed slightly.

The war ensigns of other countries are either variations of the national flag (Thailand, Egypt, Saudi Arabia and Bulgaria) or have totally different designs in national colours (Israel, South Korea and Belgium).

Generally the war ensign is worn by naval ships and by vessels that provide services to the navy. In some countries there are special ensigns for auxiliary vessels: the Royal Fleet Auxiliary Service has the British blue ensign charged with a yellow anchor, and the Russian auxiliaries fly a dark blue flag with the war ensign in the canton.

THE JACK

The second flag denoting the nationality of a naval vessel is a flag hoisted from the jackstaff, the top mast on the bow. The jack is usually square and is flown exclusively by ships in harbour or when the ship lies in the roadstead.

Most of the early jacks were identical with the flag used at sea by merchant and naval ships. The first English flag, white with the red cross of St George, was used as the jack of ships of war until 1606 and as the jack of merchant ships until the middle of the 19th century. Like the ensign, it influenced the design of jacks in other European countries and in America. The first to borrow the English design, in reversed colours, was Peter the Great, Tsar of Russia, followed by the Baltic States, which began to organize their navies after World War I. The British jack with a cross and saltire inspired the Dutch to divide the field gyronny in their national colours.

Several jacks are based on armorial banners. Spain has such a long tradition of using armorial banners at sea that it is not surprising that its

◆ LEFT
Great Britain (1606–1801).

current jack displays the arms of Castile, León, Aragon and Navarre. The first Italian jack displayed the cross of Savoy; the present one, adopted in 1954, displays the Venetian lion of St Mark and the crosses of the ancient maritime republics Genoa, Amalfi and Pisa. The Croatian jack of 1941–1945 was an armorial banner, charged with the badge of the ruling Ustasha.

Other jacks bear the state arms or emblem as the charge. The shield of the Portuguese arms is

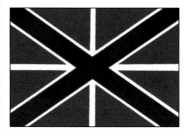

Russia (c.1700–1920 and since 1992).

Bulgaria.

Latvia.

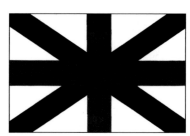

Estonia.

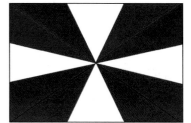

The Netherlands (since the end of the 17th century).

Paraguay (since 1934).

Germany (1867–1919).

Soviet Union (1924–1935).

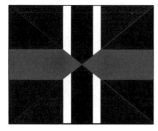

Sweden-Norway (1844–1905).

Norway (since 1905).

Confederate States of America (1863–1865).

Italy (since 1954).

Finland (since 1978).

placed on an armillary sphere (a navigational instrument in the Age of Discovery). State arms have also appeared on the jacks of Finland, Romania, Persia (Iran) and Peru. A few jacks have white stars on a dark blue field; the Chilean jack has one star, while the jacks of Brazil and the United States display as many stars as they have states (currently 27 and 50 respectively). The second jack of the Soviet Union displayed the main communist emblems from the arms and national flag, the red star and the hammer and sickle.

The last group of jacks are the national flag defaced with an emblem. The German jack, for example, was defaced with the Iron cross and the jack of Thailand with the navy's emblem. In many countries the war ensign takes the place of a distinctive jack (Denmark, Sweden, France, Germany and South Korea), in others it is the same as the national flag (Turkey, Bangladesh, Japan, Australia, New Zealand, Mexico, Dominican Republic, Colombia and Ecuador) or a square version of the national flag (Belgium). The jack often has the design of the canton of the national flag (Great Britain, Greece, Taiwan, Chile and the United States). In some countries in Latin America it has the design of a historic revolutionary flag (Cuba, Mexico and Uruguay).

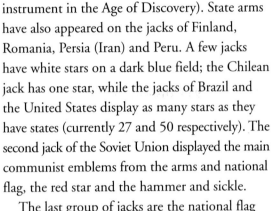

Portugal (since 1910).

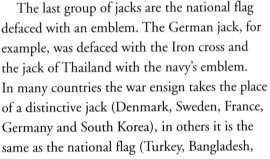

Taiwan (since 1949), (China 1912–1949).

Italy (1879–1946).

Argentina (since the end of the 19th century).

Spain (since 1945).

United States (since 1960).

Philippines (since 1955).

Croatia (1941–1945).

RANK FLAGS

In a few countries there are distinguishing flags for the commander-in-chief of the navy and the chief of staff of the navy. The predecessors of these flags were admiralty flags, adopted in the early 18th century by the Boards of the Admiralty in Great Britain and Russia. The admiralty managed naval affairs and also functioned as an operational authority, and its prerogatives were transferred in time to the navy or defence department.

In Norway, Finland and Ukraine the commanders-in-chief of the navy use war ensigns with emblems in the canton: a white saltire, a blue anchor over crossed yellow cannons and three stars respectively. The flag of the commander of the Russian Navy is the war ensign with the state arms on a disc surrounded by a garland of laurel. The flags of the chiefs of naval staff in France and Thailand are the national flag with an emblem in the centre.

Distinguishing flags are quite recent but the system of identifying the rank of ships' commanders is more than 400 years old. The English Navy was divided in 1545 into the van, the centre and the wing. The lord admiral (commander of the centre) flew the royal banner at the main and the flag of St George at the fore; the admiral of the van squadron flew the flag of St George at the main and fore; and the admiral of the wing squadron flew the flag of St George at the mizzen and bonaventure mizzen. The fleet sent to attack Cadiz in 1596 was divided into

◆ **ABOVE**
Flags of the commander-in-chief of the navy:
(*top*) Portugal,
(*bottom*) Ukraine.

◆ **ABOVE LEFT**
British Admiralty.

◆ **LEFT**
Russian Admiralty.

◆ **ABOVE**
Flags of the chiefs of staffs of the navy:
(*top*) France, (*middle*) Italy, (*bottom*) Russia.

four squadrons, each with three flag officers. The admiral's command flag was flown at the main, a vice-admiral's at the fore and a rear-admiral's at the mizzen. This system of identifying ranks was retained after the restoration of the monarchy, when there were only three squadrons – red, blue and white. The admiral of the fleet, commanding the red squadron, flew the Union flag at the main, unless he was the lord high admiral and was entitled to fly the royal standard. The vice-admiral and rear-admiral of the red squadron flew plain red flags on the fore and mizzen respectively; the admirals, vice-admirals and rear-admirals of the blue and white squadrons flew plain blue or white flags at the main, fore and mizzen respectively. This system was copied by fleets in other European countries and survived to the 19th century, when it became impractical because of changes in ships' architecture. Command flags of different designs for each flag officer were introduced at this point instead.

Throughout history there have been four basic methods of distinguishing rank among flag officers: (i) the same flag at different mastheads; (ii) the same design in different colours; (iii) the same basic design charged with additional devices for the lower ranks, and (iv) the same basic design charged with additional devices, the number of which increases with the rank. All four methods were employed in the United States Navy from 1817 to 1876. The order of colours denoting seniority was established in 1817. It was used in the Navy until 1870 and is still valid for distinguishing the flags of secretaries, deputy secretaries and under-secretaries in government departments.

Today the first two methods of distinguishing rank are obsolete. The only exceptions to this are the rank flags in the Yugoslav and French navies, which follow the second method. In France an admiral uses the national flag with four blue stars in the centre, and a vice-admiral displays three white stars in the upper hoist of the national flag. A rear-admiral uses the national flag, but with an additional white horizontal stripe of the same width as the vertical one and two white stars in the upper hoist. The third method is used only in the navies of Germany, Great Britain, Greece, Japan and Portugal; all other countries use the fourth method. Five-pointed stars are mostly used but other devices include circles (as in the case of Great Britain, Germany, Portugal, Spain and Colombia); six-pointed stars (the Netherlands); horizontal stripes (Japan and Taiwan), and suns (Peru). The field of a rank flag is generally unicoloured, mostly blue, and occasionally the field is charged with a cross (Great Britain, Germany, Portugal and Colombia) or other device (Japan). In some countries the field has the design of the war ensign (Denmark, Norway and Sweden), the national flag (the Netherlands, Spain, Romania and Mexico) or has adopted the design of its canton (Greece).

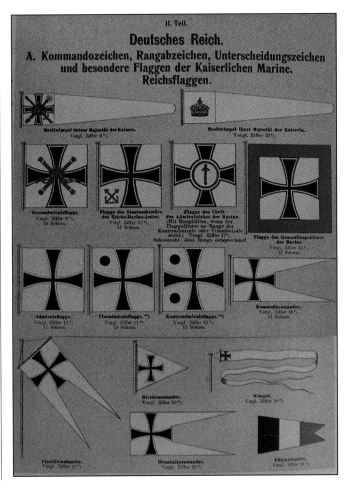

◆ LEFT
Distinguishing and rank flags in the German Navy. Plate from the *Flaggenbuch*, 1905. The rank flags are still in use.

◆ BELOW
Rank and other naval flags as presented in the *National Geographic* in 1917.

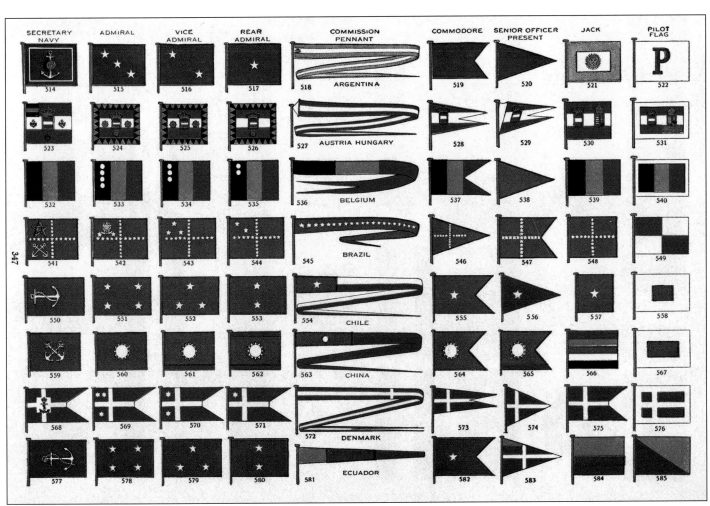

97

CURRENT RANK FLAGS

GREAT BRITAIN

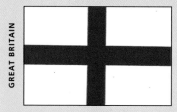

ADMIRAL

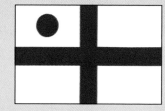

VICE ADMIRAL

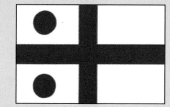

REAR ADMIRAL

NORWAY

ADMIRAL OF THE FLEET

ADMIRAL

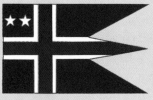

VICE ADMIRAL

REAR ADMIRAL

THE NETHERLANDS

ADMIRAL

ADMIRAL LIEUTENANT

VICE ADMIRAL

REAR ADMIRAL

YUGOSLAVIA

ADMIRAL OF THE FLEET

ADMIRAL

VICE ADMIRAL

REAR ADMIRAL

UNITED STATES

ADMIRAL OF THE FLEET

ADMIRAL

VICE ADMIRAL

REAR ADMIRAL

TURKEY

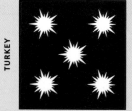

ADMIRAL OF THE FLEET

ADMIRAL

VICE ADMIRAL

REAR ADMIRAL

SAUDI ARABIA

ADMIRAL

VICE ADMIRAL

REAR ADMIRAL

Commission pennants

In the 13th century it was the custom to attach long streamers to the mastheads of ships purely for decoration, and four centuries later it became a duty of all men-of-war to fly a masthead pennant to distinguish them from merchant ships. Until the late 19th century each English or Russian warship used a pennant of its squadronal colour, either red, white or blue. Today there is only one commission pennant for all naval vessels, which should fly continuously day and night during the period the ship is in commission. If the ship is commanded by a flag officer, the appropriate rank flag replaces the commission pennant. The commission pennant is the longest, but narrowest, flag on a ship. Its width is 6–20 cm (2½–8 in) and its length 15–50 times greater. The largest pennant used during World War II by German warships was 20 cm (8 in) wide and 16 m (17½ yd) long. Most commission pennants copy the design of the national flag or display the national flag in the hoist. Some arrange the national colours differently or display in the hoist only the main design element from the national flag or war ensign.

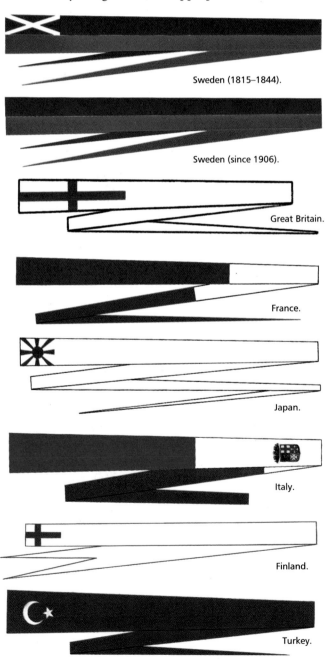

Sweden (1815–1844).

Sweden (since 1906).

Great Britain.

France.

Japan.

Italy.

Finland.

Turkey.

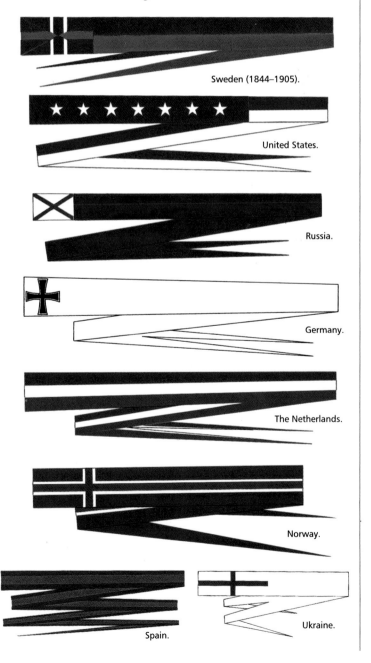

Sweden (1844–1905).

United States.

Russia.

Germany.

The Netherlands.

Norway.

Spain.

Ukraine.

Flag Families

Flags are a universal characteristic of human civilization. With the exception of the most primitive societies and nomadic peoples, it appears that every culture has invented for itself flags of one kind or another – with a remarkable similarity of form observable throughout the world. The functions of flags are nearly identical in all societies, and parallels in flag usages may be observed in diverse regions and eras.

So strong is the tradition of flags, we may not be far from the truth in surmising that there is a law – not of nature, but of human society – which impels man to make and use flags. There is perhaps no more striking demonstration of this than the fact that, despite the absence of any international regulation or treaty requiring of a national flag, without exception every country has adopted at least one.

WHITNEY SMITH, *FLAGS THROUGH THE AGES AND ACROSS THE WORLD,* 1975.

In the Middle Ages flags on land denoted mainly rulers and the military, but at sea they were used to denote nationality. With the growth of international trade in the 17th and 18th centuries, more countries began to adopt merchant ensigns and these became well known not only in their home ports but also inland. Thus in most countries with access to the sea the merchant ensign, or a flag similar to it, eventually became the national flag.

Looking at the various flags hoisted at the UN headquarters in New York, at the NATO headquarters in Brussels or at stadiums during international sporting events, we may wonder why the flags of nations in different parts of the world have such similar designs. In most cases the similarity is deliberate. It may be an expression of common history, traditions or interests, or it may be a statement that a country modelling its flag on that of another country sees that country as a religious or political role model.

The similarity of flags is as old as the use of flags themselves, but flag use did not develop on a large scale until the 19th century and continued during the 20th. Out of some 195 independent countries only 12 have flags whose designs were adopted before 1800. Seven of these (Denmark, Great Britain, the Netherlands, Russia, the United States, France and Turkey) have influenced the designs and colours of over 130 national flags and ensigns, which are grouped into ten large and three smaller "flag families". Some flags may belong to more than one flag family, for example flags displaying the pan-Arab colours and the Muslim crescent, or those displaying the French colours and the cross.

◆ **BELOW**
Flags at the Rockefeller Center in New York, 1968, show the similarities between many flags.

THE CHRISTIAN CROSS

The cross is an ancient magical sign and decorative motif known in many parts of the world, such as Mesopotamia, China, Scandinavia and Greece, but today it is universally recognized as the symbol of Christianity. In the first centuries after the death of Christ the main Christian symbol was a fish, often with the Greek word ΙΧΞΥΣ (fish). This can be made into an acrostic: I (I) = Ieus, X (Ch) = Christos, Ξ (Th) = Theou, Y (U) = Uios, Σ (S) = Soter, meaning "Jesus Christ God's Son Saviour". In the 3rd century Christian communities began to use cross-like emblems, such as an anchor with a crosspiece or a human figure with outstretched arms. A breakthrough came in 326 when St Helena, mother of Emperor Constantine, was said to have discovered the cross on which Christ was crucified. This stimulated an increase in the devotion of the faithful and led to the cross being gradually introduced as a symbol of martyrdom, resurrection, redemption and salvation.

From the 9th century to the end of the 12th century a metal cross on the top of a mast was the only device marking

merchant ships in northern Europe. Later the cross became the most common charge of the merchant ensigns of cities and countries in both Northern and southern Europe, for example Cologne, Riga, Elbing, Danzig, Königsberg, Geneva and Marseilles.

The oldest flags with a cross are those of Portugal and the kingdom of Jerusalem. From 1140 to 1185 the Portuguese flag was white with a blue cross on a white field, and from 1185 to 1250 it was white with a cross made of five blue shields; this latter arrangement remains to this day in the centre of the coat of arms of Portugal. The flag of the kingdom of Jerusalem under King Amalrich (1162–1173) displayed five golden yellow crosses on a white field.

Other flags and ensigns dating from the 13th and 14th centuries are charged with a simple

♦ **BELOW**
(from left to right)
Portugal (1140–1185);
Jerusalem; Genoa;
Constantinople (14th century);
Barcelona (14th century);
Sardinia (14th century);
Savoy (14th century).

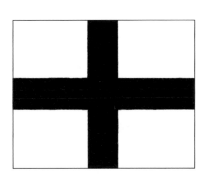

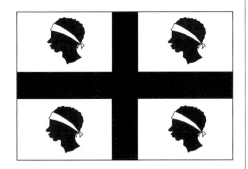

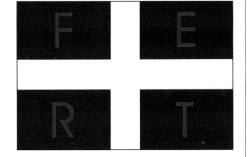

THE CROSS

The current national flags of the following countries and territories belong to this family:
ÅLAND ISLANDS, DENMARK, DOMINICA, DOMINICAN REPUBLIC, FAROES, FINLAND, GUERNSEY, ICELAND, JERSEY, MADEIRA, MARTINIQUE, NORWAY, SHETLAND, SWEDEN, SWITZERLAND, TONGA, WALLIS AND FUTUNA ISLANDS.

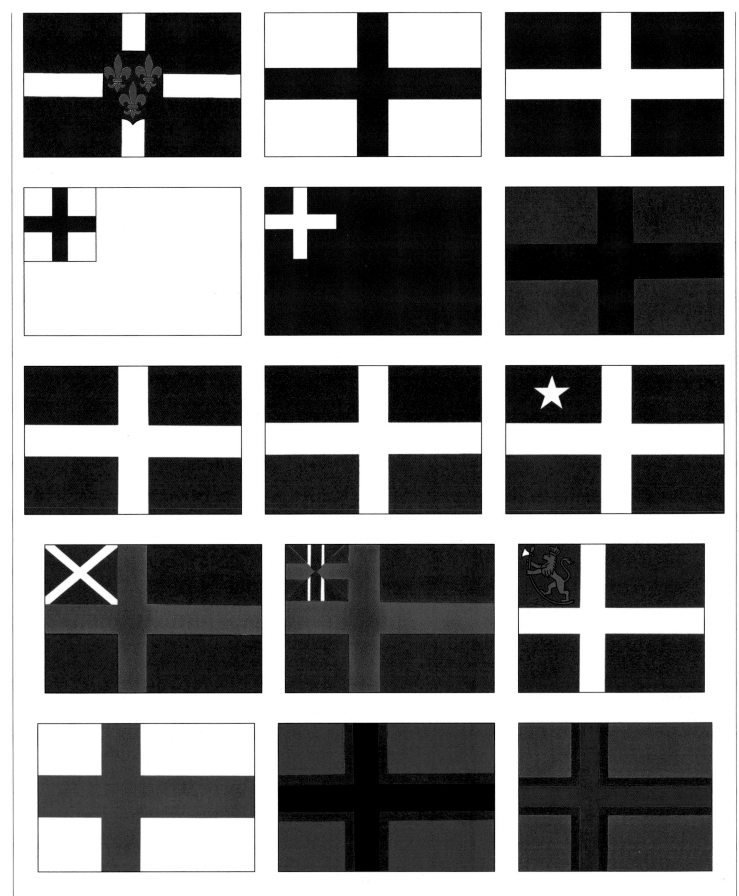

cross including the Teutonic Order, England, France, Denmark, Savoy and Malta, and the flags of Barcelona and Constantinople, which display additional devices. The flag of Barcelona has two quarters with the cross and two

displaying the armorial banner of Catalonia. The flag of Constantinople has four letters "B" between the arms of the cross, which are believed to stand for the Greek motto *Basileis Basileon Basileion Basileisi* ("King of Kings ruling

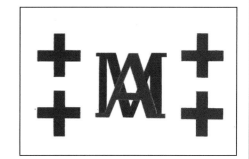

◆ **ABOVE**
(left to right from top left)
Switzerland, civil ensign
(since 1941); Livorno;
Malta (civil ensign since
1965); Samoa (1873–1885);
Rimatara (c.1856–1891);
Tongatapu (c.1858–1862).

◆ **OPPOSITE**
(left to right from top left)
France civil ensign
(1661–1790); Provence;
Calai;, Picardy; Marseilles;
Oldenburg (1774–1935);
Greece, national flag (1822–
1970); Samos (1832–1913);
Crete (1898–1913); Sweden,
civil ensign (1815–1844);
Sweden, civil ensign (1844–
1905); Norway, civil ensign
(1815–1844); Finland, civil
ensign (since 1918);
East Karelia (1920–1922);
Ingermanland.

over Kings"). It inspired the flags adopted in subsequent centuries by at least two other countries in the Mediterranean: in the Sardinian flag there are Moorish heads between the arms of the cross, and in the Savoy flag the letters "FERT" stand for *Fortitudo Ejus Rhodum Tenuit* (His Courage Saved Rhodes).

In the 17th and 18th centuries the cross was the main charge of the civil ensign of France, and of several French provinces (Provence and Picardy) and ports (Marseilles and Calais). The official French civil ensign was blue with a white cross, with the royal arms overall, but it was not popular and most French merchant vessels used either provincial or port ensigns or the banned white ensign. Such widespread use of the cross in the Mediterranean also influenced the flags of nations created in the 19th and 20th centuries such as Greece, Samos and Crete.

Until the end of the 14th century the centre of the cross corresponded with the centre of the field. Denmark was the first to position the cross in such a way that the parts of the field between the arms of the cross formed squares in the hoist and rectangles in the fly. This example was followed by Sweden (1569), Norway (1821), Iceland (1915), Finland (1918), the Faroes (1919), East Karelia (1920), and Ingermanland and the Åland Islands (1921). Thus a large sub-family, called the Scandinavian cross, came into being. Modern flags with the Scandinavian Cross are illustrated in *Flags of Europe*.

As well as simple symmetrical or Latin crosses, there were some more elaborate versions of the Christian cross. One of the first, a red Maltese cross on a white field, is known from the war ensign of the Cavalieri di Santo Stefano Order, founded in 1561. A modification of this cross appeared in the 17th and 18th centuries on the merchant ensign of Livorno.

Four very old crosses have only appeared on civil ensigns and flags during the last 100 years. In Switzerland a white cross on a red field had already appeared in the 13th century on the flag of Schwyz and on red schwenkels added to the flags of other cantons. However, it did not become the national symbol until 1889 (national flag) or for use at sea until 1941 (civil ensign). The 900-year-old white Maltese cross of the Order of the Knights of St John of Jerusalem appears on the red field of the civil ensign of Malta. Finally the cross of the Portuguese Order of Christ, founded in the early 14th century, became the central emblem on the flag of Madeira in 1978.

In various forms, the Christian cross also appears on the flags and ensigns of nations in other parts of the world. It is a charge of the flags of Dominica and the Dominican Republic, and it was placed in the canton of the Liberian flag of 1827–47. In Oceania it was the charge of the civil ensigns of Samoa, Rimatara and Tongatapu, and it is still used by Tonga and by Wallis and Futuna.

THE MUSLIM CRESCENT

The crescent is one of the oldest symbols known to humanity. Together with the sun, it appeared on Akkadian seals as early as 2300 BC and from at least the second millennium BC it was the symbol of the Mesopotamian moon gods Nanna in Sumer and Sin in Babylonia, Sin being the "Lamp of Heaven and Earth". The crescent was well known in the Middle East and was transplanted by the Phoenicians in the 8th century as far as Carthage (now in Tunisia). In the 12th century it was adopted by the Turks and since then the crescent, often accompanied by a star and mentioned in the 53rd *surah* (chapter) of the Koran, has been the main symbol of Islam.

The oldest representations of flags with the crescent are on 14th-century navigational charts, or *portolanos*, and the manuscript of a Franciscan friar. There are discrepancies between these sources as far as the colours of fields or

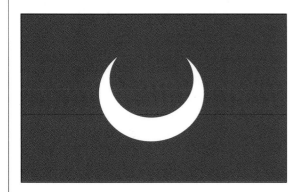

◆ **LEFT**
(left to right from top left)
Gabes; Tlemcen; Tunis; Turkey (16th–18th century); Turkey (1793–1844); Egypt (1914–1922).

crescents are concerned. However, an account of flags from the Middle East and North Africa by the author of *Libro de Conoscimento* confirms the widespread use of the crescent on flags in that region. These include: the flags of the kings of Damascus and Lucha (yellow with a white crescent); Cairo (white with a blue crescent); Mahdia in Tunisia (white with a purple crescent); Tunis (white with a black crescent); and Buda (white with a red crescent). Some of the 14th- and 15th-century *portolanos* show the flag of Tunis as red with one or two crescents, which is presented on several *portolanos* as the flag of the Ottoman Empire. From the 16th to the 18th centuries this flag is usually shown with three white crescents; in 1793 the number of crescents was reduced to one and an eight-pointed white star was added.

After the rule of the Ottoman Empire ended, Turkey was the only Muslim state regarded as a world power. Its flag was known from West Africa to the Far East, and helped to popularize the crescent and star among the Muslim populations of many countries of Asia and Africa. Muhammad Ali, who became Pasha of Egypt in 1805, introduced the first national flag of Egypt, red with three white crescents, each accompanied by a white star. This flag, in turn,

◆ **RIGHT**
(from left to right)
Egypt (1923–1958);
Rif Republic (1921–1926);
Hatay (1938–1939);
Cyrenaica (1947–1950);
Tripolitania (1951) and
Libya (1951–1969);
South Arabia (1959–1967).

◆ ABOVE
(left to right from top left)
Azerbaijan (1917–1920);
Kokand (1917);
Dagestan (1918–1921);
Turkestan (1918–1924);
North Caucasia (1919–1920);
Bokhara (1920–1921);
Khoresm (1920–1922);
Maldives (1934);
East Turkestan (1943–1949);
Comoros (1975–1978);
Singapore civil ensign
(since 1966).

influenced the design of the first flag of
independent Egypt, which was green with a
white crescent and three white stars to symbolize
the peaceful co-existence of Muslims, Christians
and Jews. During the past two centuries the
crescent and star featured on the flags of
other Arab countries in North Africa and the
Middle East. These include Tunisia (c.1835), the
Rif Republic (1921–1926), Hatay (1938–1939),
Cyrenaica (1947–1950), Tripolitania (1951),
Libya (1951–1969), South Arabia (1959),
Mauritania (1959), Algeria (1962) and
Western Sahara (1976). Other regions heavily
influenced by the Turks were the Caucasus and
Central Asia. Several countries which achieved
independence during World War I adopted flags
with the crescent and star, or the crescent alone:
Azerbaijan (1917), Kokand (1917), Dagestan
(1918), North Caucasia (1919), Khoresm
(1920), Bokhara (1920), Turkestan (1922),
Uzbekistan (1991) and Turkmenistan (1992).
Several countries in Central and South-east Asia
also adopted flags with the crescent and star: the
Maldives (1934), East Turkestan (1943),
Pakistan (1947), the Federation of Malaya
(1950), Singapore (1959) and Comoros (1963).

THE UNION JACK

Until the early 17th century and since the 13th century the English flag and jack, used by both merchant and navy ships, had been white with the red cross of St George. The Scottish flag was blue with the white cross of St Andrew. Then, on 12 April 1606 King James I of England and Scotland issued a proclamation:

That from henceforth all our Subjects of this Isle and Kingdome of Great Britaine, and the members thereof, shall beare in their Maintoppe the Red Crosse, commonly called S. Georges Crosse, and the White Crosse, commonly called S. Andrewes Crosse, joyned together, according to a forme made by our Heralds...

This was the birth certificate of what soon became the best-known flag in the world.

Until 1634 the flag was used by both merchant and navy ships, thereafter its use was restricted to the king's own ships or ships in the king's immediate service; English merchant ships reverted to flying the St George's cross and Scottish ships the St Andrew's cross. At the same time the merchant ensign, red with the St George's cross in the canton, came into use and was later legalized in a proclamation of 1674. This proclamation retained the "Flag and Jack White, with a Red Cross (commonly called Saint George's Cross)", and repeatedly warned that use of the Union Jack was illegal. Nevertheless, many merchant captains

GENEALOGY OF THE UNION JACK

ST GEORGE'S CROSS

ST ANDREW'S CROSS

ST PATRICK'S CROSS

UNION FLAG 1606–1801

UNION FLAG SINCE 1801

♦ LEFT AND FAR LEFT
Red ensign (since 1801),
blue ensign (since 1801).

continued to use the "King's jack" in order to gain advantages such as better protection, exemption from port duties in France as well as exemption from the requirement to use a pilot in Holland.

When the United Kingdom of Great Britain and Ireland came into existence on 1 January 1801, a red saltire called the cross of St Patrick was chosen to represent Ireland. It originated in the coat of arms of the Anglo-Irish family of Fitzgerald and was the main emblem of the Order of St Patrick, adopted in 1783. The idea of counterchanging the white and red saltires assured almost equal status for both of them, and was excellent from an artistic point of view. The new Union flag replaced that of 1606 in the cantons of the merchant ensign, and the red, white and blue ensigns used by the three squadrons of the Navy. On 9 July 1864 an Admiralty order abolished the division of the Navy into squadrons and assigned the white ensign exclusively to the Royal Naval Service, while the red ensign became "the national

colours for all British ships". It was decided that the blue ensign would

be carried by all vessels employed in the service of any public office; by vessels employed under the Transport Department, and the Civil Departments of the Navy (with the Seal or Badge of the office to which they belong at the present), and, under our permission, by ships commanded by Officers of the Royal Naval Reserve Force...

The use of the blue ensign was extended by the Colonial Defence Act of 1865, which allowed "all vessels belonging to, or permanently in, the service of the Colonies" to use this ensign, "with the Seal or Badge of the Colony in the Fly thereof". This Act made possible the enormous future growth in the number of flags with the Union Jack in the canton. More than 100 colonial ensigns have been in use during the last century and some of them, such as those of Australia, New Zealand, Fiji and Tuvalu, became

♦ BELOW
(from left to right)
Saint Lucia (19th century–1938); Barbados (19th century–1966); British Honduras (19th century–1981); Turks and Caicos Islands (end of the 19th century–1968); New Zealand (1900–1902); Australia (1903–1908).

◆ **BELOW**
(from left to right) Grenada (1903–1967); Nyasaland (1914–1953); Tanganyika (1919–1964); Gilbert and Ellice Islands (1937–1979); Burma (1939–1941); Sarawak (1947–1963); Federation of Rhodesia and Nyasaland (1954–1963); Guyana (1954–1966); Solomon Islands (1956–1977); Seychelles (1961–1976); the Bahamas (1964–1973); Dominica (1965–1978).

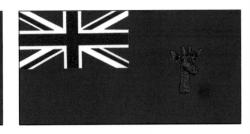

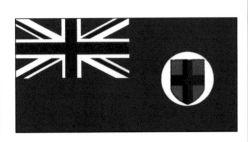

after some alteration the national flags of independent countries.

Formally the civil ensign of a British colony was always, and still is, an undefaced red ensign. Only a few dominions and one colony obtained the right to use the British red ensign defaced with a badge. The privilege was first granted to Canada (1892), then to New Zealand (1899), Australia (1903), South Africa (1910), Bermuda

(1915), the Isle of Man (1971), Guernsey (1985), the Cayman Islands (1988) and Gibraltar (1996). The charges on the last two flags mentioned are of ancient origin. The golden cross on the civil ensign of Guernsey was the main charge of William the Conqueror's gonfanon, accorded to him by the Pope before he embarked on the campaign that ended in victory at the battle of Hastings in 1066. The ensign of Gibraltar

◆ **BELOW**
(from left to right)
Canada (1922–1957),
Canada (1957–1965),
Union of South Africa
(1912–1928).

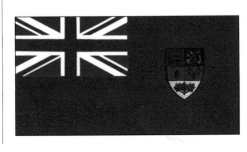

displays the arms granted by King Ferdinand and Queen Isabella of Spain on 10 July 1502. Several former British colonies were so accustomed to the red ensign that after gaining independence they introduced a civil ensign in the form of a red flag with the national flag in the canton. As well as the examples illustrated here, the civil ensigns of Sri Lanka, Bangladesh and the Solomon Islands also have this design.

The British innovation of putting the national flag in the canton of a flag or ensign greatly influenced the merchant ensigns of many countries that did not have formal ties with the British Empire. The example of the striped Elizabethan

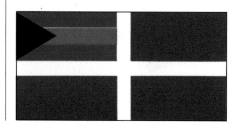  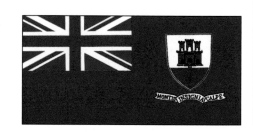

GREAT BRITAIN
COLONIES (CONTINUED)

TASMANIA

SOLOMON
ISLANDS

FIJI
ISLANDS

TERRITORY
OF PAPUA

BRITISH RESIDENT,
GILBERT & ELLIS ISLANDS

WESTERN PACIFIC
HIGH COMMISSIONERS

AFRICA

BRITISH CENTRAL AFRICA

BRITISH EAST AFRICA

SAMOLILAND

UNION OF SOUTH AFRICA

SIERRA LEONE

GOLD COAST

GAMBIA

ST. HELENA

CHINA

NIGERIA

UGANDA

HONG KONG

WEIHAIWEI

EAST INDIES

CEYLON

MAURITIAS

STRAITS SETTLEMENTS

SEYCHELLES

ensigns induced the Portuguese to adopt a similar ensign in 1640. The blue and red ensigns served as models for the civil ensigns or national flags of Hanover (1801–1866), Sardinia (1821–1848), Greece (1822–1828), China (1928–1949), Taiwan (since 1949), Spanish Morocco (1937–1956), Samoa (1948–1949), the Khmer Republic (1970–1975), and flags of the French colonies (see *The French Tricolore*).

The flag of the United States, a discussion of which follows, was one of the first flags to be modelled on the British ensign.

◆ **ABOVE AND LEFT**
(left to right from top left)
Burma (1948–1974);
Ceylon (1954–1972);
India, civil ensign
(since 1950); Pakistan,
civil ensign (since 1958);
Ghana, civil ensign
(since 1961); Greece,
civil ensign (1822–1828);
Taiwan, civil ensign
(since 1949); Spanish
Morocco (1937–1956).

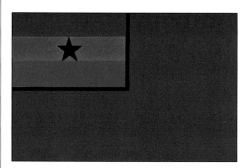

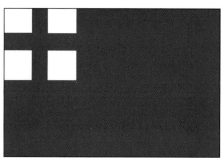

THE FLAG FAMILY

The current national flags of the following countries and territories belong to this family:
ANGUILLA, AUSTRALIA, BERMUDA, BRITISH ANTARCTIC TERRITORY, BRITISH INDIAN OCEAN TERRITORY, BRITISH VIRGIN ISLANDS, CAYMAN ISLANDS, COOK ISLANDS, FALKLANDS, FIJI, HEBRIDES, MONTSERRAT, MYANMAR, NEW ZEALAND, NIUE, PITCAIRN, ST HELENA, SAMOA, SOUTH GEORGIA AND SOUTH SANDWICH ISLANDS, TAIWAN, TONGA, TURKS AND CAICOS ISLANDS, TUVALU.

THE STARS AND STRIPES

From the end of the 15th century North America was colonized by British settlers and the best-known flag was the British red ensign, which in America was used also on land. It was only natural that it should influence the design of the United States flag, often called the Stars and Stripes or Star-spangled Banner.

The first American flag was the merchant ensign, introduced in 1775. It consisted solely of 13 red and white stripes, very similar to the flag of the Revolutionary Society of the Sons of Liberty. The flag hoisted on 2 January 1776 by the Continental Army also had 13 red and white stripes, with the Union Jack in the canton. Called the Grand Union flag or the Continental Colors, it was identical to the flag of the British East India Company although this was probably just coincidence. The Union Jack in the canton symbolized continuing loyalty to Britain, but the stripes were probably taken from the merchant ensign rather than from the flag of the East India Company and symbolized the rebellion of the 13 colonies against British rule.

Some circumstances indicate that the Union Jack had already been replaced by the star-filled canton in 1776, and that the Continental Congress's Resolution of 14 June 1777 only confirmed the design already in use. Substantiating this theory is the terse wording of the Resolution:

Resolved, That the Flag of the United States be 13 stripes alternate red and white, that the Union be 13 stars white in a blue field representing a new constellation.

There is no mention of the size of the Union (the canton) or the shape or configuration of the stars. In fact, from that date there were two different designs for the canton of the American national flag. The so-called Betsy Ross design has the stars arranged in a circle, while Francis Hopkinson's design shows the stars arranged in parallel staggered rows. In both cases the stars were five-pointed, which was a revolutionary innovation in flag design.

◆ **RIGHT**
Grand Union flag.

◆ **RIGHT**
Betsy Ross design.

◆ **RIGHT**
Francis Hopkinson's design.

One of the earliest accounts of the symbolism of the flag is by Alfred B. Street, who in October 1777 witnessed the flag at the surrender of the British General Burgoyne at Saratoga:

The stars were disposed in a circle, symbolizing the perpetuity of the Union; the ring, like the circling serpent of the Egyptians, signifying eternity. The thirteen stripes showed with the stars the number of the United Colonies, and denoted the subordination of the States to the Union, as well as equality among themselves.

The growth of the Union posed the question of how the new states should be represented in the flag. After the admission of Vermont (1791) and Kentucky (1792) to the Union, the flag

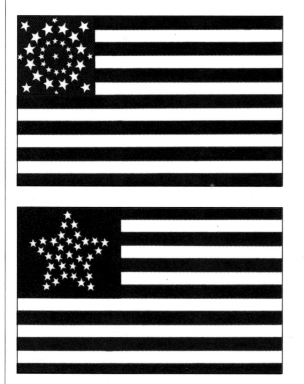

◆ **LEFT**
(from left to right)
Stars forming rings; stars forming ovals; stars forming a star; an early civil ensign.

created on 13 January 1794 displayed fifteen stars and 15 stripes. Between 1796 and 1817 five more states joined the Union but the flag was not modified until 4 April 1818, when the Flag Act raised the number of stars to 20 and reverted the number of stripes to the original 13. Section 2 of the act established the principle for future modifications:

And be it further enacted, that on the admission of every new State into the Union, one star be added to the union of the flag; such addition shall take effect on the fourth of July next succeeding such admission.

Since then the number of stars in the canton of the national flag has been increased 24 times, the latest being on 4 July 1960. From 1818 to this day the number of stars represents the

number of states in the Union, while the 13 stripes symbolize the 13 colonies that achieved independence and formed the United States of America.

For more than 130 years there was no official regulation of the arrangement of the stars in the canton of the national flag. At any given time the flags displayed dozens of designs, the most popular were concentric rings, ovals, diamonds and large stars made of smaller stars. Then, in 1818, President Monroe stipulated that the stars should be arranged in parallel rows. This arrangement was followed by the navy and was officially adopted for all flags in 1912.

◆ **BELOW**
Flag with 48 stars (1912–1959).

THE FLAG FAMILY

The current national flags of the following countries and territories belong to this family:
ABKHAZIA, CHILE, CUBA, GREECE, LIBERIA, MALAYSIA, PUERTO RICO, TOGO, UNITED STATES, URUGUAY.

◆ BELOW
(left to right from top left)
Hawaii (1815–1825);
Uruguay (1828–1830);
Texas (1836–1845);
Confederate States of
America (1861–1863);
Vermont (1837–1923);
Louisiana (1861–1962);
Orange Free State
(1857–1902);
Liberia (1827–1847);
El Salvador (1865–1912);
Brazil (1889);
North Caucasia (1918–1919);
Malaya (1950–1963).

The first country to adopt a similar flag to the American one was Hawaii. In an astute political move, the Hawaiian king combined in his country's flag the symbols of the two most influential powers in the Pacific, that is the British Union Jack with the tricolour stripes of the American ensign. Other countries adopted flags inspired by the American design to manifest their adherence to republican ideals of liberty and democracy. These countries included Chile (1817), Uruguay (1828), Texas (1836), Vermont (1837), Cuba (1850), the Confederate States of America (1861), Louisiana (1861) and Puerto Rico (1891). Alternatively, some countries used the stars and/or stripes to represent the number of their subdivisions: Greece (1822); Liberia (1827); El Salvador (1865); Brazil (1889) and seven of its states (Amazonas, Bahia, Goiás, Maranhão, Piauí, São Paulo, Sergipe); as well as North Caucasia (1918); the Federation of Malaya (1950), Togo (1960) and Abkhasia (1992).

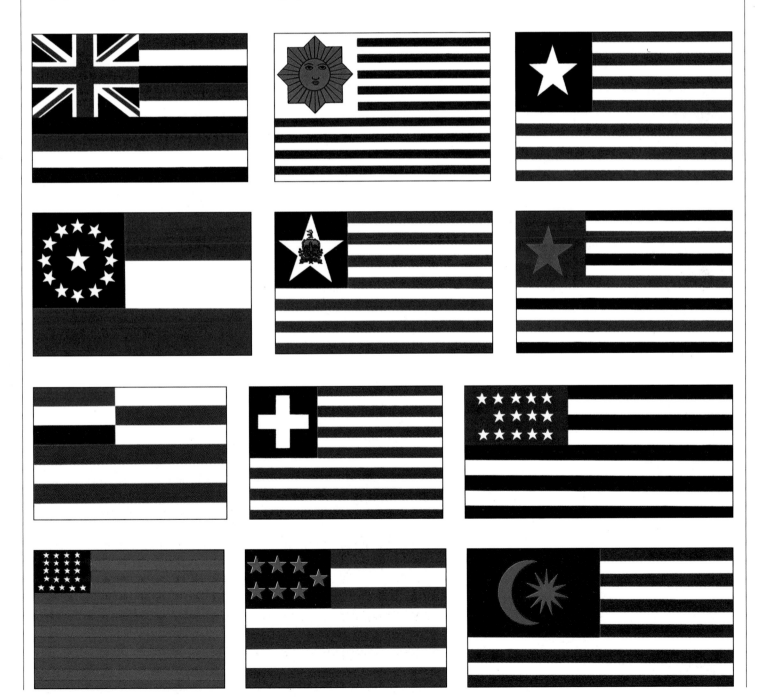

THE DUTCH AND PAN-SLAV COLOURS

Orange, white and blue were the livery colours of William I, Prince of Orange (1533–1584). Armbands in these colours were worn by his soldiers at the siege of Leiden in 1574, and in the 1580s they were used on the horizontal tricolour of the ensign and the flag used on land. Thus was created the first modern flag, displaying simple stripes instead of heraldic devices.

During the 17th century the orange was gradually replaced by red. This may have been because red is more visible at sea, or the reason may have been political: a manifestation of the Dutch estates-general's wish to exclude the House of Orange. The original tricolour survived until at least 1795, when the orange was officially replaced by red.

In the 18th century the Dutch ensign was one of a few that were well known in many parts of the world, especially South-east Asia, North America and South Africa. In South Africa seven political entities adopted flags based on the Dutch design: Natalia (1839), Transvaal (1857), Orange Free State (1857), Lyndenburg Republic (1857), Goshen Republic (1882), New Republic (1884) and the Union of South Africa (1928). In the Americas the original Dutch colours appear on the flag of New York, which is widely used in the city, while the modern colours (using

red instead of orange) appear on the flag of the Netherlands Antilles.

The Dutch flag had an even greater impact on the flags of Slav nations in central and southern Europe. It was a model for the merchant flag of Russia, personally designed in 1699 by Tsar Peter the Great (1672–1725). Eager to modernize his country, he travelled incognito to western Europe in 1697 to gather first-hand information on advanced technology, especially in shipbuilding. He worked for four months as a shipwright in the shipyard of the Dutch East India Company in Saardam, and

♦ **ABOVE**
Flag of the Netherlands
(late 16th century–1795).

♦ **BELOW**
(from left to right)
Natal (1839–1843);
Transvaal (1857–1877);
Goshen Republic
(1882–1885);
New Republic (1884–1888);
South Africa (1928–1994);
Netherlands Antilles
(1959–1985).

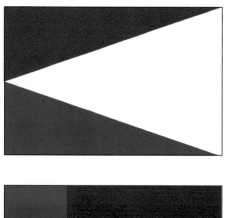

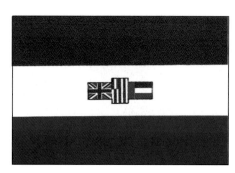

THE FLAG FAMILY

The current national flags of the following countries belong to this family: BULGARIA, CROATIA, CZECH REPUBLIC, THE NETHERLANDS, THE NETHERLANDS ANTILLES, RUSSIA, SLOVAKIA, SLOVENIA, YUGOSLAVIA.

spent some time in the British Navy shipyard at Deptford. On his return to Russia he introduced an elaborate system of naval flags, based on Dutch and British flags and ensigns. The merchant flag, which became the national flag of Russia, was a horizontal tricolour of white-blue-red.

This flag, in turn, inspired other Slav countries to adopt horizontal tricolours displaying the same colours in different arrangements. Nations living under foreign (but not Russian) domination also followed suit. In 1835 the Serbs were the first to adopt a red-blue-white tricolour for their ships on inland waters. In 1848, during the first pan-Slav Congress in Prague, these were proclaimed the pan-Slav colours and were adopted of horizontal tricolours by several Slav provinces of Austria. The Slovaks and Slovenes placed the colours in the same order as Russia, the Serbs adopted a blue-red-white tricolour and the Croats

positioned the colours as in the Dutch flag. The flag adopted by Bulgaria in 1878 was the same as that of Russia, the only difference being the substitution of green for the red. In 1880 Montenegro adopted a merchant ensign, a tricolour similar to that of Serbia with a white cross in the centre of the red stripe. A year later the cross had been removed and a crown with the royal cipher "H.I", for Nikola I, placed in the centre. The Kingdom of Serbs, Croats and Slovenes, established in 1918, adopted a national flag and ensign in the form of a horizontal blue-white-red tricolour, which remained unchanged when the name of the country was changed to Yugoslavia.

A somewhat different flag belonging to this flag family is that of Czechoslovakia (currently the Czech Republic), adopted in 1920.

There are other flags that do not belong to this family, but are worth mentioning because their design (horizontal tricolour) is copied from that of the Russian flag. These are the flags and ensigns of nations that were once part of the Russian Empire and gained independence either temporarily or permanently: Belarus (1918–1919 and 1991–1995), some Cossack states, Lithuania, Estonia, Azerbaijan, Armenia, Uzbekistan and Tajikistan.

◆ **BELOW**
(from left to right)
Russia (c.1700–1858, 1883–1918, since 1991); Bulgaria (since 1878); Slovakia (1848); Montenegro (1881–1918); Serbia (1882–1918); Croatia (1941–1945).

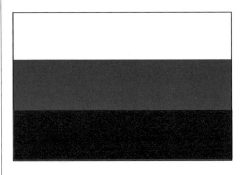
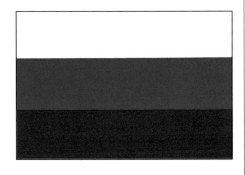
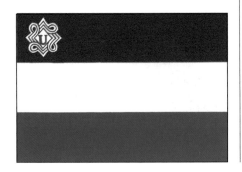

THE FRENCH *TRICOLORE*

The colours red, blue and white have been successively used on French flags from the time of Charlemagne. Red was the imperial flag from the 9th century; blue was the field of the armorial banner of France from the 13th century to 1589, and of the merchant ensign from 1661 to 1790; and white was the French flag and ensign from 1589 to 1790. Nevertheless, it is surprisingly only a coincidence that these three colours appear together on the French national flag; they are, in fact, the colours of the coat of arms of the city of Paris, combined with the white of the Bourbons.

On 13 July 1789, on the eve of the French Revolution, the Paris militia were given blue and red cockades. Four days later in the City Hall the Marquis de Lafayette presented a similar cockade to King Louis XVI, who attached it to the royal white one. The leaders of the Revolution approved the Marquis' proposal to adopt the cockade in the "colours of liberty". The new cockade was received enthusiastically by the people and in the following days the streets of Paris were full of ribbons and flags in the "colours of liberty" in various arrangements.

In spite of this fervour, the official flag and ensign remained unchanged. The addition of a tricolour streamer to the war ensign in 1790 did not satisfy the rebellious sailors, who demanded the introduction of a new one displaying the colours that were already perceived as the national ones. The ensign that was subsequently adopted on 24 October 1790 was white with the canton composed of a red-white-blue vertical tricolour and a white border separating it from the outer border, which was half-red and half-blue. The vertical arrangement of three colours was revolutionary, both geometrically and politically. The order of colours was changed to the present one on 15 February 1794.

A few decades after the French Revolution the colours of the *Tricolore*, as the flag is called, were perceived in Europe and elsewhere as the

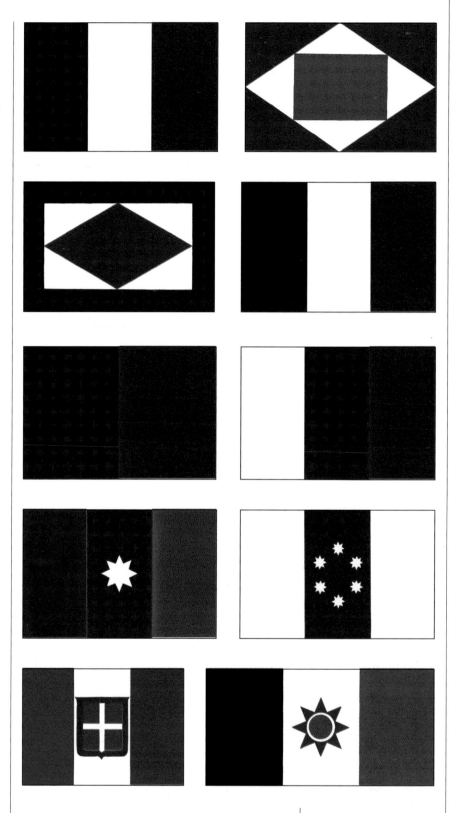

◆ **ABOVE**
(left to right from top left)
France (1794–1815 and since 1830); Italian Republic (1802–1805); Lucca (1803–1805); Rome Republic; Haiti (1804–1805); Mexico (1815–1821); Colombia, civil ensign (1834–1861); Ecuador, civil ensign (1845–1860); Italy, national flag and ensign (1848–1946); Iraq (1959–1963).

colours of the republican movement. They were adopted by Lucca (1803), Uruguay (1825–1828), the Dominican Republic (1844), Costa Rica (1848) and the Polish insurgents of 1863. Even more influential was the *Tricolore* design introduced by Napoleon in some Italian states. This later inspired revolutionaries and leaders of independence movements in many parts of the world to adopt flags with a vertical arrangement of colours. The first was the French colony of Saint Domingue where the revolutionaries had already in 1803 adopted a blue-red flag: the French flag without the white which they perceived as a symbol of their oppressors. On 1 January 1804 this became the first national flag of independent Haiti. Flags with three vertical stripes were adopted by revolutionary movements or governments in Mexico (1815), Belgium (1831), Colombia (1834), Ecuador (1845), Ireland (1848), Italy (1848) and Iraq (1958), and the King of Romania (1867).

A large group of flags with the French *Tricolore* in the canton are those of the French colonies created in the 19th and 20th centuries. When Saarland was part of the French occupation zone in Germany after World War II, the French authorities introduced a flag displaying the French colours.

The next large addition to the family of vertical tricolours came in the second half of the 20th century, when many former French colonies in Africa adopted flags following the *Tricolore* design.

THE FLAG FAMILY

The current national flags of the following countries belong to this family: ANDORRA, BELGIUM, CAMEROON, CHAD, FRANCE, GUINEA, IRELAND, ITALY, IVORY COAST, MALI, MEXICO, MOLDOVA, PERU, ROMANIA, RWANDA, SENEGAL, WALLIS AND FUTUNA.

FLAGS OF THE FRENCH COLONIES

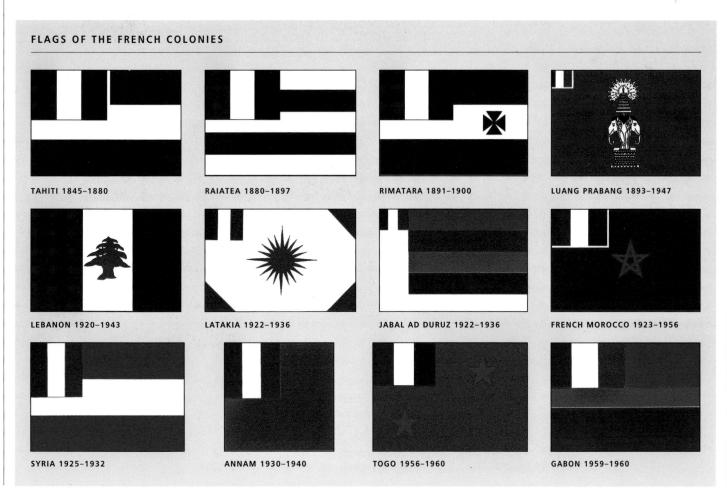

TAHITI 1845–1880

RAIATEA 1880–1897

RIMATARA 1891–1900

LUANG PRABANG 1893–1947

LEBANON 1920–1943

LATAKIA 1922–1936

JABAL AD DURUZ 1922–1936

FRENCH MOROCCO 1923–1956

SYRIA 1925–1932

ANNAM 1930–1940

TOGO 1956–1960

GABON 1959–1960

THE LIVERY COLOURS

The simplest national flags, introduced by several European countries during the last two centuries, are those composed of livery colours arranged in two or three horizontal stripes. In most cases the upper stripe is in the colour of a heraldic charge, while the lower stripe displays the colour of the shield, although the reverse order of colours was customary in Austria. When translating coats of arms into flags, gold becomes yellow and silver becomes white. The only exception to this rule is the German flag, called *Schwarz-Rot-Gold* (black-red-gold), which has a golden yellow stripe instead of yellow.

From 1785 to 1931, and since 1936, the colours of the Spanish ensigns have been yellow and red, the armorial colours of Castile, Aragón, Catalonia and Navarre. The Spanish republican

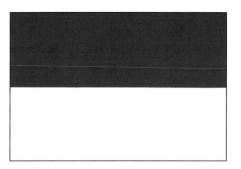

colours (1931–1939) were red, yellow and purple (the colour of the lion in the arms of León). The flag of Portugal from 1821 to 1910 displayed livery colours dating from the 12th century. National flags in livery colours were most widespread in central Europe, especially in the German states and parts of Austria-Hungary. The colours of the proper arms of Austria (a white fess on red field) were

◆ **ABOVE AND LEFT**
(from left to right) Spain, civil ensign (1785–1928); Spain, civil ensign (1931–1939); Portugal (1821–1910); Württemberg (1816–1935); Brunswick (1748–1814); Saxony (1815–1935); Saxony-Weimar-Eisenach (1815–1920); Mecklenburg (1863–1935); Prussia, civil ensign (1823–1863); Germany 1867–1919.

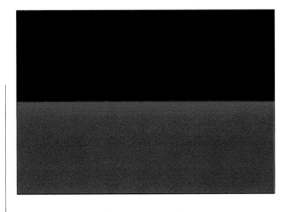

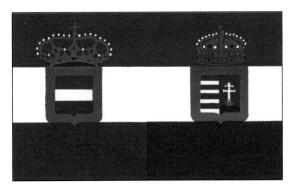

employed on the civil ensign of 1869-1918 and thereafter on the national flag. The national flag of Austria, used from 1804 to 1918, displayed the colours of the imperial arms (a black double-headed eagle on a golden field). A few other examples are the flags or ensigns of Brunswick, Saxony, Saxony-Weimar-Eisenach, Württemberg, Prussia, Mecklenburg, Germany, Galicia and Lodomeria, Hungary and Austria-Hungary. The first flag of Romania displayed the livery colours of Valachia and Moldavia. For a short period the Russian national flag displayed the colours of the imperial arms (black double-headed eagle on a golden field) and white from the charge of the arms of Moscow. Other flags with livery colours are those of San Marino, Luxembourg, Monaco, the Vatican, Poland and Ukraine.

THE FLAG FAMILY

The national flags of the following countries belong to this family:

AUSTRIA, GERMANY, HUNGARY, LUXEMBOURG, MONACO, POLAND, SAN MARINO, SPAIN, UKRAINE, VATICAN.

THE PAN-ARAB COLOURS

The early Arab flags were of one colour, often charged with religious inscriptions. Biographers of the Prophet Muhammad ascribe to him two flags, one black and one white; his followers are said to have fought under the white flag for seven years and with this flag they entered Mecca. White was also the colour of the Muslim dynasty of the Umayyads, the immediate successors of the Prophet and an influential family of the Quraish tribe to which he belonged. Under a white flag the Umayyads ruled the Muslim Empire from AD 661 to 750, and were Muslim rulers of Spain from AD 756 to 1031. Black, the second colour used by Muhammad, was the colour of the Abbasid dynasty that overthrew the Umayyads and ruled the Muslim Empire from AD 750 to 1258.

Green, perceived as the colour of Islam, was the traditional colour of the Fatimid dynasty of caliphs, which ruled in North Africa from AD 909 to 1171. The Fatimids were leaders of the Ismaili sect and claimed descent from Fatima, the daughter of the Prophet Muhammad. Red is the colour of the Hashemites, descendants of Hashim, the great-grandfather of the Prophet Muhammad, and for centuries the hereditary amirs of Mecca. The founder of the modern Hashemite dynasty was Husayn ibn Ali, the amir of Mecca, King of Hejaz (1916–1924) and father of the kings of Iraq and Jordan.

In 1911 a group of young Arabs met in the Literary Club in Istanbul to choose a design for a modern Arab flag, and decided it should be composed of these four colours – white, black, green and red. The symbolism was explained by the poet Safi al-Din al-Hili:

White are our deeds, black are our battles,
Green are our fields, red are our knives.

In 1914 the central committee of the Young Arab Society in Beirut declared that the flag of the future independent Arab state should display the colours of the Umayyads (white), Abbasids (black) and Fatimids (green). However, the Arab Revolt began in Hejaz on 10 June 1916 under a plain red flag, traditional for that area. Several months later Sharif Hussein, leader of the revolt, accepted suggestions to adopt the colours white, black and green, and added red, a symbol of his family. The flag was hoisted on 30 May 1917,

◆ LEFT
Hijaz (1917–1920).

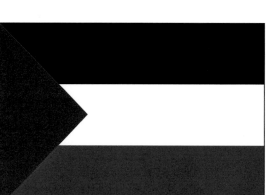

◆ LEFT
Hijaz (1920–1926) and Iraq (1921–1924).

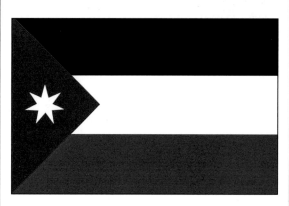

◆ LEFT
Syria (1920).

THE FLAG FAMILY

The current national flags of the following countries and territories belong to this family:
EGYPT, IRAQ, JORDAN, KUWAIT, PALESTINE, SOMALILAND, SUDAN, SYRIA, UNITED ARAB EMIRATES, WESTERN SAHARA, YEMEN.

a day that might be considered the birthday of the pan-Arab colours.

The flag family started to grow when this modern Arab flag was adopted by Syria in March 1920 and by Iraq in 1921. By adding a white star (Syria) or two stars (Iraq) to the flag, both countries manifested that they were the first and second state to emanate from the "mother-state". The designs of these flags were later modified, but the four pan-Arab colours were retained and were adopted by Transjordan (1921), Palestine (1922), Kuwait (1961), the United Arab Emirates (1971), Western Sahara (1976) and Somaliland (1996).

After the revolution of 1952 in Egypt, the young officers who abolished the monarchy introduced the Arab Liberation Flag, a horizontal red-white-black tricolour, which symbolized the period of oppression (black) overcome through bloody struggle (red) to be replaced by a bright future (white). This flag was the inspiration for the flags of several Arab nations which chose the republican political system, so it could be considered to be the first of the second generation of pan-Arab colours. With the addition of two green stars (for Egypt and Syria), in 1958 it became the national flag of the United Arab Republic. Later similar flags, with or without stars, were adopted by Yemen (1962), Syria and Iraq (1963), South Yemen (1967), Libya (1969) and Sudan (1970).

◆ **ABOVE**
(left to right from top left)
Iraq (1924–1959);
Syria (1932–1958 and 1961–1963);
United Arab Republic (1958–1961) and Egypt (1961–1972);
Iraq (1963–1991) and Syria (1963–1971);
Yemen (1962–1990);
Libya (1969–1972);
South Yemen (1967–1990).

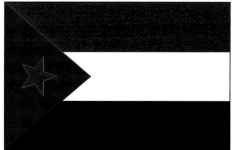

THE PAN-AFRICAN COLOURS

Two factors have influenced the choice of colours for the flags of independent countries south of the Sahara. The first, and main, source of inspiration was the green, yellow and red flag of Ethiopia, the oldest independent state in Africa. The second was the red, black and green flag designed in 1917 by Marcus Garvey, the organizer of the first important black unification movement in the United States. He created the flag for the United Negro Improvement Association, but wanted it to become the national flag of a new unified black state he dreamt of creating. In 1957, Ghana became the

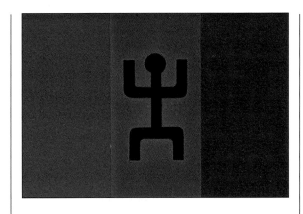

◆ **RIGHT**
(from top to bottom)
Mali Federation (1959–1961);
Biafra (1967–1970);
Cape Verde (1975–1992).

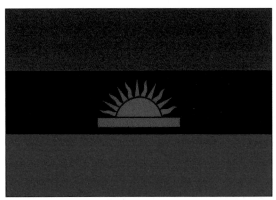

◆ **FAR LEFT**
The national flag of Ethiopia.

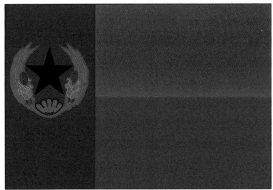

◆ **FAR LEFT**
Marcus Garvey's flag.

THE FLAG FAMILY

The current national flags of the following countries belong to this family:
ANGOLA, BENIN, BURKINA FASO, CAMEROON, CENTRAL AFRICAN REPUBLIC, CONGO, ETHIOPIA, GHANA, GUINEA, GUINEA-BISSAU, KENYA, MALAWI, MALI, MOZAMBIQUE, RWANDA, SÃO TOMÉ AND PRÍNCIPE, SENEGAL, SOUTH AFRICA, TOGO, UGANDA, ZAMBIA, ZIMBABWE.

first independent country in western Africa to adopt a flag in these colours. Its flag, in the Ethiopian colours with a black star, was inspired by the flag of the Black Star Line shipping company established by Garvey in Accra.

The Ethiopian colours and pan-Africanism ideas heralded by President Kwame Nkrumah influenced many other African leaders. Indeed, President Sékou Touré of Guinea's extensive description of the symbolic meaning of the red, yellow and green in 1958 helped to consolidate the conviction that these three colours may also be regarded as pan-African.

Ghana's example was followed by other African countries which adopted flags displaying the same colours: the Mali Federation (1959-1961), Rwanda (1961), Zambia (1964), Guinea Bissau (1973), São Tomé and Príncipe (1975), Cape Verde (1975-1992), Zimbabwe (1980), Mozambique (1983) and South Africa (1994).

The first country in Africa to adopt Garvey's colours as its main flag colours was Kenya in 1963, which was closely followed by Malawi in 1964 and Biafra in 1967. In all three flags the black stands for the people, the red symbolizes the blood shed in the struggle for independence, and the green represents the land with its fertile fields and forests.

The Ethiopian colours in various arrangements were adopted by Benin, Burkina Faso, Cameroon, Congo (Brazzaville) and Togo. Some other countries (Angola, Central African Republic, Namibia, Seychelles, Tanzania and Uganda) display on their flags three of the four pan-African colours.

Most of the flags displaying the pan-African colours are still in use (see *Flags of Africa*).

◆ RIGHT
(left to right)
South Kasai (1960–1962);
Cameroon (1961–1975).

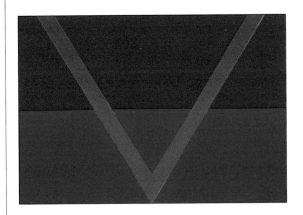

◆ RIGHT
Zanzibar (1963–1964).

◆ RIGHT
(left to right)
Burundi (1962–1966);
Zaire (1971–1997).

THE RED BANNER

A red flag has been used as a flag of defiance since the beginning of the 17th century, but its real role as a revolutionary flag began in 1830 in France, and during the Revolution of 1848 the mob in Paris even wanted it to be the national flag. It was again used by the Paris Commune of 1870, and soon after became the flag associated with the socialist movement. It then appeared during the Russian Revolutions of 1905 and 1917, and in 1918, with the addition of golden initials, was adopted by the Russian Republic. Similar flags were adopted by a few independent or semi-independent Bolshevik republics such as Belarus, Ukraine and the Far Eastern Republic, formed in the early years of the Civil War. In 1924 a red flag featuring a red star, a golden hammer and a sickle became the national flag of the Soviet Union. Soon the red star and the hammer and sickle (the crossed tools of workers and peasants) were regarded as the

symbols of communism, appearing also on the flags of the Soviet republics.

Before World War II only two other communist countries had adopted national flags based on that of the Soviet Union: Mongolia

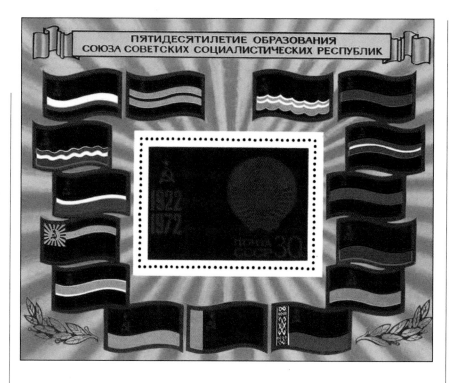

◆ **ABOVE**
Flags of the Soviet Republics as depicted on a Soviet souvenir sheet:
(*clockwise from top centre*) Estonian SSR; Armenian SSR; Kirghiz SSR; Moldavian SSR; Azerbaijan SSR; Kazakh SSS; Belarus SSR; Russian SFS; Ukrainian SSR; Uzbek SSR; Georgian SSR; Lithuanian SSR; Latvian SSR; Tajik SSR; Turkmen SSR.

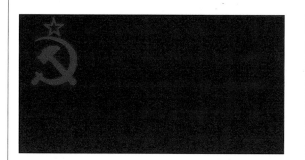

◆ **FAR LEFT**
(*from top to bottom*)
Soviet Russia (1918–1937);
Soviet Union (1924–1955);
Soviet Union (1955–1991).

◆ **LEFT**
(*top to bottom*) Soviet Byelorussia (1920–1924);
Far Eastern Republic (1920–1922);
Mongolia (1924–1940).

◆ **RIGHT TOP**
Yugoslavia (1946–1992).

◆ **RIGHT BOTTOM**
Hungary (1949–1956).

◆ **BELOW**
(from left to right)
Bulgaria (1948–1967);
East Germany, civil ensign
(1959–1990);
Afghanistan (1980–1987).

THE FLAG FAMILY

The current national flags of the following
countries belong to this family:
CHINA, VIETNAM.

(1924–40) and Tannu-Tuva (1926–1930). After
the war the Soviet Union installed communist
regimes in central and eastern Europe but their
national flags were retained, although East
Germany, Yugoslavia, Bulgaria, and Hungary
modified theirs by adding a state emblem.

In Asia, several communist countries adopted
red flags with yellow emblems. The first was the

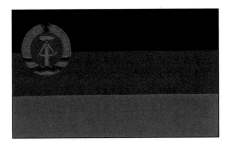
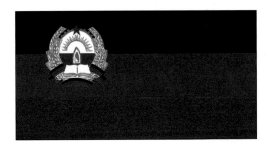

national flag and ensign of Vietnam (1945–
1955), followed by the flags of China (1949),
Cambodia (1976–1989) and Afghanistan
(1978–1980). In 1980 the traditional colours of
the Afghan flag were restored, with the addition
of the state emblem and a red star.

In Africa, only the Congo with its capital in
Brazzaville (1969–1991) copied the Soviet Red
Flag; Angola (1975), Benin (1975–1990),
Zimbabwe (1980), Mozambique (1983) and
Burkina Faso (1984) adopted a red or yellow
communist star. The hammer and sickle became
a hammer and hoe in the flag of the Congo,
and a cog wheel and machete in that of Angola.

◆ **ABOVE AND RIGHT**
(clockwise from above)
Vietnam (1945–1955),
Cambodia (1979–1989),
Cambodia (1976–1979).

◆ **BELOW**
(from left to right)
Afghanistan
(1978–1980);
Congo (Brazzaville)
(1969–1991);
Benin (1975–1990).

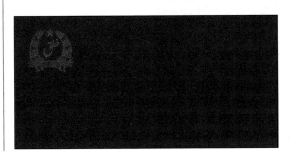
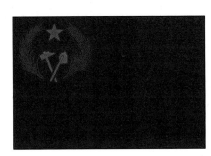

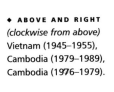

SMALLER FLAG FAMILIES

Two smaller families of regional character came into being in the first quarter of the 19th century during the struggle for the liberation of Latin America from Spanish rule.

The famous Venezuelan revolutionary, Francisco de Miranda (c.1750–1816), personally designed a horizontal tricolour that symbolized golden America (yellow) separated by the Atlantic Ocean (blue) from bloody Spain (red). It was hoisted for the first time on 4 August 1806 on Colombian soil and, despite the defeat of the revolutionary forces, was not forgotten. So, when Venezuela formally declared independence, a flag in these colours with the yellow the same width as both of the two other stripes became the national flag on 5 June 1811. Miranda's forces were defeated again in 1812 but finally became victorious in 1821. The Venezuelans joined with the victorious Creoles of neighbouring Colombia and Ecuador to form the Republic of Gran Colombia under the same flag. When this fell apart in 1830, Venezuela retained the flag, which with minor modifications is still in use. For a few decades Ecuador and Colombia used flags of different designs but they restored Miranda's tricolour in 1860 and 1861 respectively.

The second of the Latin American flag families encompasses the flags of Argentina and the five states of Central America: El Salvador, Honduras, Nicaragua, Guatemala and Costa Rica. In May 1810 blue and white colours were adopted by revolutionaries in Buenos Aires and a blue-white-blue flag was hoisted by General Belgrano in Rosario on 27 February 1812, and formally adopted by the Argentine government on 25 July 1816. The flag became known in Central America when Louis Aury led a maritime expedition there in 1816 and six years later Manuel José Arce, commander-general of the province of San Salvador, decided to adopt the "Argentinian colours of Belgrano" as the national flag of San Salvador. It was consecrated on 20 February 1822 and a year later served as a model for the flag of the newly created United Provinces of Central America. The centre of the national ensign was charged with the motto *Dios, Unión, Libertad* ("God, Union, Liberty") in golden letters, and the emblem of the United Provinces was placed in the centre of the state flag. Both flags were decreed on 21 August 1823. The main feature of the emblem was a triangle with five volcanoes between the waters of two oceans. The triangle

♦ **BELOW**
(from left to right)
Ecuador, civil flag and ensign (since 1860);
Colombia, national flag, and government flag and ensign (since 1861);
Venezuela, civil ensign (since 1930);
Argentina, national flag and civil ensign (1812–1818);
United Provinces of Central America, state flag (1823–1838);
El Salvador, civil ensign (1838–1865 and since 1912).

is a Masonic symbol of equality and its three angles represent the three branches of the government: legislative, executive and judicial. The five volcanoes stand for the five states of the Provinces, situated between the Atlantic and the Pacific. After the dissolution of the United Provinces of Central America in 1838, the five countries used various flags. The first to restore the blue-white-blue flag was Nicaragua in 1854, followed by El Salvador in 1865. Costa Rica added a wide red stripe (1848), Honduras added five blue stars (1866) and, finally, in 1871, Guatemala arranged the colours in vertical stripes.

The last family of flags contains three recent flags based on the United Nations flag. The first to adopt such a flag was Eritrea in 1952, using a design that was a compromise between emblems favoured by the Muslims and Coptic Christians. The blue background was chosen as a complement to the flag of the United Nations and was charged with a green wreath composed of two olive branches, with a third olive branch positioned vertically.

The Trust Territory of the Pacific Islands was administered by the United States under a 1947 trusteeship agreement with the Security Council of the United Nations. In July 1965 the High Commissioner revised the Code of the Trust Territory to allow all vessels registered and licensed there to fly the flag of the Territory. The flag was adopted by the Congress of Micronesia at its first session in July 1965, and became official on 19 August. It was a natural choice to adopt the United Nations blue for the field as it also symbolized the Pacific Ocean. The six white stars represented the six districts of the Trust Territory which were Mariana Islands, Marshall Islands, Ponape, Truck, Yap and Palau. In 1978 voters in the Marshall Islands and Palau rejected the proposed constitution for the Federated States of Micronesia. Since then the flag of Micronesia, introduced on 30 November 1978, has displayed four stars only.

The newest addition to the United Nations family of flags was the flag of Cambodia, used from 1991 to 1993. It was designed at the peace conference in Paris on 23 October 1991 as a transitional flag for the reconstruction of the country after many years of civil war and foreign intervention, so it did not display traditional Cambodian emblems or colours. Its colour was the United Nations blue and the only charge was a map of Cambodia with the country's name.

◆ **BELOW**
(from left to right)
Guatemala (1851–1858); Guatemala, civil ensign (since 1871); Costa Rica, state flag (1906–1934); Eritrea (1952–1959 and on liberated territory until 1993); Pacific Islands (1965–1978) Cambodia (1991–1993).

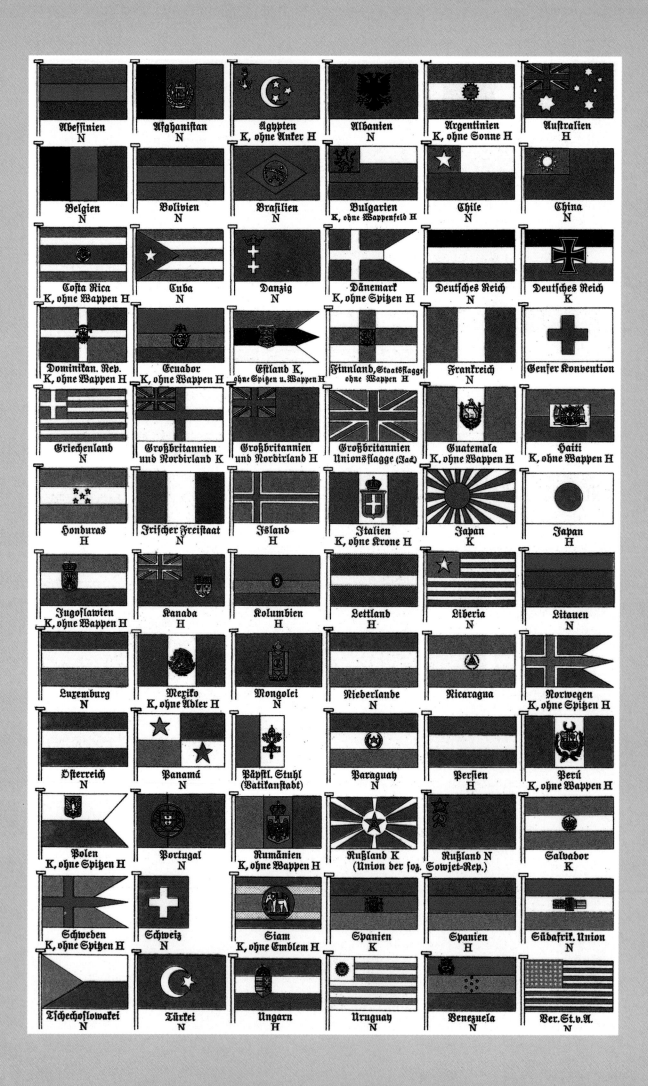

Abessinien N	Afghanistan N	Ägypten K, ohne Anker H	Albanien N	Argentinien K, ohne Sonne H	Australien H
Belgien N	Bolivien N	Brasilien K, ohne Wappenfeld H	Bulgarien	Chile N	China N
Costa Rica K, ohne Wappen H	Cuba N	Danzig N	Dänemark K, ohne Spitzen H	Deutsches Reich N	Deutsches Reich K
Dominikan. Rep. K, ohne Wappen H	Ecuador K, ohne Wappen H	Estland K, ohne Spitzen u. Wappen H	Finnland, Staatsflagge ohne Wappen H	Frankreich N	Genfer Konvention
Griechenland N	Großbritannien und Nordirland K	Großbritannien und Nordirland H	Großbritannien Unionsflagge (Jack)	Guatemala K, ohne Wappen H	Haiti K, ohne Wappen H
Honduras H	Irischer Freistaat N	Island H	Italien K, ohne Krone H	Japan K	Japan H
Jugoslawien K, ohne Wappen H	Kanada H	Kolumbien N	Lettland N	Liberia N	Litauen N
Luxemburg N	Mexiko K, ohne Adler H	Mongolei N	Niederlande N	Nicaragua	Norwegen K, ohne Spitzen H
Österreich N	Panamá N	Päpstl. Stuhl (Vatikanstadt)	Paraguay N	Persien H	Perú K, ohne Wappen H
Polen K, ohne Spitzen H	Portugal N	Rumänien K, ohne Wappen H	Rußland K (Union der soz. Sowjet-Rep.)	Rußland N	Salvador K
Schweden K, ohne Spitzen H	Schweiz N	Siam K, ohne Emblem H	Spanien K	Spanien H	Südafrik. Union
Tschechoslowakei N	Türkei N	Ungarn H	Uruguay N	Venezuela N	Ver.St.v.A. N

The World of Flags

A thoughtful mind, when it sees a nation's flag, sees not the flag only, but the nation itself; and whatever may be its symbols, its insignia, he reads chiefly in the flag the government, the principles, the truths, the history which belongs to the nation that sets it forth.

HENRY WARD BEECHER (1813–1887), *THE AMERICAN FLAG.*

This comprehensive survey of modern flags is designed to be clear and informative. The national flags of countries of the world are grouped under each continent, with a map of the continent at the beginning to give their location. The word "nation", however, describes not only a state recognized by the international community, but also a community of people of mainly common descent, history, culture, language, and religion who inhabit a territory. So included here are also flags of de facto independent states, autonomous or semi-autonomous territories, and flags of subdivisions of federations and confederations.

Many flags have an interesting story to tell. Even simple colours provide an insight into the symbolic "language" of flags. Some flags show the colours of their natural environment, such as blue for the sea or sky, while in others the colour red may represent the blood spilt by the people in defence of their country. The colours may also refer to an important crop or feature of the landscape, or it may symbolize a virtue or characteristic.

To complete the survey of flags of the world, there are descriptions of regional and local municipal flags used extensively in some countries, and the flags of people and causes. In the 19th and 20th centuries yacht and private flags became very popular and today there are numerous flags for business, commerce and personal or organizational use, including the high-profile flags of sporting events such as the Olympic Games.

◆ **OPPOSITE**
In 1935 one page was enough to show all the national flags of countries around the world. Today there are four times the number of independent countries. *Courtesy of F.A. Brockhaus GmbH.*

Flags of Europe

In the pages that follow, the current national flags of the countries of Europe, from Iceland and the Faeroes Islands to Russia and Chechnya, and their territories, states and provinces are illustrated and described.

For ease of reference, the countries of Europe have been grouped into geographical areas. We begin with the countries of northern Europe before moving on through central and western Europe and down to south-west Europe, and south and south-east Europe. Finally we look at the flags of the Eastern European countries. There are some geographical anomalies, for example, all Russia's flags are illustrated together in this section. The flags of Turkey, Cyprus and Northern Cyprus are all illustrated here.

For each entry, the country or territory's name is given in its most easily recognized form and then in all its official languages. This is followed by a description of its political status and geographic position. The basic data for each flag contains the status of the flag, date of adoption, proportions, and the symbolic meaning.

NORTHERN EUROPE

ICELAND

Republic of Iceland,
Icelandic **Lýdveldid Ísland**.
Republic comprising an island in the N Atlantic.

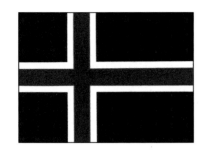

CIVIL FLAG AND ENSIGN

In use since 1913, officially approved 19 June 1915 for use on land and territorial waters, after 1 December 1918 also at sea. Proportions 18:25. State flag and ensign are swallow-tailed.

The design of the flag is based on that of Norway, with the colours reversed. Blue and white are the traditional national colours of Iceland and red symbolizes links with Norway, where most of their ancestors originated. The Scandinavian cross shows that Iceland belongs to the family of Scandinavian countries (see *Flag Families*).

Other symbolic meanings refer to the natural features of Iceland. Blue is the colour of the Atlantic Ocean, white represents the snow and ice covering the island for most of the year, and red the volcanoes on the island.

FAEROES ISLANDS

Danish **Færøerne**.
Island group in N Atlantic, outlying part of Denmark with full self-government.

NATIONAL FLAG AND CIVIL ENSIGN

Introduced in 1919, recognized by the local parliament in 1931 and officially approved by the King of Denmark 25 July 1948. The shade of blue was changed to lighter blue 5 June 1959. Proportions 8:11.

The flag was designed by two Faeroese students in Copenhagen, using Norwegian and Icelandic colours with the Scandinavian cross. Red and blue are also traditional Faeroese colours and the white represents the foam of the sea and the clear, bright sky of the Faeroes Islands.

Until 1940 the Faeroese flag was used only on land but in April 1940, after the Germans occupied Denmark, Faeroese ships began to use it at sea. The first to recognize the Faeroese flag were the British authorities; it was officially announced in a BBC broadcast on 25 April 1940 by Winston Churchill, at that time First Lord of the Admiralty, and ever since 25 April has been celebrated as Faeroese Flag Day.

NORWAY

Kingdom of Norway,
Norwegian **Kongeriket Norge**.
Constitutional monarchy in NW Europe.

CIVIL FLAG AND ENSIGN

Adopted 17 July 1821 as a civil ensign only in N Atlantic, since 1838 usage unrestricted. Proportions 8:11. Since 1899 state and war flag and ensign have been triple swallow-tailed.

From 1748 to 1814 Norwegian ships flew the Danish *Dannebrog*. In 1814, when Norway was united with Sweden, the Norwegians obtained the right to carry the *Dannebrog* with the canton charged with the Norwegian golden lion, crowned and holding an axe. Nevertheless, the struggle for a purely Norwegian flag continued and in 1821 the parliament adopted a new design, the *Dannebrog* with a dark blue cross positioned within the white one. The combination of red, white and blue followed the French revolutionary *Tricolore* as well as the flags of the United States and the United Kingdom, and was at that time regarded as a symbol of freedom. The cross was a common symbol of the national flags of Denmark and Sweden.

DENMARK

Kingdom of Denmark,
Danish **Kongeriget Danmark**.
Constitutional monarchy in NW Europe.

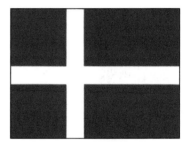

CIVIL FLAG AND ENSIGN

In use since the 13th century, officially confirmed in 1625. Proportions 28:37. State flag and war ensign are swallow-tailed.

The Danish flag, called the *Dannebrog,* is probably the oldest national flag in the world. According to legend, its history begins when the Danish crusaders, led by King Valdemar II the Victorious, were conducting a crusade against the pagan Estonians. The struggle had been going on for some time when the Estonians called all their warriors to arms on St Viti Day, 15 June 1219. The Danes were thrown into confusion by the fierce and unexpected attack, but suddenly a sign from heaven, a great blood red flag with a white cross floated down from the sky. The retreating Danish soldiers caught the flag, counter-attacked with the cry of "Forward to victory under the sign of the Cross", and eventually won the battle.

There is no definite proof that the *Dannebrog* was used at such an early date; the first picture of it appeared in *Wapenboek Gelre* in the second half of the 14th century. However, the *Dannebrog* may originally (in the 12th century) have been a crusade banner or even an ensign. The most probable theory is that the *Dannebrog* evolved in the same way as the flags for the border territories of the Holy Roman Empire (Hanseatic cities or cities in northern Italy), most of which displayed a white cross on red or red on white.

SWEDEN

Kingdom of Sweden,
Swedish **Konungariket Sverige**.
Constitutional monarchy in NW Europe.

CIVIL FLAG AND ENSIGN

Introduced in the 16th century, usage regulated on 6 November 1663, the most recent regulations of colours and proportions laid down in the Flag Act of 1982. Proportions 5:8.

In the royal warrant of 1569, King John III decreed that the golden cross should always be borne on Swedish battle banners. The oldest recorded pictures of the blue flag with a yellow cross date from the end of the 16th century, while reliable evidence that it was also the ensign of Swedish vessels dates from the 1620s. According to the oldest existing flag warrant from 1663, a triple-tailed flag was to be used by all except merchant ships, whose ensign was rectangular. Nowadays, use of the triple-tailed flag is reserved for the royal family and armed forces. The design of the flag was influenced by the Danish *Dannebrog*; its colours were from the coat of arms.

The main shield of the Great Arms of Sweden is divided quarterly and charged with the three crowns of Sweden (in the first and fourth quarters) and the lion of the Folkung dynasty (in the second and third quarters). This arrangement, with a golden cross separating four blue fields, was introduced by King Karl VIII Knuttson in 1448, and set the pattern for the flag.

There are very close ties between Sweden and Denmark, so it cannot be a concidence that the Swedes added the cross to the arms, as the Danes did in the 14th century, and adopted a flag of the same pattern as the Danish *Dannebrog*.

ÅLAND ISLANDS

Finnish **Ahvenanmaa**, Swedish **Åland**.
Autonomous province of Finland comprising an archipelago in the Baltic Sea.

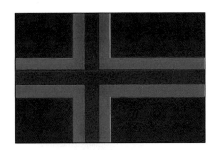

NATIONAL FLAG

In use since 1921, officially adopted 7 April 1954 for use on land only. Proportions 17:26.

The adoption of the Swedish flag charged with an additional red cross reflects the fact that the population of the islands is predominantly of Swedish origin. The colours are those of the arms of the Åland Islands (golden stag in blue field) and the arms of Finland (golden lion in red field).

FINLAND

Republic of Finland,
Finnish **Suomen Tasavalta,**
Swedish **Republiken Finland**.
Republic in N Europe.

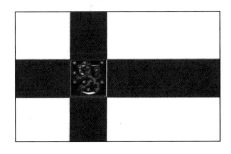

STATE FLAG AND ENSIGN

Adopted 29 May 1918, the most recent regulations came into force 1 June 1978. Proportions 11:18. Civil flag and ensign are without the arms, war ensign is triple swallow-tailed with the arms.

Finland was a part of Sweden from the 12th century until 1809 and, after gaining independence, adopted a national flag patterned on the Swedish one. Similar flags were introduced by Finnish yacht clubs more than half a century earlier, when Finland was under Russian rule. The first yacht club, the *Nyländska Jaktkluben*, was established in 1861 in Helsinki and adopted a white flag with a blue cross, with the arms of the county of Nyland in the canton. The other yacht clubs followed suit, adopting the same design with different arms in the canton. The first to propose the blue and white as national colours of Finland was a poet called Zachris Topelius in 1862. In 1863 the newspaper *Helsinfors Dagblat* suggested that the national flags should be white with a blue cross.

The blue represents the thousands of lakes in Finland and its clear sky; the white stands for the snow that covers the country in the long winters.

ESTONIA

Republic of Estonia, Estonian **Eesti Vabariik**.
Republic in N Europe.

NATIONAL FLAG, CIVIL AND STATE ENSIGN

Approved 4 July 1920, re-adopted 8 May 1990.
Proportions 7:11.

The blue-black-white horizontal tricolour was adopted on 29 September 1881 by the Vironia, the Estonian students' association, and was displayed in great numbers at national song festivals in both 1894 and 1896. During the revolutions in 1905 and 1917 it was used by the populace as a national flag, and when independence was proclaimed on 24 February 1918 it became the Estonian civil flag.

In Estonian folk songs the colours of the flag symbolize the sky (blue), the soil (black) and the aspiration to freedom and hope for the future (white). Another interpretation is blue for mutual confidence and fidelity; black for the supposed ancestors of the Estonians, the black-cloaked people mentioned in Herodotus' *Histories*; and white for the snow that covers the country for half the year.

LATVIA

Republic of Latvia.
Latvian **Latvijas Republika**.
Republic in N Europe.

NATIONAL FLAG, CIVIL AND STATE ENSIGN

Approved 15 June 1921, re-adopted
15 February 1990. Proportions 1:2.

In 1279, long before it became the national flag of Latvia, the red-white-red banner was used by the home guard of Cesis. It was revived in 1870 by a group of Latvian university students in Estonia and used in 1873 at a national song festival in Riga. During World War I these colours became popular and were used by Latvian units of the Russian army, by boy scouts and by civil organizations. In 1917 prominent Latvian artists agreed that the shade of red should be crimson and that the width of the white stripe should be one-fifth of the flag's width. Use of the flag was forbidden under the Soviet occupation, which started on 17 June 1940. On 29 September 1988 its use as a civil flag was legalized and in 1990 it again became the national flag.

LITHUANIA

Republic of Lithuania,
Lithuanian **Lietuvos Respublika**.
Republic in N Europe.

NATIONAL FLAG, CIVIL AND STATE ENSIGN

Hoisted 11 November 1918, re-adopted
20 March 1989. Proportions 1:2.

Since the end of the 14th century the historic flag of Lithuania was red with a white knight and, in 1918, this became the state flag. The Lithuanian Council appointed a special commission to design a national flag and on 19 April 1918 it approved a horizontal tricolour using the colours most popular in traditional Lithuanian cloth.

The yellow is the colour of the sun, symbolizing light, prosperity, nobility, honesty and spiritual greatness. The green is the colour of vegetation, symbolizing the beauty of nature, life, hope, freedom and joy. The red is the colour of the land and of blood, symbolizing love, daring, courage and blood shed for the Fatherland.

THE *VYTIS*

The Lithuanian arms were adopted in the late 14th century. They are called *vytis* in Lithuanian which means "dispatch rider" or "knight". However, since the verb *vyti* means "to pursue, to follow hastily in order to overtake", the name of the arms in English can be translated as "the pursuit".

The Lithuanian arms or "pursuit" depict an armoured medieval knight riding hard on a galloping horse with a sword above his head.

Until the end of the 18th century "the pursuit" appeared on a red field on all Lithuania's battle and state banners. Then,

when Lithuania regained its independence in 1918, the *vytis* or "pursuit" became the main figure on the obverse of both the state and the presidential flag.

The arms were restored again in 1991 and appeared on the presidential standard and military colours.

CENTRAL EUROPE

POLAND

Republic of Poland,

Polish **Rzeczpospolita Polska**.

Republic in central Europe.

In use since 1916, approved 1 August 1919.
Proportions 5:8. Civil flag is without arms.

This is the only state flag in the world that is not used by all of the government authorities. According to the law, it may be used only by Polish representations abroad, civil airports and airfields, harbour authorities and civil aircraft abroad.

The Polish arms are over 700 years old and show a white eagle on a red shield. Officially approved in 1831 as the colours of the national cockade, they became popular during World War I.

SLOVAKIA

Slovak Republic,

Slovak **Slovenská Republika**.

Republic in Central Europe.

NATIONAL FLAG

Adopted 1 September 1992. Proportions 2:3.

The first Slovak flag, a horizontal tricolour of white-blue-red, appeared in 1848. The colours are those of the arms (white patriarchal cross, blue triple mountain,

red shield). The same flag was adopted on 23 June 1939 as the national flag of independent Slovakia and remained in use until 1945. It again became official on 1 March 1990 and was used in Slovakia, which at that time was part of Czechoslovakia. The present flag was described in the constitution of 1 September 1992, four months before Slovakia became an independent republic.

CZECH REPUBLIC

Czech **Česká Republika**.

Republic in central Europe.

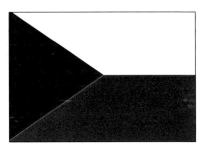

NATIONAL FLAG

Adopted 20 March 1920 as the flag of
Czechoslovakia, proclaimed the flag of the Czech
Republic 17 December 1992. Proportions 2:3.

White and red are the traditional colours of Bohemia; they stem from the arms (which feature a white lion on a red field), which date back to 1192. The first Czech white and red bicolour flag appeared during World War I and in 1918 became the first national flag of Czechoslovakia. As it displayed only the colours of Bohemia, the blue from the arms of Moravia and Slovakia was added in 1920.

HUNGARY

Republic of Hungary, Hungarian **Magyar**
Köztársaság. Republic in Central Europe.

NATIONAL AND STATE FLAG

Adopted in 1848, re-introduced 1 October 1957.
Proportions 2:3.

The first recorded instance of the Hungarian national colours (red, white, green) dates from a drum cover of the mid-16th century. From the beginning of the 17th century they were used in the seal cord, and later were an important part of the decorations used at coronations. In the 1830s patriotic elements started to use flags with these colours, and during the revolution of 1848 the Hungarian tricolour was proclaimed as the national flag. The colours are those of the Hungarian arms (red shield, white stripes and patriarchal cross, green triple mountain).

AUSTRIA

Republic of Austria,
German **Republik Österreich**.

Federal republic in central Europe.

STATE FLAG

Adopted 1 May 1945. Civil flag and ensign
are without arms.

From at least 1230 the Austrian arms consisted of a red shield with a wide horizontal white bar. The red-white-red stripes first appeared on the state and war ensign, introduced on 1 January 1787. The red-white-red horizontal bicolour with no charge was adopted in 1918 as the national flag and in 1921 as the civil ensign. After the German occupation of 1938–1945, the flag was re-introduced in 1945.

AUSTRIAN STATES

Austria is divided into nine states (Bundesländer) which have their own flags.

BURGENLAND

STATE FLAG

Adopted 25 June 1971. Proportions 2:3.

The arms in the centre of the horizontal bicolour of livery colours were introduced in 1922. They combine the arms of two families, the counts of Güssing-Bernstein and the counts of Mattersdorf-Forchtenstein, who had extensive estates in Burgenland before they died out in the 15th century.

CARINTHIA

STATE FLAG

Officially adopted 18 June 1946. Proportions 2:3.

This flag has been in use since the 19th century. The colours stem from the arms, which date back to the 13th century.

They were officially adopted in 1930 as the arms of the province.

LOWER AUSTRIA

STATE FLAG

*Officially adopted 9 August 1954.
Proportions 2:3.*

The flag was introduced in the 19th century. The colours are those of the arms (five golden eagles on a blue field), adopted in 1359.

SALZBURG

STATE FLAG

*Officially adopted 16 February 1921.
Proportions 2:3.*

The red-white bicolour has been in use since the 19th century. The colours derive from the second field of the provincial arms and bear the colours of Austria.

STYRIA

STATE FLAG

Officially adopted in 1960. Proportions 2:3.

In the 19th century the flag of Styria was a green-white bicolour; the colours then were reversed in 1960. They are the colours of the arms, which date back to the 13th century and display a silver panther on a green field.

TYROL

STATE FLAG

*Officially adopted 10 March 1949.
Proportions 2:3.*

A red eagle on a silver (white) field has been the arms of Tyrol since the 13th century. A crown was added in 1416, and a green wreath in 1567. The present form of the arms was introduced in 1946.

UPPER AUSTRIA

STATE FLAG

*Officially adopted 25 April 1949.
Proportions 2:3.*

The arms date back to the 14th century and were confirmed in 1930. The colours of the flag stem from the second field of the arms (white and red pallets).

VIENNA

STATE FLAG

Approved in 1946. Proportions 2:3.

The red-white flag has been in use since the first half of the 19th century. The colours are those of the arms (white cross on red field).

VORARLBERG

STATE FLAG

Approved in 1946. Proportions 2:3.

Introduced in the 19th century, the flag's colours are those of the provincial arms, based on the arms of the dukes of Montford, which date back to the end of the 12th century (red gonfanon on silver field).

LIECHTENSTEIN

Principality of Liechtenstein,
German **Fürstentum Liechtenstein.**
Constitutional monarchy in W Central Europe.

NATIONAL FLAG

Adopted 24 June 1937, the crown modified 18 September 1982. Proportions 3:5.

The national colours of Liechtenstein probably derive from the blue and red livery used in the 18th century by the servants of Prince Joseph Wenzel of Liechtenstein. The horizontal bicolour was confirmed as the national flag in the constitution signed on 5 October 1921. In 1937 the prince's crown was introduced to distinguish it from the civil flag of Haiti.

SWITZERLAND

Swiss Confederation,
German **Schweizerische Eidgenossenschaft,**
French **Confédération Suisse,**
Italian **Confederazione Svizzera,**
Romansch **Confederaziun Svizra.**
Federal republic in W Central Europe.

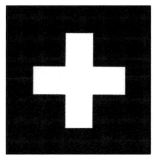

NATIONAL FLAG

Officially adopted 12 December 1889.
Proportions 1:1. Proportions of civil ensign 2:3.

In 1339 every soldier and officer of the troops leaving for the battle of Laupen was marked with the sign of the Holy Cross. The white cross on a red field has been a common Swiss emblem ever since. From the end of the 15th century a red banner charged with a white cross has been the accepted flag of the Confederation. The current flag was introduced in 1848 as the military colours, and its exact proportions were established in a military regulation of 1852. It became the national flag in 1889.

SWISS CANTONS

The official flags of all Swiss cantons are square armorial banners (*Kantonsfahnen*). Other types of Swiss flags are: (i) a long, vertical, swallow-tailed banner with a square armorial flag in the hoist and vertical stripes in livery colours (*Wappenflagge*); (ii) a long, vertical, rectangular banner of the same design as above, hanging from a traverse projecting at a right angle from a mast (*Knatterfahne*); (iii) a long, vertical, swallow-tailed banner in livery colours (*zweizipflige Farbenfahne*); (iv) a rectangular flag of proportions 2:3 in livery colours (*querrechteckige Farbenfahne*).

AARGAU

CANTONAL FLAG

Adopted in 1803, present form since 1930.

The white waves symbolize the River Aare, and the stars stand for the districts of Baden, Freien Ämter and Fricktal. The livery colours are black and blue.

APPENZELL INNER-RHODES

CANTONAL FLAG

In use since the beginning of the 15th century.

The bear was taken from the arms of the Abbey of Sankt Gallen. The livery colours are white and black.

APPENZELL OUTER-RHODES

CANTONAL FLAG

Adopted in 1597.

When the canton separated from Appenzell, the bear was retained and the letters "VR" (the initial letters for Ussroden – Outer-Rhodes) were added. The livery colours are white and black.

BASEL-LAND

CANTONAL FLAG

Introduced in 1834, the present form established 1 April 1947.

The arms are based on the civic arms of Liestal. The livery colours are white and red.

BASEL-STADT

CANTONAL FLAG

In use since at least the 15th century.

The oldest known representation of the bishop's crozier is on a coin minted in the 11th century; the current shape of the crozier

has been in use since the 13th century. The livery colours are white and black.

BERN

CANTONAL FLAG

In use since at least the 14th century.

These are canting arms, i.e. they contain an allusion to the name of the canton (the German word for "bear" is *Bär*). The oldest representation of the bear is on a coin minted in 1224. The livery colours are red and black.

FRIBOURG

CANTONAL FLAG

In use since the beginning of the 15th century.

The arms, based on the banner, were adopted in 1477. The livery colours are black and white.

GENEVA

CANTONAL FLAG

In use since the 15th century.

The black eagle is the emblem of the Holy Roman Empire and the key is a symbol of St Peter. The oldest representations of the arms are in two books published in 1451. The livery colours are yellow and red.

GLARUS

CANTONAL FLAG

In use since the 14th century. The present form adopted 25 June 1959.

The patron saint of the canton is St Fridolin, an Irish missionary who settled there in 500. The livery colours are black, white and red. The black and white together are the same width as a red stripe.

GRAUBÜNDEN

CANTONAL FLAG

Adopted 8 November 1932.

The arms display the symbols of the three parts of the canton, which united in the 15th century: *Grauer Bund* (black and white), *Zehgerichtenbund* (cross) and *Gotteshausbund* (ibex). The livery colours are black, white and blue.

JURA

CANTONAL FLAG

Adopted in 1951, approved in 1976, official since 1978.

The crozier recalls that Jura was part of Basel-Land. The stripes represent seven districts interested in being part of a new canton. In the end only three formed Jura. The livery colours are white and red.

LUCERNE

CANTONAL FLAG

In use since the 13th century.

The canton's colours are older than the arms (adopted in 1386). In the arms the colours are arranged vertically: blue, white. The livery colours are white and blue.

NEUCHÂTEL

CANTONAL FLAG

Adopted 11 April 1848.

The green represents liberty, the white and red are traditional Swiss colours. The livery colours are green, white and red.

NIDWALDEN

CANTONAL FLAG

In use since the beginning of the 15th century.

The key is the emblem of St Peter. The livery colours are red and white.

OBWALDEN

CANTONAL FLAG

Adopted 12 August 1816.

Since the 13th century the canton's arms and banner have been a red-white bicolour. The key of St Peter appeared for the first time on the seal in the 13th century. The livery colours are red and white.

SAINT GALL

CANTONAL FLAG

Adopted 4 April 1803.

The fasces is a symbol of sovereignty and unity; the eight rods (five are visible) represent the eight districts of the canton. The livery colours are green and white.

SCHAFFHAUSEN

CANTONAL FLAG

In use since the 14th century.

The ram (*Schafsbock* in German) alludes to the name of both the city and the canton. Since the 15th century the canton's colours have been green and black.

SCHWYZ

CANTONAL FLAG

In use since the 15th century.

Since the end of the 13th century the banner has been plain red. The oldest recorded picture of a banner with a white cross in the canton dates from 1470. The livery colour is red. The white cross appears on the *zweizipflige Farbenfahne*.

SOLOTHURN

CANTONAL FLAG

In use since the 14th century.

The livery colours are red and white.

THURGAU

CANTONAL FLAG

Adopted 13 April 1803.

The lions are from the arms of the counts of Kyburg. Green represents freedom. The livery colours are green and white.

TICINO

CANTONAL FLAG

Adopted 23 May 1803.

The colours (vertical in the arms, horizontal on the banner) were established in 1930. The livery colours are red and blue.

URI

CANTONAL FLAG

In use since the 14th century.

From the 13th to the 15th century the aurochs's head was without the nose-ring. The emblem (*Uroch* in Old German) alludes to the name of the canton. The livery colours are yellow and black.

VALAIS

CANTONAL FLAG

In use since the 16th century, present form adopted 12 May 1815.

The stars represent the 13 districts of the canton. The livery colours are white and red.

VAUD

CANTONAL FLAG

Decreed 16 April 1803.

The motto is "Freedom and Fatherland" and the green is a symbol of freedom. The livery colours are white and green.

ZUG

CANTONAL FLAG

In use since the mid-14th century.

The arms and banner were originally identical to those of Austria (red field with white band) and were changed when Zug joined the Confederation in 1352. The livery colours are white, blue and white.

ZÜRICH

CANTONAL FLAG

In use since the 13th century.

The oldest known representation of the arms dates from 1389. The livery colours are blue and white.

GERMANY

Federal Republic of Germany, German **Bundesrepublik Deutschland**.

Federal republic in Central Europe.

STATE FLAG

Introduced 23 March 1848, re-introduced in 1919 and again 23 May 1949. Civil flag and ensign are without arms.

The German national colours are those of the arms, which are the same as the arms of the Holy Roman Empire: black for the eagle, red for its beak and claws, and yellow for the golden shield. They featured in the uniform worn by the Lützow Free Corps (black greatcoats, red facings and hems, golden buttons) during the war of liberation in 1813–15, when the trend towards the unification of Germany was growing. The horizontal tricolour of black-red-gold became the national flag of the German Federation in 1848 and was replaced in 1867 with a tricolour of black-white-red, which was in use until 1919 and again in 1933–5.

GERMAN STATES

From 1949 to 1990 West Germany comprised 11 states (Bundesländer). Since reunification with East Germany there are now 16 states.

BADEN-WÜRTTEMBERG

STATE FLAG

Adopted 29 September 1954. Proportions 3:5.

Black and yellow have been the colours of the arms of the Duchy of Swabia since the end of the 12th century. They display three black lions on a golden shield.

BAVARIA

STATE AND CIVIL FLAG

Adopted 2 December 1946. Proportions 3:5.

The Bavarian flag is a horizontal bicolour in the livery colours. The arms of Bavaria, which date back to the beginning of the 13th century, have white and blue lozenges.

BERLIN

STATE FLAG

Adopted 13 May 1954. Proportions 3:5.

The bear first appeared on the second city seal in 1280. A red-white-red flag with a black bear was introduced in 1913, and the current design of the bear was established in 1954.

CIVIL FLAG

BRANDENBURG

STATE AND CIVIL FLAG

Adopted 30 January 1991. Proportions 3:5.

The arms date back to 1330. The flag is in the livery colours.

BREMEN

STATE AND CIVIL FLAG

In use without arms since 1691, approved 21 November 1947. Proportions 2:3.

The originally plain red flag was charged in the second half of the 14th century with a white key, the symbol of St Peter, the patron saint of the city. The current forms of the great and small arms, and two state flags, were enacted in 1891.

HAMBURG

STATE FLAG

Civil flag adopted 14 May 1751, state flag introduced 8 October 1897, confirmed 6 June 1952. Proportions 2:3.

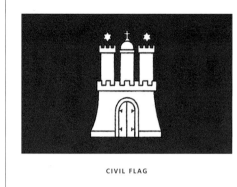

CIVIL FLAG

The castle represents Hammaburg Castle, built by Emperor Charles the Great in AD 808, and the arms date back to 1254. The three towers stand for the Trinity, the cross is a symbol of Christ, and the stars symbolize God the Father and the Holy Spirit. Red flags with the castle were already in use in the first half of the 14th century.

HESSE

STATE AND CIVIL FLAG

Both flags adopted 22 November 1949. Proportions 3:5.

The colours of the flag are taken from the lion in the arms. These stem from the arms of the landgraves (ruling counts) of Thuringia, who from 1130 to 1247 were also landgraves of Hesse.

LOWER SAXONY

CIVIL FLAG

Adopted 13 April 1951. State flag is swallow-tailed. Proportions 2:3.

The flag is in the German national colours and is charged with the arms of the state. The horse (*Niedersachsenross*) has been the symbol of Lower Saxony since the 14th century.

MECKLENBURG-WEST POMERANIA

CIVIL FLAG

Adopted 29 January 1991. Proportions ±3:5.

The flag is a combination of the colours of Pomerania (blue, white), Hansa (white, red) and former flags of Mecklenburg – the national flag (blue, yellow, red) and the civil ensign (blue, white, red).

NORTH RHINE-WESTPHALIA

STATE FLAG

Adopted 10 March 1953. Civil flag is without arms. Proportions 3:5.

The colours of the flag are taken from the arms, which combine the symbols of three parts of the state which are Rhineland (river), Westphalia (horse) and Lippe (rose).

RHINELAND-PALATINATE

STATE AND CIVIL FLAG

Adopted 10 May 1948. Proportions 2:3.

The flag is in the colours of Germany and the state arms. The arms combine the arms of Trier (cross), Koblenz (wheel) and Palatinate (lion), all dating back to the 13th century.

SAARLAND

STATE AND CIVIL FLAG

Adopted 9 July 1956, introduced 1 January 1957. Proportions ±3:5.

This is the national flag of Germany with the state arms. The arms are quarterly: (i) countship of Saarbücken, (ii) Trier, (iii) Lorraine, (iv) Palatinate.

SAXONY

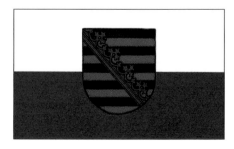

STATE FLAG

Adopted 16 June 1815. Civil flag is without arms. Proportions 3:5.

The civil flag, used 1815–1935 and 1947–1952, was re-adopted in 1991. The arms are those of the duchy of Saxony and date back to the 13th century.

SAXONY-ANHALT

STATE FLAG

Civil flag (without arms) adopted 29 January 1991. State flag described in the constitution of 1992. Proportions 3:5.

The black and yellow bicolour was the flag of the Prussian province of Saxony from 1884–1935 and 1945–1952. The order of the colours has been reversed to differentiate the flag from that of Baden-Württemberg. The arms used are a combination of the arms of Saxony (black and yellow bands, green crown of rue), Anhalt (black bear on red wall) and Prussia (black eagle).

STATE FLAG

Adopted 18 January 1957. Civil flag is without the arms. Proportions 3:5.

The blue-white-red horizontal tricolour became the civil flag for use on land in 1842. This flag was used until 1854, and again in 1864–1935. The colours were taken from the arms, which depict the blue lion of Schleswig and the white nettle leaf of Holstein.

THURINGIA

STATE FLAG

Adopted 10 January 1991. Civil flag is without the arms. Proportions 1:2.

The flag shows the colours of the Thuringian white and red lion, dating from the 12th century. The white stars were added to the arms to commemorate the seven small states that formed the province of Thuringia in 1920.

WESTERN EUROPE

LUXEMBOURG

Grand Duchy of Luxembourg,
French **Grand-Duché de Luxembourg**,
Letzeburgesch **Groussherzogtum Lëtzebuerg**,
German **Grossherzogtum Luxemburg**.
Constitutional monarchy in W Europe.

NATIONAL FLAG

Introduced in the present form 12 June 1845, adopted 16 August 1972. Proportions 3:5.

It is only coincidence that this flag is so similar to that of the Netherlands. The colours of the national flag of Luxembourg are those of the arms (red lion, white and blue stripes). Note the lighter shade of blue. An armorial banner has been in use since 1853 as the flag of the Army, and since 1972 as the flag of inland shipping and civil aviation.

FRANCE

Republic of France,
French **République Française**.
Republic in W Europe.

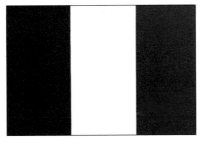

NATIONAL FLAG

*Introduced 20 May 1794, uninterrupted use since 5 March 1848.
Proportions 2:3. Civil and war ensign have stripes of different width.*

The colours of the French national flag, known as the *Tricolore*, were introduced during the French Revolution when the King added the royal white cockade of the House of Bourbon to the revolutionary cockade of blue and red (the livery colours of Paris).

BELGIUM

Kingdom of Belgium, Flemish **Koninkrijk
België**, Walloon **Royaume de Belgique**.
Federal constitutional monarchy in W Europe.

NATIONAL FLAG

*Introduced August 1830, officially adopted
23 January 1831. Proportions 13:15, proportions
of civil ensign 2:3.*

The flag, inspired by the French *Tricolore*,
displays the colours of the arms of the
duchy of Brabant, which date back to the
12th century. The war of independence
started in Brabant and found its greatest
support there, so its arms became the arms
of Belgium (golden lion with red claws and
tongue on black field).

BELGIAN REGIONS

In 1993 Belgium became a federal state
comprising three nearly autonomous
regions: Flanders (Flemish-speaking),
Wallonia (French-speaking), and Brussels
(bilingual). Each has its own parliament,
regional council and government.

BRUSSELS

REGIONAL FLAG

Adopted on 22 June 1991. Proportions ±2:3.

The blue is that of the flag of the European
Union. The iris is a well-known flower of
the fields along the river Senne which flows
through Brussels.

FLANDERS

REGIONAL FLAG

Introduced 11 July 1985. Proportions 2:3.

This is an armorial flag, the basic design of
which dates from the 12th century.

WALLONIA

REGIONAL FLAG

Introduced in 1913. Proportions 2:3.

The cock is a traditional Gallic emblem and
recalls Wallonia's linguistic and cultural ties
with France.

THE NETHERLANDS

Kingdom of the Netherlands,
Dutch **Koninkrijk der Nederlanden**.
Semi-federal constitutional monarchy
in W Europe.

NATIONAL FLAG AND ENSIGN

*Officially introduced 14 February 1796,
confirmed 19 February 1937. Proportions 2:3.*

The first flag of the Netherlands,
introduced in 1574 during the struggle for
independence, was a horizontal tricolour of
orange-white-blue. Orange was the colour
of William I, Prince of Orange, who led the
rebellion against Spanish rule and
eventually in 1581 established an
independent country. During the 17th
century red gradually replaced the orange,
and in 1796 the red-white-blue was
officially confirmed.

Nevertheless, orange is still the Dutch
national colour and when the flag is
displayed during state holidays or by
diplomatic missions abroad it is
accompanied by a long orange streamer
fastened just above the flag.

THE NETHERLANDS PROVINCES

While all Dutch port cities had their own
flags already in the 17th century, the
provincial flags came into being during the
last 50 years. Nevertheless, they display
livery colours or arms that are several
centuries old.

DRENTHE

PROVINCIAL FLAG

Adopted 19 February 1947. Proportions 9:13.

White and red are the colours of the
bishopric of Utrecht, to which the province
once belonged. The black castle is the castle
of Coevorden, where in 1227 the rebellion
against the bishopric started. The stars
represent the former six *fehmic* courts.

FLEVOLAND

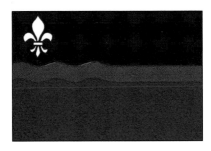

PROVINCIAL FLAG

Adopted 9 January 1986. Proportions 2:3.

The flag recalls how the new province was reclaimed from the waters of the IJsselmeer. The dark yellow central stripe, wavy then straight, symbolizes the transformation of the sea into land. Its colour is that of rape, planted in the new polders to stabilize the land; the blue represents water, the green the land. The fleur-de-lis honours C. Lely, who designed the original polders.

FRIESLAND

PROVINCIAL FLAG

Adopted 9 July 1957. Proportions 9:13.

The design is based on the arms from the 15th century. The stripes and waterlily leaves represent the districts of Friesland.

GELDERLAND

PROVINCIAL FLAG

Adopted 13 April 1953. Proportions 9:13.

The colours are those of the provincial arms, combining the arms of the old dukedoms of Gelre (golden lion in blue field) and Gulik (black lion in golden field).

GRONINGEN

PROVINCIAL FLAG

Adopted 17 February 1950. Proportions 2:3.

Green and white are Groningen's colours; red, white and blue are Ommerland's.

LIMBURG

PROVINCIAL FLAG

Adopted 28 July 1953. Proportions 1:2.

The blue stripe stands for the river Meuse and the lion comes from the arms of the duchy of Limburg. Yellow and red are the colours of the arms of Valkenburg, Gulik, Horn and Gelre.

NORTH BRABANT

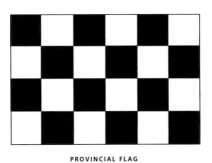

PROVINCIAL FLAG

Adopted 21 January 1959. Proportions 2:3.

This is the flag of the duchy of Brabant and dates back to the 17th century.

NORTH HOLLAND

PROVINCIAL FLAG

Adopted 22 October 1958. Proportions 2:3.

The colours stem from the arms of Holland (red lion in golden field) and West Friesland (golden lions in blue field).

OVERIJSSEL

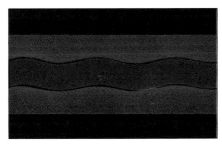

PROVINCIAL FLAG

Adopted 21 July 1948. Proportions 10:17.

The wavy blue stripe symbolizes the river IJssel. The colours are those of the arms (red lion in golden field charged with a blue fesse wavy). They also recall the historic association of the province with Holland.

SOUTH HOLLAND

PROVINCIAL FLAG

Adopted 1 January 1986. Proportions 2:3.

This is the armorial banner of the former countship of Holland.

UTRECHT

PROVINCIAL FLAG

Adopted 15 January 1952. Proportions 9:13.

White and red are the colours of the city of Utrecht. The white cross in a red field is the arms of the bishopric of Utrecht and dates back to the 16th century.

ZEELAND

PROVINCIAL FLAG

Adopted 14 January 1949. Proportions 2:3.

The wavy blue and white stripes symbolize the stripes of sea and land in the coastal area. The arms in the centre date back to the 16th century.

IRELAND

Republic of Ireland,
Irish **Poblacht Na h'Éireann.**
Republic comprising most of the territory of the island of Ireland, NW Europe.

NATIONAL FLAG AND ENSIGN

In use since 1916, recognized in 1922, formally confirmed 29 December 1937. Proportions 1:2.

The flag is based on the French *Tricolore* and displays colours that were used in reverse order during the revolutionary year of 1848. The green represents the Catholics, the orange the Protestants (originally supporters of William of Orange) and the white stands for peace between both parts of the population.

ISLE OF MAN

Isle of Man, Manx **Ellan Vannin.**
Dependency of the British crown in the Irish Sea, NW Europe.

NATIONAL FLAG

Introduced in 1929, present design adopted 9 July 1968. Proportions 1:2.

The distinctive "Three Legs of Man" have been the emblem of the island since at least the 13th century. At the end of the 14th century they were armed and in this form were the main charge of the Manx flags and ensigns.

UNITED KINGDOM

United Kingdom of Great Britain and Northern Ireland.
Constitutional monarchy in NW Europe.

STATE FLAG AND JACK

Adopted 1 January 1801. Proportions 1:2.

The Union flag, also called the Union Jack, is a combination of the crosses of the patron saints of England (St George's cross, red cross on white field), Scotland (St Andrew's cross, white saltire on blue field) and Ireland (St Patrick's cross, red saltire on white field).

UNITED KINGDOM TERRITORIES

Presented here are the flags of the four parts of the United Kingdom (England, Scotland, Wales and Northern Ireland), as

TRISKELION

The *triskelion* (from the Greek for "three-legged") is one of the oldest symbols known to mankind. The earliest representations of it were found in prehistoric rock carvings in northern Italy. It also appears on Greek vases and coins from the 6th and 8th centuries BC, and was revered by Norse and Sicilian peoples. The Sicilian version has a representation of the head of Medusa in the centre.

The Manx people believe that the *triskelion* came from Scandinavia. According to Norse mythology, the *triskelion* was a symbol of the movement of the sun through the heavens.

well as flags of three areas within Scotland that enjoy a limited autonomy (Orkneys, Shetland and the Hebrides).

ENGLAND

NATIONAL FLAG

In use since the 13th century. Proportions ±2:3.

The red cross of St George on a white field was an emblem of the English Army and (until 1606) an ensign of merchant and naval ships. From 1606 to 1801 it was a jack of merchant ships. According to legend, St George saved a princess from a dragon and with its blood made the sign of the cross on his white shield.

SCOTLAND

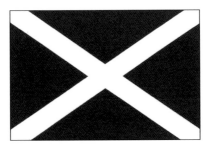

NATIONAL FLAG

In use since the 12th century. Proportions ±2:3.

St Andrew, brother of St Peter, was a missionary in the area around the Black Sea. He was crucified in Patras on an X-shaped cross, and legend says that some of his relics were taken to Scotland and buried there. Since the 11th century St Andrew has been the patron saint of Scotland, and since the 12th century a white saltire of St Andrew has been the Scottish national symbol (since the 15th century on a blue field).

ORKNEY ISLANDS

NATIONAL FLAG

Introduced in 1975. Proportions 2:3.

In this banner of arms, granted on 3 March 1975, the boat (a traditional galley) is taken from the arms of the countship of the Orkneys. The arms of Norway (a lion holding an axe) recall that the Orkneys originally belonged to Norway and were one of two provinces entitled to use the royal arms.

SHETLAND ISLANDS

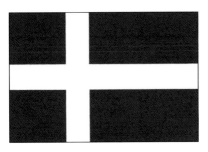

NATIONAL FLAG

In use since 1969. Proportions 2:3.

White and blue are the colours of Scotland. The Scandinavian cross is a reminder that the Shetlands were once settled by the Vikings and indicates that the islands are part of the Nordic countries.

HEBRIDES

NATIONAL FLAG

Granted 9 September 1976. Proportions 1:2.

The British blue ensign is charged with a badge depicting a lymphad (traditional rowing boat) in black. The heraldic boat symbolizes the seafaring traditions and skills of the population.

WALES

NATIONAL FLAG

Approved in 1959. Proportions 2:3.

The red dragon (*Y Ddraig Goch*) dates from the 4th century. In the 7th century it was adopted by Cadwaladr, Prince of Gwynedd, as the charge of his battle standard. White and green were the livery colours of the Welsh Prince Llewellyn, and later of the House of Tudor.

NORTHERN IRELAND

NATIONAL FLAG

Adopted 29 May 1953. Proportions 2:3.

The banner of arms of Northern Ireland was granted by King George V on 2 August 1924. The star representing the six counties is ensigned with the royal crown and charged with the red hand of Ulster. There is a flag of the same design, with a yellow field instead of white.

JERSEY

Bailiwick of Jersey.

Dependency of the British crown in the
English Channel, NW Europe.

NATIONAL FLAG

*Granted by royal warrant of 10 December 1980,
introduced 7 April 1981. Proportions unspecified.*

For about 200 years the flag of Jersey was
white with a red saltire. The arms, added in
1980, are those granted about 1290 by
Edward I, King of England, to the Bailiff of
Jersey. The shield is ensigned with an
ancient crown, similar to that attributed to
the House of Plantagenet.

GUERNSEY

Bailiwick of Guernsey and Dependencies.

Dependency of the British crown in the
English Channel, NW Europe.

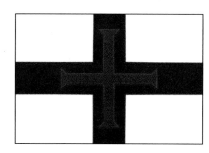

NATIONAL FLAG

*Adopted 13 March 1985, officially hoisted
9 May 1985. Proportions 2:3.*

The St George's cross symbolizes
constitutional ties with the British crown,
and the yellow cross of William the
Conqueror recalls that Guernsey was once
part of Normandy. William's banner with
this cross appears several times in the
Bayeaux Tapestry, made in the 11th century.

THE DEPENDENCIES OF GUERNSEY

The Bailiwick of Guernsey comprises
Guernsey, Alderney, Great and Little
Sark, Herm, Brechou, Jethou and
Lihou. Some of the dependencies
have their own flags which are white
with the cross of St George and some
additional devices. The flag of Alderney
(proportions 1:2) has a badge of the
island in the centre. The badge is a
British lion with three leaves in his right
paw on a green disc, framed with a
yellow ornamental border. The flag of
Sark (proportions 1:2) displays two
yellow lions in the red canton. The
canton of the flag of Herm (proportions
3:5) is the banner of arms which
features three monks and two dolphins.
The flag of Leonard Joseph Matchan,
the owner of Brechou (proportions 1:2)
is like that of Sark but has his personal
arms in the lower fly.

SOUTH-WEST EUROPE

PORTUGAL

Republic of Portugal,
Portuguese **República Portuguesa**.
Republic in SW Europe.

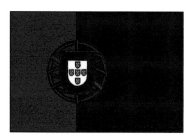

NATIONAL FLAG AND ENSIGN

Adopted 19 June 1911. Proportions 2:3.

The red stands for revolution, the green for
hope. The armillary sphere (a navigational
instrument of the Age of Discovery)
commemorates Prince Henry the
Navigator, who inspired the sea voyages
that led to the discovery of new lands and
created Portugal's colonial empire.

The central part of the shield shows the
arms of Portugal, adopted by Alfonso
Henriques after the Battle of Ourique in
1139. The five blue shields represent the
defeated Moorish kings of Lisbon, Badajoz,
Beja, Elvas and Évora. The divine assistance
that enabled Henriques to be victorious is
commemorated on each shield by white
dots representing the five wounds of Christ.

The red border which is charged with
seven yellow castles was added to the arms
after the annexation of Algarve and the
wedding of King Alfonso III and Beatriz
of Castile in 1252.

AZORES

Portuguese **Região Autónoma dos Açores**.
Group of islands in N Atlantic, autonomous
region of Portugal.

NATIONAL FLAG

Adopted 10 April 1979. Proportions 2:3.

The colours of the flag are those of the flag
of Portugal from 1830 to 1911; in the
canton is a shield with the arms of Portugal.
The goshawk (*açor* in Portuguese) refers to

the name of the islands. The nine stars represent the islands of Flores, Corvo, Terceira, São Jorge, Pico, Faial, Graciosa, São Miguel and Santa Maria.

MADEIRA

Portuguese **Região Autónoma da Madeira**.
Island group in E Atlantic, autonomous region of Portugal.

NATIONAL FLAG

Adopted 28 July 1978. Proportions 2:3.

The blue represents the sea, the yellow stands for the land. The cross of the Order of Christ is a reference to Prince Henry the Navigator, who colonized the uninhabited islands.

GIBRALTAR

British dependency in SW Europe.

NATIONAL FLAG

Introduced in 1966. Proportions 1:2.

This banner of arms was granted on 10 July 1502 by King Ferdinand and Queen Isabella of Spain, and was confirmed by the British authorities in June 1936. The castle and the key symbolize the strategic importance of the Gibraltar fortress as the key to the Mediterranean.

SPAIN

Kingdom of Spain, Spanish **Reino de España**.
Constitutional monarchy in SW Europe.

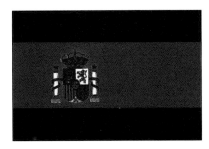

· STATE FLAG AND ENSIGN

Adopted 28 October 1981. Proportions 2:3.
Civil flag is without arms.

The basic design of the flag (the yellow stripe is twice as wide as each of the red) was introduced on 28 May 1785. With the state arms placed near the hoist, it was until 1931 the war ensign. Without the arms, it was the merchant flag from 1 January 1928 to 27 April 1931. On 29 August 1936 General Franco decreed that it should be the flag and civil ensign of Spain. Since then the state flag is always with the arms, which changed in 1938, 1945, 1977 and 1981.

The colours of the flag are the livery colours of the oldest Spanish kingdoms: the red of León and both colours of Castile, Aragón and Navarre.

SPANISH AUTONOMOUS COMMUNITIES

In 1977–1982 Spain was divided into 17 autonomous communities. They were formed on an ethnic and/or historic basis.

ANDALUSIA

COMMUNITY FLAG

Adopted 30 December 1981. Proportions 2:3.

The colour white represents the homes, the green represents the land.

ARAGÓN

COMMUNITY FLAG

Adopted 14 October 1981. Proportions 2:3.

The armorial banner of Aragón dates from the 14th century. The regional arms display the emblem of the legendary kingdom of Sobrarbe, the white cross of Iñigo Arista, the proper arms of Aragón as used in the 14th century, and the proper arms of Aragón.

ASTURIAS

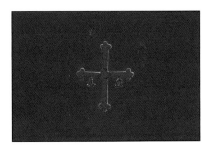

COMMUNITY FLAG

Adopted 30 December 1981. Proportions 2:3.

The traditional Asturian emblem is the Cross of Victory. From it hang the Greek letters "alpha" and "omega", symbolizing Christ as the Beginning and the End. Blue is the colour of the Virgin Mary.

BALEARES

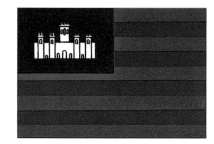

Adopted 25 February 1983. Proportions 2:3.

The flag closely resembles the flag of the kingdom of Mallorca, adopted in 1312. The stripes denote that Baleares has belonged to Aragón since 1228. The castle in the canton is that of Almoraima.

BASQUE COUNTRY

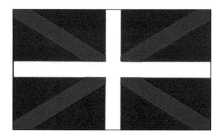

In use since 1894, officially approved 18 December 1979. Proportions 14:25.

The white cross is a symbol of the Catholic faith, the green saltire stands for the holy oak of Guernica and the red field commemorates the blood shed in the struggle for independence. The flag, called *Ikkurina*, was illegal from 1936 to 1977. Persecution for displaying it in public ended on 21 September 1976 and on 19 January 1977 the flag was legalized.

CANARY ISLANDS

Adopted 10 April 1989. Proportions 2:3.

The white represents the snow covering the volcano Pico de Teide on the island of Tenerife, the blue stands for the sea and the yellow for the sun.

CANTABRIA

Adopted 30 December 1981. Proportions 2:3.

White and red are the traditional colours of the region.

CASTILLA-LA MANCHA

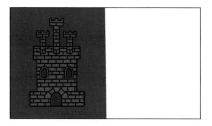

*Adopted 30 June 1983.
Proportions 1:2, actual flags differ.*

This banner of arms displays the arms of Castile in the hoist and in the fly the colour of the surcoats worn by the crusaders.

CASTILLA-LEÓN

Adopted 25 February 1983. Proportions 76:99.

This regional armorial banner is the same as that used by Spain from 1230 to 1479. It displays canting arms referring to Castile (castle) and León (lion).

CATALONIA

*In use since the 13th century, confirmed in 1932.
Proportions 2:3.*

The flag displays the stripes of the medieval arms of Catalonia (four red pallets on a golden field), arranged horizontally. Use of this flag was illegal from 1939 to 1975.

EXTREMADURA

Adopted 3 June 1985. Proportions 2:3.

The colours of the flag are those of the two parts of the region, Cáceres (green and white) and Badajoz (white and black).

GALICIA

COMMUNITY FLAG

Adopted 5 May 1984. Proportions 2:3.

White and blue are the colours of the Virgin Mary. The design of the flag is based on that of the maritime flag of the city of La Coruña.

LA RIOJA

COMMUNITY FLAG

Adopted 31 May 1985. Proportions 2:3.

The colours are taken from the first field of the regional arms. (Above a green mountain on a golden (yellow) field is a red cross between two silver (white) shells.)

MADRID

COMMUNITY FLAG

Adopted 25 February 1983. Proportions 7:11.

Red is the colour of Castile. The stars appear in the arms of the city of Madrid.

MURCIA

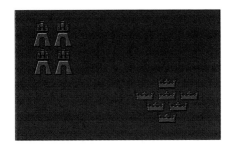

COMMUNITY FLAG

Adopted 9 June 1982. Proportions 2:3.

The castles recall that Murcia once belonged to Castile. The seven crowns stand for the seven provinces of Murcia.

NAVARRE

COMMUNITY FLAG

Adopted 10 August 1982. Proportions 2:3.

The flag displays the shield of the arms of Navarre, which date from the 13th century, ensigned with the royal crown.

VALENCIA

COMMUNITY FLAG

Adopted 1 July 1982. Proportions 2:3.

The flag is almost an exact copy of the flag granted by King James I the Conqueror to the City of Valencia in 1238.

ANDORRA

Principality of Andorra, Catalonian **Principat d'Andorra**, Spanish **Principado de Andorra**, French **Principauté d'Andorre**.
Independent co-principality in the Pyrenees, SW Europe.

NATIONAL FLAG

Adopted in present form in 1993. Proportions 2:3.

The blue-yellow-red tricolour has been in use since the second half of the 19th century. Blue and red are the colours of France, yellow and red are those of Spain, and together they reflect Franco-Spanish protection. The arms combine the arms of the bishopric of Urgel, the counts of Foix, Catalonia and Béarn. The motto is "United strength is stronger".

MONACO

Principality of Monaco,
French **Principauté de Monaco**.
Constitutional monarchy under French protectorate, SW Europe.

CIVIL FLAG AND ENSIGN

Adopted 4 April 1881. Proportions 4:5.

The colours are those of the ducal arms of Grimaldi (lozengy (diamond-shaped) white and red). Since the 17th century the flag has been white with the shield of arms.

SOUTH AND SOUTH-EAST EUROPE

ITALY

Republic of Italy, Italian **Repubblica Italiana**.
Republic in S Europe.

CIVIL ENSIGN

Officially adopted 19 June 1946. Proportions 2:3.
The state and civil flag is without arms.

Originally this was the national flag of the
Cisalpine Republic, founded by Napoleon.
The flag's design was influenced by the
French *Tricolore* and was in use from
11 May 1798 to 20 August 1802. It was
reintroduced in 1848 by the King of
Sardinia, who charged the white stripe with
his arms of Savoy and in 1861 this became
the national flag of the united Italy. In
1946 the arms were removed from the flag.

VATICAN

Holy See, Vatican City State, Italian **Santa
Sede, Stato della Cittá del Vaticano**.
Papal state in S Europe.

STATE FLAG

Officially adopted 7 June 1929. Proportions 1:1.

A flag of this design was introduced as the
merchant flag of the Pontifical State at the
beginning of the 19th century. The colours
are those of the keys of St Peter, which are
the keys to the kingdom of heaven and a
symbol of papal authority. The crossed keys

with the papal tiara have been the emblem
of the papal state since the 14th century.

Although the official proportions are
1:1, the actual flags flown in the Vatican
City are 2:3.

SAN MARINO

Most Serene Republic of San Marino, Italian
Serenissima Repubblica di San Marino.
Republic in central Italian peninsula, S Europe.

CIVIL FLAG

Adopted 6 April 1862. Proportions 3:4.
National flag is with arms.

As an emblem of sovereignty, San Marino
adopted in 1797 a white and blue national
cockade. The colours were taken from the
coat of arms, which displays three white
towers on a blue field. The towers represent
three castles built on three summits of
Mount Titano: Guaita, Cesta and Montale.

The white stands for peace, exemplified by
the white clouds and the snow; the blue is a
symbol of liberty and the sky over San Marino.

MALTA

Republic of Malta,
Maltese **Repubblika Ta'Malta**.
Insular republic in the Mediterranean, S Europe.

NATIONAL FLAG

Adopted 21 September 1964. Proportions 2:3.

The colours are those of the Knights of St
John of Jerusalem (the white Maltese cross
on a red field), who ruled Malta from 1530
to 1798. In April 1942 King George VI of
the United Kingdom awarded the islanders
the George cross for heroism in World War
II. Since 1964 the George cross bordered in
red has been placed directly on the
white field.

SLOVENIA

Republic of Slovenia, Slovene **Republika
Slovenija**. Republic in S Europe.

NATIONAL FLAG AND ENSIGN

Adopted 24 June 1991. Proportions 1:2.

The national flag, showing the same
arrangement of the pan-Slavic colours as
the flags of Russia or Slovakia, was adopted
by the Slovenian patriots in 1848. In 1991
the newly created arms of Slovenia were
added to the tricolour of white-blue-red.
The main feature of the arms is a stylized
silhouette of Triglav, the highest mountain
in the Slovene Alps. The three yellow stars
on a blue field are from the arms of the
former Duchy of Celje. The wavy lines
symbolize the rivers and the Adriatic Sea.

CROATIA

Republic of Croatia, Croat **Republika
Hrvatska**. Republic in S Europe.

NATIONAL FLAG

Adopted 22 December 1990. Proportions 1:2.

Following the example of other Slavic nations, the Croats in 1848 adopted a red-white-blue horizontal tricolour. When Croatia proclaimed independence in 1941, the arms (checked white and red) were placed in the centre of the tricolour and the badge of Ustasha in the canton. Under communist rule the Croat tricolour was charged with a red star.

The crown surmounting the present state arms is composed of shields with the historic arms of Croatia (golden star above silver crescent), Dubrovnik (two red stripes on a blue field), Dalmatia (three golden lions' heads), Istria (golden goat with red horns and hooves) and Slavonica (golden star above red stripe, fimbriated silver, and charged with black marten).

BOSNIA-HERZEGOVINA

Republic of Bosnia-Herzegovina, Serbian and Croat **Bosna i Hercegovina**.
Federal republic in S Europe.

NATIONAL FLAG AND ENSIGN

Adopted 4 February 1998. Proportions 1:2.

This flag was one of three proposals presented to parliament by a commission appointed by a special envoy of the United Nations. All three employed the same colours; the blue was to stand for the United Nations but it was changed to a darker blue to correspond with the European Union flag. The blue and the stars represent Europe and the yellow, the colour of the sun, symbolizes hope. The triangle stands for the three ethnic groups: Muslims, Croats and Serbs.

TERRITORIES OF BOSNIA AND HERZEGOVINA

After the civil war, on the basis of the 1996 agreement reached in Dayton (Ohio), Bosnia and Herzegovina was transformed into a federal state with two autonomous provinces.

CROAT-MUSLIM FEDERATION

NATIONAL FLAG

Adopted 6 November 1996. Proportions 2:3.

Red stands for the Croats, green for the Bosnian people and white for purity and peace. The golden fleur-de-lis is from the arms of Tvrtko, who was crowned in 1376 as Stephen I, King of Bosnia, Serbia and the sea-coast. It is a symbol of the Bosnians, while the historic arms of Croatia represent the Croat population. The ten stars symbolize the ten provinces that make up the Federation.

SERBIAN REPUBLIC

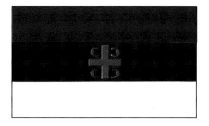

STATE AND NATIONAL FLAG

Adopted 9 January 1992. Proportions 1:2.

The tricolour has the Serbian historic arms in the centre, a golden cross with four golden flints each resembling the Cyrillic letter "S". They stand for the first letters of the Serbian motto, which translates as: "Only unity will save the Serbs".

YUGOSLAVIA

Federal Republic of Yugoslavia, Serbian **Federativna Republika Jugoslavija**.
Federal republic in SE Europe.

NATIONAL FLAG AND CIVIL ENSIGN

Adopted 1 December 1918, readopted 27 April 1992. Proportions 1:2.

From 1918 to 1941 the Yugoslav version of the pan-Slavic tricolour without any emblem was the civil flag and ensign. Under communist rule the national flag and civil ensign used the same tricolour, which from 1945 to 1946 was charged with a red star and from 1946 to 1992 with the red star bordered in yellow.

YUGOSLAVIAN REPUBLICS

From 1945 to 1991 Yugoslavia comprised six republics; now only two remain: Serbia and Montenegro.

SERBIA

STATE AND NATIONAL FLAGS

Introduced 28 January 1839, re-adopted 1992. Proportions 1:2.

The first Serbian horizontal tricolour of pan-Slavic colours, introduced in 1835, was white-blue-red. In 1838 the present order of colours was adopted, and in this form the tricolour served as the national flag of semi-independent Serbia and of the kingdom of Serbia (1882–1918).

MONTENEGRO

NATIONAL FLAG

Introduced in 1992. Proportions 1:3.

The flag is identical to that of Serbia, but it has different proportions. From 1860 to 1918 the same tricolour, but with the proportions 2:3, was the civil flag of the kingdom of Montenegro.

ALBANIA

Republic of Albania,
Albanian **Republika e Shqipërisë**.
Republic in SE Europe.

NATIONAL FLAG

Adopted 28 February 1912, re-established 7 April 1992. Proportions 5:7.

The red banner with the black double-headed eagle was the ensign of George Castriota, known as Skanderbeg, the hero of the uprising against the Turks and founder of the independent state in 1443. He probably chose the eagle on account of a tradition that the Albanians are the descendants of the eagle. They call themselves *Shkypetars* which translates as: "the sons of the eagle".

MACEDONIA

Republic of Macedonia, Macedonian
Republika Makedonija.
Republic in SE Europe.

NATIONAL FLAG

Adopted 5 October 1995. Proportions 1:2.

This is the second national flag of Macedonia since the country proclaimed independence in 1991 (the controversy provoked by the first flag is explained at the end of *All About Flags*). The present flag displays a yellow sun of eight rays instead of the former Star of Vergina with 16 rays.

GREECE

Hellenic Republic,
Greek **Elliniki Dimokratia**.
Republic in SE Europe.

NATIONAL FLAG AND ENSIGN

Adopted 15 March 1822, re-introduced 21 December 1978. Proportions 2:3.

The common device of all the flags used in the war for independence in 1821 was a white cross, the symbol of Christian faith. When in 1822 the Greek government adopted flags for the Army, and merchant and war ensigns, all of them displayed the same Greek cross. The flag of the Navy, and the later flag used on land, was a blue square with a white cross. The war ensign,

in use until 1833, was the same design as the present national flag.

The nine stripes represent the nine syllables of the war cry of independence, *Eleutheria i Thanatos* ("Freedom or Death"). The blue stands for the pure Greek sky, and recalls that God inspired the Greek people to fight for independence in spite of all odds. The white symbolizes the purity and sacred character of the struggle for liberation from Turkish tyranny.

MOUNT ATHOS

Greek **Hagion Oros**.
Self-governing theocratic republic under Greek protectorate, SE Europe.

STATE FLAG

*Date of introduction unknown.
Proportions 2:3.*

The first monastery on Mount Athos, the Great Laura, was founded in AD 963 by St Athanasius the Athonite. In the 11th century several more monasteries were built with the help of the Byzantine Empire, and in 1060 the Byzantine Emperor gave the monastic community its first constitution.

The golden yellow flag is charged with the black Byzantine eagle holding an orb and a sword in its claws. An imperial crown appears above its two heads.

BULGARIA

Republic of Bulgaria,
Bulgarian **Republika Bulgariya**.
Republic in SE Europe.

NATIONAL FLAG AND CIVIL ENSIGN

Adopted in 1878, re-introduced 22 November 1990. Proportions 3:5.

Because Russia supported the Bulgarians in their struggle for independence from Turkey, the Constitutional Assembly adopted an almost identical tricolour, although this one had a green stripe in place of the blue one. The colour of the new green stripe symbolizes freedom. The white symbolizes peace and Slavic thought, and the red represents the bravery of the Bulgarian people. Under communist rule (from 1947–1990) the state emblem was displayed on the white stripe near the hoist.

ROMANIA

Romania, Romanian **România**.
Republic in SE Europe.

NATIONAL FLAG, CIVIL AND STATE ENSIGN

Introduced in 1848, adopted in 1867, re-adopted 27 December 1989. Proportions 2:3.

Blue, yellow and red are the colours of the arms of the principalities of Walachia (red and yellow) and Moldavia (red and blue). These colours appeared together for the first time in 1848 on a revolutionary vertical tricolour of blue-yellow-red which was based on the French *Tricolore*. Walachia and Moldavia united in 1861 under the name of Romania, and adopted a red-yellow-blue horizontal tricolour. In April 1867 the colours were reversed and arranged vertically. From 1867 to 1989 the state flag was always charged with the actual state arms.

NORTHERN CYPRUS

Turkish Republic of Northern Cyprus,
Turkish **Kibris Cumhuriyeti**.
Republic in NE part of the island of Cyprus, SE Europe and W Asia.

NATIONAL FLAG

Adopted 13 March 1984. Proportions 2:3.

The national flag of Northern Cyprus retains the white field of the flag of Cyprus. The crescent with the star is the symbol of Islam.

CYPRUS

Greek Republic of Cyprus,
Greek **Kypriaki Dimokratia**.
Republic in NW and S part of the island of Cyprus, SE Europe and W Asia.

NATIONAL FLAG AND ENSIGN

Adopted 16 August 1960. Proportions 3:5..

The map of the island is dark yellow, symbolizing copper which has been mined here since the 3rd millennium BC. Copper takes its name from the Greek name for the island, *Kupros*, and the crossed olive branches stand for peace between the Greeks and Turks. The white is also a symbol of peace.

TURKEY

Republic of Turkey,
Turkish **Türkiye Cumhuriyeti**.
Republic in SE Europe and W Asia.

NATIONAL FLAG AND ENSIGN

Adopted in 1793, officially confirmed 5 June 1936. Proportions 2:3.

Red was the colour of Umar I, the caliph who ruled from AD 634 to 644 and was known as a great consolidator of the Islamic Empire. In the 14th century red became the colour of the Ottoman Empire. The crescent and star is the symbol of Islam.

EASTERN EUROPE

MOLDOVA

Republic of Moldova,
Moldovan **Republica Moldoveneasca**.
Republic in E Central Europe.

NATIONAL FLAG

Adopted 12 May 1990. Proportions 2:3.

In 1940 Bessarabia and Bukowina, a substantial part of historic Moldavia, have torn out of Romania and forcibly incorporated into the Soviet Union under the name of the Moldavian SSR. Striving for independence and eventual reunification with Romania, the Moldavian authorities adopted the flag of Romania and charged it with the state arms (the eagle of Walachia with the shield of Moldavia).

MOLDOVAN TERRITORIES

The Gagauzians and the inhabitants of the territory east of the Driester river were proclaimed independent republics in 1990 and 1992 respectively. Since 1994, Gagauzia has been an autonomous part of Moldova. The status of the Trans-Dniester Republic is not clear.

GAGAUZIA

NATIONAL FLAG

Adopted 31 October 1995. Proportions 1:2.

Blue is the traditional colour of the Turkic peoples. It symbolizes the sky, hope, kind-heartedness and allegiance to the Fatherland. For the Turkic people the white represents the west and symbolizes where the Gagauzians live; it is also a symbol of friendly co-existence with the Moldavians, Bulgarians, Ukrainians and Russians. The red is a symbol of gallantry and courage in the fight for freedom; it stands for the rebirth of the Gagauzians as a nation and represents their generosity. The three stars represent their past, present and future.

TRANS-DNIESTER REPUBLIC

NATIONAL FLAG

Date of introduction unknown. Proportions 1:2.

This former territory of the Moldavian SSR on the east side of the river Dniester and inhabited mainly by Russians and Ukrainians, proclaimed independence on 2 September 1991. It retained the Soviet flag but several years later removed the hammer and sickle.

UKRAINE

Ukrainian **Ukraina**.
Republic in E Central Europe.

NATIONAL FLAG AND CIVIL ENSIGN

Adopted 1918, re-adopted 21 January 1992.
Proportions 2:3.

The national colours derive from the arms of the medieval principality of Galicia (golden lion on a blue field). The first Ukrainian flag, adopted by the Supreme Council in 1848, was a yellow-blue horizontal bicolour and this was the first flag of the independent Ukraine, adopted in January 1918. However, in the 19th century most of the flags displayed by the public were bicolours, with the blue at the top, and this order of colours has been official since March 1918. The blue stands for the sky and the yellow for wheat, the main source of the wealth of Ukraine.

AUTONOMOUS TERRITORY

The only autonomous part of Ukraine is Crimea. The peninsula was conquered and settled by Tartars in the 13th century, annexed by Russia in 1783 and transferred in 1954 from the Russian SFSR to the Ukrainian SSR. It proclaimed independence on 5 May 1992 under the name of the Crimean Republic but later agreed to be an autonomous part of the Ukraine.

CRIMEA

NATIONAL FLAG

Adopted 24 September 1992. Proportions 1:2.

The Crimea was transferred in 1954 from the Russian SFSR to the Ukrainian SSR. It proclaimed independence on 5 May 1992 but later agreed to be an autonomous part of Ukraine. The flag displays the Russian colours in a different order. The colours represent the future (blue), the present (white), and the Crimea's heroic and tragic past (red).

BELARUS

Republic of Belarus,

Belorussian **Respublika Belarus**.

Republic in E Central Europe.

NATIONAL FLAG

Introduced 7 June 1995. Proportions 1:2.

When Belarus proclaimed independence in 1991 it readopted the white-red-white tricolour, first introduced in 1918. This was used in great numbers during rallies and demonstrations against the regime of the pro-Russian president. In response a presidential decree was issued introducing the current flag, which is similar to the flag of Soviet Belorussia (1951–1991). A white and red national ornament appears on the vertical stripe at the hoist.

RUSSIA

Russian Federation,

Rusian **Rossiyskaya Federatsiya**.

Federal republic in E Europe and N Asia.

NATIONAL FLAG AND CIVIL ENSIGN

Introduced 1699, re-adopted 22 August 1991. Proportions 2:3 (decreed 11 December 1993).

The Russian civil ensign was personally designed by Peter the Great, Tsar of Russia, in 1699 and became the national flag of Russia on 7 May 1883. In 1918 it was replaced by a red flag with the golden initials RSFSR in the upper hoist. Since 1990 the white-blue-red tricolour has been used in great numbers by pro-democracy forces.

RUSSIAN REPUBLICS

According to the constitution Russia comprises 21 republics, 49 provinces, six territories, ten administrative areas, two cities with federal status and one autonomous region. Flags of 20 republics follow. Since Chechnya is a de facto independent former republic and did not sign the Russian constitution, it is shown separately.

ADYGEA

NATIONAL FLAG

Adopted in 1830, re-adopted 24 March 1992. Proportions 1:2.

The green is a symbol of Islam; the 12 stars recall the tribes of Adygeans, united in the 19th century in the struggle for independence. The arrows originally symbolized the brotherhood and bravery of those tribes; today they symbolize the brotherhood and unity of all nationalities in Adygea.

ALANIA

NATIONAL FLAG

Adopted 10 December 1991. Proportions 1:2.

The white and red reflect qualities of the Alanian people – ethical purity and gallantry respectively. The yellow stands for abundance and prosperity.

ALTAY

NATIONAL FLAG

Adopted 2 July 1992. Proportions 1:2.

The white symbolizes faithfulness, as well as mutual understanding between the various nationalities of Altay. The blue stands for the purity of the skies, mountains, rivers and lakes.

BASHKORTOSTAN

NATIONAL FLAG

Adopted 25 February 1992. Proportions 1:2.

The stylized *kurai* flower (*Salsola kali*) is a symbol of friendship. Its seven petals represent the tribes who laid foundations of unity and consolidation for the Bashkir people. The blue symbolizes the integrity and virtue of the thoughts of the people; the white represents their peacefulness, openness and readiness to co-operate; the green stands for freedom and eternal life.

BURYATIA

NATIONAL FLAG

Adopted 29 October 1992. Proportions 1:2.

The traditional Buryat *Soyonbo*, consisting of the moon, sun and fire, is a symbol of eternal life. The blue stands for the sky and Lake Baykal, the white symbolizes purity, and the yellow represents freedom and prosperity.

CHUVASHIA

NATIONAL FLAG

Adopted 29 April 1992. Proportions 5:8.

The main charge of the flag is a stylized tree of life, a symbol of rebirth, with the three suns, a traditional emblem popular in Chuvash art. The purple stands for the land, the golden yellow for prosperity.

DAGESTAN

NATIONAL FLAG

Adopted 26 February 1994. Proportions 1:2.

The green is the symbol of Islam, the blue represents the Caspian Sea and the red stands for courage and fidelity.

INGUSHETIA

NATIONAL FLAG

Adopted 15 July 1994. Proportions 1:2.

In the religion and philosophy of the Ingushetians, the solar emblem (in the centre of the flag) represents not only the sun and the universe but also awareness of the oneness of the spirit in the past, present and future.

The red recalls the struggle of the Ingush people for existence and in the defence of their homeland. The white symbolizes the divine purity of the thoughts and views of the nation. The green is the symbol of Islam.

KABARDINO-BALKARIA

NATIONAL FLAG

Adopted 21 July 1994. Proportions 1:2.

The blue stands for the sky, the white represents the snow-topped Caucasus Mountains and the green symbolizes the fields. In the centre is a white silhouette of Mount Elbrus, the highest peak in Europe.

KALMYKIA

NATIONAL FLAG

Adopted 30 July 1993. Proportions 1:2.

The yellow stands for the sun, the people and the religious faith of the nation. The blue represents the sky, eternity and steadiness. The lotus is a symbol of purity, spiritual rebirth and happiness. Its five upper petals represent the continents and the lower four stand for the quarters of the globe. Together they symbolize the will of the Kalmyks to live in friendship and to co-operate with all the nations of the world.

KARACHAYEVO-CHERKESIYA

NATIONAL FLAG

Adopted 3 February 1994. Proportions 1:2.

The blue is the colour of peace, good intentions and serenity. The green represents nature, fertility and wealth; it is the colour of youth, and also of wisdom and restraint. The red is a symbol of warmth and friendship between nations. The sun rising above the mountains represents the hope of the peoples in the Caucasus for a bright future.

KARELIA

NATIONAL FLAG

Adopted 16 February 1993. Proportions 2:3.

Warm feelings, unity and co-operation between the peoples of Karelia are represented by the red stripe. The blue stands for the lakes and the green for the forests.

KHAKASSIA

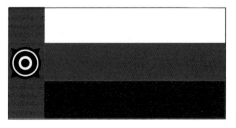

NATIONAL FLAG

Adopted 8 July 1992. Proportions 1:2.

The use of the Russian colours shows that the republic is part of the Russian Federation. The green, the traditional colour of Siberia, is a symbol of eternal life and rebirth. The emblem is a sign of respect to the ancestors who used the solar symbol; its black colour symbolizes their wisdom.

KOMI

NATIONAL FLAG

Adopted 27 November 1991. Proportions 1:2.

The colours of the flag reflect the geographical location of the republic and its physical features. The blue stands for the sky, the green for the taiga landscape and the white for the snow.

MARI EL

NATIONAL FLAG

Adopted 3 September 1992. Proportions 1:2.

The colours are those of Russia but in different shades. The name of the republic appears below a solar sign, which is part of the traditional national emblem.

MORDOVIA

NATIONAL FLAG

Adopted 30 March 1995. Proportions 1:2.

This republic uses the national colours of Russia in different shades. A local form of the solar emblem is placed in the centre.

SAKHA

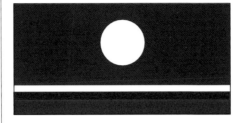

NATIONAL FLAG

Adopted 14 December 1992. Proportions 1:2.

The white disc represents the northern sun. The blue, white and green stand for the sky, snow and taiga landscape. The red symbolizes the courage and constancy of the people.

TATARSTAN

NATIONAL FLAG

Adopted 29 November 1991. Proportions 1:2.

The green, the colour of Islam, represents the Tatars; the red stands for the Russians. The white stripe symbolizes peace between the Tatar majority and the Russian minority.

TUVA

NATIONAL FLAG

Adopted 17 September 1992. Proportions 1:2.

Three days after it was adopted this flag was consecrated by the Dalai Lama, who was

visiting Tuva at the time. The colours stand for prosperity (yellow), courage and strength (blue), and purity (white).

UDMURTIA

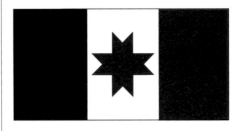

NATIONAL FLAG

Adopted 3 December 1993. Proportions 1:2.

The black is a symbol of the earth and of stability, the white stands for the universe and the purity of moral foundations, and the red represents the sun and life. The solar emblem protects the people against ill fortune.

CHECHNYA

Chechen Republic,
Chechen **Republika Ichkeriya**.
De facto independent former republic of Russia in the Caucasus Mountains, E Europe.

NATIONAL FLAG

Adopted 2 November 1991. Proportions 2:3.

The green is the colour of Islam, the red symbolizes the blood shed in the struggle for independence and the white represents the road to a bright future.

Flags of Asia

Illustrated here are the current national flags of the countries of Asia, from Georgia and Abkhazia to South Korea and Japan, as well as the flags of their territories, states and provinces.

Because Asia is so vast, we have grouped together its countries into geographical sections. We begin in western Asia, then move on to the Middle East, South-west Asia and then Central Asia. Finally, we look at the flags of the countries of southern and South-east Asia and the Far East. There are some geographical anomalies: the flags of Russia, Turkey, Cyprus and Northern Cyprus can all be found in *Flags of Europe*.

For each entry, the country or territory's name is given in its most easily recognized form and then in all its official languages. This is followed by a description of its political status and geographic position. The basic data for each flag contains the status of the flag, date of adoption, proportions, and the symbolic meaning.

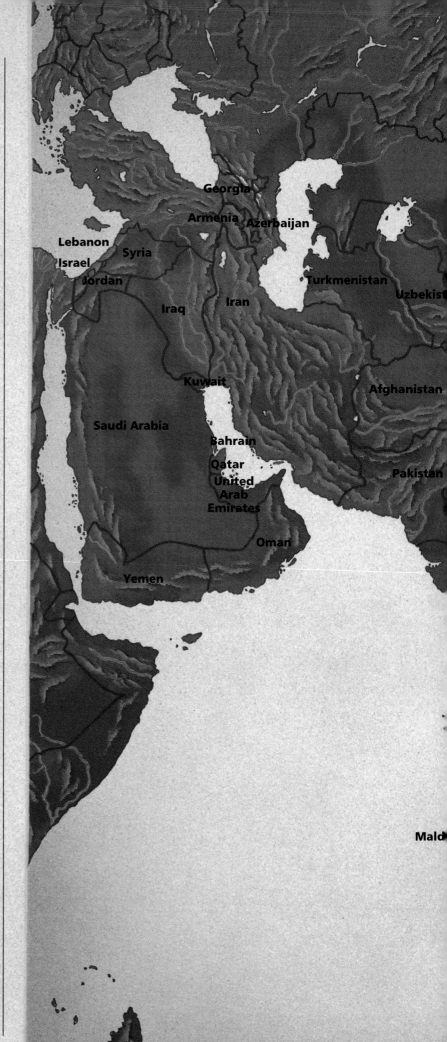

WESTERN ASIA

GEORGIA

Republic of Georgia,
Georgian **Sakartvelos Respublika**.
Republic in W Asia.

NATIONAL FLAG AND CIVIL ENSIGN

Introduced 25 March 1918, re-adopted 14 November 1990. Proportions 3:5.

Dogwood red is the national colour of Georgia. The black and white represent the tragic past under Russian rule and hope for a peaceful future.

ABKHAZIA

Republic of Abkhazia,
Abkhaz **Arespublika Apsni**.
De facto independent former autonomous republic in Georgia, W Asia.

NATIONAL FLAG

Adopted 23 July 1992. Proportions 2:2.

The design of the flag is based on the flag of North Caucasia, which was in use 1918–1919. The palm of a hand was a symbol of Abkhaz statehood in the 8th–10th centuries and the stars and stripes represent the seven historic districts of Abkhazia. (Seven is a sacred number, often found in Abkhaz mythology, religion and folk art.) The stripes in green and white symbolize the tolerance of the Caucasus

people and the peaceful co-existence of Islam (green) and Christianity (white).

ARMENIA

Republic of Armenia,
Armenian **Haikakan Hanrapetoutioun**.
Republic in W Asia.

NATIONAL FLAG AND ENSIGN

Introduced 22 April 1918, re-adopted 1 September 1991. Proportions 1:2.

The red recalls the blood shed in the struggle for national existence. The blue stands for the skies, hope and the unchanging character of the land. The orange represents the courage of the people.

NAGORNO-KARABAKH

Armenian **Artsakh**
De facto independent former autonomous republic of Azerbaijan, W Asia.

NATIONAL FLAG

Adopted in June 1992. Proportions unspecified.

The flag displays the colours of Armenia but has slightly different symbolic meaning: the blood spilt in the struggle to preserve the nation (red), love of liberty (blue) and bread (orange). The westwards-pointing arrow is a graphic representation of the country's current separation from Armenia proper and its hopes for union with the Fatherland.

AZERBAIJAN

Republic of Azerbaijan,
Azeri **Azarbajchan Respublikasy**.
Republic in W Asia.

NATIONAL FLAG AND ENSIGN

Adopted 5 February 1991. Proportions 1:2.

The main features of the flag are based on the flag introduced in autumn 1917 and used until the occupation of the country by the Red Army in 1920. The colours represents the Turkic world (blue), contemporary life (red) and the Islamic religion (green). The crescent and star is the symbol of Islam. The eight points of the star stand for the Turkic peoples: Azerbaijani, Ottoman, Jagatay, Tatar, Kazakh, Kipchak, Seljuk and Turkoman.

THE REGION OF CAUCASIA

The republics on this page belong to the region of Caucasia which comprises 13 political entities including Chechnya, six Russian republics (Adygea, Alania, Dagestan, Ingushetia, Kabardino-Balkaria, Karachayevo-Cherkesiya) and South Ossetia, an autonomous subdivision of Georgia. It is home to over 40 different nations and ethnic groups of which only a few had or have their own states.

Historic flags of Azerbaijan, Dagestan and North Caucasia can be found in *Flag Families: The Muslim crescent;* the flags of the modern Soviet Republics of Armenia, Azerbaijan and Georgia can be found in *Flag Families: the red banner.* The flag of the Balkars is in the section *Flags of Peoples and Causes: Nations and ethnic groups.*

SYRIA

Republic of Syria,
Arabic **al-Jumhuriya al-Arabiya as-Suriya.**

Republic in W Asia.

NATIONAL FLAG AND ENSIGN

Adopted 30 March 1980. Proportions 2:3.

The present flag is that of the United Arab Republic, used from 1958 to 1961 in both Syria and Egypt. In 1972 Egypt, Syria and Libya formed the Federation of Arab Republics, with a common flag. The policy of reconciliation between Egypt and Israel caused Libya to withdraw from the Federation in 1977, and Syria followed suit in 1980. The Syrian authorities changed the flag because they felt that the Federation flag had been disgraced when it was dipped to the Prime Minister of Israel by an Egyptian guard of honour.

LEBANON

Republic of Lebanon,
Arabic **al-Jumhuriya al-Lubnaniya.**

Republic in W Asia.

NATIONAL FLAG AND ENSIGN

Adopted 7 December 1943. Proportions 2:3.

The red symbolizes sacrifices in the struggle for independence, and the white stands for purity and peace. The cedar is a symbol of

holiness, eternity and peace, and since the 19th century it has been the symbol of the Maronite Christian community in Lebanon.

ISRAEL

State of Israel, Hebrew **Medinat Israel.**

Republic in W Asia.

NATIONAL FLAG

Adopted 28 October 1948. Proportions 8:11.

The flag was designed for the Zionist movement in 1891. The basic design recalls the *tallith*, the Jewish prayer shawl, which is white with blue stripes. The hexagram in the centre is the *Magen David* ("Shield of David"), often erroneously called the Star of David. It became the Jewish symbol in the 17th century and was adopted by the First Zionist Congress in 1897.

PALESTINE

State of Palestine,
Arabic **Daulat Filastin.**

Semi-autonomous state comprising Gaza and part of the West Bank of Jordan in W Asia.

NATIONAL FLAG

Introduced 1922. Proportions 1:22.

The flag is based on a flag used in the Arab revolt of 1917 and displays the pan-Arab colours.

JORDAN

Hashemite Kingdom of Jordan, Arabic **al-Mamlaka al-Urdunniya al-Hashemiya.**

Constitutional monarchy in W Asia.

NATIONAL FLAG, CIVIL AND STATE ENSIGN

Introduced in 1921, officially confirmed 16 April 1928. Proportions 1:2.

The flag displays the pan-Arab colours, with the seven points of the star representing the seven verses that make up the *Fatiha* of the Koran: the Fundamental Law of Life, Thought and Aspiration.

SAUDI ARABIA

Kingdom of Saudi Arabia,
Arabic **al-Mamlaka al-Arabiya as-Saudiya.**

Absolute monarchy in SW Asia.

NATIONAL FLAG

Introduced in 1932, present design adopted 15 March 1973. Proportions 2:3.

The flag is very similar to that of the Wahabi sect, in use since 1901. The green is the colour of Islam. The inscription in white *tulth* script reads "There is no God but Allah and Muhammad is the Prophet of Allah", the Muslim Statement of Faith. The sword is a symbol of justice.

YEMEN

Republic of Yemen,
Arabic **al-Jumhuriya al-Yamaniya**.
Republic in SW Asia.

NATIONAL FLAG AND CIVIL ENSIGN

Adopted 22 May 1990. Proportions 2:3.

After the unification of North and South Yemen, the flag retained the common element of stripes in the pan-Arab colours.

OMAN

Sultanate of Oman, Arabic **Saltanat Uman**.
Absolute monarchy in SW Asia.

NATIONAL FLAG AND ENSIGN

Adopted 18 November 1995. Proportions 1:2.

The national emblem of Oman is composed of two crossed swords surmounted by a ceremonial dagger and an ornate belt. The white symbolizes peace and prosperity. The red is the colour of the pre-1970 Omani flag, which was plain red, and recalls the battles against the foreign invaders. The green represents the Jebel Akhdar (the Green Mountains) and stands for fertility.

UNITED ARAB EMIRATES

Arabic **Dawlat Ittihad al-Imarat al-Arabiyah
al-Muttahidah**.
Federal monarchy in SW Asia.

NATIONAL FLAG AND CIVIL ENSIGN

*Adopted 2 December 1971, officially hoisted
1 January 1972. Proportions 1:2.*

The flag displays the pan-Arab colours. Red is the traditional colour of the emirates and red flags of several tiny Arab states along the southern coast of the Persian Gulf were modified for the first time in 1820 following the General Treaty that was signed by the British and the rulers of eight sheikhdoms. It required that these states "should carry by land and sea a red flag, with or without letters on it, at their option, and this shall be in a border of white". Such were the flags of Sharjah and Ras al Khaimah, while Abu Dhabi, Ajman, Dubai and Umm al Qaiwain used a red flag with a white vertical stripe along the hoist. In 1958 Abu Dhabi exchanged the white stripe for a white canton and in 1961 the flag of Umm al Qaiwain was charged with a white crescent and star. In 1975 the ruler of Sharjah decided to replace his emirate's flag with that of the Union.

ABU DHABI

STATE FLAG

AJMAN, DUBAI

STATE FLAG

AL FUJAIRAH

STATE FLAG

RAS AL KHAIMAH

STATE FLAG

UMM AL QAIWAIN

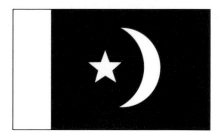

STATE FLAG

QATAR

State of Qatar, Arabic **Dawlat Qatar**.

Absolute monarchy in SW Asia.

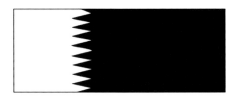

NATIONAL FLAG AND ENSIGN

Adopted in 1948. Proportions 11:28.

The flag used in the 19th century was red with a white vertical stripe along the hoist. In the first half of the 20th century the line separating the two colours became serrated, and the name of the country was often inscribed in white on the red portion of the flag. The local red dyes used in making flags darken when exposed to sun, so the red was officially changed to maroon in 1948.

BAHRAIN

State of Bahrain, Arabic **Dawlat al-Bahrayn**.

Absolute emirate in SW Asia.

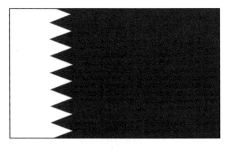

NATIONAL FLAG AND ENSIGN

Adopted in 1933, officially confirmed 19 August 1972. Proportions 3:5.

In the 19th century the flag of Bahrain was red with a white vertical stripe along the hoist. In 1933 the line dividing the colours was serrated to distinguish the flag of Bahrain from those of other Trucial States.

KUWAIT

State of Kuwait, Arabic **Dawlat al-Kuwait**.

Absolute monarchy in SW Asia.

NATIONAL FLAG AND CIVIL ENSIGN

Adopted 7 September 1961. Proportions 1:2.

The flag displays the pan-Arab colours. The black stands for the defeat of the enemy on the battlefield, the red is the blood of the enemy left on the Arab swords. The green represents the fertile land, and the white the pure Arab deeds.

IRAQ

Republic of Iraq,
Arabic **al-Jumhuriya al-Iraqiya**.
Socialist republic in SW Asia.

NATIONAL FLAG AND ENSIGN

Adopted 14 January 1991. Proportions 2:3.

Since 1963 the flag of Iraq has been a red-white-black horizontal tricolour, with three green stars on the white stripe. During the Gulf War, the Revolutionary Command Council chaired by President Saddam Hussein decided to place the words *Allahu Akbar* ("God is Great") between the stars.

IRAN

Islamic Republic of Iran,
Farsi **Jomhori-e-Islami-e-Irân**.
Authoritarian Islamic republic in SW Asia.

NATIONAL FLAG AND ENSIGN

Adopted 29 July 1980. Proportions 4:7.

One of the consequences of the Islamic revolution in Iran was the addition of religious symbols to the Iranian horizontal tricolour. The central emblem is a composite of Arab letters in the form of four crescents and a vertical line in the middle. The five principal parts of the emblem represent the five principles of Islam and together they form the word *Allah*. Other combinations of these elements represent the Book (Koran), the Sword (the symbol of power and solidarity), man's growth, the negation of all idolatrous values, the negation of all powers and super-powers, and the struggle to establish a unified society. The symmetrical form of the emblem signifies balance and equilibrium.

The words *Allahu Akbar* ("God is Great"), written in highly stylized Kufic script, appear 22 times to commemorate Bahman 22, 1357 (11 February 1979), the day of victory for the revolution.

CENTRAL ASIA

TURKMENISTAN

Republic of Turkmenistan,
Turkmen **Türkmenistan**.
Republic in W Central Asia.

NATIONAL FLAG

*Adopted 19 February 1992, modified
1 February 1977. Proportions 1:2.*

The flag of Turkmenistan has the most intricate design of all national flags in the world. It is also one of the most interesting. The green field with the crescent and stars is clearly the symbol of Islam; the crescent and stars represent faith in a bright future, while the white symbolizes serenity and kind-heartedness. The five stars symbolize the five *velayats* (regions): Ahal, Balkan, Dashhowuy, Lebap and Mary. They also stand for the five senses. The five points of each star symbolize the five states of matter: solid, liquid, gaseous, crystalline and plasmatic.

The vertical stripe along the hoist bears five major *guls* of the Turkmenian carpets. Each *gul* is a symmetrical medallion, in some cases divided into four quarters in counterchanging colours. Major *guls* are repeated in rows or in a chequered pattern on the central field of the carpet, and minor *guls* appear on the border. They reflect the national identity of Turkmenistan where carpets were part of traditional nomadic life, used for floor-covering, furniture, sacks and bags, and to decorate camel and horse trappings.

In 1995 the President of Turkmenistan declared a policy of neutrality, which was acknowledged by a unanimous vote of the United Nations General Assembly on 12 December 1995. To immortalize this, crossed olive branches similar to those on

the UN flag were placed below the *guls*. The new law stated, "The State Flag of Turkmenistan is a symbol of the unity and independence of the nation and of the neutrality of the state."

UZBEKISTAN

Republic of Uzbekistan,
Uzbek **Uzbekistan Respublikasy**.
Republic in W Central Asia.

NATIONAL FLAG

Adopted 18 November 1991. Proportions 1:2.

Blue is the colour of the Turkic peoples and also of the banner of Tamerlane, who ruled an Uzbek empire in the 14th century. It is a symbol of eternal skies and of the people as one of the fundamental sources of life. The white signifies peace, the traditional Uzbek wish for a safe journey and striving for purity of thoughts and deeds. The green is the colour of nature, fertility and new life, as well as being the colour of Islam. The red stripes stand for the vital force in all living organisms, which links good and pure ideas with the eternal sky and deeds on earth.

The crescent symbolizes the new republic. The stars stand for the twelve months of the solar Uzbek calendar and are named after the 12 constellations, reflecting the astronomical knowledge of Uzbeks in ancient times.

KAZAKHSTAN

Republic of Kazakhstan,
Kazak **Kazak Respublikasy**.
Republic in W Central Asia.

STATE AND CIVIL FLAG AND ENSIGN

Adopted 4 June 1992. Proportions 1:2.

Blue is the common colour of the Turkic peoples. Here it stands for the endless skies over all people as a symbol of well-being, tranquillity, peace and unity. The sun and a golden eagle represent the love of freedom and the lofty thoughts and ideals of the Kazakhs. Along the hoist is a typical national ornament.

KYRGYZSTAN

Republic of Kyrgyzstan,
Kyrgyz **Kyrgyz Respublikasy**.
Republic in W Central Asia.

NATIONAL FLAG

Adopted 3 March 1992. Proportions 3:5.

The word *kyrgyz* originally meant "red" and red has been the national colour from time immemorial. Red was also the colour of the banner of Manas the Noble, who struggled for unity and formed the Kyrgyz nation. The sun is a symbol of light, eternity and infinite nobility, and the 40 rays stand for the 40 Kyrgyz tribes united by Manas. The sun is charged with a representation of the device covering the roof of a typical *yurt*, the tent used by the Kyrgyz nomads. It symbolizes hearth and home, the unity of time and space, the origin of life and solidarity.

TAJIKISTAN

Republic of Tajikistan,
Tajik **Jumhuri Tojikiston**.
Republic in W Central Asia.

NATIONAL FLAG

Adopted 24 November 1992. Proportions 1:2.

The crown represents the Tajik people. The name is derived from *tajvar*, which means "crowned". In traditional Tajik culture the magic word "seven" is a symbol of perfection, the embodiment of happiness and the provider of virtue. According to Tajik legend, heaven is composed of seven beautiful orchards, separated by seven mountains each with a glowing star on top.

The red is a symbol of the sun and victory; the white stands for purity, cotton and the snow on the mountains, and the green represents the spiritual meaning of Islam and the generosity of nature.

AFGHANISTAN

Islamic Emirate of Afghanistan,
Autocratic Islamic state in Central Asia.

NATIONAL FLAG

Adopted 27 October 1997. Proportions 1:2.

The white flag with the *Shahada* (the Muslim Statement of Faith) in green is the 17th Afghanistan national flag since 1900. This flag, introduced by the Taliban regime, is not yet recognized internationally; the United Nations Headquarters in New York and the Afghan embassies still fly the former green-white-black horizontal

tricolour with the golden national emblem. Since it was impossible to obtain the exact data on design and proportions of the flag of the current regime, the internationally recognized flag is reproduced here.

KASHMIR

Kashmiri **Azad Jammu o Kashmir**.
Northern, autonomous part of Kashmir within Pakistan, Central Asia.

NATIONAL FLAG

Adopted in 1947. Proportions unspecified.

The flag displays the Pakistani colours, white and green, with the symbols of the Muslim majority (crescent and star) and the Hindu and Sikh minorities (a saffron square). The four white stripes symbolize the four main rivers of Kashmir.

JAMMU AND KASHMIR

Kashmiri **Jammu o Kashmir**.
Southern part of Kashmir, state of India, Central Asia.

NATIONAL FLAG

Adopted in 1952. Proportions 2:3.

The native plough is a symbol of labour, and the three stripes represent the three provinces of the state.

AFGHANISTAN: FLAGS REFLECT POLITICAL CHANGES

Political change in countries that gained independence in the 20th century are often reflected in the change of the national flag. In Afghanistan, the Taliban regime's current flag is the 17th national flag since 1900.

The first three flags (1900–1928) were black with three different state emblems. In July 1928 a horizontal black-red-green tricolour was introduced, and in September of the same year these colours were re-arranged vertically. The colours symbolized the past (black), the blood shed for independence (red), and the wealth and hope for the future (green). In January 1929, the black flag was revived but was soon replaced by the vertical tricolour with three different emblems (from October 1930 to 1974).

In 1974 the monarchy was forcibly abolished and the republican regime changed the emblem and restored the horizontal arrangement of the national colours (from April to October 1978 the flag had no emblem). When the communists came to power in October 1978 they adoped a red flag with a new emblem. From 1980-1992, two flags used under the Soviet occupation were horizontal tricolours with an emblem, which until 1987 displayed a red star.

After the liberation of Kabul in 1992 the national flag became a horizontal tricolour of green, white and black with the golden inscription "God is Great" (on the top stripe), and the Muslim Statement of Faith (on the second stripe).

SOUTHERN ASIA

PAKISTAN

Islamic Republic of Pakistan,
Urdu **Islami Jamhuriya e Pakistan.**
Republic in S Asia.

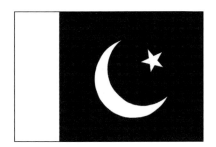

NATIONAL FLAG

Adopted 14 August 1947. Proportions 2:3.

The flag of the All-India Moslem League, introduced in 1906, was green with the white crescent and star, the colours symbolizing Islam. A white vertical stripe at the hoist was added to symbolize the non-Muslim minorities after independence. The white and green portions of the flag symbolize peace and prosperity, the crescent progress and the star light and knowledge.

INDIA

Republic of India, Hindi **Bharatiya Ganarajya.**
Federal republic in S Central Asia.

NATIONAL FLAG

Adopted 22 July 1947. Proportions 2:3.

The central figure is *chakra* (wheel) from the capital of the ancient Asokan column at Sarnath. To a Buddhist the wheel represents the inevitability of existence: *Dharma Chakra* (Wheel of Law). The saffron (orange) symbolizes courage and sacrifice, while the white stands for peace and truth, and the green faith and chivalry.

NEPAL

Kingdom of Nepal, Nepali **Nepal Adhirajya.**
Constitutional monarchy in S Central Asia.

NATIONAL FLAG

Adopted 16 December 1962. Proportions 4:3.

Nepal is the only country in the world to have a flag that is not rectangular or square. The two triangles symbolize the Himalaya Mountains and they also stand for two religions, Hinduism and Buddhism. Crimson is the national colour of Nepal. The moon and sun originally symbolized the families of the king and the prime minister, and the wish that the nation might live as long as these celestial bodies.

BHUTAN

Kingdom of Bhutan, Dzongkha **Druk-yul.**
Constitutional monarchy in S Central Asia.

NATIONAL FLAG

In use since the 19th century. Proportions 2:3.

The present design of the flag was established *c.*1965, when the maroon was replaced by orange and the shape of the dragon was modified. The dragon represents the name of the country (*druk* means "dragon") and its colour stands for purity

and loyalty. Its snarling mouth expresses the stern strength of the deities protecting Bhutan, and the jewels clasped in its claws symbolize the wealth and perfection of the country. The yellow stands for the fruitful action of the king in affairs of religion and state; the orange represents religious practice.

BANGLADESH

People's Republic of Bangladesh,
Bengali **Gana Prajatantri Bangladesh.**
Republic in S Asia.

NATIONAL FLAG

Adopted 13 January 1972. Proportions 3:5.

The green represents the greenery of the country, its vitality and youthfulness. The red disc is a symbol of the rising sun of independence after the dark night of a blood-drenched struggle.

SRI LANKA

Democratic Socialist Republic of Sri Lanka,
Sinhala **Sri Lanka prajathanthrika samajawadi janarajaya,**
Tamil **Ilankayc cananayaka sosalisak kutiyarucu.**
Socialist republic consisting of an island in Indian Ocean, S Asia.

NATIONAL FLAG

Adopted 7 September 1978. Proportions 1:2.

In traditional Sanskrit and Pali literature the island is called Sinhaladvipa, the word *sinhala* deriving from the Sinhalese word *sinha* (lion), and since the 15th century a golden lion holding a sword of authority has appeared on the crimson field of the state banner. This flag with a yellow border, a symbol of Buddhism, was adopted as the first flag of independent Ceylon on 4 February 1948. The lion denotes the desire for peace, while the crimson symbolizes national pride. In 1950 the stripes of green (for the Muslims) and saffron (for the Tamils) were added. In 1972 and 1978 the finials in the corners were modified to represent the leaves of the fig tree (*Ficus religiosa*) under which Siddartha Gautama sat when he received enlightenment and became the Buddha. The four leaves stand for love, compassion, sympathy and equanimity, which are virtues extolled by Buddhism.

MALDIVES

Republic of the Maldives, Divehi **Divehi Rajje ge Jumhuriya**. Republic comprising 19 clusters of coral islands in Indian Ocean, S Asia.

NATIONAL FLAG AND ENSIGN

Adopted 26 July 1965.
Proportions 2:3.

The crescent is the symbol of Islam. The green stands for peace and prosperity, and the red symbolizes blood shed in the struggle for independence.

BRITISH INDIAN OCEAN TERRITORY

British colony consisting of the Chagos Archipelago in N Indian Ocean.

STATE FLAG AND ENSIGN

Adopted in 1990. Proportions 3:5.
Ensign is in proportions 1:2.

The white and blue wavy stripes represent the Indian Ocean. The palm tree stands for the islands, of which only Diego Garcia is inhabited. The Union flag in the canton and the crown are there to symbolize British sovereignty.

SOUTH-EAST ASIA

MYANMAR

Union of Myanmar, Burmese **Pyidaungsu Myanma Naingngandaw**. Military republic in SE Asia.

NATIONAL FLAG

Adopted 3 January 1974. Proportions 5:9.

The white represents purity and virtue, the blue symbolizes peace and integrity, and the red signifies courage and decisiveness. The pinion and padi leaves stand for industry and agriculture, and for workers and peasants. The stars represent the 14 constituent member states of the union.

THAILAND

Kingdom of Thailand, Thai **Muang Thai** or **Pratet Thai**. Constitutional monarchy in SE Asia.

CIVIL AND STATE FLAG AND ENSIGN

Adopted 28 September 1917. Proportions 2:3.

The flag adopted in 1916 was red with two white stripes, but the central red portion was altered to blue. It was an expression of solidarity with World War I allies (United Kingdom, France, United States and Russia), whose flags used the red, white and blue. The flag is given the name *Trairanga* which means tricolour.

The colours symbolize the blood shed for their country (red), the purity of the people protected by their religion (white) and the monarchy (blue).

CAMBODIA

State of Cambodia,

Khmer **Roat Kampuchea**.

State in Indo-China, SE Asia.

NATIONAL FLAG AND ENSIGN

Adopted 30 June 1993. Proportions 2:3.

The present flag is the seventh since 1948, when the country became independent. All of them except one bore a representation of Angkor Wat, built in the 12th century, which is one of the most impressive temples in the world.

LAOS

Lao People's Democratic Republic, Lao **Sáthálanalat Pasathipatay Pásáson Lao**.

Socialist republic in Indo-China, SE Asia.

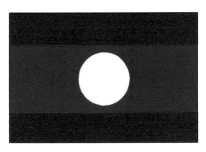

NATIONAL FLAG

Adopted 2 December 1975. Proportions 2:3.

The flag has been used since 1956 by Pathet Lao, the communist guerrilla movement, and became the national flag when it gained control of the country in 1975. The red symbolizes the blood spilt by the Lao people in defence of their Fatherland, the blue stands for the country's wealth, and the white represents the unity of the multi-ethnic society under communist rule.

VIETNAM

Socialist Republic of Vietnam,

Vietnamese **Công Hòa Xã Hôi Chu Nghia Viêt Nam**.

Socialist republic in Indo-China, SE Asia.

NATIONAL FLAG AND ENSIGN

Adopted 30 November 1955. Proportions 2:3.

The red symbolizes the revolution and the blood shed in the struggle for independence. The five-pointed star represents the unity of workers, peasants, intellectuals, young people and soldiers in building socialism.

MACAO

Macao Special Administrative Region of the People's Republic of China.

Former Portuguese colony in SE Asia.

REGIONAL FLAG

Adopted 31 March 1993, will be in use from 20 December 1999. Proportions 2:3.

The five stars, taken from the flag of China, recall that Macao is an inseparable part of China. The stylized lotus flower stands for the people, and its three petals represent the three islands of Macao. The bridge and the waves are emblematic of the natural environment surrounding Macao.

HONG KONG

Hong Kong Special Administrative Region of the People's Republic of China.

Former British crown colony in SE Asia.

REGIONAL FLAG

Officially hoisted 1 July 1997. Proportions 2:3.

The stylized bauhinia (orchid tree) flower represents the people of Hong Kong. The five red stars, taken from the flag of China, state that the Territory is an inseparable part of China.

PHILIPPINES

Republic of the Philippines,

Tagalog **Republika ng Pilipinas**.

Republic consisting of an archipelago in the Pacific Ocean, SE Asia.

NATIONAL FLAG AND ENSIGN

Adopted 19 May 1898. Colours modified 16 September 1997. Proportions 1:2.

The golden sun with eight rays symbolizes liberty and was championed by the first eight provinces to revolt against Spain. The stars represent the three major regions: Luzon, the Visayas and Mindanao. The white triangle stands for purity and peace while the blue and red symbolize patriotism and bravery respectively. The flag is the only one in the world to change the position of its colours: in time of war the upper stripe is red and the lower blue.

MALAYSIA

Federation of Malaysia,
Malay **Persekutuan Tanah Malaysia**.
Federal constitutional monarchy
in SE Asia.

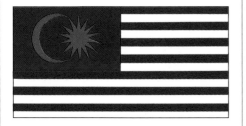

NATIONAL FLAG AND STATE ENSIGN

Adopted 16 September 1963. Proportions 1:2.

The crescent and star is the symbol of
Islam, and the 14 points of the star and the
14 stripes represent the 14 members of the
Federation of Malaysia. (Singapore left the
Federation in 1965 but the flag remains
unchanged.) The blue canton symbolizes the
unity of the peoples of Malaysia and yellow
is the colour of Their Highnesses the rulers.

MALAYSIAN STATES
AND TERRITORIES

Malaysia comprises 13 states and two
federal territories (Kuala Lumpur and
Lebanon). All flags have the proportions
1:2. The crescent and star appear on seven
flags and symbolizes Islam, the faith of the
majority of the population.

JOHOR

NATIONAL FLAG AND ENSIGN

Adopted in 1870.

The white and blue represent the ruler and
the government respectively. The red stands
for the warrior caste Hulabalang.

KEDAH

NATIONAL FLAG

Adopted in 1912.

The red is the traditional colour of the
state. The *padi* represents the main crop
of the state, the crescent stands for Islam
and the shield is a symbol of authority.

KELANTAN

NATIONAL FLAG

Adopted in 1924.

The red symbolizes the loyalty of the people
who are faithful to the ruler. The spears and
daggers represent their strength.

KUALA LUMPUR

FLAG OF THE TERRITORY

Adopted on 15 May 1990.

The blue symbolizes the unity of the
population of this federal territory. The
colour red stands for courage and vigour,
the white for purity, and the yellow for
sovereignty and prosperity.

LABUAN

FLAG OF THE TERRITORY

Date of adoption unknown.

The symbolism of the colours is the same as
the national flag.

MELAKA

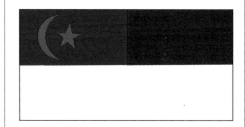

NATIONAL FLAG

Adopted in 1961.

The colours signify that Melaka is a
component state of Malaysia.

NEGERI SEMBILAN

NATIONAL FLAG

Adopted in 1895.

The colours represent the authorities:
the ruler (yellow), the ruling chiefs of
districts (black), and the people (red).

PAHANG

STATE FLAG

Adopted 28 December 1903.

The white stands for the ruler, whose powers depend on the people. Because white can be changed into any other colour, the ruler can be swayed to meet the wishes of the people. The black represents the people, whose rights should not be alienated by the ruler.

PERAK

STATE FLAG

Adopted c.1920.

The colours represent the authorities – the Sultan (white), the Raja Muda (yellow) and the Raja di-Hilir (black).

PERLIS

STATE FLAG

Adopted in 1870.

The yellow stands for the ruler, the blue represents the people. Together the colours symbolize co-operation between the ruler and his subjects.

PINANG

STATE FLAG

Adopted in 1949.

The tree is *pokok pinang*, the betel nut tree (*Areca catechu*) after which the state is named. The blue represents the sea that surrounds the island, the white stands for the state itself in its serenity and the yellow represents prosperity.

SABAH

STATE FLAG

Adopted 16 September 1988.

This is the only flag in the world with displays three different shades of blue: royal (silhouette of Mount Kinabalu), icicle (canton) and zircon (upper stripe). Mt Kinabalu represents the state of Sabah. The zircon blue symbolizes peace and tranquillity, the white purity and justice, the red courage and conviction, the icicle blue unity and prosperity, and the royal blue strength and co-operation.

SARAWAK

STATE FLAG

Adopted 31 August 1988.

The flag displays the colours established in 1870 and used until 1973. At that time the flag was yellow charged with a cross divided vertically into black and red portions. The yellow denotes the supremacy of law and order, and unity and stability in diversity. The black represents the natural resources (petroleum, timber etc), that provide the foundation for the advancement of the people. The red stands for the courage, determination and sacrifices of the people in their tireless pursuit to attain and maintain progress and esteem in the course of creating a model state. The star embodies the aspiration of the people to improve their quality of life; its nine points represent the nine divisions of the state.

CHANGING FLAGS

While Johor, Negeri Sembilan and Perlis still use flags adopted more than a hundred years ago, Sabah and Sarawak have changed their flags several times over the last half a century. In the 1980s both states had flags similar to Czechoslavakia's (now the Czech Republic). From 1973 to 1988, the flag of Sarawak had red and white stripes and a blue triangle. From 1982 to 1988, the flag of Sabah had blue and white stripes and a red triangle.

From 1925 to 1933, the national flag of Terengganu was black with a vertical white stripe at the hoist. In 1933 a white Muslim crescent and star was placed in the centre of the black portion of the flag, and in 1947 the design of the flag was changed to the current one.

SELANGOR

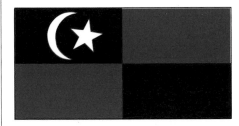

STATE FLAG

Adopted in 1965.

The yellow and red symbolize flesh and blood respectively, giving life and strength to the state.

TERENGGANU

STATE FLAG

Adopted in 1947.

The flag is a graphic representation of the protection that the sultan (white) spreads around his subjects (black).

BRUNEI

State of Brunei,
Malay **Negara Brunei Darussalam**.
Absolute monarchy in SE Asia.

STATE FLAG, CIVIL AND STATE ENSIGN

Adopted 29 September 1959. Proportions 1:2.

The flag in its present form, except for the crest, has been in use since 1906 when Brunei became a protected state. The colours are those of the flags of the principal signatories to the agreement between Brunei and the United Kingdom: the Sultan (yellow), Pengiran Bendahara (white) and Pengiran Pemancha (black). The crest was added in 1959. The mast and pedestal represent the three levels of government, and the four feathers symbolize justice, tranquillity, peace and prosperity. The hands signify that the government preserves and promotes the welfare of the citizens. The crescent stands for Islam, the state religion. The state motto, written in Arabic script, means "Always render service by God's guidance". The name of the state appears on the ribbon.

SINGAPORE

Republic of Singapore,
Malay **Repablik Singapura**,
Chinese **Xinjiapo Gongheguo**,
Tamil **Sinkappur Kutijarasu**.
Republic comprising mainly Singapore Island in SE Asia.

STATE FLAG

Officially hoisted 3 December 1959.
Proportions 2:3.

The colours represent universal brotherhood (red), and purity and virtue (white). The crescent stands for "a young country on the ascent in its ideals of establishing democratic peace, progress, justice and equality as indicated by the five stars".

INDONESIA

Republic of Indonesia,
Bahasa **Indonesia Republik Indonesia**.
Republic consisting of an archipelago in SE Asia.

NATIONAL FLAG AND ENSIGN

Adopted 17 August 1945. Proportions 2:3.

The flag, officially called *Sang Dwiwarna* (exalted bicolour), symbolizes a living person. The red represents the body and physical life, the white the soul and spiritual life.

STATES OF INDONESIA

Since 1945 Indonesia has been a unitary republic made up of 28 provinces. Before 1945, however, under Dutch rule, Indonesia was composed of more than 200 states, many of which were sultanates. Most of these had their own national flags and ensigns as well as flags of the ruler and other state dignitaries. For example the state of Sambas on the Island of Sumatra had a grand total of 28 distinguishing and rank flags. So, at any time in the 19th century there were thousands of flags in use over vast areas of current Indonesia.

Until 1881, Indonesian seafaring vessels used the flag of whichever state they represented; after this time, however, the Dutch authorities began to enforce the law that they must use the Dutch ensign.

MONGOLIA

State of Mongolia,
Mongolian **Mongol Uls**.
Republic in E Central Asia.

NATIONAL FLAG

Introduced 12 February 1992. Proportions 1:2.

The basic design of the flag dates from 1940. In 1992 the star surmounting the emblem was removed and the design of the *Soyonbo*, an ancient Mongolian symbol, was modified. The blue is the traditional colour of the Mongols and other Turkic peoples and the two red vertical stripes symbolize the double joys of liberty and independence.

The *Soyonbo* is accompanied by several other ancient symbols. The arrowheads, or triangles, pointing downwards mean "Death to the enemy"; two signifying "Death to the enemies of the people". The triangle is a symbol of straightforwardness, honesty and adherence to principles. The two fish in the centre represent men and women. As fish never sleep they are a reminder that

SOYONBO

Marco Polo was the first European to report that Mongolian flags were charged with the sun and moon. In fact, the ancient sign of *Soyonbo* is composed of the sun, moon and fire. Together they represent the wish, "May you live and flourish forever". Fire denotes prosperity, regeneration and ascent, and the three tongues of flame stand for the past, present and future. The sun and moon symbolize the belief that the Mongolians are children of the sun (mother) and moon (father).

the people should always be vigilant for their country. The horizontal bars above and below this image indicate that the highest and the lowest in society should be honest and straightforward in the service of the people. A vertical bar represents a fortress; the two bars illustrate the proverb, "Two friends are stronger than stone".

TIBET

Tibetan **Bod rang-skyong ljongs**,
Chinese **Xi-zang**.
Region of China with limited autonomy,
E Central Asia.

CIVIL FLAG

Adopted in 1912. Proportions unspecified.

The white triangle represents a mountain covered with snow, symbolizing Tibet's location in the Himalaya Mountains. The two lions represent harmony between temporal and spiritual rule. They are holding the wishing gem. This symbolizes the rule of law based on the principle of cause and effect underlying the Ten Golden Precepts and the Sixteen Humane Principles of Buddhism, which are the source of infinite benefit and peace. Above the gem stand the three flaming jewels", representing Buddha (God), Dharma (the Doctrine) and Sangha (the saints, guardians of the Doctrine).

The sun is a symbol of freedom, happiness and prosperity. Its 12 rays represent the 12 descendants of the six aboriginal tribes of Tibet. Their colours are symbolic of the two guardian deities (male and female) protecting the flag. The yellow border of the flag indicates the spread of the golden ideals of Buddhism.

CHINA

People's Republic of China,
Chinese **Zhonghua Renmin Gonghe Guo**.
Socialist republic in E and Central Asia.

NATIONAL FLAG AND ENSIGN

Adopted 1 October 1949. Proportions 2:3.

The red stands for the communist revolution and the large star is a symbol of the communist party. The four smaller stars represent the workers, peasants, bourgeoisie and patriotic capitalists who are united in building communism.

TAIWAN

Republic of China,
Chinese **Chung Hua Min Kuo**.
Republic consisting of an island in Pacific Ocean, E Asia.

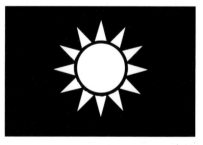

NATIONAL FLAG AND STATE ENSIGN

*Adopted 28 October 1928.
Proportions 2:3.*

The flag, adopted as the national flag and war ensign of China, was retained by the nationalist forces, which were defeated by the communists and in 1949 found refuge on the island of Taiwan. The 12 rays of the white sun represent the 12 two-hour periods of the day, and together they symbolize the spirit of unceasing progress.

YIN-YANG

The two elements, the feminine yin and the masculine yang, together form a disc, a figure enclosed by a circle, which is a symbol of infinity, perfection and eternity. The red part is the positive element yang, representing the sun, light, day, heaven, movement and activity. The blue part is the negative element yin, symbolizing the moon, darkness, night, earth, immobility and passivity. The yin-yang reflects the immemorial relationship of contradictions and encompasses all opposites such as good and evil, truth and lies, warmth and coldness, life and death. This dualism (yin-yang) in the absolute (the circle) reflects the paradoxes of life and suggests that it is impossible to comprehend fully the complexities of existence and the universe.

The colours stand for the three principles of the people – democracy (blue), the people's livelihood (white) and nationalism (red). The colours also have a dual meaning: blue stands for equality and justice, the white for fraternity and frankness, and the red for liberty and sacrifice.

NORTH KOREA

People's Democratic Republic of Korea,
Korean **Chosun Minchu-chui Inmin Konghwa-guk**.
Socialist state in N part of Korean Peninsula, E Asia.

NATIONAL FLAG AND ENSIGN

Adopted 8 September 1948. Proportions 1:2.

The star symbolizes the revolutionary traditions established by President Kim Il Sung. The red represents revolutionary patriotism and the fighting spirit, and the white stands for the Korean nation and its culture. The blue stripes symbolize "the aspiration of the Korean people to unite with the revolutionary people of the whole world and fight for the victory of the idea of independence, friendship and peace".

SOUTH KOREA

Republic of Korea,
Korean **Taehan Min-guk**.
Republic in S part of the Korean Peninsula, E Asia.

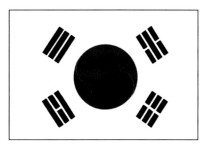

NATIONAL FLAG, CIVIL AND STATE ENSIGN

Adopted in 1882, last time modified 21 February 1984. Proportions 2:3.

The white is the Korean national colour, a symbol of purity, peace and justice. The central emblem is a reflection of Chinese cosmogony, in which the opposites of yin and yang unify and co-operate. The yin-yang, a synthesis of the Great Beginning, is called *taeguk* in Korean and from this the flag derives its name *Taeguki*. In the corners are four trigrams, which are also composed of the yin (broken bars) and yang (unbroken bars). Clockwise from the upper hoist, the trigrams symbolize:
(i) heaven, the south and summer,
(ii) the moon, the west, autumn and water,
(iii) the earth, the north and winter, and
(iv) the sun, the east, spring and fire. The black stands for vigilance, perseverance, justice and chastity.

JAPAN

Japanese **Nippon (Nihon)**.
Constitutional monarchy consisting of an island chain in Pacific Ocean, E Asia.

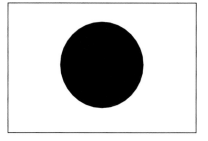

CIVIL AND STATE FLAG AND ENSIGN

Officially adopted 5 August 1854. Proportions 2:3.

This flag, called *Hinomaru* (disc of the sun) has been in use at least since the 14th century. The red sun recalls the name of Japan (the Land of the Rising Sun) and worship of Amaterasu Omikami (the Sun Goddess), the most venerated goddess in the Shinto religion. The colours also reflect the spirit of Shinto ethics, based on a bright, pure, just and gentle heart. The white stands for purity and integrity, the red for sincerity, brightness and warmth.

SOLAR DISC

The most common feature appearing on flags in the Far East is the disc, which usually represents the sun. The disc appears in many different colours. For example, in Sakha, North Korea and Laos the disc is white; the Mongol banners in the 13th century and the civil ensign of China 1872-1912 feature a yellow disc. In Japan and Bangladesh it is red; in South Korea the disc is red-blue.

The sun is one of humanity's oldest symbols and symbolizes divinity, majesty, life, beauty and goodness. So it is no surprise that the solar disc is often used on flags to represent a ruler.

Flags of Australia and Oceania

The current national flags of the
countries of Australasia and Oceania,
from Christmas Island and Australia to
French Polynesia and the Pitcairn Islands,
are illustrated and described in the
following pages, together with the flags
of their territories, states and provinces.

The countries of this continent, scattered
throughout the Pacific Ocean, have
been grouped together for ease of reference.
We begin in Australia and move swiftly
on to the vast Pacific Ocean which
is harnessed into the west Pacific,
central Pacific, south-west Pacific and
finally, the south-east Pacific Ocean.

For each entry, the country or territory's
name is given in its most easily recognized
form and then in all its official languages.
This is followed by a description of its
political status and geographic position.
The basic data for each flag contains the
status of the flag, date of adoption,
proportions, and the symbolic meaning.

Guam

Palau

Pap[

Christmas Island

Torres Strait Islands

Australia

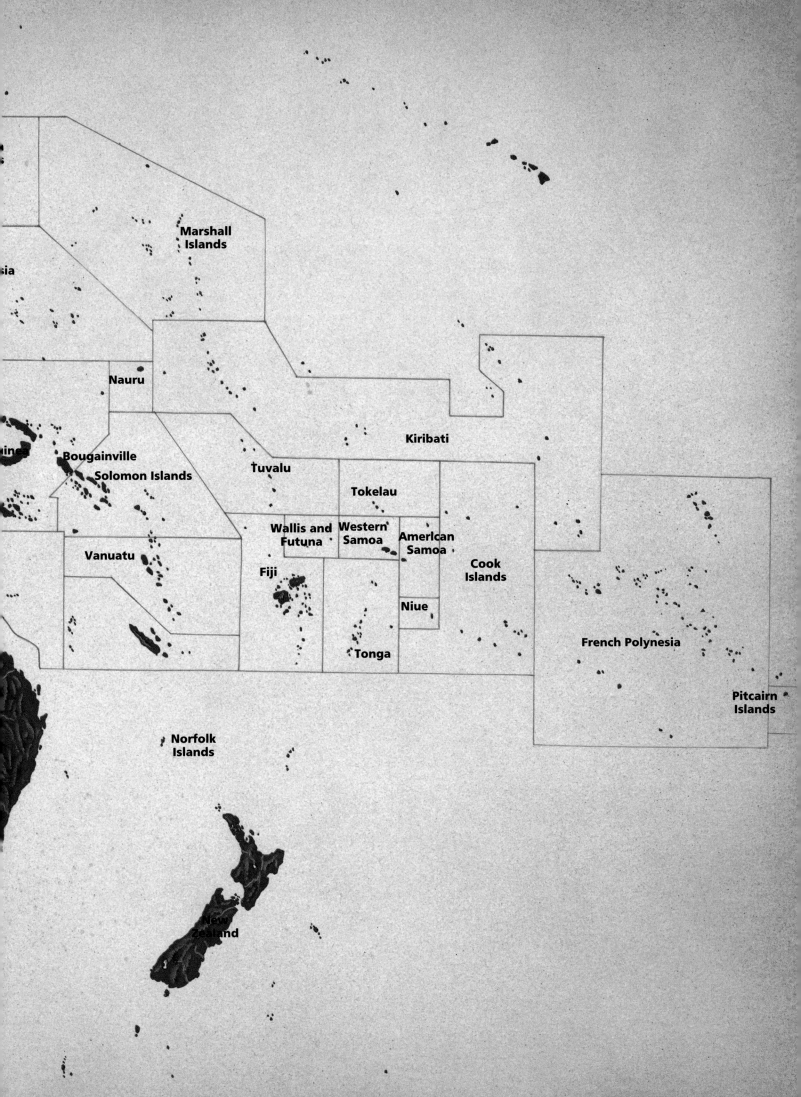

AUSTRALIA

CHRISTMAS ISLAND

Territory of Christmas Island
Autonomous external territory of Australia in
E Indian Ocean.

NATIONAL FLAG

Introduced in 1987. Proportions 1:2.

The yellow and green, the national colours
of Australia, and the stars of the Southern
Cross constellation symbolize the island's
association with Australia. The blue stands
for the Indian Ocean, the green for the
tropical rainforest and the bird is a golden
bosun, unique to the island. A graphic
representation of the island appears on the
yellow disc in the centre of the flag.

TORRES STRAIT ISLANDS

Part of Queensland (Australia)
with limited autonomy.

NATIONAL FLAG AND CIVIL ENSIGN

Introduced in May 1992. Proportions 23:31.

The traditional *dhari* headdress symbolizes
the inhabitants of the islands, which are
represented by the star. The green stands for
the land, the blue for the sea and the black
for the indigenous people.

AUSTRALIA

Commonwealth of Australia.
Federal constitutional monarchy comprising the
continent of Australia.

NATIONAL FLAG

*Introduced in 1901, approved by the
King of Great Britain in 1903. Proportions 1:2.*

The British blue ensign, charged with five
stars forming the Southern Cross and a
sixth to represent the Commonwealth of
Australia, was the design chosen in a
competition in 1901, which attracted
30,000 entries. Subsequently there were
some changes to the stars until their shape,
size and position were precisely specified
on 15 April 1954. The six points of the
Star of the Commonwealth represent the
six states, and the seventh stands for the
Northern Territory and the six external
territories of Australia.

THE SOUTHERN CROSS

The crux is the most distinctive
constellation of the southern
hemisphere. It is visible in the night
skies from south of about 30°N
latitude. Of the main four stars the
largest is the bottom one, the double
star acrux, and the brightest is the star
on the left, the *Alpha crucis*. This bright
constellation was used as a navigational
aid by the islanders in Oceania and by
the European discoverers. It became a
popular emblem among the settlers,
and since the 19th century has been
displayed on many flags in the
southern hemisphere.

AUSTRALIAN STATES AND TERRITORY

The state flags follow the design of the
British colonial flags, i.e. the blue ensign
in proportions 1:2, charged with a badge.
Almost all of them are older than the
national flag of Australia.

NEW SOUTH WALES

STATE FLAG

Granted 11 July 1876.

The cross of St George is charged with
the English lion and the four stars of the
Southern Cross.

NORTHERN TERRITORY

FLAG OF THE TERRITORY

Adopted 1 July 1978.

Black and ochre are the official colours of
the territory. The stars form the Southern
Cross constellation. The seven petals of
the highly stylized Sturt's desert rose
(*Gossypium sturtianum*) and the seven-
pointed star in its centre represent the
seven states-to-be of Australia.

QUEENSLAND

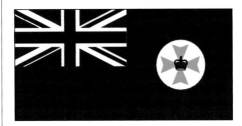

STATE FLAG

Granted 29 November 1876.

The badge displays a blue Maltese cross surmounted by a royal crown. The shape of the cross resembles the insignia of the military award for valour, known as the Victoria Cross.

SOUTH AUSTRALIA

STATE FLAG

Adopted 13 January 1904.

The golden disc, which symbolizes the rising sun, is charged with a black and white piping shrike (*Gymnorhina tibicen hypoleuca*) perched on the branch of a gum tree. The piping shrike, or white-backed magpie, is the South Australian bird emblem.

TASMANIA

STATE FLAG

Adopted 25 September 1876.

The badge on Tasmania's flag is white with a heraldic lion in red. The same red lion appears in the crest of the Tasmanian coat of arms and the arms of the city of Hobart.

VICTORIA

STATE FLAG

Adopted 30 November 1877.

The flag of Victoria is the only state flag that does not bear a badge. Since 1870 it has been charged with the five stars of the constellation of the Southern Cross. The Tudor crown was added in 1877 and originally signified the state's ties to Queen Victoria and Britain. In 1952 it was replaced by St Edward's crown.

WESTERN AUSTRALIA

STATE FLAG

Adopted in 1953.

As early as 1830, a black swan (*Cygnus atratus*) became the emblem of the colony, which was also known as "the Swan River Colony". Aboriginal legend tells how the ancestors of a section of the Bibbulman tribe of western Australia were originally black swans who changed into men.

The badge, introduced on 27 November 1875, was yellow with the black swan turned out to the fly; in 1953 a mirror image of this was introduced instead.

THE CHANGING STARS

The first recorded attempt to adopt the national flag of Australia occurred in 1824 when Captain John Bingle and Captain John Nicholson charged the British white ensign with four stars. Each of the white eight-pointed stars was placed in the middle of each arm of the St. George's Cross.

In 1831, Captain J. Nicholson introduced a New South Wales ensign of very similar design. The colour of the cross was changed to dark blue and the fifth star was positioned in the centre of the cross. This flag became

very popular in Australia and in the 1880s and 1890s was the chief symbol of the political movement towards the federation of Australian territories.

The first national flag of Australia was hoisted for the first time on 3 September 1901. It was the British blue ensign charged with a large star underneath the canton and five stars forming the constellation of the Southern Cross in the fly. The larger star, called the Commonwealth Star, had six points representing the six states of the new

nation. The five stars in the fly had nine, eight, seven, six and five points, reflecting the brightness of the Southern Cross. In 1903, after minor modification, this flag became the current national flag of Australia.

In the last two decades there were several attempts to design and introduce a new national flag without the Union Jack in the canton. It is quite probable that in the near future Australia will have a new flag and it is almost certain that any new design will incorporate the stars of the Southern Cross.

WEST PACIFIC OCEAN

PAPUA NEW GUINEA

**Independent State of
Papua New Guinea**, Pidgin **Papua Niugini.**
Constitutional monarchy in E part of
New Guinea, W Pacific Ocean.

NATIONAL FLAG, STATE AND CIVIL ENSIGN

Approved 11 March 1971. Proportions 3:4.

Young student Susan Hareho Karike, designer of the flag, chose red and black because of the widespread use of these colours in traditional native art. The Empress of Germany's bird of paradise (*Paradisaea raggiana augustae-victoriae*) is peculiar to the island of New Guinea. The five stars form the constellation of the Southern Cross, symbolizing the relationship with Australia and also referring to a local legend about five sisters.

The flag was only for use on land from 1971 to 16 September 1975, when the country became independent.

BOUGAINVILLE

Republic of Bougainville.
Secessionist province of Papua New Guinea
in W Pacific Ocean.

NATIONAL FLAG

Introduced 1 September 1975. Proportions 1:2.

When the province of North Solomons broke ties with Papua New Guinea in May 1990 and proclaimed independence under the name of Bougainville, its flag remained unchanged. The blue background symbolizes the Pacific Ocean surrounding Bougainville, which is represented by the centrally positioned emblem. The black disc recalls the native Bougainvillean people. In its centre is an *upe*, head-dress associated with the transition of young men from adolescence to manhood. The red stripes on the *upe* generally suggest leadership. A broad central stripe and two narrower lateral stripes represent men and women, since for ceremonial occasions all men paint the centre of their hair red, whilst the women decorate the sides of their hair red and leave the centre black. The disc is framed by a green ring representing the island. The white triangles allude to the carved turtle shells worn by local chiefs and their queens on ceremonial occasions.

SOLOMON ISLANDS

Constitutional monarchy comprising a group
of islands in SW Pacific Ocean.

NATIONAL FLAG

Adopted 18 November 1977. Proportions 1:2.

The stars originally represented the five districts of the country, but in 1982 when the country was divided into seven provinces, it was decided that the stars would instead symbolize the five main groups of islands. The yellow stands for the sun, the blue for water (the sea, rivers and the rain) and the green for land, its trees and food crops.

VANUATU

Republic of Vanuatu,
Bislama **Ripablik blong Vanuatu.**
Republic comprising a group of islands
in SW Pacific Ocean.

NATIONAL FLAG AND ENSIGN

*Officially hoisted 30 July 1980.
Proportions 11:18.*

The national emblem consists of two crossed *namele* leaves (*Phoenix sylvestris*) surrounded by a boar's tusk. The leaves symbolize peace and their 39 fronds represent the 39 members of the Representative Assembly. The boar's tusk is a symbol of prosperity. The black represents the people and the rich soil, the yellow (shaped like the archipelago) symbolizes peace and the light of Christianity, the green represents the islands and the red is a symbol of the unity of the Vanuatu people.

NAURU

Republic of Nauru, Nauruan **Naoero.**
Republic comprising an island in
W Central Pacific Ocean.

NATIONAL FLAG AND ENSIGN

Adopted 31 January 1968. Proportions 1:2.

The blue stands for the Pacific Ocean and blue skies. The yellow line stands for the Equator and immediately below it lies the island, represented by a white star. Its 12 points symbolize the 12 original tribes of Nauru.

MICRONESIA

Federated States of Micronesia.

Federal republic comprising most islands of the Caroline group in N Pacific Ocean.

NATIONAL FLAG AND ENSIGN

Adopted 30 November 1978. Proportions 1:2.

The blue represents the Pacific Ocean. The stars stand for the groups of islands forming the Federation.

MICRONESIAN STATES

Since 1947 the Caroline Islands (Chuuk, Kosrae, Palau, Pohnpei and Yap) have been administered by the USA as part of the United Nations Trust Territory of the Pacific Islands. Palau did not join the Federated States of Micronesia created in 1979.

Although some of the four constituent states have established proportions for their flags, the flags are manufactured in the United States in the standard proportions of 2:3 and 3:5.

CHUUK

Adopted 7 September 1979, approved 28 January 1980.

The blue stands for peace. The 38 stars represent the 38 municipalities and the coconut tree in the centre is a symbol of the local agriculture.

KOSRAE

Adopted 30 July 1981.

The blue represents the Pacific Ocean. The *fafa* pounding stone symbolizes local culture, custom, knowledge and prosperity. The olive branches denote peace and unity among the state and municipal government and the people. The four stars stand for the four main municipalities.

POHNPEI

Adopted in December 1977.

The half coconut shell represents the *sakau* cup. (*Sakau* is a local drink extracted from kava roots and hibiscus bark, and used during traditional ceremonies.) The stars represent the municipalities. The coconut branches signify the people's dependence on coconut resources.

YAP

Adopted 30 May 1980, officially hoisted 1 March 1981.

The blue stands for the Pacific Ocean, the white for peace and brotherhood. The highly stylized outrigger canoe is a symbol of the means and ways of accomplishment. The large circle symbolizes unity, while the smaller one represents the state and the people. The star is symbolic of guidance and the state's goals.

PALAU

Republic of Palau, Palauan Belau.

Federal republic comprising a group of islands in NW Pacific Ocean.

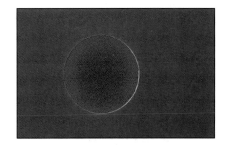

NATIONAL FLAG AND ENSIGN

Adopted 13 June 1980. Proportions 3:5.

The blue stands for the final transition from foreign domination to independence. The disc in the centre represents the full moon, which is the time for fishing, cutting trees, canoe-carving, planting, harvesting and celebrating.

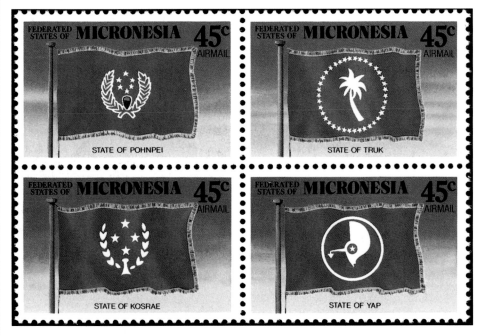

ABOVE
State flags on Micronesian postage stamps: (*clockwise from top left*)
Pohnpei; Truk (Chuuk); Kosra; Yap.

GUAM

Territory of Guam.

Unincorporated United States territory comprising the largest of the Mariana Islands in NW Pacific Ocean.

CIVIL AND STATE FLAG

Approved 9 February 1948. Proportions 22:41.

The basic design of the flag was approved on 4 July 1917, and in 1948 a narrow red border was added. The blue stands for the Pacific Ocean. The seal is in the shape of a sling-shot used by the ancient Chamorros for hunting and warfare. It is a symbol of the protection and endurance of the home government. The seal depicts a typical landscape in Guam, seen from the mouth of the Agana River. The lonely coconut palm tree escaped being uprooted during the destructive typhoon of 1918 and therefore it symbolizes perseverance, courage, strength and usefulness (coconut is the main crop of the island). In the distance is "Two Lovers' Point" which represents faithfulness to a good cause. According to legend, two lovers preferred to kill themselves by jumping from the Point rather than be forced to marry someone they did not love. The outrigger canoe recalls the fame of the native people, the Chamorros, for their nautical skills. It stands for bravery and skill in making the best of one's environment.

NORTHERN MARIANAS

Commonwealth of the Northern Mariana Islands.

Self-governing incorporated United States territory in NW Pacific Ocean.

NATIONAL FLAG AND ENSIGN

Introduced 1 July 1989. Proportions 20:39 (de facto 2:3 or 3:5).

The first flag, adopted in 1972 and introduced in 1976, was blue with a large white star in the centre, superimposed over a grey *latte* stone in silhouette (*latte* stones, columns of limestone, were used to support traditional houses). In 1989 the emblem was surrounded with a garland of flowers and shells. It underwent some modification in 1991 and 1995.

The blue symbolizes the Pacific Ocean, which surrounds the islands with love and peace, and the star represents the Commonwealth. The *latte* stone symbolizes the culture of the Chamorro people. The circular head wreath made from four flowers (*ylang-ylang*, *seyur*, *ang'gha* and *teibwo*) is a symbol of the indigenous Carolinian culture.

CENTRAL PACIFIC OCEAN

KIRIBATI

Republic of Kiribati.

Republic comprising three groups of islands in E Central Pacific Ocean.

NATIONAL FLAG AND ENSIGN

Officially hoisted 12 July 1979. Proportions 1:2.

This is the heraldic banner of arms of Kiribati. The frigate bird (*Fregata minor*) is a symbol of authority, freedom and traditional dances. The rising sun stands for the Equator, whose length within the borders of Kiribati is more than 4000 km (2500 miles). The white and blue waves symbolize the Pacific Ocean, of which some 5 million sq km (2 million sq miles) belong to Kiribati.

TOKELAU

Overseas territory of New Zealand comprising a group of islands in Central Pacific Ocean.

NATIONAL FLAG

Adopted in October 1986. Proportions 1:2.

The blue represents the Pacific Ocean. The silhouette of a palm tree represents the local flora and the three stars stand for the atolls of Atafu, Fakaofo and Nukunonu.

AMERICAN SAMOA

Territory of American Samoa.
Self-governing United States overseas territory in Central Pacific Ocean.

CIVIL AND STATE FLAG

Adopted 27 April 1960. Proportions 1:2.

The colours are those of the United States flag, the *Stars and Stripes*. The American bald eagle, a symbol of protection, is holding in its talons a *fue*, or fly switch, the Samoan chief's attribute and a symbol of wisdom, and a *nifo oti*, a Samoan dancing knife. The fact that the eagle holds these symbols of Samoan authority and culture indicates the friendship between Samoan and American people.

SAMOA

Independent State of Samoa,
Samoan **Malotutu'atasi o Samoa i Sisifo.**
Constitutional monarchy in Central Pacific Ocean.

NATIONAL FLAG AND ENSIGN

Adopted 26 April 1949. Proportions 1:2.

On 26 May 1948, before adoption of the current flag, a similar flag with four stars was approved for use on land only. The five stars represent the constellation of the Southern Cross. The colours represent the qualities of freedom (blue), purity (white) and courage (red).

WALLIS AND FUTUNA

French **Territoire des Îles Wallis et Futuna.**
Autonomous French overseas territory in Central Pacific Ocean.

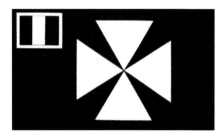

NATIONAL FLAG AND CIVIL ENSIGN

Introduced in 1888.

Originally a red flag with a white cross pattée was used in the 19th century in Uvea. The cross was introduced by the first Marist Brothers, the French missionaries who established the missions. When, in 1886, the Queen of Wallis accepted the French Protectorate it was agreed to charge the canton with the French *Tricolore*.

TUVALU

South West Pacific State of Tuvalu.
Constitutional monarchy comprising an island group in Central Pacific Ocean.

NATIONAL FLAG AND ENSIGN

Officially hoisted 1 October 1978, re-established 11 April 1997. Proportions 1:2.

The British blue ensign, with the field changed to light blue, is charged with nine yellow stars, representing the nine islands of the nation (Nanumea, Niutao, Nanumanga, Nui, Vaitupua, Nukufetau, Funafuti, Nukulaelae and Niulakita). The arrangement of the stars reflects the positions of the islands on the map, oriented to the east (east is at the top of the flag instead of north).

MARSHALL ISLANDS

Republic of the Marshall Islands,
Marshallese **Republic eo an Aelon in Majel.**
Republic consisting of two chains of islands in NW Pacific Ocean.

NATIONAL FLAG AND ENSIGN

Officially hoisted 1 May 1979. Proportions 10:19.

The blue stands for the Pacific Ocean. The star represents the nation, and its 24 points stand for the 24 municipalities. The four longer rays stand for Majuro (the capital), Wotji, Jaluit and Kwajalein. These rays form a cross, the symbol of the Christian faith of the islanders. The position of the star reflects the geographical position of the Marshall Islands a few degrees north of the Equator, which is represented by two stripes. Their shape (widening to the fly) symbolizes the increase in growth and vitality of life. The orange stands for wealth and bravery, the white for brightness.

FIJI

Republic of Fiji.

Republic comprising a group of islands
in S Pacific Ocean.

NATIONAL FLAG

Officially hoisted 10 October 1970.
Proportions 1:2.

For the first time in history, the colour of
the blue ensign was changed to distinguish
this flag from the flags of Australia and
New Zealand. The light blue symbolizes the
Pacific Ocean. The central device on the
shield of arms, granted in 1908, is the cross
of St George separating local agricultural
products (sugar cane, coconuts and
bananas) and a flying dove with a breadfruit
leaf in its beak, the emblem of the
Kingdom of Fiji (1871–1874). On the
upper part of the shield is a British lion
holding a coconut between its paws.

TONGA

Kingdom of Tonga.

Constitutional monarchy in S Pacific Ocean.

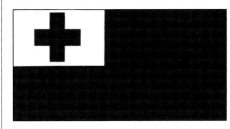

NATIONAL FLAG, CIVIL AND STATE ENSIGN

Adopted 4 November 1875. Proportions 1:2.

The flag reflects the deep-rooted
Christianity in Tonga. The cross reminds
the people that they owe their salvation to
the sacrifice made by Jesus on the Cross,
the red represents the blood Jesus shed
and the white stands for purity

NIUE

Associated State of New Zealand, an island
in S Pacific Ocean.

NATIONAL FLAG

Adopted in 1975. Proportions 1:2.

The larger star stands for Niue, the smaller
ones symbolize links with New Zealand.
The Union flag recalls the protectorate
Great Britain established in 1899 following
a request made by the kings and chiefs of
Niue. The golden yellow symbolizes "the
bright sunshine of Niue and the warm
feelings of the Niuean people toward New
Zealand and her people".

COOK ISLANDS

Associated State of New Zealand, a group
of islands in S Pacific Ocean.

NATIONAL FLAG

Officially hoisted 4 August 1979.
Proportions 1:2.

The British blue ensign stands for links
with New Zealand. The 15 stars represent
the 15 islands. The stars symbolize heaven,
faith in God and the power that has
guided the inhabitants of the islands
throughout their history. The circle stands
for unity and strength.

OCEANIA

For many years Oceanic societies did not
use flags and only some of them used
vexilloids. This began to change, however,
when the Europeans discovered this area
of the world, bringing their influences
with them. The Spanish first explored the
Pacific Ocean in the 16th century, the
Dutch in the 17th and the British in the
18th. The French were the first to establish
a protectorate in Polynesia, followed by the
Germans in Samoa and then the British and
the Americans. Most of the French colonies
had their own flags and the British had
state ensigns and governor's flags. Most
American colonies have only adopted their
own flags in the last few decades.

Looking at the flags of this area can be a
history lesson in itself. Many flags from the
colonial period are featured in *Flags
through the Ages*. The flag of the governor
of the German colonies is shown in context
in *Government Flags: governors and envoys*
and closely follows the German national
flag of that time. Other flags clearly show
their colonial roots in the chapter *Flag
Families*: Rimatara and Tongatapu are part
of the family of the *Christian cross*; the
Gilbert and Ellice Islands and the Soloman
islands are based on the *Union Jack*, and
Tahiti, Raiatea and Rimatara show
influences from the *French Tricolore*. Many
flags from the Pacific Islands have adopted
the United Nations blue as this colour also
symbolizes the Pacific Ocean.

The royal flag of Tonga is the oldest
example of an armorial banner used as the
flag of a head of state and dates from
1862; it is still in use today: see the chapter,
Emperors, Sovereigns and Presidents.
Tonga's war ensign is clearly based on
the British white ensign: see *Navy Ensigns
and Flags*.

SOUTH-WEST PACIFIC OCEAN

NORFOLK ISLANDS

Territory of Norfolk Islands.
External territory of Australia with full internal autonomy, SW Pacific Ocean.

NATIONAL FLAG

Adopted 11 January 1980.
Official proportions 1:2.

The central emblem of the flag is a Norfolk Island pine (*Araucaria heterophylla*). It appeared on the official seal for the first time in 1856.

NEW ZEALAND

Dominion of New Zealand.
Constitutional monarchy consisting of several islands in SW Pacific Ocean.

NATIONAL FLAG AND STATE ENSIGN

Adopted 12 June 1902. Proportions 1:2.

On 23 October 1869 this flag was adopted as the ensign of government vessels, and from 1902 it has also been the civil and state flag. The fly is charged with the four main stars of the Southern Cross constellation.

MAORI FLAGS

The native inhabitants of New Zealand adopted their first flag in 1857 when they chose their *kingi* (king) of *Niu Tireni* (New Zealand). Actually, there were three flags hoisted jointly one above another. The upper and the lower flags were long red rectangles with a white hoist portion charged with the red cross and three white squares with a red cross. In the middle was a red triangular flag with three white squares charged with a red cross.

More Maori flags appeared in the 1860s during the war against the colonists who were taking Maori land. The main feature of these flags was a red cross.

SOUTH-EAST PACIFIC OCEAN

FRENCH POLYNESIA

French **Territoire d'outre-mer de la Polynésie Française**.
Autonomous French overseas territory in SE Pacific Ocean.

NATIONAL FLAG

Adopted 23 November 1984. Proportions 2:3.

The red-white-red horizontal stripes recall the second national flag of the kingdom of Tahiti which was used from 1829 to 1847. The same flag with the addition of a French *Tricolore* became the flag of the protectorate and was used until 1880. After World War II a version without the canton was in popular, but unofficial, use. In 1975, the authorities agreed to allow the use of the flag with a 1:2:1 ratio of stripes.

To distinguish the flag of French Polynesia from that of Tahiti, the emblem was placed in the centre. Its main feature is a *piragua*, which is a status symbol as well as an indispensable boat used for fishing and transportation. Polynesian society is often compared to a *piragua* and the figures in the *piragua* stand for the five parts of French Polynesia: the Windward Islands, the Leeward Islands, the Tuamotu Archipelago, the Austral Islands and the Marquesas Islands. The golden yellow rays symbolize the sun and light, and the blue and white waves represent the riches of the Pacific on which the people have always relied for their livelihood.

PITCAIRN ISLANDS

British colony in SE Pacific Ocean.

STATE FLAG

Adopted 2 April 1984. Proportions 1:2.

The fly of the British blue ensign is charged with the coat of arms, granted on 4 November 1969. The centrepieces are the Bible and the anchor of the ship the *Bounty*. The green triangle represents the rugged cliffs of the island, the blue stands for the sea. The wheelbarrow in the crest stands for the first settlers, while a miro plant represents the wood the islanders use for carving souvenirs for tourists.

Flags of the Americas

The current national flags of the countries of the Americas, from Greenland and Canada to Argentina and the islands of the South Atlantic, are illustrated and described in the following pages, together with their territories, states and provinces.

For ease of reference, the countries of this huge continent have been grouped into geographical areas. We begin in North America and move on through Central America and the West Indies and the Caribbean. Finally, we look at the flags of the countries of South America and the islands of the South Atlantic.

For each entry, the country or territory's name is given in its most easily recognized form and then in all its official languages. This is followed by a description of its political status and geographic position. The basic data for each flag contains the status of the flag, date of adoption, proportions, and the symbolic meaning.

NORTH AMERICA

GREENLAND

Dan. **Grønland**,

nat. **Kalaalit Nunaat**.

Island NE of North America, outlying part of Denmark with full self-government.

NATIONAL FLAG AND CIVIL ENSIGN.

Adopted 6 June 1985. Proportions 2:3.

The colours derive from the flag of Denmark. The white stands for the ice covering 83 per cent of the island, and the red-white disc symbolizes the northern sun with its lower half sunk in the sea.

CANADA

Federal constitutional monarchy in N America.

NATIONAL FLAG AND ENSIGN

Adopted 15 December 1964, officially hoisted 15 February 1965. Proportions 1:2.

The maple leaf has been the symbol of Canada since at least the middle of the 19th century. Red and white were approved as the official colours of Canada in 1921.

CANADIAN PROVINCES AND TERRITORIES

When the dominion of Canada was created in 1867 there were only four provinces (Ontario, Quebec, Nova Scotia and New Brunswick). Today Canada comprises ten provinces and two territories. Their flags have different official proportions, but in practice almost all are made and displayed in the proportion 1:2.

ALBERTA

PROVINCIAL FLAG

In use since 1967, officially approved 1 June 1968. Proportions 1:2.

The blue field of the flag is charged with the shield of arms, granted on 30 May 1907. The shield displays the cross of St George and a typical landscape in Alberta.

BRITISH COLUMBIA

PROVINCIAL FLAG

Adopted 20 June 1960. Proportions 3:5.

This banner of arms was granted on 31 March 1906. The Union Jack is a reminder of British Columbia's origins as a British colony and stands for its continued links with the United Kingdom. The crown represents the sovereign power that links, in free association, the countries of the Commonwealth. The sun setting over the Pacific Ocean, symbolized by the wavy stripes, reminds us that British Columbia is the most westerly province of Canada.

MANITOBA

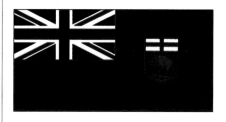

PROVINCIAL FLAG

Adopted 12 May 1966. Proportions 1:2.

The fly of the British red ensign is charged with the shield of arms, granted on 10 May 1905. The shield displays the cross of St George and a buffalo standing on a rock.

NEW BRUNSWICK

PROVINCIAL FLAG

Adopted 24 February 1965. Proportions 5:8.

This is the banner of arms, granted on 26 May 1868. The golden lion symbolizes ties with the United Kingdom. The boat signifies the importance of shipbuilding and seafaring to the province.

NEWFOUNDLAND

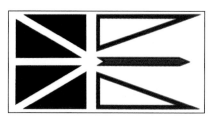

PROVINCIAL FLAG

Adopted 28 May 1980. Proportions 1:2.

The design is based on that of the British Union flag. The colours symbolize snow and ice (white), the sea (blue), human effort (red) and confidence in the future (golden yellow). The two red triangles represent the mainland and island parts of the province. The yellow arrow stands for hope for the future. The trident (formed by the triangles and the arrow) refers to Newfoundland's continued dependence on fishing and the sea.

NOVA SCOTIA

PROVINCIAL FLAG

Officially approved 19 January 1929. Proportions 3:4.

This banner of arms was in use from 1625 to 1868, and was reinstated on 19 January 1929. The field shows the flag of Scotland in reversed colours. The shield displays the Royal Arms of Scotland.

ONTARIO

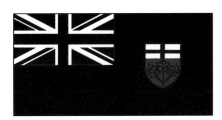

PROVINCIAL FLAG

Approved 21 May 1965. Proportions 1:2.

The fly of the British red ensign is charged with the shield of arms, granted on 26 May 1868. The shield displays the cross of St George and three maple leaves.

PRINCE EDWARD ISLAND

PROVINCIAL FLAG

Adopted 24 March 1964. Proportions 2:3.

The banner of arms was granted on 30 May 1905, having been used on the provincial Great Seal since 1769. The lion symbolizes ties with the United Kingdom. The larger tree is the oak of England and the tree saplings represent the three counties of the province. The green island reminds us that both Britain and the province are islands.

QUEBEC

PROVINCIAL FLAG

Adopted 21 January 1948. Proportions 2:3.

The white cross is taken from an ancient French military colour. The four fleurs-de-lis are based on the emblem of France under the reign of the Bourbons. The flag is called the *Fleurdelisé*.

SASKATCHEWAN

PROVINCIAL FLAG

Adopted 22 September 1969. Proportions 1:2.

The green represents the northern forested areas of the province and the yellow symbolizes the southern grainfield areas. The shield of arms, granted on 25 August 1906 appears in the upper hoist. The fly is charged with the western red lily, which is the floral emblem of the province.

NORTH-WEST TERRITORIES

FLAG OF THE TERRITORY

Adopted 1 January 1969. Proportions 1:2.

The blue vertical stripes represent the lakes and waters of the Territories and the white stands for the snow and ice. In the centre is the shield of arms, granted on 24 February 1956. The white symbolizes the polar icepack, the blue wavy stripe the Northwest Passage, the green the forested areas and the red the tundra. The head of an arctic fox represents the local fauna. The yellow rectangles symbolize mineral riches.

YUKON

FLAG OF THE TERRITORY

Adopted 1 December 1967. Proportions 1:2.

The colours stand for the natural features of the province – the *taiga* forests (green), the winter snows (white) and the northern waters (blue). In the centre are the full arms adopted on 5 November 1956. The cross of St George stands for the first explorers and fur traders from England, the roundel of *vair* (heraldic fur) symbolizes the fur trade, the white and blue wavy lines symbolize the Yukon River and the rivers and creeks where gold was discovered, and the red triangles represent the mountains. The golden balls symbolize the territory's mineral resources, and the malamute dog, noted for its loyalty, stamina and courage, emphasizes the important role these animals played in the early history of the territory. Below the shield are two crossed branches of fireweed. This was adopted in 1956 as the floral emblem of Yukon.

SAINT-PIERRE ET MIQUELON

French **Collectivité territoriale des Îles Saint-Pierre et Miquelon**.
Dependency of France comprising two islands N of North America.

NATIONAL FLAG

This is a heraldic banner of arms. The blue is for the Atlantic Ocean and the ship commemorates French discoverer Jacques Cartier, who came to the islands in 1535. The emblems placed on the vertical stripe at the hoist are a reminder that the colonists came from the Basque Country (*ikkurina*), Brittany (ermine) and Normandy (two lions).

UNITED STATES

United States of America.
Federal republic in Central N America.

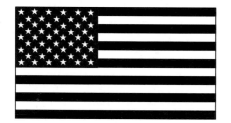

NATIONAL FLAG

Adopted 4 July 1960. Proportions 10:19.

The blue canton symbolizes the union. The 50 stars stand for the 50 states. The 13 stripes represent the 13 colonies which formed the independent nation (New Hampshire, Massachusetts, Rhode Island, Connecticut, Delaware, Maryland, Virginia, North Carolina, South Carolina, Georgia, New York, New Jersey and Pennsylvania). The blue symbolizes loyalty, devotion, friendship, justice and truth; the red stands for courage, zeal and fervency; and the white represents purity and rectitude of conduct.

The *de jure* proportions of the national flag and the state flags are followed only by the government and the armed forces; the flags used by the general public are manufactured in the proportions of 2:3, 3:5 and 5:8.

AMERICAN STATES

The union formed in 1776 by 13 former British independent colonies has grown over the years, and since 1960 comprises 50 states and the federal District of Columbia. Most of the state flags displaying the arms or seal on a blue background are based on state military colours; some of them retain the proportions of these colours (26:33).

ALABAMA

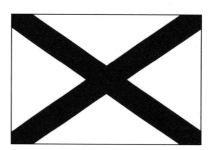

STATE FLAG

Adopted 16 February 1895.
Official proportions 1:1, actual flags 2:3.

The red saltire stands for the most distinctive feature of the Confederate battle flag (a blue saltire with white stars).

ALASKA

STATE FLAG

Adopted 2 May 1927. Proportions 125:177.

This is the winning design in a flag contest. The blue represents the evening sky, the sea and mountain lakes, and the wild flowers that grow in Alaska. The golden yellow symbolizes the wealth that lies hidden in Alaska's hills and streams. The stars form the most conspicuous constellation in the northern sky, *Ursa major* (the Great Bear). The eighth star is Polaris, the North Star, "the ever-constant star for the mariner, explorer, hunter, trapper, prospector, woodsman and surveyor".

ARIZONA

STATE FLAG

Adopted 27 February 1917. Proportions 2:3.

Blue and gold are the colours of Arizona and the flag represents the copper star of Arizona rising from a blue field in front of the setting sun; mining is the most important industry of Arizona and copper is its main product. The red and yellow are the colours of Spain and are a reminder that the first whites to enter Arizona in 1540 were the Spanish *conquistadores*, headed by Coronado.

ARKANSAS

STATE FLAG

Adopted 10 April 1924. Proportions not specified.

The colours of the flag are those of both the United States and the Confederate States of America. The 25 white stars record that Arkansas was the 25th state admitted to the Union. The diamond shape indicates that Arkansas was the only diamond producing state of the Union, and the star above the name of the state commemorates the Confederacy. The other blue stars have a double meaning: they represent Spain, France and the United States, to which Arkansas successively belonged, and note that Arkansas was the third state formed out of the Louisiana Purchase.

CALIFORNIA

STATE FLAG

Adopted 3 February 1911. Proportions 2:3.

The design is based on the flag hoisted in Sonoma on 14 June 1846 when a group of Americans proclaimed an independent California republic. The grizzly bear is a symbol of strength.

COLORADO

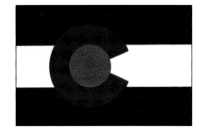

STATE FLAG

Adopted in 1911, officially approved 31 March 1964. Proportions 2:3.

The colours stand for the skies (blue), the gold (yellow), the mountain snows (white) and the soil (red). The capital "C" represents the name of the state.

CONNECTICUT

STATE FLAG

Introduced in 1895, adopted 3 June 1897. Proportions 26:33.

This is the design of the military colours from the Civil War period. The arms were granted on 25 October 1711. The three grapevines symbolize the three original settlements (Hartford, Windsor and Wethersfield), which formed the Colony of Connecticut in 1639. The motto means "He Who Transplanted Still Sustains".

DELAWARE

STATE FLAG

Adopted 24 July 1913. Proportions not specified.

The diamond stands for the state's nickname, the "Diamond State". The arms, adopted in 1777, indicate that the main industry is agriculture. The blue wavy stripe stands for the Delaware River. The ship in the crest recalls the fact that Delaware has access to the sea and to the benefits of commerce. The date recalls the day on which Delaware was the first state to ratify the Federal Constitution.

FLORIDA

STATE FLAG

Adopted 6 November 1900, seal modified in 1966 and 1985.

The red saltire is based on the battle flag of the Confederacy. The seal depicts a typical landscape in Florida, with an American Indian woman representing the original inhabitants of the peninsula.

GEORGIA

STATE FLAG

Adopted 13 February 1956 (effective 1 July 1956). Proportions 2:3.

The flag prominently displays the battle flag of the Confederacy and the state seal, with its tenets of wisdom, justice and moderation. The blue stands for reverence to God, loyalty, sincerity and justice; the white stands for purity; and the red for valour and sacrifice.

HAWAII

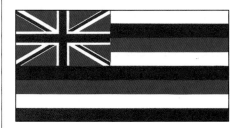

STATE FLAG

Adopted 20 May 1845. Proportions 1:2.

The flag is based on that adopted by the Kingdom of Hawaii in 1816. It combines the symbols of the United Kingdom (the Union Jack) and the United States (stripes of an early 19th-century ensign). The eight stripes represent the eight main islands: Hawaii, Kahoolawe, Kauai, Lanai, Maui, Molokai, Niihau and Oahu.

IDAHO

STATE FLAG

Introduced in 1907, formally adopted 15 March 1927. Proportions 26:33.

The female figure is a symbol of women's suffrage. She also represents liberty and justice, as denoted by the Phrygian cap (a symbol of liberty) and scales. The miner notes Idaho's chief occupation; the tree represents its timber interests; the ploughman and grain represent agriculture, and the cornucopias stand for horticulture. The elk's head refers to state game laws protecting elk and moose.

ILLINOIS

STATE FLAG

Basic design introduced in 1915. Proportions 3:5.

The bald eagle perched on an American shield indicates the allegiance of Illinois to the Union. The water stands for Lake Michigan. The name of the state was added on 1 July 1970.

INDIANA

STATE FLAG

Adopted 31 May 1917. Proportions 26:33.

The torch stands for liberty and enlightenment and the rays symbolize their far-reaching influence. The largest star represents Indiana, the 19th state of the Union. The outer circle of stars represents the original 13 states, and the inner circle of stars stands for the next five states admitted to the Union.

IOWA

STATE FLAG

Adopted 29 March 1921.
Proportions 3:4.

The French *Tricolore* signifies ties with France before the Louisiana Purchase. The bald eagle denotes Iowa's allegiance to the Union; it holds in its beak a ribbon with the state motto "Our liberties we prize and our rights we will maintain".

KANSAS

STATE FLAG

Adopted 30 June 1963. Proportions 3:5.

This design, without the word "Kansas", was adopted on 23 March 1927. The sunflower is the state flower, the wreath symbolizes the Louisiana Purchase and the 34 stars record the fact that Kansas was the 34th state admitted to the Union. The state motto "To the stars through difficulties" reflects the political trials of Kansas prior to joining the Union. A man ploughing with horses represents agriculture as the basis of the future prosperity of the state, and the steamboat is a symbol of commerce. The past of Kansas is represented by a settler's cabin, a train of ox wagons going west and a herd of buffalo retreating, pursued by two native Americans on horseback.

KENTUCKY

STATE FLAG

Adopted 26 March 1918. Proportions 10:19.

The seal of the state was adopted in 1792. Above it appears the name of the state and below the seal are two crossed branches of golden rod, the state flower. The two friends embracing exemplify the state motto "United we stand, divided we fall".

LOUISIANA

STATE FLAG

Adopted 1 July 1912. Proportions 2:3.

The emblem is taken from the state seal, adopted in 1902. The pelican is the state emblem of Louisiana and is shown nourishing its young on blood from its own breast, signifying self-sacrifice. The scroll bears the state motto, "Union, Justice and Confidence".

MAINE

STATE FLAG

Adopted 24 February 1909. Proportions 26:33.

The state arms display a white pine (*Pinus strobus*), which stands for the state and its nickname "the Pine Tree State". The moose, native to Maine, is a symbol of large areas of unpolluted forests. The water symbolizes the sea. The farmer resting on a scythe represents the land and agriculture; the sailor resting on an anchor represents the sea, as well as commerce and fisheries. The star and the motto *Dirigo* (I direct) refer to the fact

that the North Star was a guiding star for sailors, trappers and settlers.

MARYLAND

STATE FLAG

Adopted 9 March 1904. Proportions 2:3.

This armorial banner is unique among the flags of the 50 states. It is derived from the arms of two English families, Calvert and Crossland. Sir George Calvert was granted arms in 1622. His sons founded Maryland in 1634 and to create the arms of Maryland they adopted the quarterly arms of Calvert with the arms of Crossland, which belonged to their grandmother's family.

MASSACHUSETTS

STATE FLAG

Adopted 18 March 1908. Proportions 3:5.

A Native American holding a bow and arrow is an old emblem of the colony, dating back to the first half of the 17th century. The star represents the Commonwealth of Massachusetts. The motto was adopted in 1775 by the provincial congress as a message for England, "By the sword we seek peace, but peace only under liberty". The crest (an arm with a sword) was added in 1780.

MICHIGAN

STATE FLAG

Adopted 1 August 1911. Proportions 2:3.

Since 1837 this has been a flag of the Michigan militia. The bald eagle represents the superior authority and jurisdiction of the United States; the elk and moose represent the local fauna. The word *Tuebor* ("I will defend") refers to Michigan's geographic position on the frontier. The sun rising over the lake calls attention to a man standing on a peninsula. His upraised right hand symbolizes peace but his left hand holds a rifle, indicating readiness to defend the state and the nation. On the scroll appears the state motto – "If you seek a pleasant peninsula look about you".

MINNESOTA

STATE FLAG

Adopted 19 March 1957. Proportions 3:5.

The 19 stars are because Minnesota was the 19th state to be admitted to the Union. The motto *L'Etoile du Nord* (the North Star) refers to the fact that Minnesota was once the northernmost state of the Union. The central scene displays a Native American giving way to a white settler.

MISSISSIPPI

STATE FLAG

Adopted 7 February 1894. Proportions 2:3.

The flag displays the national colours. The enlarged canton is charged with the battle flag of the Confederacy. The flag's features were specified on 6 September 1996.

MISSOURI

STATE FLAG

Adopted 23 March 1913. Proportions 7:12.

The 24 stars recall that Missouri was the 24th state to be admitted to the Union. The bears indicate the size and strength of the state. The national arms symbolize the allegiance of Missouri to the union and the crescent stands for a new state, the second to be carved from the Louisiana Purchase.

MONTANA

STATE FLAG

Introduced 1 July 1981.
Proportions 2:3, 3:5 or 5:8.

The basic design of the flag has been unchanged since 1905; the word "Montana" was added in 1981. The seal, dating from 1865, displays the Great Falls of Missouri and the Rocky Mountains. The plough, shovel and pick indicate the state's reliance on agriculture and mining.

NEBRASKA

STATE FLAG

Adopted 2 April 1925. Proportions unspecified.

The main natural features displayed on the seal are the Rocky Mountains and the Missouri River. The smith symbolizes the mechanical arts and agriculture is represented by shocks of grain, growing grain and a settler's cabin. The steamboat and train represent the role of transport.

NEVADA

STATE FLAG

Adopted 8 June 1991.
Proportions 2:3, 3:5 or 5:8.

The star symbolizes the state; its colour stands for silver, the main mineral product of Nevada. The state motto "Battle Born" is a reminder that Nevada was admitted to the Union during the Civil War. The emblem is flanked by two sprays of sagebrush which is the state flower.

NEW HAMPSHIRE

STATE FLAG

Adopted 1 January 1932.
Proportions unspecified.

The sun rises behind a broadside view of the frigate *Raleigh*, which was one of the first 13 vessels ordered for the American navy. It was built at Portsmouth in 1776, the year New Hampshire achieved independence. The nine stars refer to the fact that New Hampshire was the ninth state admitted to the Union.

NEW JERSEY

STATE FLAG

Adopted 26 March 1896.
Proportions unspecified.

Buff is the regimental colour of the New Jersey Continental Line, prescribed by General G. Washington in 1779. Buff became the colour of the field of state regimental colour in 1780. The main device of the arms is three ploughs, as New Jersey was the third state admitted to the Union. The figures of Liberty and Ceres (the goddess of agriculture) support the arms. The horse's head symbolizes vigour.

NEW MEXICO

STATE FLAG

Adopted 11 March 1925. Proportions 2:3.

The colours of the flag are those of Spain. The Zia sun symbol is that of the ancient Zia Pueblo Native Americans.

NEW YORK

STATE FLAG

Adopted 2 April 1901. Proportions 10:19.

The shield displays a landscape with the Hudson River and the rising sun symbolizes a bright future. It is supported by the figures of Liberty and Justice.

NORTH CAROLINA

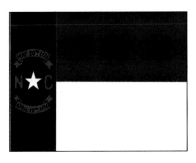

STATE FLAG

Adopted 9 March 1885. Proportions 3:4.

The flag displays the national colours. The star and the letters "NC" symbolize the state. The dates recall two important documents from the era of the Revolution:

the Mecklenburg Declaration of Independence and the Halifax Resolutions.

NORTH DAKOTA

STATE FLAG

Adopted 3 March 1911. Proportions 26:33.

The flag conforms in all respects to the regimental colours carried by the First North Dakota Infantry in the Spanish American War and the Philippine Insurrection, except for the name of the state on the scroll below the eagle.

OHIO

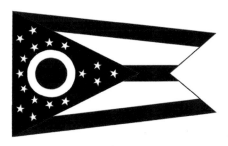

STATE FLAG

Adopted 9 May 1902. Proportions 8:13.

The flag displays the national colours. The white circle suggests the name "Ohio". The 17 stars signify that Ohio was the 17th state to enter the Union. The white circle with the red centre represents a buckeye (*Aesculus glabra*), the state tree, which gave the state its nickname, "the Buckeye State". The shape of the flag represents the hills and valleys of the state. The stripes symbolize the roads and waterways of Ohio.

OKLAHOMA

STATE FLAG

Adopted 9 May 1941. Proportions unspecified.

The blue symbolizes loyalty and devotion, the shield stands for protection, and the crossed olive branch and pipe of peace symbolize the desire for peace.

OREGON

STATE FLAG, OBVERSE

STATE FLAG, REVERSE

Adopted 26 February 1925.
Proportions 500:833.

The arms are accompanied by the date of the state's admission to the Union. The 33 stars signify that Oregon was the 33rd state admitted to the Union and the American eagle represents protection. The shield shows the Pacific Ocean in the setting sun with two ships, the British departing and the Americans arriving. The covered wagon represents the settlers, the wheatsheaf and plough are symbols of agriculture, and the pick represents mining.

PENNSYLVANIA

STATE FLAG

Adopted 13 June 1907. Proportions 27:37.

The American eagle denotes allegiance to the Union. The ship, the plough and the three wheatsheaves were taken from the arms of the counties of Philadelphia, Chester and Sussex (which is now part of Delaware) respectively.

RHODE ISLAND

STATE FLAG

Adopted 19 May 1897. Proportions 29:33.

The anchor has the motto "Hope" below it and has appeared on the seals of Rhode Island since 1664. The 13 stars represent the 13 original states.

SOUTH CAROLINA

STATE FLAG

Adopted 28 January 1861. Proportions unspecified.

The crescent refers to the badge with the inscription "Liberty or Death" worn on the caps of the soldiers of two regiments formed in South Carolina in 1775, who fought during the American Revolution. The palmetto tree is a symbol of victory, adopted in 1776 after the fort at Sullivan's Island, in Charleston harbour, defeated the British fleet. The fort was built out of palmetto tree trunks, which grow abundantly on Sullivan's Island.

SOUTH DAKOTA

STATE FLAG

Adopted 11 March 1963, modified 1 July 1992. Proportions 3:5.

The sun alludes to the former nickname of the state, "the Sunshine State". Its new nickname, "the Mount Rushmore State", has featured since 1992 around the lower portion of the sun. The seal depicts a typical landscape, in which the ploughman symbolizes agriculture, the steamboat transportation, the smelting furnace the mining industry, the cattle dairy farming, and the trees lumbering.

TENNESSEE

STATE FLAG

Adopted 17 April 1905. Proportions 3:5.

The flag is in the national colours, which symbolize purity (white), lofty aims (blue) and the fame of Tennessee (red). The three stars represent the three geographical divisions of the state. They also refer to the fact that Tennessee was the third state to join the Union after the original 13. The circle symbolizes unity.

TEXAS

STATE FLAG

Adopted 25 January 1839. Proportions 2:3.

The Lone Star flag was designed for the Republic of Texas, and was retained as the state flag after Texas joined the Union in 1845. The colours represent loyalty (blue), purity (white) and bravery (red).

UTAH

STATE FLAG

Adopted 11 March 1913. Proportions unspecified.

The beehive represents industry, the main virtue of the first settlers, and the sego lily, the state flower, is a symbol of peace. The American eagle symbolizes protection and the flags denote Utah's support to the nation.

VERMONT

STATE FLAG

Adopted 1 June 1923. Proportions unspecified.

The pine tree is the traditional emblem of New England; the sheaves of wheat and the cow represent agriculture. The two crossed pine branches symbolize the pine sprigs worn at the Battle of Plattsburgh in 1814.

VIRGINIA

STATE FLAG

Adopted 30 April 1861. Proportions unspecified.

Sic Semper Tyrannis ("Thus Ever to Tyrants") is the message of the Virginian seal. Virtus, the symbol of the Commonwealth, is dressed as an Amazon with her foot on Tyranny, represented by the prostrate body of a man holding a broken chain and a scourge in his hands.

WASHINGTON

STATE FLAG

Adopted 7 June 1923.
Proportions 2:3, 3:5 or 5:8.

The green reflects the state's nickname, "the Evergreen State". The present design of the seal, with the vignette of General George Washington, was adopted in 1967. It is an improved version of the seal which was adopted in 1889 when Washington became a state of the Union.

WEST VIRGINIA

STATE FLAG

Adopted 7 March 1929. Proportions 10:19.

The white is for the purity of the state institutions; the blue stands for the Union. The rock is a symbol of stability and continuity, and the date is the day the state was founded. The farmer and miner symbolize the two main industries, and the Phrygian cap (a symbol of liberty) and rifles indicate that the state won its freedom and will defend it by force of arms.

WISCONSIN

STATE FLAG

Introduced 1 June 1981. Proportions 2:3.

The blue flag with the arms was adopted on 29 April 1913. In 1981 the word "Wisconsin" and the date "1848" (admission to the Union) were added. The shield of arms displays symbols of agriculture, mining, manufacture and navigation. The arms and motto of the United States symbolize the allegiance of

the state to the union, and the badger refers to its nickname, "the Badger State". The main branches of the economy, mining and agriculture, are represented by lead ore and a cornucopia. The sailor and the miner symbolize labour on water and on land.

WYOMING

STATE FLAG

Adopted 31 January 1917. Proportions 7:10.

The red symbolizes the Native Americans and the blood of the pioneers who gave their lives. The white is a symbol of purity and uprightness; the blue is the colour of the skies and distant mountains, and also a symbol of fidelity, justice and virility. The bison represents the local fauna while the seal on it symbolizes the custom of branding livestock. The woman holding a banner with the words "equal rights" symbolizes the political position of women in the state, and the men represent the livestock and mining industries. The lamps signify the light of knowledge.

DISTRICT OF COLUMBIA

FLAG OF THE DISTRICT

Adopted 15 October 1938. Proportions 10:19.

The state flag is the banner of arms of George Washington.

BERMUDA

British colony comprising a group of islands
in the Atlantic Ocean, E of North America.

CIVIL FLAG AND ENSIGN

Introduced in 1915. Proportions 1:2.

Bermuda was the first British colony to fly
the defaced red ensign. The fly is charged
with the arms, granted on 4 October 1910.
The British lion supports a shield
portraying the wreck of the *Sea Venture*,
which in 1609 carried the first settlers and
came to grief on a reef.

MEXICO

United States of Mexico,
Spanish **Estados Unidos Mexicanos**.
Federal republic S of North America.

NATIONAL FLAG AND ENSIGN

Adopted 17 August 1968. Proportions 4:7.

After Mexico achieved independence, it
adopted on 2 November 1821 a flag based
on the French *Tricolore*. The green-white-
red flag was charged with the national
emblem, a modern interpretation of an
ancient Aztec symbol. According to Aztec
legend, an eagle grasping a serpent in its
claws and standing on a flowering nopal
cactus growing from a rock in the middle of
the Tenochtitlan Lake appeared on the site
where the Aztecs decided to build their capital
city in 1325. The emblem has changed its
form several times, the last time in 1968.

Originally the colours symbolized
independence (green), purity of religion
(white) and striving for unity between the
native races and the Spaniards (red). Today
they stand for hope (green), purity (white)
and religion (red).

CENTRAL AMERICA

BELIZE

Constitutional monarchy in Central America.

NATIONAL FLAG AND ENSIGN

*Officially hoisted 21 September 1981.
Proportions unspecified.*

Blue and red are the colours of the ruling
and opposition parties respectively, and the
50 leaves in the wreath symbolize 1950,
when the independence movement began.
The arms retain the main features of the
arms granted to British Honduras on 28
January 1907: sailors' and woodsmen's tools
and a sailing ship. The tree behind the
shield is a mahogany tree and supporting it
are two men, denoting racial diversity. The
motto means "Flourish in the Shade".

GUATEMALA

Republic of Guatemala,
Spanish **República de Guatemala**.
Republic in Central America.

STATE FLAG AND ENSIGN

*Decreed on 26 December 1997.
Proportions 5:8. National flag and ensign
are without arms.*

Guatemala, like the other four former
members of the United Provinces of
Central America, has retained the colours
of the Federation's flag. The blue-white-
blue vertical tricolour with the state
emblem was introduced in 1871 and the
form of the emblem was changed in 1968
and again in 1997. The blue stands for
justice and steadfastness, and the white
for purity and uprightness. The main device
of the emblem is a quetzal, the national
bird of Guatemala and a symbol of liberty.
The inscription on the scroll, "Liberty 15
September 1821", is the date when Central
America broke with Spain. The rifles
symbolize the will of the people to defend
freedom, the swords stand for justice and
sovereignty, and the wreath is a symbol of
victory. The latest change involved the
spelling of the date of independence. Since
December 1997 the inscription reads
"15 de Septiembre" instead of "15 de
Setiembre".

HONDURAS

Republic of Honduras,
Spanish **República de Honduras**.
Republic in Central America.

NATIONAL FLAG, CIVIL AND STATE ENSIGN

Adopted 16 February 1866. Proportions 1:2.

The flag is based on the flag of the United Provinces of Central America. The five stars refer to the members of the Federation: Costa Rica, El Salvador, Guatemala, Honduras and Nicaragua. The blue stands for the skies and brotherhood; the white for the desire for peace and purity of thoughts.

EL SALVADOR

Republic of El Salvador,
Spanish **República de El Savador.**
Republic in Central America.

STATE FLAG

Adopted 15 September 1912. Proportions 3:5. Civil flag is without arms. Civil ensign, an alternative civil flag and state flag and ensign are without arms, with the inscription "Dios, Union, Libertad" in gold letters on the white stripe.

The flag and the emblem are based on those of the United Provinces of Central America. The Masonic triangle symbolizes equality; its angles represent three branches of government: legislative, executive and judicial. The volcanoes stand for the five

nations of Central America flanked by the Pacific and the Atlantic Oceans. Within the triangle are symbols of liberty (a Phrygian cap), the ideals of the people (golden rays) and peace (rainbow). The motto, *"Dios, Union, Libertad"* ("God, Unity, Liberty") reflects faith in God, harmony in the family and the independence of the people. The 14 clusters of leaves represent the number of departments of El Salvador.

NICARAGUA

Republic of Nicaragua,
Spanish **República de Nicaragua**.
Republic in Central America.

STATE FLAG

Adopted 4 September 1908. Proportions 3:5. The alternative civil flag is without emblem.

The flag is based on that of the United Provinces of Central America. The triangle is a symbol of equality. The five volcanoes represent the five nations of Central America flanked by the Atlantic and Pacific Oceans. The Phrygian cap is a symbol of liberty; the rainbow symbolizes peace.

COSTA RICA

Republic of Costa Rica,
Spanish **República de Costa Rica**.
Republic in Central America.

STATE FLAG AND ENSIGN

Adopted 13 June 1964. Proportions 3:5. Civil ensign is without emblem.

In 1848 the present design of the flag with five stripes was adopted. The red was added to obtain the colours of revolutionary France and the national emblem was positioned in the centre. The current design of the flag and the emblem were adopted in 1964. The seven stars represent the seven provinces of Costa Rica and the volcanoes denote the geographical position of Costa Rica between the Pacific and the Atlantic. The sun is a symbol of freedom and the ships symbolize commerce.

PANAMA

Republic of Panama,
Spanish **República de Panama**.
Republic in Central America.

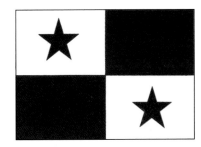

NATIONAL FLAG AND ENSIGN

Introduced 3 November 1903, officially approved 4 June 1904. Proportions 2:3.

The blue and red are the colours of the main political parties (Conservatives and Liberals respectively) and the white denotes peace between them. The blue also symbolizes the Pacific Ocean and the Caribbean, and the red stands for the blood of those who lost their lives for their country. The blue star represents the civic virtues of purity and honesty, and the red star is a symbol of authority and law.

201

WEST INDIES AND THE CARIBBEAN

THE BAHAMAS

Commonwealth of the Bahamas.
Constitutional monarchy comprising a chain of islands NW of West Indies.

NATIONAL FLAG

Adopted 10 July 1973. Proportions 1:2.

The flag is a graphic representation of the golden beaches of the Bahama Islands surrounded by the aquamarine sea. The black represents the vigour and force of a united people. The triangle indicates the enterprise and determination of the Bahamian people to develop the rich resources of land and sea.

TURKS AND CAICOS ISLANDS

British crown colony in the N Central West Indies.

STATE FLAG AND ENSIGN

*Introduced in 1968. Proportions 1:2.
Civil ensign has a red field.*

The fly is charged with the shield of arms, granted on 26 September 1965. It displays local flora and fauna: a queen conch shell, a spiny lobster and a Turk's head cactus.

CUBA

Republic of Cuba,
Spanish **República de Cuba**.
Socialist republic comprising an island in the W West Indies.

NATIONAL FLAG AND ENSIGN

*Introduced in 1850, officially approved
20 May 1902. Proportions 1:2.*

The flag was designed by a Cuban poet Teurbe Tolón in 1849 and was patterned on the design of the Stars and Stripes. The star, called *La Estrella Solitaria* ("the Lone Star"), was selected to light the way towards freedom and was taken from the flag of Texas. In time, the Cuban flag itself began to be known as *La Estrella Solitaria*. The flag was hoisted for the first time on 19 May 1850 in Ordenas on the north coast of Cuba where General Francisco Lopez landed with 600 men and staged an abortive attempt to free the country from colonial rule.

The triangle is a Masonic symbol of liberty, equality and fraternity, and the three blue stripes stand for the three sectors into which Cuba was divided by the Spaniards. The white symbolizes the pure intentions of the revolutionaries and for justice; the red is for the blood that was shed in the struggle for independence.

CAYMAN ISLANDS

British colony in the W West Indies.

STATE FLAG AND ENSIGN

*Introduced in 1958. Proportions 1:2.
Civil ensign has a red field.*

The badge displays the whole achievement of the arms, granted on 14 May 1958. The three stars represent the three main islands: Grand Cayman, Cayman Brac and Little Cayman. The lion denotes loyalty to Great Britain. A turtle and a pineapple represent the fauna and flora of the islands.

JAMAICA

Constitutional monarchy comprising an island in the W West Indies.

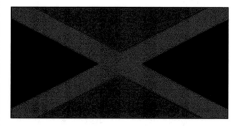

NATIONAL FLAG, STATE AND CIVIL ENSIGN

*Officially hoisted 6 August 1962.
Proportions 1:2.*

The green stands for hope and agriculture, the black for hardships overcome and to be faced, and the yellow for natural resources and the beauty of sunlight.

HAITI

Republic of Haiti, French **République d'Haiti**.
Republic consisting of the W part of Hispaniola Island in the Central West Indies.

STATE FLAG

*Introduced in 1897, reintroduced
25 February 1986. Proportions 3:5. Civil flag
and ensign are without arms.*

The blue and red are taken from the French *Tricolore* and represent the union of blacks and mulattoes. The arms are composed of a cabbage palm surmounted by the Phyrgian cap of liberty and ornamented with trophies (rifles, flags, hatchets, cannons, cannonballs, trumpets, anchors etc). The motto means "Union Makes Strength".

DOMINICAN REPUBLIC

Spanish **República Dominicana**.
Republic consisting of the E part of Hispaniola Island in the Central West Indies.

STATE FLAG AND ENSIGN, WAR ENSIGN

*Adopted 6 November 1844.
Civil flag and ensign are without arms.
Proportions 5:8.*

In 1839 the Trinitarians struggling for independence added a white cross to the flag of Haiti to form their flag. Later the blue and red were reversed at the fly portion of the flag. The cross stands for the Catholic faith, the blue is the colour of liberty and the red symbolizes blood. The arms display the national colours and flags, the Cross and the Bible. The motto above the shield means "God, Fatherland, Liberty".

PUERTO RICO

Free Associated State of Puerto Rico,
Spanish **El Estado Libre y Asociado de Puerto Rico**.
Self-governing incorporated territory of the United States of America, an island in the Central West Indies.

NATIONAL FLAG

*In use since 22 December 1895, official since
24 July 1952. Proportions 2:3.*

The flag, designed in 1891, is that of Cuba with reversed colours. The star symbolizes the Fatherland. The triangle and the colours represent the republican ideals of liberty, equality and fraternity.

VIRGIN ISLANDS

Virgin Islands of the United States.
Organized, unincorporated territory of the United States of America comprising a group of islands in the E West Indies.

NATIONAL FLAG

Adopted 17 May 1921. Proportions unspecified.

The white is a symbol of purity. The emblem is a simplified version of the United States arms and the letters "V" and "I" stand for the Virgin Islands.

BRITISH VIRGIN ISLANDS

British colony in the E West Indies.

STATE FLAG AND ENSIGN

Proportions 1:2.

The arms, granted on 15 November 1960, appear in the centre of the British blue ensign. The central figure is St Ursula, the "wise virgin" and namesake of the islands. The eleven lamps represent the 11 virgins murdered with St Ursula by the Huns.

ANGUILLA

Dependency of the United Kingdom in the E West Indies.

STATE FLAG AND ENSIGN

Officially hoisted 30 May 1990. Proportions 1:2.

The British blue ensign is defaced with the shield of arms, which displays three dolphins, symbolizing unity and strength. The blue base stands for the Caribbean Sea surrounding the island.

ST KITTS AND NEVIS

Federation of St Kitts and Nevis.
Federal constitutional monarchy comprising
two islands in the E West Indies.

NATIONAL FLAG AND ENSIGN

Adopted 19 November 1983.
Proportions 2:3.

The two stars stand for hope and liberty,
and the black symbolizes the African
heritage of a major part of the population.
The green represents the fertility of the
land, the yellow the constant sunshine, and
the red symbolizes the struggle to end
slavery and colonialism.

MONTSERRAT

British crown colony consisting of a volcanic
island in the E West Indies.

STATE FLAG AND ENSIGN

Adopted in 1960. Proportions 1:2.

The British blue ensign is defaced with the
arms, adopted in 1909. The cross stands for
Christianity. The woman with a harp refers
to the Irish immigrants who settled on the
island in 1632.

ANTIGUA AND BARBUDA

State of Antigua and Barbuda.
Constitutional monarchy comprising
three islands in the E West Indies.

NATIONAL FLAG AND ENSIGN

Introduced 27 February 1967. Proportions 2:3.

The sun symbolizes the new era of
independence in the history of the island.
The colours represent its African heritage
(black), hope (blue) and the dynamism of
the people (red). The "V" stands for victory.
The yellow, blue and white indicate the
country's main tourist attractions: the sun,
sea and sandy beaches.

DOMINICA

Commonwealth of Dominica.
Republic comprising an island in the E West Indies.

NATIONAL FLAG AND ENSIGN

Adopted 3 November 1990. Proportions 1:2.

The basic design of the flag was introduced
on 3 November 1978. Since then it has
undergone several modifications. The red
circle symbolizes socialism. The sisserou
parrot (*Psittacus imperialis*) is the national
bird, unique to Dominica, and symbolizes
flight towards greater heights and fulfilment
of aspirations. The ten stars represent the
ten parishes of equal status, thus the
equality of the people. The green

symbolizes the lush vegetation; the triple-
coloured cross represents the Trinity of God.
The yellow represents the sunshine, the
main agricultural products (citrus and
bananas) and the Carib people, the first
inhabitants of the island; the black is a
symbol of the rich black soil and African
heritage; the white symbolizes the rivers
and waterfalls, and purity of aspirations.

MARTINIQUE

French **Département de la Martinique.**
French overseas department and administrative
region, an island in the E West Indies.

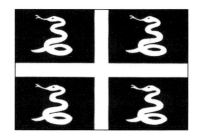

NATIONAL FLAG

Adopted 4 August 1766. Proportions 2:3.

The flag is the old French merchant ensign
charged with four white serpents.

ST LUCIA

Constitutional monarchy consisting of an island
in the SE West Indies.

NATIONAL FLAG AND ENSIGN

Officially introduced 1 March 1967.
Proportions 1:2.

The triangle represents the twin peaks of
the Pitons, a geological formation of
volcanic origin. The black and white
symbolize the "two races living and working
in unity", the yellow symbolizes the

constant sunshine and the blue stands for the Caribbean and the Atlantic Ocean.

ST VINCENT AND THE GRENADINES

Constitutional monarchy comprising several islands in the SE West Indies.

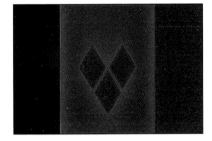

NATIONAL FLAG AND ENSIGN

Officially hoisted 22 October 1985.
Proportions 2:3.

"The Gems", as the green lozenges and the flag itself are commonly called, is an abbreviation of "the Gems of the Antilles", which is the islands' nickname. They also represent the nature of the country, with numerous islands and peoples. The blue symbolizes the sky and the sea, and the green represents the lush vegetation and the vitality of the people. The yellow stands for the golden sands, the bright spirit of the people and warmth.

BARBADOS

Constitutional monarchy consisting of an island in the SE West Indies.

NATIONAL FLAG AND ENSIGN

Introduced 30 November 1966. Proportions 2:3.

The blue stands for the sea and the sky, and the yellow represents the sandy beaches.

The trident, an attribute of the mythical sea god Neptune, symbolizes some of the traditions of the past but the shaft is broken, indicating the break with the historical and constitutional ties of the past.

GRENADA

State of Grenada.
Constitutional monarchy comprising several islands in the SE West Indies.

CIVIL AND STATE FLAG

Officially hoisted 7 February 1974.
Proportions 3:5. Proportions of the ensign 1:2.

The yellow represents the sun and the friendliness of the people, the green stands for the agriculture and the red is a symbol of harmony, unity and courage. The seven stars represent the island's seven parishes. The nutmeg recalls that this small island is the second-largest producer of nutmeg in the world.

TRINIDAD AND TOBAGO

Republic of Trinidad and Tobago.
Republic of several islands in the S West Indies.

STATE FLAG

Officially hoisted 31 August 1962.
Proportions 3:5. Proportions of the ensign 1:2.

The black represents the dedication of the people, joined together by one strong

bond; it also symbolizes strength, unity, purpose and the wealth of the land. The red stands for the vitality of the people, the warmth and energy of the sun, and the courage and friendliness of the people. The white symbolizes the sea, purity of aspirations and the equality of all men under the sun.

NETHERLANDS ANTILLES

Dutch **De Nederlandse Antillen**.
Autonomous part of the Netherlands consisting of 5 islands in the E and S West Indies.

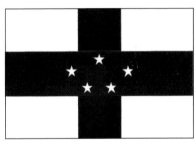

CIVIL AND STATE FLAG AND ENSIGN

Adopted 1 January 1986. Proportions 2:3.

The colours are based on those of the Netherlands flag. The blue represents the Caribbean and the stars stand for the five constituent parts of the Netherlands Antilles: Curaçao and Bonaire off the coast of Venezuela, St Maarten, St Eustatius and Saba in the Leeward Islands.

ISLANDS OF THE NETHERLANDS ANTILLES

The Netherlands Antilles are an integral part of the Netherlands realm. They consist of five islands: Curaçao, Bonaire, St Maarten, St Eustatius and Saba. St Eustatius does not have its own flag.

BONAIRE

FLAG OF THE ISLAND

Hoisted 15 December 1981. Proportions 2:3.

The star represents the island itself, while its six points recall the six neighbourhoods of Bonaire. The black ring around it, which represents a compass, symbolizes the seamanship of Bonaireans and their purposefulness in orienting themselves between the spirit (which is symbolized by the colour yellow) and the world (symbolized by the colour blue). The red is a symbol of energy, the blood of the people of Bonaire, and their struggle during their daily lives. The yellow stands for brilliant sunshine and the beauty of nature, especially the yellow flowers of brasilia and *Kibrahacha* (axe-breaker) plants. The white symbolizes liberty, tranquillity and peace. The blue is for the sea which provides a basis for their livelihood.

CURAÇAO

FLAG OF THE ISLAND

Adopted 2 July 1984. Proportions 2:3.

Two stars represent the islands of Curaçao and Klein Curaçao. They are also seen as a symbol of peace and happiness. The five points of each star recall the five continents from which people came and settled the islands. The blue stands for the loyalty of the people; the upper blue symbolizes the sky, the lower stripe the sea. The yellow stripe stands for the tropical sun and reflects the joyful character of the Curaçao population.

SABA

FLAG OF THE ISLAND

Adopted 6 December 1985. Proportions 2:3.

The star represents Saba. Its colour stands for the wealth of natural beauty found on the island and symbolizes hope for the future. The colours symbolize historical and political ties with the Netherlands and the Netherlands Antilles. In addition, the white stands for peace, friendship, purity and serenity; the red for unity, courage and determination. The blue represents the sea which has played a significant role in the survival of the people of Saba. Blue also symbolizes the heavens which remind the people of Saba of God Almighty who created the island.

ST MAARTEN

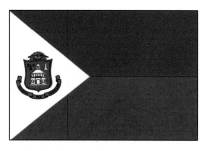

FLAG OF THE ISLAND

Adopted 13 June 1985. Proportions 2:3.

The colours are those of the flag of the Netherlands. The arms show an old courthouse, a bouquet of yellow sage (the national flower), and a silhouette of the monument honouring Dutch-French friendship and the unity of both parts of the island. The orange border symbolizes loyalty to the ruling Dutch house of Orange-Nassau. The crest is formed by a yellow disc which represents the sun, and a grey silhouette of a pelican in flight. The motto in Latin, "Semper Progrediens" means "Always Progressing".

ARUBA

Autonomous overseas territory of the Netherlands, an island in the S West Indies.

NATIONAL FLAG AND CIVIL ENSIGN

*Officially hoisted 1 January 1986.
Proportions 2:3.*

The blue stands for the Caribbean and the skies. The star symbolizes Aruba, with its red soil and white beaches. The four points of the star represent the four major languages (Papiamento, Dutch, Spanish and English) and the four points of the compass, indicating that the inhabitants came from all over the world to live here in unity and strength. The stripes represent the sun and tourism, and the mineral resources of the island.

COLOMBIA

Republic of Colombia,
Spanish **República de Colombia**.

Republic in NW South America.

CIVIL ENSIGN SINCE 1890

*Adopted 26 November 1861. Proportions 2:3.
National flag and state ensign are
without the emblem.*

The colours symbolize sovereignty and justice (yellow); nobility, loyalty and vigilance (blue); and valour, honour, generosity and victory achieved at the cost of bloodshed (red). According to another interpretation, the colours stand for universal liberty (yellow), the equality of all races and social classes before God and the law (blue), and fraternity (red).

VENEZUELA

Republic of Venezuela,
Spanish **República de Venezuela**.

Republic in NW South America.

STATE FLAG AND ENSIGN, WAR ENSIGN

*Adopted 17 February 1954. Proportions 2:3.
Civil ensign is without arms.*

This flag, with yellow, blue and red stripes of equal width, was introduced in 1836 and has since undergone several modifications in the arms and the arrangement of the stars. The seven stars represent the seven provinces that began the fight for independence. The emblems on the arms symbolize the unity of the 20 provinces (a wheatsheaf with 20 ears), the struggle for independence (flags and weapons) and liberty (a running horse). The cornucopias stand for the country's wealth and prosperity, and the wreath of laurel and palm is a symbol of glory and peace.

ECUADOR

Republic of Ecuador,
Spanish **República del Ecuador**.

Republic in NW South America.

STATE FLAG AND ENSIGN

*Adopted 10 January 1861. Proportions 1:2.
Civil flag and ensign are without arms.*

The colours of the flag represent the sunshine, grain and wealth (yellow), the sky, sea and rivers (blue), and the patriots and their blood shed in the struggle for freedom and justice (red). Mount Chimborazo and the river symbolize the ties between the interior of the country and the coastal areas; the steamship recalls the first South American steamship, built in 1841 in Guayaquil. The sun is a symbol of liberty and the signs of the zodiac denote the four memorable months (March-June) of the revolution in 1845. The condor is a symbol of strength and valour, and the *fasces* represents the sovereignty of the republic. The flags mounted on lances refer to the duty to defend the Fatherland with arms.

GUYANA

Co-operative Republic of Guyana.

Republic in N South America.

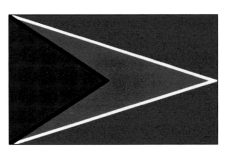

NATIONAL FLAG

*Adopted 20 May 1966. Proportions 3:5.
Proportions of national ensign are 1:2.*

Whitney Smith, the designer of the flag, chose green for the background because green forests and fields cover more than 90 per cent of Guyana. The red represents zeal and sacrifice, which are part of the nation-building process that the Guyanese are striving towards. The black border indicates the perseverance needed to reach their goal. The "golden arrowhead" represents the golden future the citizens hope will be built upon Guyana's mineral resources. The country's extensive water resources are symbolized by the white border.

SURINAM

Republic of Surinam,
Dutch **Republiek Surinam**.

Republic in N South America.

NATIONAL FLAG AND ENSIGN

*Officially hoisted 25 November 1975.
Proportions 2:3.*

The golden star is a symbol of the golden future that can be achieved through unity.

The green stands for the fertile land, the white for justice and freedom, and the red for progress in the struggle for a better life.

BRAZIL

Federative Republic of Brazil, Portuguese **República Federativa do Brasil**.
Federal republic in Central South America.

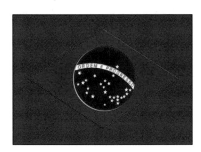

NATIONAL FLAG AND ENSIGN

Adopted 12 May 1992. Proportions 7:10.

The original design, with 21 stars, was adopted on 19 November 1889. The number of stars was increased to 22 in 1960, to 23 in 1968 and to 27 in 1992. The central device represents the sky above Rio de Janeiro at 8.30 a.m. on 15 November 1889, the date of the proclamation of the republic. The 27 stars correspond to the stars of the constellations of the Virgin, Water Snake, Scorpio, Southern Triangle, Octant, Southern Cross, Keel of Argo, Greater Dog and Smaller Dog. Each of 26 stars represents one state of the Federation and the 27th star represents the Federal District. The curved band with the national motto "Order and Progress" stands for the Equator. The green and yellow symbolize the forests and mineral resources respectively.

BRAZILIAN STATES

Since 1989 Brazil has been a federal republic. Currently it comprises 26 states and the federal district where Brasilia, the capital of the country, is located.

ACRE

STATE FLAG

Flag introduced in 1899, officially confirmed 1 March 1963. Proportions 11:20.

Yellow and green are the national colours of Brazil. The red stands for courage.

ALAGOAS

*Adopted 23 September 1963.
Proportions 4:7.*

The colours are taken from the state arms, which display the arms of the cities of Alagoas, Penedo and Porto Calvo. The pictures of a stalk of sugar cane and a

branch of cotton represent the state's two chief agricultural products.

AMAPÁ

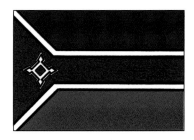

STATE FLAG

Adopted in 1984. Proportions 4:7.

The colours symbolize the sky and law (blue), the green land, faith in the future, freedom and love (green), the natural riches (yellow), purity and tranquillity (white), regard to the past being the source of good (black). The emblem represents the fort of São José de Macapá. The blue star stands for the state.

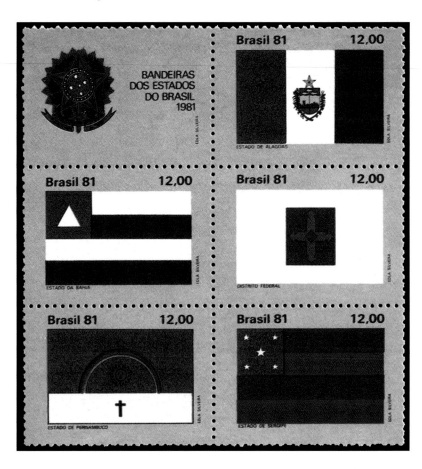

◆ **ABOVE** State flags on Brazilian postage stamps, 1981 (*from left to right beginning top right*) Alagoas; Bahia; Federal District; Pernambuco; Sergipe.

AMAZONAS

Flag introduced in 1897. Proportions 7:10.

The red stripe represents the state and the white stripes stand for the Amazon and Negro Rivers. The larger star symbolizes Manaus, the capital of the state, and the other stars represent the 43 other municipalities that form the state.

BAHIA

Flag adopted 26 May 1889. Proportions 7:10.

The red triangle represents the Masonic symbol of the *Inconfidencia Mineira*, the miners' revolt of 1789. Blue, white and red were the colours of the Bahian Revolution of 1798.

CEARÁ

Flag adopted 31 August 1967. Proportions 7:10.

Green and yellow are the national colours of Brazil. The central portion of the arms displays the bay and lighthouse at Mucuri. The stars represent the municipalities of the state.

ESPIRITO SANTO

Flag officially hoisted 24 April 1947. Proportions 7:10.

The colours of the flag represent peace (blue), harmony and sweetness (white), and joy (rose). The motto means "Work and Hope".

FEDERAL DISTRICT

Flag officially hoisted 7 September 1969. Proportions 13:18.

The white stands for purity, and green and yellow are the national colours of Brazil. The four arrows symbolize the balance of centralization and devolution in Brazil.

GOIAS

Flag adopted 30 July 1919. Proportions 7:10.

The stars are those of the Southern Cross constellation. Green and yellow are the national colours of Brazil.

MARANHÃO

Adopted 21 December 1889. Proportions 2:3.

The white star stands for the state. The colours of the stripes represent the three components of the population: the descendants of the Portuguese discoverers and colonizers (white), the native Indians (red) and the African slaves.

MATO GROSSO

Flag adopted in 1890, officially confirmed 11 July 1947. Proportions 7:10.

The flag has the colours of the national flag but in a different arrangement. The star stands for the state.

MATO GROSSO DO SUL

Flag officially hoisted 1 January 1979. Proportions 7:10.

The state is represented by a golden star shining in the blue sky of hope, symbolizing the wealth of the people's labour. The green stands for the forests and fields. The white band symbolizes the future and friendship among peoples.

MINAS GERAIS

Flag adopted 27 November 1962. Proportions 7:10.

The triangle recalls the Inconfidencia Mineira, the miners' revolt of 1789.

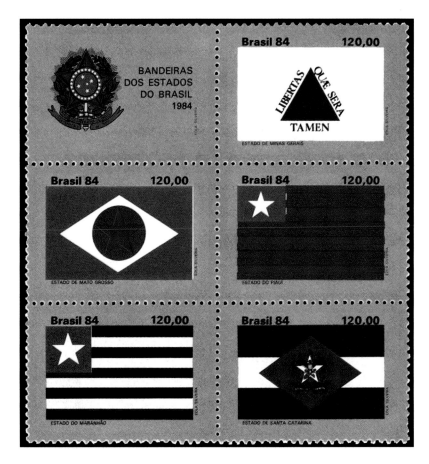

◆ **ABOVE** State flags on Brazilian postage stamps, 1982 (*from left to right beginning top right*) Minas Gerais; Mato Grosso; Piaui; Maranhão; Santa Catarina.

PARÁ

STATE FLAG

Flag introduced 17 November 1889.
Proportions 7:10.

The star represents the state and the white symbolizes the river Amazon.

PARAÍBA

Flag introduced 27 October 1965.
Proportions 7:10.

The motto *Nego* ("I deny it") refers to the revolution of 1930, in which the state played a leading part.

PARANÁ

Flag officially adopted 31 March 1947.
Proportions 2:3.

The basic design of the flag was adopted in 1892. The green symbolizes the country's natural wealth, the white stands for its mineral resources. The main device of the emblem is the Southern Cross constellation. The branches of araucaria and maté represent forestry and agriculture.

PERNAMBUCO

Flag officially adopted 23 February 1917.
Proportions 2:3.

The flag was adopted by the republic of Pernambuco in 1817. The star represents the state, the three arches of the rainbow symbolize peace, friendship and union, and the sun signifies that the people of Pernambucos are the children of the sun. The cross refers to the name Santa Cruz (Holy Cross) which was given to Brazil by the European discoverers.

◆ **BELOW**
State flags on Brazilian postage stamps, 1983 (*from left to right beginning top right*) Amazonias; Goias; Rio de Janeiro; Mato Grosso Do Sul; Paraná.

PIAUÍ

Flag adopted 24 July 1922.
Proportions 7:10.

The star represents the state. The national colours of Brazil, yellow and green symbolize its allegiance to that country.

RIO DE JANEIRO

Flag introduced in 1947.
Proportions 7:10.

The flag displays the pre-1910 colours of Portugal; the arms were adopted on 29 June 1892. The main feature is an eagle holding in its talons branches of sugar cane and olive.

RIO GRANDE DO NORTE

Flag adopted 3 December 1957.
Proportions 2:3.

The colours of the flag represent the forests and the chalk cliffs. The arms were adopted on 1 July 1909.

RIO GRANDE DO SUL

STATE FLAG

Flag introduced in 1891.
Proportions 7:10.

This design was adopted by the republic of Rio Grande do Sul in 1836. The arms, displaying a Phrygian cap of liberty and suits of armour, were added in 1891.

◆ **BELOW**
State flags on Brazilian postage stamps (*from left to right beginning top right*) Ceará; Espririto Santo; Paraíba; Rio Grande do Norte; Rondônia.

An almost identical flag with 21 stripes, designed in 1888, was one of several proposed flags for the Republic of Brazil. It did not become the national flag but was used unofficially as the flag of the state of São Paulo. The number of stripes was reduced in 1932. The white, black and red represent whites, blacks and Native Americans living peacefully together. Blue and white are the historic colours of Portugal, and blue, white and red are the republican colours.

SERGIPE

Flag introduced 1897. Proportions 7:10.

The colours of the flag are those of the national flag of Brazil. The stars are those of the Southern Cross constellation.

TOCANTINS

STATE FLAG

Flag adopted 1 January 1989. Proportions 3:5.

The sun represents the state, which split from Goías in 1988. The blue symbolizes river Tocantins.

RONDÔNIA

Flag adopted 31 December 1981.
Proportions 7:10.

The flag shows the colours of the Brazilian flag, yellow and green. The star stands for the state.

RORAIMA

STATE FLAG

Flag adopted 31 December 1981.
Proportions 7:10.

The flag displays the colours of the national flag of Brazil, yellow and green. The star represents the state and the red line symbolizes the Equator.

SANTA CATARINA

Flag adopted 23 October 1953. Proportions 3:4.

The green lozenge represents the vegetation of the state; the arms were adopted on 15 August 1895. The star symbolizes the state and the Phrygian cap is a symbol of liberty. The eagle represents productivity, the anchor denotes the maritime character of the state and the key indicates that it is the key to southern Brazil. The wreath, made of grain and coffee plants, symbolizes agriculture.

SÃO PAULO

STATE FLAG

Flag adopted 18 November 1932.
Proportions 7:10.

URUGUAY

Oriental Republic of Uruguay,
Spanish **República Oriental del Uruguay.**
Republic in SE South America.

NATIONAL FLAG AND ENSIGN

Adopted 12 July 1830. Proportions 2:3.

The creators of the flag were inspired by the national colours of Argentina, and by the design of the American Stars and Stripes. It was adopted on 16 December 1828, with nine blue and ten white stripes. In 1830 the number of stripes was reduced to four blue and five white; these nine stripes represent the nine original regions of Uruguay. The sun is a symbol of freedom.

PARAGUAY

Republic of Paraguay,

Spanish **República del Paraguay**.

Republic in S Central South America.

NATIONAL FLAG AND ENSIGN, OBVERSE

EMBLEM IN THE CENTRE OF THE REVERSE OF
THE NATIONAL FLAG AND ENSIGN

Adopted 25 November 1842. Proportions 1:2.

This is the only national flag in the world with a different design on the obverse and reverse. The state seal appears on the obverse and the reverse is charged with the treasury seal. Red, white and blue are the republican colours. They symbolize patriotism, courage, equality and justice (red), steadfastness, unity, peace and the purity of ideas (white), kindliness, love, sharpness, sense of reality, and liberty (blue). The star symbolizes the date of independence, 14 May 1811. The lion guarding the Phrygian cap symbolizes the defence of liberty. The national motto is "Peace and Justice".

BOLIVIA

Republic of Bolivia,

Spanish **República de Bolivia**.

Republic in W Central South America.

STATE FLAG

Adopted 5 November 1851. Proportions 2:3.
Civil flag and ensign are without arms.

The red symbolizes the blood of the national heroes, sacrifice and love. The yellow stands for the mineral resources and for the Incas, who were the first to make use of them. The green is a symbol of eternal hope, evolution and progress.

The arms display symbols of dignity and independence (condor), liberty (sun) and republic (Phrygian cap). The animal kingdom is represented by an alpaca, the mineral kingdom by Mount Potosi and the vegetable kingdom by a breadfruit tree. The wheatsheaf symbolizes agriculture. The ten stars represent the nine departments of Bolivia and the one lost to Chile. The flags and weapons symbolize the will to defend the country.

PERU

Republic of Peru,

Spanish **República del Perú**.

Republic in W South America.

STATE FLAG AND ENSIGN

Adopted 25 February 1825. Proportions 2:3.
The civil flag and ensign do not have arms.

According to legend, General José de San Martin saw a great number of flamingos when he arrived in Peru in 1820. Taking this as a good omen, he decided that white and red should be the colours of the Peruvian Legion that he founded to liberate Peru. The white represents peace, dignity and progress; the red symbolizes war and courage. The arms show symbols of the animal kingdom (*vicuña*), vegetable kingdom (cinchona tree) and mineral kingdom (a cornucopia full of gold and silver coins). The laurel wreath above the shield symbolizes the republic. The palm and laurel wreath around the shield is a symbol of peace and the will to defend the country.

CHILE

Republic of Chile,

Spanish **República de Chile**.

Republic in SW South America.

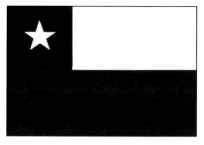

NATIONAL FLAG AND ENSIGN

Adopted 18 October 1817. Proportions 2:3.

The flag was designed by an American, Charles Wood, who fought for Chilean independence as an officer in the army of General José de San Martin. The design is clearly influenced by the Stars and Stripes. The white star is the guiding star on the path of progress and honour. The blue symbolizes the sky; the white symbolizes the snow of the Andes, and the red stands for all the blood shed in the struggle for independence.

ARGENTINA

Republic of Argentina,

Spanish **República Argentina**.

Republic in S South America.

NATIONAL FLAG AND ENSIGN

Adopted 25 February 1818.
Proportions unspecified.

In May 1810 the pro-independence movement initiated the use of the blue and white cockade. It was decreed the national cockade on 18 February 1812, and nine days later a flag in these colours was adopted. The blue and white symbolize the clear skies and snow of the Andes. The sun, added in 1818, is the *Sol de Mayo* ("May Sun"), the national symbol of Argentina. It commemorates the appearance of the sun in cloudy skies on 25 May 1810, when the first mass demonstration in favour of independence took place.

The flag with the sun was the state flag and the state and war ensign. Since 16 August 1985 it may also be used as the civil flag and ensign.

THE SOUTH ATLANTIC

FALKLAND ISLANDS

British crown colony in the S Atlantic.

STATE FLAG AND ENSIGN

Introduced in 1948. Proportions 1:2.

The badge in the centre of the fly portion of the British blue ensign contains the arms, granted on 29 September 1948. The ram, standing on tussock grass, denotes that wool is the principal product of the islands. The ship is *Desire* which was commanded by Captain John Davis in 1592 when he discovered the Falklands. The five stars on its sail allude to the Southern Cross constellation.

SOUTH GEORGIA AND SOUTH SANDWICH ISLANDS

British crown colony in the S Atlantic.

STATE FLAG AND ENSIGN

Introduced in 1992. Proportions 1:2.

The British blue ensign is charged with the shield of arms, granted on 14 February 1992. The colours white, blue and green represent ice, snow and grass respectively. The lion is a symbol of British protection and the torch symbolizes exploration. The stars are from the arms of Captain James Cook, who discovered the islands in 1775.

BRITISH ANTARCTIC TERRITORY

British dependent territory in the S Atlantic.

FLAG AND ENSIGN OF THE RESEARCH STATIONS
AND THEIR VESSELS

Adopted in 1963. Proportions 1:2.

This ensign is flown by Natural Environment Research Council vessels engaged on British Antarctic survey work. The ensign features the only use of a white field with the Union Jack in the canton. The arms were granted to the Falkland Islands' Dependencies on 11 March 1952 and with the crest added in 1963 they were assigned to the new colony. The torch is a symbol of exploration; the white field with wavy blue stripes is the ice-covered land and the Antarctic waters. The shield is supported by the British lion and a penguin which represents the local fauna. The crest shows the research ship "Discovery".

SAINT HELENA

British crown colony in the SE Atlantic.

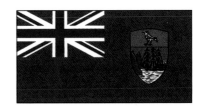

STATE FLAG AND ENSIGN

Introduced in 1984. Proportions 1:2.

The British blue ensign is charged with the shield of arms, granted on 30 January 1984. The ship recalls that in 1659 the island became the possession of the British East India Company. The wirebird is endemic to the island.

213

Flags of Africa

The current national flags of the countries of Africa, from Morocco and Algeria to Anjouan and Mauritius, and their territories, states and provinces are illustrated and described in the following pages.

For ease of reference, the countries of this continent have been divided into geographical areas. We begin in northern Africa and move on through western, central and eastern Africa. Finally we look at the flags of the countries of southern Africa and the islands of the Indian Ocean.

For each entry, the country or territory's name is given in its most easily recognized form and then in all its official languages. This is followed by a description of its political status and geographic position. The basic data for each flag contains the status of the flag, date of adoption, proportions, and symbolic meaning.

NORTH AFRICA

MOROCCO

Kingdom of Morocco,
Arabic **al-Mamlaka al-Maghrebia**.
Constitutional monarchy in NW Africa.

NATIONAL FLAG, CIVIL AND STATE ENSIGN

Adopted 17 November 1915. Proportions 2:3.

The red is the colour of the sheriffs of Mecca. The pentagram, called the "Seal of Solomon", is an ancient symbol of life and good health.

ALGERIA

Democratic and Popular Republic of Algeria, Arabic **al-Jumhuria al-Jazariya ad-Dimuqratiya ash-Shabiya**.
Republic in N Africa.

NATIONAL FLAG AND ENSIGN

Adopted 3 July 1962. Proportions 2:3.

The colours of the flag symbolize Islam (green), purity (white) and liberty (red). The crescent and star is a symbol of Islam, with the crescent being more closed than in other Muslim countries because the Algerians believe that the long horns of the crescent bring happiness.

TUNISIA

Tunisian Republic,
Arabic **al-Jumhuriya at-Tunisiya**.
Republic in N Africa.

NATIONAL FLAG AND ENSIGN

Introduced c.1835. Proportions 2:3.

The flag is based on that of Turkey. Until 1850 the star had six points. The star and crescent stand for Islam.

LIBYA

Great Socialist People's Libyan Arab Republic, Arabic **al-Jamahariya al-Arabiya al-Libya al-shabiya al-Ishtirakiya al-Uzma**.
Socialist republic in N Central Africa.

NATIONAL FLAG AND ENSIGN

Introduced in 1977. Proportions 1:2.

This is the only monochromatic national flag in the world. The green is the colour of Islam and is a manifestation of the Green Revolution proclaimed by President Mu'ammar al Qaddafi.

EGYPT

Arab Republic of Egypt,
Arabic **Jumhuriyat Misr al-Arabiya**.
Republic in NE Africa.

CIVIL AND STATE FLAG AND ENSIGN

Officially hoisted 5 October 1984.
Proportions 2:3.

The red-white-black horizontal tricolour was introduced in Egypt after the revolution of 1953. The central white stripe was charged with two green stars from 1958 to 1972, and with the hawk of Quraish from 1972 to 1984. In 1984 it was replaced by the eagle of Saladin, standing on a panel that carries the name of the country. The eagle bears on its breast a shield, sometimes in the national colours.

SOME HISTORIC FLAGS

While formally part of the Ottoman Empire, in the 18th and 19th centuries Algeria, Tunisia and Tripoli (Libya) each had their own civil ensigns. All the ensigns displayed between five and seven horizontal stripes: white-red-green (Algeria), blue-red-green (Tunisia) and red-green-white (Tripoli). While under foreign domination, Algeria (which was under French rule from 1830-1962) and Libya (under Italian rule from 1912-1947) did not have their own flags. After achieving independence, however, they have made changes to their national flags several times.

WESTERN AFRICA

WESTERN SAHARA

Sahara Arab Democratic Republic,
Arabic **al-Jumhuriya as-Sahrawiya ad-Dimukratiya al-Arabiya**.

State in W Africa currently occupied by Morocco.

NATIONAL FLAG

Introduced 27 February 1976. Proportions 1:2.

Western Sahara proclaimed independence and adopted its flag the day after the formal Spanish withdrawal. The design of the flag is based on that of Palestine, with pan-Arab colours and a red crescent and star, the symbol of Islam. The red symbolizes blood shed in the struggle for independence, the black recalls the period of colonialism, the white stands for liberty and the green is a symbol of progress.

MAURITANIA

Islamic Republic of Mauritania, French **République Islamique Arabe et Africaine de Mauritanie**, Arabic **al-Jumhuriya al-Islamiya al-Mauritaniya**.

Islamic republic in W Africa.

NATIONAL FLAG AND ENSIGN

Adopted 1 April 1959. Proportions 2:3.

The green and the crescent and star are both symbols of Islam; the green also represents hope for a bright future. The yellow stands for the Sahara Desert.

MALI

Republic of Mali,
French **République du Mali**.

Republic in W Africa.

NATIONAL FLAG AND ENSIGN

Adopted 1 March 1961. Proportions 2:3.

The flag, based on the French *Tricolore*, displays the pan-African colours. They stand for nature (green), purity and mineral resources (yellow), and for bravery and blood shed in the struggle for independence (red).

SENEGAL

Republic of Senegal,
French **République du Sénégal**.

Republic in W Africa.

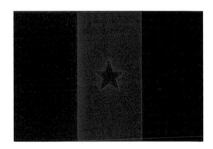

NATIONAL FLAG AND ENSIGN

Introduced in 1960. Proportions 2:3.

After the dissolution of the federation with Mali, Senegal retained the colours of the flag and placed a green star in the centre, symbolizing unity and hope. The green is an expression of hope for undisturbed progress, the yellow represents the verdant land and the wealth which will be the fruit of collective labour. The red recalls the martyrs and the common struggle of the African nations for independence; it is also a symbol of life and socialism.

THE GAMBIA

Republic of the Gambia.

Republic in W Africa.

NATIONAL FLAG, CIVIL AND STATE ENSIGN

Introduced 18 February 1965. Proportions 2:3.

The original idea for the flag came from the Gambia, but the design was prepared by the College of Arms in London. The red stands for the sun, the blue represents the river Gambia and the green symbolizes the fertile land and agriculture. The white stripes stand for unity and peace.

GUINEA-BISSAU

Republic of Guinea-Bissau,
Portuguese **República da Guiné-Bissau**.

Republic in W Africa.

NATIONAL FLAG AND ENSIGN

Introduced 24 September 1973. Proportions 1:2.

In August 1961 the African Party for the Independence of Guinea and Cape Verde adopted a flag in pan-African colours with the party initials (PAIGC) beneath a black star. When independence was proclaimed the flag, without the initials, became the national flag of Guinea-Bissau.

The red stands for the suffering under colonial rule and for the blood shed in the struggle for independence. The yellow symbolizes the fruits of work that contribute to well-being. The green represents the tropical forests of the country and hope for a bright future. The star is a symbol of Africa and its people.

GUINEA

Republic of Guinea,
French **République de Guinée**.
Republic in W Africa.

NATIONAL FLAG AND ENSIGN

Adopted 10 November 1958. Proportions 2:3.

The first French colony to achieve independence, Guinea patterned its flag on the French *Tricolore*. Sékou Touré, the first President of Guinea, stated that by choosing the same colours as those of Ghana his country intended to show its dedication to African unity. The colours reflect the national motto "Work, Justice, Solidarity". The red is the colour of blood and reflects the spirit of sacrifice and hard work, and symbolizes the will for progress. The yellow is the colour of the gold of Guinea and of the African sun, which is the source of energy, generosity and equality as it shines on everyone. The green is the colour of the vegetation, agriculture, the productivity of the peasants and the spirit of solidarity in collective enterprises. Thus the three colours of the flag symbolize the three bases of the republic: labour, justice and solidarity.

SIERRA LEONE

Republic of Sierra Leone.
Republic in W Africa.

NATIONAL FLAG

Officially hoisted 27 April 1961. Proportions 2:3.

The green represents the agriculture, natural resources and the mountains. The white stands for unity and justice. The blue is a symbol of hope that the only natural harbour in Freetown will be able to make its contribution to peace throughout the world.

LIBERIA

Republic of Liberia.Republic in W Africa.

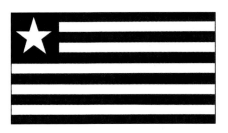

NATIONAL FLAG

Adopted 27 August 1847. Proportions 10:19.

The design of the flag copies that of the United States, from where since 1822 freed slaves came to settle in Liberia. The white star represents the shining light of the new republic in the dark continent, represented by a blue square. The 11 stripes symbolize the 11 signatories of the Liberian Declaration of Independence.

IVORY COAST

Republic of Côte d'Ivoire, French
République de la Côte d'Ivoire.
Republic in W Africa.

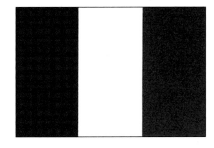

NATIONAL FLAG AND ENSIGN

Adopted 3 December 1959. Proportions 2:3.

The flag is based on the French *Tricolore*. The orange represents the savannahs of the north and the spirit of national development. The green stands for the forests in the south and for the hope of a better future based on natural resources. The white is the colour of the sky and purity, symbolizing unity between the north and south of the country.

BURKINA FASO

**The People's Democratic Republic of
Burkina Faso**, French **République
Démocratique Populaire de Burkina Faso**.
Socialist republic in W Africa.

NATIONAL FLAG

Adopted 4 August 1984. Proportions 2:3.

The red is a symbol of revolutionary concern to transform the country and the green symbolizes hope and abundance. The star stands for the revolution, leading the nation to a golden future. The yellow represents the undiscovered mineral resources.

GHANA

Republic of Ghana. Republic in W Africa.

NATIONAL FLAG AND STATE ENSIGN

Adopted 6 March 1957. Proportions 2:3.

Ghana was the first country in black Africa to use the Ethiopian colours, which have since been called pan-African. The black star symbolizes the lodestar of African freedom. The red commemorates those who worked for independence, the gold (yellow) represents the wealth of the country (its former name was the Gold Coast) and the green stands for forests and farms.

TOGO

Republic of Togo,
French **République Togolaise**.
Republic in W Africa.

NATIONAL FLAG AND ENSIGN

Adopted 27 April 1960. Proportions 2:3.

The green symbolizes hope and the yellow signifies faith in work as the way to achieve material, moral and spiritual well-being. The red is a symbol of charity, fidelity and love, the virtues that make people love their neighbours and sacrifice their own lives, if necessary, for the triumph of the principles of humanity and the lessening

of human misery. The white is the colour of purity, reminding all citizens to be worthy of their nation's independence.

BENIN

People's Republic of Benin, French
République Populaire du Benin.
Socialist republic in W Africa.

NATIONAL FLAG AND ENSIGN

Adopted 16 November 1959, re-established 1 August 1990. Proportions 2:3.

The green denotes hope for renewal, the red evokes the ancestors' courage and the yellow refers to the country's riches.

CAPE VERDE

Republic of Cape Verde, Portuguese
República de Cabo Verde.
Republic comprising an archipelago
in the Atlantic, W Africa.

NATIONAL FLAG AND ENSIGN

*Officially hoisted 25 September 1992.
Proportions 10:17.*

The ring of stars symbolizes the unity of all parts of the country. The ten stars represent the ten main islands of the archipelago: São Tiago, Santo Antão, São Vincente, São Nicolau, Sal, Boa Vista, Fogo, Maio, Brava and Santa Luzia. The colours symbolize the

sky and the sea (blue), peace (white) and the efforts of the people (red).

NIGERIA

Federal Republic of Nigeria.
Federal republic in W Africa.

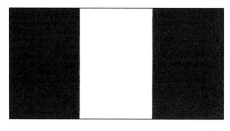

NATIONAL FLAG

Officially hoisted 1 October 1960. Proportions 1:2.

The green reflects the green land of Nigeria and stands for its agriculture. The white symbolizes peace.

SÃO TOMÉ AND PRÍNCIPE

Democratic Republic of São Tomé and Príncipe, Portuguese **República Democrática de São Tomé and Príncipe**.
Republic consisting of several islands
in the Gulf of Guinea.

NATIONAL FLAG AND ENSIGN

Adopted 5 November 1975. Proportions 1:2.

The two stars represent the two main islands of the nation: São Tomé and Príncipe. The red stands for the blood shed in the struggle for independence, the green is the colour of the rich vegetation and the yellow represents cocoa, which is one of the main agricultural products.

CENTRAL AFRICA

NIGER

Republic of Niger,

French **République du Niger.**

Republic in N Central Africa.

NATIONAL FLAG

Adopted 23 November 1959.
Proportions unspecified.

The orange represents the Sahara Desert, with the white being a symbol of purity and innocence. The orange disc represents the sun and symbolizes the sacrifices made by the people, their firm commitment and their determination to defend human rights and justice. The green, a symbol of hope, represents the fertile and productive zone of Niger.

CHAD

Republic of Chad,

French **République du Tchad.**

Republic in N Central Africa.

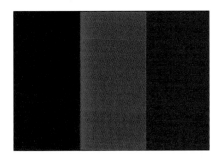

NATIONAL FLAG

Adopted 6 November 1959. Proportions 2:3.

The blue represents the rivers and forests, the yellow symbolizes sand and the desert, and the red is a symbol of sacrifice and the blood of martyrs.

CAMEROON

Republic of Cameroon,

French **République du Cameroun.**

Republic in W Central Africa.

NATIONAL FLAG AND ENSIGN

Adopted 20 May 1975. Proportions 2:3.

The green stands for the luxuriant vegetation of the south, and also represents hope for a rich, prosperous, hard-working and unified Cameroon. The red is a symbol of sovereignty and of unity between the north and the south. The yellow represents the soil of the north, wealth and the sun. The star symbolizes unity.

CENTRAL AFRICAN REPUBLIC

French **République Centrafricaine.**

Republic in W Central Africa.

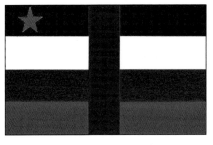

NATIONAL FLAG

Introduced 1 December 1958.
Proportions unspecified.

The flag displays the colours of France (blue-white-red) combined with the pan-African colours (green-yellow-red) to show that Europeans and Africans should have respect and friendship for one another. Their common bond, their red blood, is represented by the vertical red stripe

binding all the stripes together. The star symbolizes independence.

EQUATORIAL GUINEA

Republic of Equatorial Guinea,

Spanish **República de Guinea Ecuatorial.**

Republic in W Central Africa.

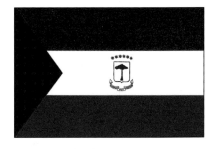

NATIONAL FLAG AND ENSIGN

Adopted 12 October 1968, re-adopted
21 August 1979. Proportions unspecified.

The blue represents the sea linking the mainland of the country with Bioko and other islands. The colour green symbolizes its tropical forests and natural riches, the white stands for peace and the red commemorates the blood shed in the struggle for independence. The main device of the arms is the tree under which King Bonkoro signed the treaty with Spain in 1843. The six stars represent the six districts of the state.

GABON

Gabonese Republic,

French **République Gabonaise.**

Republic in W Central Africa.

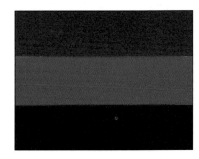

NATIONAL FLAG AND ENSIGN

Adopted 9 August 1960. Proportions 3:4.

The design of the flag was inspired by the geographical position of Gabon. The green (forests) and the blue (Atlantic Ocean) are separated by the yellow stripe, which stands for the Equator and the ever-present sun.

CONGO

Republic of Congo,
French **République du Congo**.
Republic in Central Africa.

NATIONAL FLAG

Adopted 18 August 1959, re-established 10 June 1991. Proportions 2:3.

The green stands for nature and peace. The yellow represents the natural wealth and expresses hope for a better future. The red is a symbol of independence and of the dignity of all humanity.

CONGO

Democratic Republic of Congo, French **République Démocratique du Congo**.
Republic in Central Africa.

NATIONAL FLAG AND ENSIGN

Adopted 30 June 1960, re-adopted 17 May 1997. Proportions 2:3.

The blue flag with a large yellow star in the centre was the flag of Congo from 1885 to 1960, when the six stars along the hoist were added. The blue symbolizes the river Congo and the star symbolizes a bright future. The six stars represent the six provinces existing at the time of independence.

RWANDA

Republic of Rwanda, Kinyarwanda **Republika y'u Rwanda**, French **République Rwandaise**.
Republic in E Central Africa.

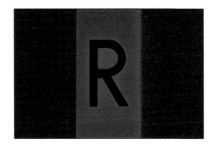

NATIONAL FLAG

Adopted 28 January 1961. Proportions 2:3.

The red represents the blood and pain suffered in the struggle for independence, the yellow is a symbol of tranquillity and peace, and the green represents hope and optimism. The initial "R" for Rwanda has been added to differentiate the flag from that of Guinea.

BURUNDI

Republic of Burundi, Kirundi **Republika y'Uburundi**, French **République du Burundi**.
Republic in E Central Africa.

STATE FLAG

Adopted 26 December 1968. Proportions 3:5 (established 27 September 1982).

The colours represent the struggle for independence (red), hope (green) and peace (white). The three stars symbolize the national motto "Unity, Work, Progress".

EASTERN AFRICA

SUDAN

Democratic Republic of Sudan,
Arabic **Jumhuriyat es-Sudan**.
Military republic in NE Africa.

NATIONAL FLAG AND ENSIGN

Officially hoisted 20 May 1970. Proportions 1:2.

The red stands for struggles and for the martyrs in the Sudan and the great Arab land. The white is the colour of peace, optimism, light and love. The black represents the Sudan and the Mahdija Revolution, during which a black flag was used. The green symbolizes Islamic prosperity and agriculture.

ERITREA

State of Eritrea,
Tigrinya **Hagere Eritrea**.
Republic in NE Africa.

NATIONAL FLAG

Adopted 24 May 1993. Proportions 1:2.

The basic design of the flag is identical to the flag of the Eritrean People's Liberation Front. The olive wreath with an upright branch in the centre recalls the emblem on the first flag of Eritrea (1952).

ETHIOPIA

Federal Democratic Republic of Ethiopia, Amharic **Hebretesebawit Ityopia**.

Republic in NE Africa.

STATE FLAG

Adopted 6 February 1996. Proportions 1:2.

The Ethiopian horizontal tricolour dates back to *c.*1895. In 1996 the new national emblem was placed in the centre of the flag. The blue symbolizes peace and the pentagram represents the unity of the nations, nationalities and peoples of Ethiopia.

The original symbolism of the colours denoted the Christian virtues. In the present official symbolism, the green represents fertility, labour and development; the yellow, hope, justice and equality, and the red, sacrifice and heroism in the cause of freedom and equality.

DJIBOUTI

Republic of Djibouti, French **République de Djibouti**, Arabic **Jumhuriya Djibouti**.

Republic in NE Africa.

NATIONAL FLAG AND ENSIGN

Officially hoisted 27 June 1977.
Proportions 21:38.

The colours of the flag stand for the sea and sky (blue), the earth (green) and peace (white). Green and blue are also the colours of the two main population groups, the Afars and Issas respectively. The red star recalls the struggle for independence and is a symbol of unity.

SOMALILAND

Republic of Somaliland, Somali **Jamhuriyadda Somaliland**.

De facto independent republic in NE Africa.

NATIONAL FLAG AND ENSIGN

Introduced 14 October 1996.
Proportions unspecified.

The flag displays the pan-Arab colours; the star stands for the republic. On the green stripe is *Shahada*, the Muslim Statement of Faith.

SOMALIA

Somali Democratic Republic, Somali **Jamhuriyadda Dimugradiga ee Soomaliya**.

Republic in E Africa.

NATIONAL FLAG AND ENSIGN

Officially introduced 12 October 1954.
Proportions unspecified.

The adoption of the blue was influenced by the blue field of the United Nations flag. The five points of the star represent the five countries in which the Somalis live: Somali (Italian colony), British Somali, Ethiopia, Kenya and Djibouti.

KENYA

Republic of Kenya, Kiswahili **Jamhuri ya Kenya**.

Republic in E Africa.

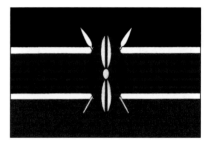

NATIONAL FLAG, CIVIL AND STATE ENSIGN

Officially introduced 12 December 1963.
Proportions 2:3.

The colours symbolize the people (black), the struggle for independence (red) and agriculture (green). The white stripes stand for peace and unity. The Masai shield and spears represent the will to defend freedom.

UGANDA

Republic of Uganda, Kiswahili **Jamhuri ya Uganda**.

Republic in E Central Africa.

NATIONAL FLAG

Officially hoisted 9 October 1962.
Proportions unspecified.

The colours of the flag derive from the flag of the Uganda People's Congress, the party that won the first elections. They symbolize the people of Africa (black), sunshine (yellow) and brotherhood (red). The crested crane (*Balearica pavonia*) is the symbol of Uganda and has already appeared on the colonial badge in the early 20th century.

TANZANIA

United Republic of Tanzania,
Kiswahili **Jamhuri ya Muungano wa Tanzania**.
Republic in E Africa.

NATIONAL FLAG AND ENSIGN

Adopted 30 June 1964. Proportions 2:3.

The colours of the flag combine those of the flags of Tanganyika (green, yellow, black) and Zanzibar (blue, black, green). They symbolize the people (black), the land (green), the sea (blue) and the mineral wealth (yellow).

TANZANIA

The red flag of the Sultanate of Zanzibar dated from the 18th century. On 12 January 1964 the sultan was overthrown and the new republic adopted a flag with three vertical stripes of blue, yellow, and green. Less than three weeks later the flag was changed to a horizontal tricolour of blue, black and green. At that time, Tanganyika's flag was green with a black horizontal stripe fimbriated yellow and positioned in the centre of the flag. In April 1964 the two formed a united republic, combining the two flags into the flag that we see today.

SOUTHERN AFRICA AND INDIAN OCEAN

MOZAMBIQUE

People's Republic of Mozambique,
Portuguese **República Popular de Moçambique**.
Republic in SE Africa.

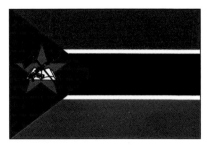

NATIONAL FLAG AND ENSIGN

Introduced in April 1983.
Proportions unspecified.

The flag follows the design of the Frelimo Party flag. The star symbolizes the spirit of international solidarity. The book, hoe and gun stand for study, production and defence. The red recalls "the centuries of resistance to colonialism, the armed national liberation struggle, and the defence of sovereignty". The other colours represent the riches of the soil (green), the African continent (black), the mineral riches (yellow), and justice and peace (white).

MALAWI

Republic of Malawi,
Chichewa **Mfuko la Malawi**.
Republic in SE Africa.

NATIONAL FLAG

Officially hoisted 6 July 1964. Proportions 2:3.

The leading force in the struggle for independence was the Malawi Congress Party. Its flag, a horizontal tricolour of

black-red-green, served as the basis for the national flag. A sun emblem was added to symbolize the dawn of hope and freedom for the whole of Africa. The black stands for the people of Africa, the red symbolizes the blood of the martyrs of African freedom, and the green represents the vegetation of Malawi.

ZAMBIA

Republic of Zambia.
Republic in S Central Africa.

NATIONAL FLAG

Officially hoisted 24 October 1964. Shape of the eagle modified in 1996. Proportions 2:3.

The eagle in flight symbolizes freedom in Zambia and the ability to rise above the country's problems. The red represents the struggle for independence, the black the people of Zambia, the orange its mineral wealth and the green its natural resources.

ANGOLA

Republic of Angola,
Portuguese **República de Angola**.
Republic in SW Africa.

NATIONAL FLAG AND ENSIGN

Introduced 11 November 1975. Proportions 2:3.

The red symbolizes the blood shed in the struggle for independence. The black stands for Africa. The cog-wheel and machete are symbols of the workers and peasants respectively. The star symbolizes international solidarity and progress. The yellow signifies the wealth of the nation.

NAMIBIA

Republic of Namibia.
Republic in SW Africa.

NATIONAL FLAG AND ENSIGN

Adopted 21 March 1990. Proportions 2:3.

The sun symbolizes life and energy. The golden yellow represents the plains and the Namib Desert. The blue represents the sky, the Atlantic Ocean, the marine resources of Namibia, and the importance of rain and water. The red stands for the people, their heroism and their determination to build a future of equal opportunity for all. The green is a symbol of the vegetation and natural resources. The white refers to peace and unity.

BOTSWANA

Republic of Botswana.
Republic in S Central Africa.

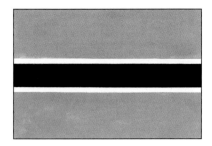

NATIONAL FLAG

*Officially hoisted 30 September 1966.
Proportions 2:3.*

The blue symbolizes the sky and reliance on water. The black and white represent the majority and minority of the country's population respectively.

ZIMBABWE

Republic of Zimbabwe.
Republic in S Central Africa.

NATIONAL FLAG AND ENSIGN

*Officially introduced 18 April 1980.
Proportions 1:2.*

The emblem displays a red star, representing socialism, and the Great Zimbabwe Bird, which represents the great past of the country. The colours of the flag symbolize the majority of the population (black), the blood shed in the struggle for independence (red), the mineral wealth (yellow), the agriculture (green) and peace (white).

SOUTH AFRICA

Republic of South Africa,
Afrikaans **Republiek van Suid-Afrika**.
Republic in S Africa.

NATIONAL FLAG, CIVIL AND STATE ENSIGN

*Officially introduced 27 April 1994.
Proportions 2:3.*

The flag combines the colours of the Boer republics (red, white, blue) with the colours of the African National Congress (black,

green, yellow), which came to power in 1994. The ANC is shown as a driving force behind the country's convergence and unification which is symbolized by the "Y" shape.

LESOTHO

Kingdom of Lesotho,
Lesotho **Mmuso wa Lesotho**.
Constitutional monarchy in S Africa.

NATIONAL FLAG

*Officially introduced 20 January 1987.
Proportions 2:3.*

The colours of the flag symbolize peace (white), rain (blue) and prosperity (green). The Lesotho shield with weapons symbolizes a will to defend the country.

SWAZILAND

Kingdom of Swaziland,
Swazi **Umbuso we Swatini**.
Absolute monarchy in SE Africa.

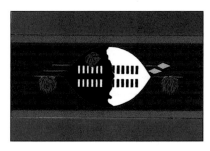

STATE FLAG

Adopted 30 October 1967. Proportions 2:3.

The red symbolizes the battles of the past, the yellow represents the wealth of the country's resources and the blue stands for peace. The black and white Swazi shield is that of the Emasotha Regiment, formed in the late 1920s. Behind the shield appear their assegais and a traditional fighting stick with *tinjobo* tassels, made from widow-bird and loury feathers.

MADAGASCAR

Democratic Republic of Madagascar,
Malagasy **Repoblika Demokratika n`i Madagaskar**.
Republic comprising an island in the Indian Ocean.

NATIONAL FLAG AND ENSIGN

Adopted in October 1958. Proportions 2:3.

The choice of colours for the national flag was influenced by the fact that white and red were the flags of the Hova Empire in the 19th century. The green was added for the peoples living on the coast. The colours symbolize purity (white), sovereignty (red) and hope (green).

COMOROS

Federal Islamic Republic of Comoros,
Arabic **Jumhuriyat al-Qumur al-Ittihadiya al-Islamiya**, Comorian **Dja Mouhouri Yamtsangagniho ya Kissilam ya Komori**.
Republic consisting of Grand Comore island in the Indian Ocean.

NATIONAL FLAG AND ENSIGN

Adopted 3 October 1996. Proportions 2:3.

The green field and the crescent stand for Islam. The four stars represent the four islands of the archipelago, despite the fact that Mayotte, Anjouan and Mohéli are separate political entities. The word "Allah" appears in the upper fly corner, and the word "Muhammad" in the lower hoist.

ANJOUAN

State of Anjouan
De facto independent country comprising an island in the Indian Ocean.

NATIONAL FLAG AND ENSIGN

Approved on 25 February 1998. Proportions 2:3.

The red flag with a right hand and a crescent was used by the Sultanate of Anjouan in the 19th century. Red was for centuries the colour of the Arab colonies along the coast of eastern Africa and on the islands in the Indian Ocean, and the crescent is the symbol of Islam.

SEYCHELLES

Republic of Seychelles,
Creole **Repibik Sesel**.
Republic consisting of a group of islands in the Indian Ocean.

NATIONAL FLAG AND ENSIGN

Adopted 8 January 1996. Proportions 1:2.

The flag is a combination of the colours of the two main political parties, the Democratic Party (which is represented by blue and yellow) and the Seychelles People's United Party (represented by red, white and green). The blue symbolizes the sky and the sea; the yellow represents the sun; red stands for the people and their determination to work in unity; white symbolizes social justice and harmony; and green stands for the land.

MAURITIUS

Republic of Mauritius.
Republic comprising an island in the Indian Ocean.

NATIONAL FLAG

Officially hoisted 12 March 1968. Proportions 2:3.

The red stripe represents the struggle for freedom and independence, the blue stripe stands for the colour of the Indian Ocean. The yellow stripe symbolizes the new light of independence, and the green stripe represents agriculture and symbolizes the colour of lush, green Mauritius throughout the year.

Flags of International Organizations

These flags are presented in chronological order, beginning with the flag of the Red Cross, which has existed since 1863. The latest addition to the family of international organizations is the Portuguese-speaking community, whose flag was adopted in 1996.

THE RED CROSS

The International Committee of the Red Cross was established in 1863. Its activities follow the Geneva Conventions of 1864, 1907, 1929, 1947 and 1977 on the treatment of prisoners of war and the protection of civilians during hostilities and natural catastrophes.

The flag was proposed by the Red Cross's founder, the Swiss philanthropist Henri Dunant, and was adopted in 1863 as the flag of Switzerland in reversed colours. The flag used in Muslim countries, which was adopted in 1876, displays a red Muslim crescent instead of the cross.

THE COMMONWEALTH

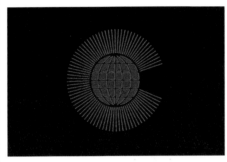

Originally the members of the Commonwealth of Nations were the United Kingdom and its self-governing Dominions. The term "British Commonwealth" began to be used after World War I. In 1949 the name was changed to the Commonwealth and in 1965 the Commonwealth Secretariat in London was established. A total of 54 independent countries from all parts of the world belong to the Commonwealth.

The flag displays the letter "C" (as the first letter of "Commonwealth") which encircles a central globe, denoting the global scope of the organization. The number of lines forming the letter "C" does not correspond to the number of member-states.

LEAGUE OF ARAB STATES

The main aim of the Arab League is to protect the independence and sovereignty of the 22 member-states, and to safeguard their interests. The flag was adopted in 1945, the year the organization was founded. The green and the crescent symbolize Islam and the name of the organization appears in the centre of the emblem. The chain is a symbol of unity and the laurel wreath stands for peace as well as dignity.

UNITED NATIONS

The United Nations was established in 1945 to promote international peace, security and co-operation. It is the largest and the most important international organization, with 185 member-states. Its specialized departments handle international issues including economic, monetary, scientific, educational, social, judicial and health matters.

The flag was adopted on 20 October 1947. The colour blue and the olive branches symbolize peace, and the map of the world represents the organization's global concerns.

SOUTH PACIFIC COMMISSION

The South Pacific Commission was set up in 1947 to advise the governments of Australia, New Zealand, Great Britain, France, the Netherlands and the United States on economic, social and health matters affecting the territories in the South Pacific administered by them. At present the Commission has 27 member-states. The emblem, formed by the letter "C" and a ring of stars, resembles an atoll. The six points of the stars symbolize the original six members of the Commission and the number of stars represents the number of member-states.

ORGANIZATION OF AMERICAN STATES

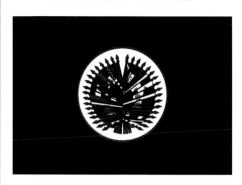

This name and the charter of the organization were adopted in 1948. The main goal of the member-states of OAS is to uphold sovereignty and to work for peace and prosperity in the region. The flag, adopted in 1965, has been modified several times as the flags of new member-states were added to the emblem; currently the emblem displays the flags of 35 member-states.

NORTH ATLANTIC TREATY ORGANIZATION

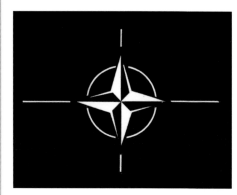

NATO was formed in 1949 by the countries of western Europe and North America, originally as a united defence against the threat of Soviet aggression. The flag was adopted in 1954. Its dark blue field represents the Atlantic Ocean, the circle is a symbol of unity and the compass symbolizes the common direction towards peace that has been taken by the 19 member-nations.

ORGANIZATION OF PETROLEUM EXPORTING COUNTRIES

OPEC was set up in 1961 by the main oil-producing countries and currently has 11 members; the flag was adopted in 1970. The emblem is formed from the stylized letters "OPEC".

ORGANIZATION OF AFRICAN UNITY

The OAU was formed in 1963 and includes all independent African countries. Its aim is mutual co-operation and peaceful settlement of conflicts. The colours of the flag, adopted in 1970, symbolize the natural environment of Africa (green), its golden future (golden yellow) and a peaceful co-existence (white). The emblem is a golden map of Africa encircled by a golden wreath.

ASSOCIATION OF SOUTH-EAST ASIAN NATIONS

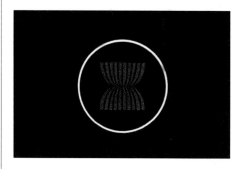

ASEAN was formed in 1967 to promote regional stability and economic co-operation. The flag, adopted in 1997, displays the colours of the flags of the member-states. The blue stands for the sea, the sky and friendship. The emblem is formed of ten *padi* stalks, representing the ten member-states.

CARIBBEAN COMMUNITY AND COMMON MARKET

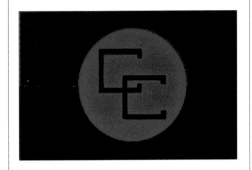

CARICOM is a regional organization, established in 1973 to promote unity, economic integration and co-operation between the small, insular countries of the Caribbean. It has a total of 14 members. The stripes of the flag represent the sky and the sea, and the yellow disc stands for the sun. The letters are the initials of the community.

ORGANIZATION OF THE ISLAMIC CONFERENCE

The main aim of the organization, founded in 1974, is to promote unity and to prevent foreign interference in the domestic affairs of the 35 member-states. The flag, in pan-Arab colours, was adopted in 1981. The green and the crescent symbolize Islam, and the inscription in the centre reads *Allah u Akbar* ("God is Great").

UNION OF THE ARAB MAGHREB

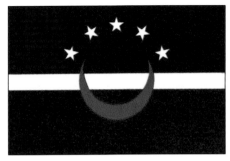

This was set up in 1989 to co-ordinate the communications and economic policies of its member-countries. The flag was adopted in 1990. The five stars represent the UAM members: Morocco, Mauritania, Algeria, Tunisia and Libya; the colours were taken from the flags of the member-countries.

COMMONWEALTH OF INDEPENDENT STATES

This was formed on the eve of the fall of the Soviet Union in 1991; the 12 member-states are all former Soviet republics. The flag was adopted on 19 January 1996 and the emblem symbolizes aspiration for an equal partnership, unity, peace and stability.

EUROPEAN UNION

The flag, originally adopted on 8 December 1955 by the Council of Europe, was taken over by the European Union on 29 May 1986. The blue symbolizes the sky, the 12 golden stars in a circle represent the union of Europe.

LA FRANCOPHONIE

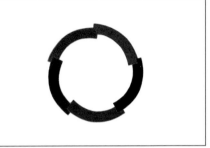

This organization provides an institutional framework of official and private organizations and associations representing the interests of the French-speaking community, encompassing 47 countries. The emblem conveys the idea of bringing together and denotes the universal character of La Francophonie. The five parts of the ring symbolize the five continents where members of the community live (North America, Europe, Africa, Asia and Oceania).

COMMUNITY OF NATIONS OF THE PORTUGUESE LANGUAGE

The main aim of the CPLP (Comunidade dos Países de Língua Portuguesa) is to promote unity and co-operation. The flag, adopted on 17 July 1996, displays the historic colours of Portugal (blue and white) and a logo symbolizing the close ties among the seven member-states.

Regional and Local Flags

In the Middle Ages many European provinces were independent or semi-independent political entities, some of which have retained their original flags. But in central Europe provincial flags as such began to appear only in the 19th century, and most of them date from the second half of the 20th century. Throughout the world provincial flags fit into a general pattern that is particular to each country or has some features in common with other countries.

Some municipal flags, such as those of Genoa or Elbing, are among the oldest flags in the world but, like provincial flags, most were designed in the 20th century. With both provincial and municipal flags the principal factors influencing design are heraldry and the use of charges, whether these are armorial devices, Japanese *mons* or modern logos.

◆ **ABOVE** Flag display on a street in Lucerne. All civic and commune flags in Switzerland are in the form of a square armorial banner.

REGIONS AND PROVINCES

The first country to provide its provinces with flags (*Landesfarben*) was Prussia. In 1882 the government of Prussia approved the flags of Brandenburg, Hanover, East Prussia, Pomerania, Posen, Rhineland, Silesia, Westphalia, West Prussia and Hohenzollern. The provincial flag of Saxony was approved in 1884, and that of Hessen-Nassau in 1892. All of these flags displayed horizontal stripes in livery colours, based on the arms approved or granted in 1881. The flag of Posen was changed in 1896 to show Prussian colours rather than Polish, and was changed

FLAGS OF PRUSSIAN PROVINCES

BERLIN (1861–1911).

BRANDENBURG (1882–1935).

EAST PRUSSIA (1822–1935).

HANOVER (1882–1935).

HESSEN-NASSAU (1882–1935).

HOHENZOLLERN (1815–1935).

POMERANIA (1882–1935).

POSEN (1882–1896).

RHEINLAND (1882–1935).

SAXONY (1884–1935).

SCHLESWIG-HOLSTEIN (1866–1935).

SILESIA (1882–1935).

WESTPHALIA (1882–1935).

WEST PRUSSIA (1882–1923).

POSEN (1896–1923).

POSEN-WEST PRUSSIA (1923–1935).

UPPER SILESIA (1925–1935).

Alsace.

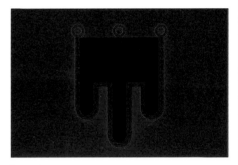

Auvergne.

Franche-Comté.

again in 1923 when Posen was united with West Prussia.

In many other European countries provincial flags are mostly heraldic banners. For example, the flags of the provinces of France and the counties of Norway are all armorial banners. Regional banners have been introduced in France during the last few decades but some, such as the flags of the duchies of Anjou and Maine or the kingdom of Burgundy, were already known in the Middle Ages. In contrast to the French armorial banners, which are quite complex, the flags of the Norwegian counties display single, simple heraldic figures. Many of them were proposed in 1930, but they were only officially adopted between the 1950s and 1989. The flags illustrated here were adopted in 1960 (Troms), 1965 (Nordland) and 1989 (Oppland). For a long time the flags of all nine provinces in Belgium were armorial banners. But now there are ten provinces,

PROVINCES OF NORWAY

Nordland.

Oppland.

Troms.

PROVINCES OF BELGIUM

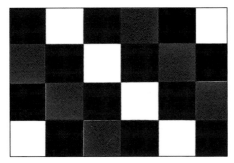

Antwerp.

East Flanders.

West Flanders.

PREFECTURES OF JAPAN

Hokkaido.

Toyama.

Tokio.

and some of the existing provinces have adopted new flags. Heraldry has influenced all the Belgian designs but the only armorial banner is the flag of West Flanders. Finland is the only country where the provincial flags, which display the livery colours, consist of very long pennants.

The flags of the Japanese prefectures are modest yet very distinctive: their chief characteristic is their uniformity of style. Nearly all of them display a *mon* or logo in the centre of a unicoloured field, often an

PENNANTS OF THE PROVINCES OF FINLAND

Uusimaa
Ruotsinkielinen Uusimaa
Varsinais-Suomi/
Ruotsinkielinen Pohjanmaa
Häme
Etelä-Pohjanmaa
Kainuu

Ahvenanmaa
Satakunta
Karjala

Savo
Keski-Pohjanmaa
Varsinais-Suomi

Pohjois-Pohjanmaa
Kymenlaakso
Lappi

Siniristi (koko Suomen yleisviiri)
Keski-Suomi
Etelä-Karjala

unusual colour such as dark brown, rust brown, plum, lavender, violet or turquoise green. These flags were adopted after World War II, mostly in the 1960s. The colourful provincial flags of Papua New Guinea, adopted in 1978–1979, are very different. Although they do not display traditional heraldic figures, their appearance resembles armorial banners. Most of the emblems contain local birds or animals, insignias of authority, leadership and bravery, or artefacts used during ceremonies.

Thai Province of Nonthaburi

Province of Mindoro Occidental, Philippines

PROVINCES OF PAPUA NEW GUINEA

East New Britain.

Madang.

Simbu.

Provincial flags in other countries are either standardized, as in the Philippines and Thailand, or display common emblems or colours. Provincial flags in Morocco are square armorial banners with a *schwenkel*

PROVINCES OF MOROCCO

Casablanca.

Ouarzazate.

in national colours, i.e. red with the green Seal of Solomon; the arms of the provinces were established in 1968. Provincial flags in Liberia have the national flag in the canton, while those in the Philippines display the seal of the province in the centre of a unicolour white, yellow or red field. The field of almost all the provincial flags in Venezuela is white and all of them are defaced with the coat of arms of the province. The only exemption is the flag of Sucre, which is a diagonal bicolour of white and blue with 14 white stars in the lower hoist and the provincial coat of arms in the upper hoist. Thai provinces use the national flag defaced with the provincial emblem, all of which are circular. The flags of some Argentinian provinces display the national colours of light blue and white.

The most diversified provincial flags are those of the United States. Most consist of a plain field embossed with the state's seal and the symbol of authority, and in many the field is also charged with inscriptions such as the name of the state and the date of its foundation or

incorporation. There are a multitude of designs based on partitions of the field and displaying various emblems, and some of them are very innovative.

France has recently developed a series of flags that are unsuccessful from a vexillological perspective. The departments and regions, which as we have already seen have beautiful armorial banners, have also adopted white flags charged with logos in shapes and colours that are difficult to recognize from a distance. In most cases the logos are accompanied by long, illegible inscriptions. This, of course, means that it is difficult to recognize and distinguish between the flags when in use.

Nord-Pas-de-Calais. Typical example of new French regional and departmental flags.

UNITED STATES COUNTIES

Franklin (Illinois).

Santa Clara (California).

Sussex (New Jersey).

Civic Flags

In several European countries there is a general design for municipal flags. In Switzerland they are all square armorial banners. In Portugal they are square, gyronny and defaced with the full achievement of the civic arms. In Slovenia all the municipal flags have the proportions 1:3 and display the main heraldic figure from the coat of arms; the field is either plain or partitioned in one of ten different ways; seven have a square field at the hoist.

Slovakia is the only European country where the flags of all 135 cities and towns were established centrally by the Heraldry Commission of the Ministry of Internal Affairs. The flags are swallow-tailed, in proportions 2:3, and display the livery colours. 105 of the flags are composed solely of two to nine horizontal stripes, ten have fields charged with a saltire and ten are quartered. The flags of rural communities are triple swallow-tailed and also display the livery colours.

In Italy and Spain municipal flags are more diverse. Some designs, however, are more frequently used than others and are characteristic of the country, namely a

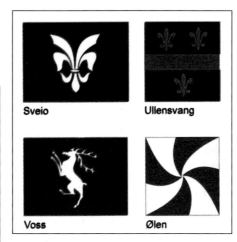

Sveio
Ullensvang
Voss
Ølen

vertical bicolour or a field charged with a cross in Italy and a plain field charged with a coat of arms in Spain. The use of a civic flag in the form of a gonfalon has survived in many Italian cities.

Municipal flags in Germany, Austria, the Czech Republic and Poland have several common characteristics. Most of them are horizontal bicolours or tricolours, they display livery colours and are often defaced with an armorial shield or the full achievement of arms. In West Germany just over 100 cities use the white-red bicolour, whereas the red-white bicolour has been adopted by more than 130 cities. Other bicolours are very popular there: blue-white (almost 90 cities), blue-yellow (65 cities), red-yellow (more than 60 cities) and black-

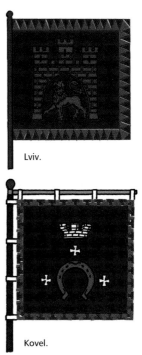

Lviv.

Kovel.

yellow (more than 50 cities). Much more inventive, distinctive and recognizable flags have been designed in recent years in Poland, the Czech Republic and the eastern part of Germany. The trend is to introduce more ingenious partitions of the field and to display some heraldic devices from the arms instead of the whole coat of arms. Ukrainian cities have begun to acquire municipal flags only in recent years and fewer than a quarter of the 1500 cities have their own flags. They are usually

Bari.

Ancona (Italy).

◆ **ABOVE**
Typical examples of flags of the communes in Hordaland (Norway).

◆ **ABOVE RIGHT**
Two typical Ukrainian municipal flags.

◆ **LEFT**
Ceremonial flag of Rome, at the town hall.

◆ **RIGHT**
Polish municipal flags.

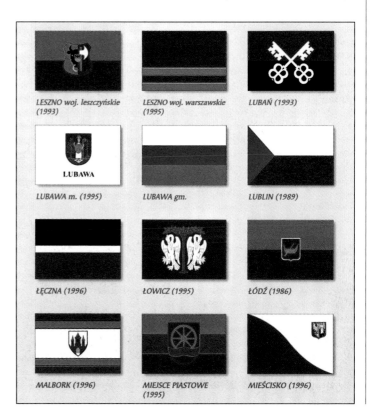

LESZNO woj. leszczyńskie (1993)

LESZNO woj. warszawskie (1995)

LUBAŃ (1993)

LUBAWA

LUBAWA m. (1995)

LUBAWA gm.

LUBLIN (1989)

ŁĘCZNA (1996)

ŁOWICZ (1995)

ŁÓDŹ (1986)

MALBORK (1996)

MIEJSCE PIASTOWE (1995)

MIEŚCISKO (1996)

Millville (New Jersey).

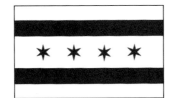

Chicago (Illinois).

Kettering (Ohio).

Lubbock (Texas).

Memphis (Tennessee).

Milwaukee (Wisconsin).

Pittsburgh (Pennsylvania).

New York.

Amsterdam (Holland).

Barcelona (Spain).

Bergen (Norway).

◆ TOP TWO ROWS
United States city flags

◆ BOTTOM TWO ROWS
European city flags

City of London (United Kingdom).

Paris (France).

St Petersburg (Russia).

square, mostly charged with the civic coat of arms and with a decorative border. Official flags are mounted on staffs with a traverse bar.

Heraldry has very much influenced the municipal flags of Norway, Sweden, Great Britain, Finland, Belgium and the Netherlands. In the Netherlands almost all of more than 800 municipalities have their own flags. Over 20 per cent of them are composed only of several stripes (up to 13), in most cases horizontal, in some vertical or diagonal. The designs of the other flags are distinctive and very recognizable, with extensive use of livery colours and the main armorial figures instead of the full arms. Some of the most beautiful municipal flags have been created in South Africa since the 1960s. There are armorial banners, flags with the armorial shield or full achievement of arms, or flags displaying one or a few heraldic figures from the civic arms. Heraldry has also greatly influenced the design of municipal flags in many countries of the Commonwealth, mainly Canada and Australia. In the countries

of Latin America most municipal flags display the whole achievement of the civic coat of arms.

In the United States the most common design of a municipal flag is a plain field, in most cases blue, defaced with the civic seal. The second characteristic is an extensive use of lettering spelling out the city's name, the date of its foundation or incorporation, its locality in a state or county, and its nickname or motto. Some flags have graphic symbols with a written explanation

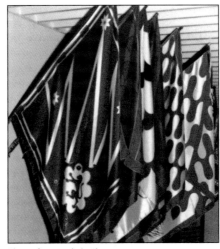

Flags of contrade in Siena.

underneath. As one vexillologist remarked, too many American flags are "literally littered by lettering". There is also a multitude of designs based on both traditional and unusual partitions of the field. The emblems are sometimes so intricate that they are imperceptible when the flag is flying; others are simple, modern and very distinctive. Many newer municipal flags as well as some older flags are excellent examples of ingenious flag design.

Some European cities have different flags for each district. The best known are the colourful flags of the *contrade* in Siena, in Italy, which date back to the beginning of the 13th century. Each *contrada* has its own mayor assisted by councillors. There have been 17 *contrade* since the end of the 17th century. Each *contrada* has its own colours, usually forming an intricate pattern, and an emblem that corresponds to the name of the district (for example, eagle, dragon, giraffe, owl, porcupine, unicorn, panther, and so on). These colours and emblems are used on the square flags which resemble armorial banners.

Flags of Peoples and Causes

Since time immemorial people have been eager to show their colours. In fact there was almost no mutiny, rebellion or defiance movement without its distinctive flag. Since the end of the first half of the 19th century, nations subjugated by world powers began to adopt their own flags. At first there were flags of nations living under the Austro-Hungarian, and then under Prussian or Russian rule. This trend continues, and today several dozen nations without statehood use their flags to denote either their identity or an aspiration to have their own state.

The 20th century witnessed the adoption of flags by political parties and fighters for freedom and independence. The flag of a political movement became the national

flag for the first time when the Nazi flag became Germany's national flag. The Nazis were also the first political movement to treat the flag as a political weapon. The use of flags during parades and rallies created an aura of might and invincibility; a tactic that was later copied by the Soviet Union and China.

Many current flags are closely associated with politics and the struggle for independence. Whether the flag belongs to the Albanians in Kosovo or the Palestinians, it manifests their defiance and aspirations.

◆ **ABOVE**
A demonstrator seen through an Albanian flag in Kosovo, March 1998.

◆ **LEFT**
Palestinian youths armed with a flag and stones approach Israeli soldiers on the West Bank, March 1988.

◆ **RIGHT**
Hoisting a giant flag to celebrate the anniversary of the liberation of Ho Chi Minh City, Vietnam.

NATIONS AND ETHNIC GROUPS

National flags for nations and ethnic or cultural entities without statehood first appeared in North America, where ethnic diversity is greatest. In the United States there are 558 federally recognized Native American nations and tribes. Twenty years ago very few had their own flags but there are currently about 180 tribal flags. Two acts passed by the Federal Government spurred the creation of flags: the United States Self-Determination and Education Assistance Act (1975) and the United States Indian Gaming Regulatory Act (1988) which allowed Native Americans to use gaming and tribal casinos as an economic resource.

The Arapahos in Wyoming adopted a flag during World War II and modified it in 1956. Red stands for the Arapahos, white for long life, black for happiness. Eleven Sioux tribes living in South Dakota have a

Arapaho.

Crow Tribe.

United Sioux Tribes.

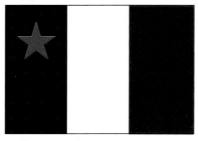

Acadians in Canada.

Acadians in Louisiana.

common white flag. The number of tepees represents the number of tribes, and the arrowheads in the central emblem symbolize the four compass directions, the four seasons and the four natural elements. One of the most distinctive flags, designed in 1967, belongs to the Crows who live in Montana. The tepee symbolizes the home and its four poles represent the original treaty area agreed with the United States Government in 1868. They also stand for the four directions and the four seasons, i.e. for the limits or framework within which life takes place. The flag depicted here has the old seal; in the new one the white star and the stars of the Big Dipper (the Plough) constellation are omitted.

The flag of the Acadians who live in Canada, mainly in northern New Brunswick, was adopted in 1884. It is the French Tricolore with a yellow star, symbol of the Virgin Mary, and symbolizes the Acadians' fidelity to their origins and their faith. The flag of the Acadians in Louisiana was adopted in 1965 when they celebrated the 200th anniversary of their arrival there. It symbolizes their French origins (three fleurs-de-lis on blue) and the Spanish rule over Louisiana at the time of their migration (yellow castle on red). The yellow star symbolizes the Virgin Mary as Our

Lady of Assumption, their patroness, and also commemorates the Acadians' participation in the American Revolution.

African-Americans use the flag created in 1917 by the famous black activist Marcus Garvey for a new homeland for American blacks in Africa. Irish-Americans prefer to use a flag specially designed for them rather than the national flag of Ireland. It is based on the flags of the 1798 rebellion and the Irish motto *Erin go bragh*, meaning "Ireland for ever".

Many nations without statehood live in Europe. Some of them use flags that have become the flags of the regions. For their national flags the Basques, Catalonians and Galicians use the flags of autonomous communities in Spain, while the flags of the

Afro-Americans.

Irish-Americans.

Flamands and Wallons have become the flags of regions in Belgium. The Alsatians are descendants of Germanized peoples of Celtic origin, and those who are striving for a greater degree of autonomy use a red-white horizontal bicolour. The Breton flag displays an ermine canton and nine horizontal stripes. The ermine has been the arms of Brittany since the 12th century, the five black stripes represent the dioceses of the French language, and the four white stripes stand for the dioceses of the Breton language. The Cornish flag is black with the white cross of St Piran, patron saint of Cornwall, and dates back to the beginning of the 15th century.

One of the oldest national flags is a white flag with a Moor's head, an armorial banner of Corsica dating back to at least the 14th century. It is still used by those Corsicans who have never reconciled themselves to French rule over their island. The emblem of the Crimean Tatars, *tarak tamga*, appears in the upper hoist of the field of their flag which is light blue, the national colour common to all Turkic peoples. Although the Kashubians have lived for many

Alsatians.

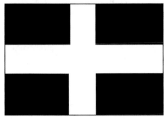

Bretons.

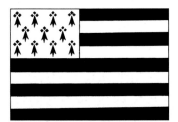

Cornish.

Corsicans.

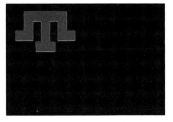

Crimea Tatars.

Gypsies.

centuries under German rule, they have preserved both their language and the consciousness that they are part of the Polish nation. Their flag displays the colours of the coat of arms of the duchy of Kashubia (black griffin on gold), not as a sign of separatism but to show their identity as an ethnic group with their own language, tradition and culture.

Normandy displays two flags: heraldic and modern. The armorial banner with two golden lions (one above the other) on a red field originated in the 12th century. The Scandinavian cross on the modern flag denotes that they are the descendants of people from Scandinavia (via the Vikings). Gypsies, or Romanies, were originally

Kashubians.

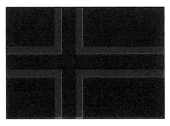

Normans.

nomadic people from India and by the end of the 16th century were living in many European countries. Their flag, not adopted until the 1970s, reflects the fact that the wheel enabled them to move freely on wide green plains under the blue sky. The wheel takes different shapes. One of the newest national flags is that adopted in 1986 by the Samis, or Lapps. For thousands of years these people lived in areas of northern Europe that now belong to Norway, Sweden, Finland and Russia. In 1956 they set up the Nordic Sami Conference, which in 1983 proclaimed the Land of Sami across international borders where they want to preserve their common language, history, traditions, culture and way of life.

Sami.

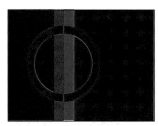

Scots.

The Scottish blue flag with a white St Andrew's cross is one of the oldest national flags in the world but the Scots prefer to use the Royal Banner of Scotland and some Scots living in the United States recognize the banner with the tressured lion as their national flag. The triskelion, an ancient emblem of Sicily known at least from the 4th century BC, is composed of three bare legs and the face of a Gorgon. It appears on the flag used by the Sicilians since 1990 as their unofficial regional flag. In 1848 the Sorbs adopted a flag in pan-Slavic colours: the blue stands for the sky, the red for love and the white for

237

innocence. The Sorbs are the descendants of the Wends, a Slavic people who in the Middle Ages occupied large areas of the eastern part of Germany. Today they predominantly live in Lusatia.

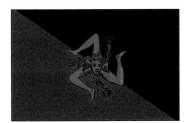
Sicilians.

Sorbs.

In 1950 the Amboinese proclaimed an abortive independent state, the Republic of South Moluccas. Although it was suppressed by the Indonesian army, their use of the national flag manifested their will to be free. The red is the colour of their traditional dress and a symbol of courage; the blue is the sea and its riches; the white represents the beaches, a symbol of purity; the green represents the fertility of the land.

Amboinese

The flag of the Balkars, a Turkic people living in the Caucasus Mountains, was adopted in 1993 and displays the Turkic light blue and a silhouette of Mount Elbrus. The white stands for purity; the upper white stripe symbolizes the heavenly and spiritual attitude of the nation, and the lower stripe stands for their way of life.

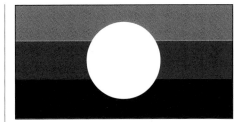
Shans.

Kurds.

Kachins.

Despite the numerous uprisings and promises by world powers that they will have their own state the Kurds, who live mainly in Iran, Iraq and Turkey, are the largest nation in the world still without statehood. Their flag displays the colours of the Iranian flag with a yellow sun in the centre. According to some sources there is also another Kurdish flag: a horizontal tricolour of red, yellow and green. There are several nationalities in Myanmar (formerly Burma) who are struggling to create separate states, among them the Arakans, Kachins, Karens, Mons and Shans. (The Arakans and the Mons in the past formed several kingdoms which existed until the 1700s.) The red and green of the Kachin flag stand for courage and the land respectively, and the crossed native swords represent the love of the homeland and the will to defend it. The flags of at least two liberation movements and parties are used by the people. The ochre in the Shan flag is the colour of the saffron robes of Buddhist monks, testifying that Buddhism

Balkars.

Australian Aborigines.

Kanaks.

is the national religion; the green stands for the land and for agriculture; the red denotes the Shans' bravery, and the white disc of the moon symbolizes their love of peace and their willingness to co-exist peacefully.

The Australian aborigines adopted their flag in 1971 but it was only decreed as their official flag in 1995. The black represents the aborigines, whose ancestors have lived in Australia for more than 40,000 years; the red stands for the earth and for the blood spilled by aboriginal people in defence of their land; and the yellow disc symbolizes the life-giving sun. The flag of the Kanaks, a people native to New Caledonia and striving for independence from France, was introduced in 1984. The colours are significant: the blue symbolizes the sky, perfection and sovereignty; the red stands for blood and the equality of all races; the green represents the land, and the yellow disc symbolizes the sun. The silhouette of an ornamented spire symbolizes tradition.

RELIGIOUS FLAGS

Out of the main religions of the world only one has its own flag, which is used wherever the faithful congregate. It is the Buddhist flag, adopted in 1950 as the internationally recognized flag of all Buddhists of the world. Its five colours represent the five auras that emanated from the Buddha when he was in the Gem Chamber in the fourth week of his enlightenment. According to Buddhist belief, the blue is the colour of the Buddha's hair, the yellow stands for all impure secretions of the human body, the red for blood, the white for bones and for purity of words and deeds, and the orange for those parts of the body that are orange.

Of the many Christian denominations only a few have flags. There is no Catholic flag, but the yellow and white of the Holy See and the white and blue of the Virgin Mary are used to decorate churches at festivals. In the United States a fringed flag

of the Vatican City is used in Catholic churches and a fringed flag of the State of Israel in synagogues; there is also a Christian flag, designed in 1897 for use in Protestant churches. Some Protestant churches do have their own flags: the flag of the Episcopal Church is white with a red cross of St George and a blue canton with nine white crosses in saltire. Since 1938, Church of England churches have displayed a white flag with the red cross of St George and, in the canton, the arms of the see to which the particular church belongs.

In the United States and Great Britain there are church pennants to indicate that a ship's company is engaged in divine service. These date back to the Anglo-Dutch wars and were used to indicate a truce so that services could be performed at sea. In Catholic countries there is a multitude of banners designed to be carried in processions and displayed during

religious holidays. They are mostly pictorial in character, bearing painted or embroidered representations of the Virgin Mary, the Trinity or various saints.

The Muslims have mostly unicoloured flags, usually green, with religious inscriptions and simple emblems such as a crescent or the hand of Fatima. There are reports that in some countries the adherents of the Ismaili sect have a green flag with a red bend. The Sikhs, who live mainly in the Indian state of Punjab have their own flag, although some reports consider this an ethnic rather than a religious flag. It is a triangular saffron (orange) flag with a black traditional Sikh emblem consisting of a ring, two crossed daggers and a spear.

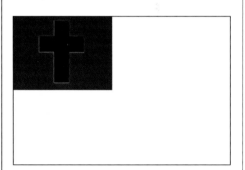

Christian flag.

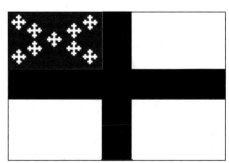

Episcopal church.

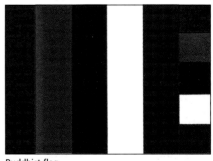

Buddhist flag.

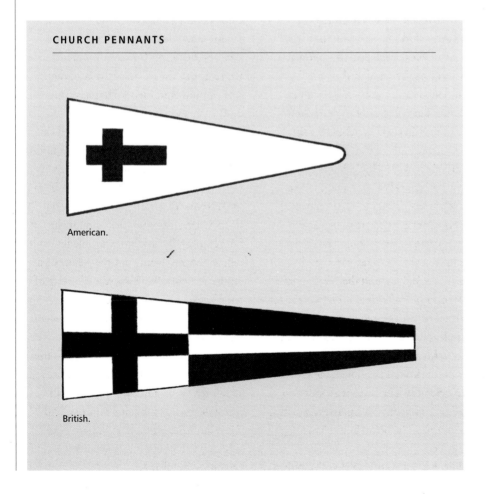

CHURCH PENNANTS

American.

British.

FLAGS OF REVOLT AND DEFIANCE

Throughout the course of history social and political upheavals, rebellions and revolutions have always been carried out under a flag. Some of these flags influenced the design of national flags and a few eventually became national symbols; many more were carried by rebels who did not succeed in their struggle. Their emblems were either symbols familiar to the rebels or new symbols created to convey their ideas. For example, at the end of the 15th century German peasants rebelled under a white pennant with the emblem of a golden peasant shoe, *Bundschuh*, which in contrast with the boots worn by the nobility was a symbol of peasantry. The Bundschuh Rebellion flared up several times until 1525, when it was finally suppressed.

The taxation imposed by the British on the American colonists was met by defiance and led in 1765 to the foundation of the Sons of Liberty, a secret patriotic and radical society that was involved in the Boston Massacre (1770) and the Boston Tea Party (1773). Their flag displayed nine red and white stripes, symbolizing the nine colonies that participated in the Stamp Act Congress of 1765. The stripes in the national flag of the United States may well stem from this defiant flag.

Bundschuh pennant.

Polish peasants with their scythes upright played an important role in the Kosciuszko Insurrection of 1794. In the battles against Russsia they carried a red standard with the motto "Feeding and Defending" above weapons crossed behind a wheatsheaf. In the first half of the 19th century there were numerous kingdoms and principalities in the territory of modern-day Germany. Inspired by the French Revolution of 1830, the students from some of these German states began to agitate for unification. They adopted a flag with three horizontal stripes in the colours of the uniforms of the *Lützow Freikorps* and the inscription *Deutschlands Wiedergeburt* (Rebirth of Germany). Without the inscription, this flag became the national flag of Germany in 1848.

Australia's most famous rebellion was that of the miners of the Ballart goldfields in Victoria in 1854 against the imposition of licence fees. They raised a blue flag with a white cross bearing the five stars of the Southern Cross constellation. A few days

later the flag was raised again by a group of diggers at the Eureka Stockade, who took an oath, "We swear by the Southern Cross to stand truly by each other, and to fight to defend our rights and liberties." The stockade was overwhelmed by the police, but the Eureka flag became a symbol of independence and liberty, and inspired the design of the Australian national flag.

The newest addition to the flags of defiance and rebellion was that of the *Solidarnosc* (Solidarity) movement in Poland. In the first days of the famous strike at the Gdansk shipyard a young artist created a logo in which he spelt the name of the movement in such a way that the letters resembled people marching close together under the Polish national flag. Since then a white flag with this logo has been the symbol of opposition against communist rule, and in a free Poland remains the flag of the trades unions. In two known instances people in revolt did not need to adopt a new flag, it was enough to cut out the communist state emblem from the flag to show what they stood for. The first instance was during the Hungarian uprising of 1956, and in 1989 a flag with a hole in it was again carried in street battles in Romanian cities.

Flag of the Sons of Liberty.

Banner of Polish peasants participating in the Insurrection of 1794.

Flag carried by advocates of the unification of Germany in the Hambach Festival of 1832.

Flag of the Eureka Stockade, Australia (1854).

Flag of Solidarność (Solidarity) since 1980.

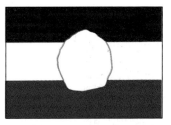

Flag of the Hungarian uprising (October to November 1956).

Flag of the Rumanian uprising (1989).

Flag of the Federal Republic of Padania, an Italian state that does not officially exist.

FLAGS OF GUERRILLA MOVEMENTS

Vietkong.

Sandinistas.

Eritrean People's Liberation Front.

The Tigre Liberation Front.

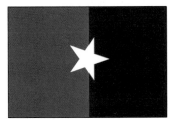

The Western Somali Liberation Front.

SWAPO (South West African People's Organization).

MPLA (Movimento Popular da Libertação de Angola).

UNITA (União Nacional para a Independência Total de Angola).

FNLA (Frente Nacional para a Libertação de Angola).

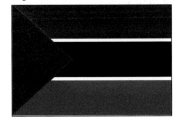

FRELIMO (Frente da Libertação de Moçambique).

RENAMO (Resistencia Nacional Moçambicana).

Kurdistan Workers' Party.

In Italy a peaceful struggle to create a new state of Padania is led by the Northern League, formed in 1984. The Federal Republic of Padania was proclaimed on 15 September 1986 in Venice, but formally does not exist. Nevertheless the flag of Padania with a green "Sun of the Alps" is carried during demonstrations in favour of the new state.

Since the 1960s in various parts of the world, mainly in Africa and Asia, armed insurrections have aimed to achieve independence or to impose a communist regime. The best known are the communist guerrillas of Vietkong in Vietnam and the Sandinistas in Nicaragua. The struggle for independence in Angola was conducted by the MPLA (People's Movement for the Liberation of Angola); the FNLA (National Front of the Liberation of Angola) and the UNITA (National Union for the Total Independence of Angola). In Mozambique the struggle for independence has been

conducted by two movements hostile to each other. The stronger one was the FRELIMO (Front for the Liberation of Mozambique) and its flag, adopted in 1962, displayed the pan-African colours. The other was the RENAMO (Mozambican National Resistance), which rejected both communist and fascist ideologies. The colours of their flag, adopted in 1977, symbolized the nation (blue) and the struggle for independence (red). The field was charged with RENAMO's seal. The Kurdistan Workers' Party is the main political and military force of Kurds fighting for their own state.

For more than a decade its flag has been seen in many cities of Europe during demonstrations for a free Kurdistan.

Two famous rebel flags are still in use. The "Jolly Roger" pirate flag is usually black with images such as a skull and crossbones, or skeletons with a scythe or hourglass. Some people claim that "Jolly Roger" is a corruption of the French *jolie rouge* and in fact the flags of pirates from the Barbary states were red. The jack of the Confederate Navy, used from 1863 to 1865, is also known as the rebel flag. It is still revered by some people and groups as a symbol of southern states' rights.

The Jolly Roger.

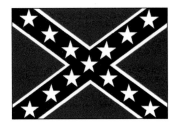

The rebel flag.

FLAGS IN POLITICS

Since late medieval times certain colours have had particular meanings. In Europe white was connected with purity and nobility. Red was originally the colour of empire and royalty but later became the colour of defiance, mutiny and revolution. The combination of red and black is used mainly by anarchosyndicalists. White was adopted by Francis I of France (reigned 1515–1547) and became increasingly popular as the colour of royalty, perceived as such since the 18th century, and today it is the main colour of royalist movements. Black is used on African flags to represent the country and the people. The colour can also have a dual symbolism, being the colour of mourning as well as defiance of law and order. Black flags were used by

Monarchists.

Anarchists.

Socialists.

Anarchosyndacilists.

FLAGS OF NATIONALIST MOVEMENTS

NSDAP 1920–1945. *Nationalsozialistische Deutsche Arbeitspartei.*

Flemish National Union.

Sudeten German Party.

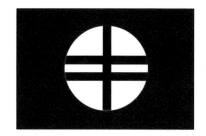

Hlinka Guard.

Arrow Cross.

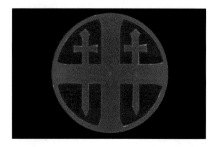

Rikshird.

Fronte della Gioventú.

Freie Arbeitspartei.

Afrikaaner Resistance Movement.

Afrikaans Student Federation.

Yedinstvo, Russian National Unity.

National Bolshevik Party, Russia.

mutineers and pirates, and today they are the flags of anarchists and are often seen at protests. Many anarchists place a large white letter "A" in a ring on the black flag. Red flags were displayed as a sign of defiance as early as the 17th century. Sailors demanding better pay and working conditions hoisted them during mutinies at Portsmouth, England, in 1797 and at St Petersburg, Russia, in 1905. The same flag was used by the revolutionaries in France in 1830, 1848 and 1870, and since the Paris Commune (1871) it has been regarded as a socialist symbol, adopted in the 1920s by the communists in Russia. At the other end of the spectrum, it was also adopted by the Nazis in Germany.

The flag of the NSDAP *(Nationalsozialist-ische Deutsche Arbeitspartei)* was designed personally by Adolf Hitler, who combined the socialist red with two other colours of pre-war Germany. A white disc charged with a black swastika became the symbol used by foreign Nazis. The flag used by the Imperial Fascist League in Britain from 1933 to 1940 had the white disc and swastika in the centre of the Union Jack. The *Parti National Social Chrétien*, founded in Montreal, from 1933 to 1938 had a blue flag charged with a red swastika on the white disc. The flag of the NSDAP also served as a model for emblems adopted by nationalist movements in several countries, during Hitler's lifetime and afterwards. The flags shown opposite were used by the Flemish National Union in the Netherlands, the Sudeten German Party in Czechoslovakia, the Hlinka Guard in

FLAGS OF COMMUNIST PARTIES

Ethiopian Workers' Party.

Revolutionary Party of Benin.

People's Democratic Party of Afghanistan (1980–1992).

FRELIMO (since 1983).

Slovakia, the Arrow Cross in Hungary and the Rikshird in Norway; those currently in use belong to the Freie Arbeitspartei in Germany, two organizations in South Africa and two in Russia. One of the emblems, a black Celtic cross on a white disc, became the international symbol of young nationalists in several European countries. It is placed in the centre of a red field, as in the flag of the Italian *Fronte della Gioventú*.

The Soviet Union was a one-party state so the communists had no need to adopt a special flag. The red flag with a star and crossed hammer and sickle served all purposes and became a model for the flags of communist parties in many countries. Shown here are the flags of the Ethiopian

Workers' Party, FRELIMO (Mozambique) the Revolutionary Party of Benin, and the People's Democratic Party of Afghanistan in which the Soviet sickle has been replaced by a hoe. The fascist movements in Italy and Spain adopted emblems recalling the great past of their countries: the ancient Roman fasces and the yoke and arrows of the Catholic monarchs, respectively.

Many non-socialist political parties have flags displaying the national colours and often charged with the party initials. In Europe and the Middle East party flags display abstract emblems; in Africa and Asia they are charged with simple devices, mainly stylized animals such as an elephant or cockerel to symbolize strength, courage and perseverance.

Featured here is the flag of the National League for Democracy of Aung San Suu Kyi, who leads the struggle for democracy in Myanmar and was awarded the Nobel Peace Prize, one out of the hundreds of flags used by political parties in Asia. The flag combines elements of the flag of the Anti-Fascist Resistance Movement (red flag with a white star) with a peacock, the traditional Burmese emblem.

Socialist party of Belgium

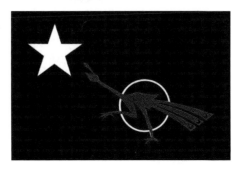

National League for Democracy (Myanmar)

243

House and Private Flags

Most of these flags were introduced in the 19th century; indeed, many of them were introduced in the last half century. The most numerous are yacht and private flags, but there is a steadily growing number of house flags for shipping and trade companies, and all kinds of commercial firms. Tens of thousands of schools, universities, associations and clubs also have their own flags.

◆ BELOW
Flags of shipping companies of North and South America in 1933. Plate from *Lloyd Reederei-Flaggen der Welt-Handelsflotte*, Bremen.

Flags of shipping companies of North and South America in 1933. Plate from *Lloyd Reederei-Flaggen der welt-Handelsflotte*, Bremen.

COMMERCE AND BUSINESS

In the Middle Ages guilds and livery companies had their own banners, used during festivities and in battle. Some of the emblems they adopted, particularly in European countries, represented their trade or occupation: a pretzel represented the bakers; scissors, the tailors; a candle, the candle-makers; a key or keys, the locksmiths; an anchor, the boatmen; and a boot or shoe, the shoemakers.

The first commercial flags were those of the English trading companies, used at the end of the 16th century. The most famous and long-lasting was the East India Company (established 1600), followed by its great rival the Dutch East India Company (established 1602). There was also the Dutch West India Company from 1621 to 1794, which established several

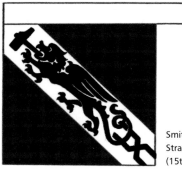
Smith's guild, Strasbourg (15th century).

colonies in the West Indies and Guiana. To distinguish them, their ensigns used national emblems, the English cross of St George and the Dutch horizontal tricolour. The Dutch ensigns differed only in their initials: "VOC" for the *Vereenigte Nederlandsche Oost Indische Compagne* and "WGC" for the *Nederlandsche Geoctroyeerde West Indische Compagnie*. A "C" above the

Smith's guild, Basel (15th century).

"VOC" stood for Capetown. The flags of the six chambers of the Dutch East India Company displayed stripes in different colours, with the initials "VOC" and an additional letter above it: "A" stood for Amsterdam; "D" for Delft; "E" for Eikhuizen; "H" for Horn; "M" for Middleburg, and "R" for Rotterdam. The Danish East India Company and the

Ensign of the British East India Company (c.1616–1707).

Ensign of the British East India Company (1707–1801).

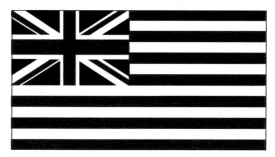
Ensign of the British East India Company (1801–1873).

Ensign of the Dutch East India Company.

Ensign of the Dutch West India Company.

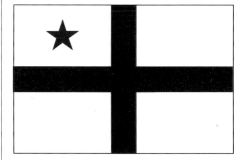
Italiana Trasporti Maritimi.

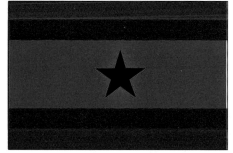
Black Star Line.

BP tanker company.

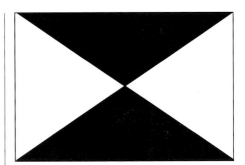

Midland Bank house flag.

Spanish Philippine Company had their own flags based on the national flag. The modern house flags of trade and shipping companies originated at the end of the 18th century. These do not use national flags as a pattern, but sometimes adopt the national colours of their home countries. A rare exception was the flag of the Hudson's Bay Company, which from the 1820s used the British red ensign with the white letters "HBC" in the fly. Since the 19th century each shipping company has had its own house flag, which identifies the company to which a ship belongs. This flag or its emblem is also usually painted on the ship's funnel. The most common characteristics of house flags are simple partitions of the field, and extensive use of initials and simple emblems. One of the simplest yet most distinctive designs for a house flag is that of P&O (Peninsular and Oriental Steam Navigation Company), which became its logo and is used on its land vehicles.

P&O house flag.

The house flags of the shipping companies inspired other commercial firms to adopt their own flags. Among the numerous airline flags, the most distinctive and attractive are (or were) those of Lufthansa, Air France, Sabena, BEA, Swissair and Qantas. Even better known are the flags of oil companies such as Shell, BP, Mobil, Texaco and Statoil, which are displayed at every filling station. Other examples of corporation flags are those of hotel chains (Hilton, Marriott, Sheraton and Holiday Inn), fast food franchises (McDonald's,

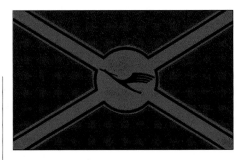

Lufthansa house flag.

Denny's and Burger King) and car manufacturers (Volkswagen, Mercedes, Volvo, Chrysler, Ford and GM). Some corporations conduct business under different names and different flags (for example, Exxon in America, Esso in Europe). Others use flags in different colour variation, for example, Volkswagen uses a white flag with its logo in blue and a blue flag with the logo in white.

The best house flags have simple designs and distinctive features, making them easy to recognize. The general characteristic of a corporate flag is a plain-colour field with a simple corporate logo in the centre. If the logo is very simple, large and has a distinctive shape it is easy to identify from a distance, but unfortunately there is a multitude of flags with intricate emblems and a lot of lettering. As most of the fields are white, hundreds of house flags look alike and are unsuitable for outdoor use because they lack the important characteristic of distinctiveness.

Esso.

Getty oil company.

Statoil.

Volkswagen.

Sheraton.

246

ORGANIZATIONAL AND PRIVATE FLAGS

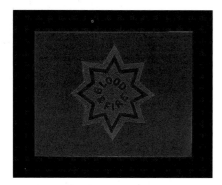

Salvation Army.

World Scouting.

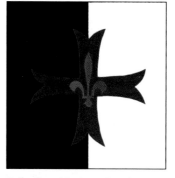

Federation of European Scouting.

Harvard University.

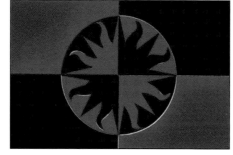

The Smithsonian Institute.

The College of Europe.

In the early 19th century many European countries set up clubs to promote national consciousness, for example gymnastic clubs in the Slavic countries run by Sokol (Falcon), students' corporations and choral clubs. Each of these clubs adopted its own flag or banner which was designed in the artistic spirit of the time. This trend became much stronger in the 20th century and flags and banners were adopted by youth, social and charitable organizations, scientific associations, clubs, schools, universities and even local fire brigades. Two examples of such flags are those of World Scouting and the Federation of European Scouting (FSE); both flags display the fleur-de-lis which is universally recognized as the scout symbol.

Universities and scientific institutions often adopt armorial banners. Their second choice is a unicoloured field defaced with a coat of arms, armorial shield or emblem. The armorial banners of Harvard University and the Smithsonian Institute show that not all flags in the United States display seals combined with lettering. The flag of the College of Europe bears a simple emblem composed of the letters "B" for Bruges, where the school is located, and "E" for Europe; the colours correspond to those of the flag of the European Union.

National colours are also displayed on the flags of vexillological associations. Just two elements – the national colours and the letter "V" (vexillology) – can create many different and distinctive designs. The

Italians made "V" part of their emblem, while the Bretons combined two "V"s (*Vannielouriezh Vreizh* – Breton Vexillological) in a saltire. In the Polish flag the partition line forms "W" for *weksylologia* (vexillology in Polish). The red saltire in the flag of the Belgian association recalls the cross of Burgundy and the yellow "V" stands for "vexillology". The Swiss vexillologists settled for an entirely different design, which resembles the Swiss military flags.

Flags of organizations are quite recent but personal flags have been in use since the beginning of the heraldic era. For example, in Great Britain the armorial banner of the Spencer family was established in 1476 and, before her marriage to Prince Charles, Lady

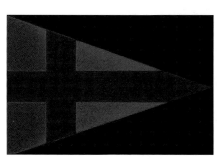

Nordisk Flaggselskab (Denmark, Norway, Sweden).

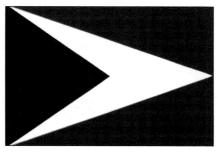

Vexilologický Klub (Czech Republic).

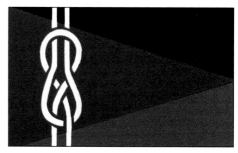

Deutsche Gesellschaft für Flaggenkunde (Germany).

FLAGS OF VEXILLOLOGICAL ASSOCIATIONS

Centro Italiano Studi Vessillologici (Italy).

Societas Vexillologica Belgica (Belgium).

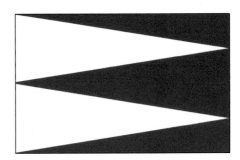

Polskie Towarzystwo Weksylologiczne (Poland).

North American Vexillological Association
(U.S.A. and Canada).

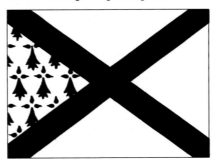

Kevarzhe Vannielouriezh Vreizh (Brittany).

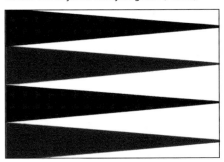

Nederlandse Verenigung voor Vlaggenkunde
(the Netherlands).

Diana Spencer was entitled to use it.
The Spencer arms also appeared in the
second and third quarters of the banner
of Winston Churchill, who inherited them
through the dukes of Marlborough. Many
modern personal flags have also been
designed by famous artists. In some
countries there are festivities for hoisting
private flags.

Two historic venues in Great Britain
permanently display the armorial banners

Sociedad Española de Vexilología
(Spain).

Société Suisse de Vexillologie
(Switzerland).

◆ LEFT
Banners of the Knights Grand
Cross of the Most Honourable
Order of the Bath situated in the
Henry VII chapel, Westminster
Abbey in London.

of the knights of two important orders. The
banners of the Knights Grand Cross of the
Most Honourable Order of the Bath are in
Westminster Abbey in London. These are
the Royal Banner, the Banner of the Prince
of Wales, Great Master of the Order, and
the banners of 33 knights. The armorial
banners of the Knights of the Order of the
Garter are displayed in the Choir of St
George's Chapel in Windsor Castle.

◆ RIGHT
Banner of the Spencer family.

FLAGS IN SPORT

One of the oldest sports is shooting, and in the Middle Ages clubs for crossbowmen had their own flags. This tradition was taken over by rifle clubs, which still exist in many countries of Central Europe. In Great Britain cricket clubs, sailing clubs and rowing clubs have their own flags; the designs are usually based on simple field partitions and some display charges such as crosses, stars, three curved swords, a rampant horse, a rose, anchors or dolphins.

The first and best-known flag used in sport is that of the Olympic Games. It was designed in 1913 and was flown for the first time in public in Paris on the 20th anniversary of the foundation of the International Olympic Committee. The flag was first hoisted at the Olympics in Antwerp in 1920. The white stands for

Flag of Olympic Games.

peace and friendship between the competing nations, and the rings represent the five continents and denote the global character of the Olympic movement. During the opening ceremony a large Olympic flag is raised on a flagpole at the stadium and remains there during the Games. The athletes take the oath holding a corner of the Olympic flag and various forms of the flag are used during the opening and closing ceremonies. At the end of the 1992 Games in Barcelona the athletes held over their heads the largest Olympic flag ever made, 75 m (82 yd) wide and 105 m (115 yd) long.

The most widespread use of flags is by football (soccer) fans. After World War II many football clubs, mainly in communist countries, adopted flags but these were

rarely used and in most cases club regulations did not allow fans to use them. Instead the fans used homemade flags displaying the clubs' colours and even today in most countries flag manufacturers produce such flags, only rarely with the

club emblem. In the United States flag manufacturers produce different flags for the American football teams, with the clubs' colours in common. These flags all serve as a means of identification but in some sports special flags are used for marking and signalling. In many field games small unicoloured flags mark the corners or boundary line of the field and larger flags are used as markers to define the path in skiing events. In soccer the linesmen use two flags (red and yellow, one for each team) to signal to the referee a breach of the rules or that the ball has gone out of play. In car racing a black and white chequered flag is used to signal the end of the race.

Flag of the Redskins, Washington DC.

◆ LEFT
Banner of the Bavarian Rifle Association.

YACHT FLAGS

The first yacht club, the Water Club of the Harbour of Cork, was formed in 1720 in Ireland. Another two clubs (Starcross Yacht Club and Cumberland Fleet) were established in England in the 1770s, but the custom of flying yacht club burgees on the main masthead was not established until early in the 19th century when several dozen yacht clubs were established in Great Britain, and more than 20 in the United

US yacht ensign.

States. Clubs were also established in many countries of the British Empire: Gibraltar, 1829; Canada, 1837; Tasmania, 1838; Bermuda, 1844; India, 1846; Australia, 1853; South Africa, 1858; New Zealand, 1871; Malta, 1873. In Europe, clubs were established in: Sweden, 1830; France, 1838; Russia, 1846; Belgium and the Netherlands, 1847; Portugal, 1856; Denmark, 1866; Germany, 1868.

Four types of flags are used in yachting: (i) ensign, (ii) club burgee, (iii) flag of a yacht club officer and (iv) private flag. The ensign denotes nationality and in Great Britain most of the yacht clubs have the privilege to use either the British red ensign or the British blue ensign, either plain or defaced with the club emblem. In 1922 this privilege was enjoyed by 52 British yacht clubs and today by almost 100 clubs. The first national yacht ensign was adopted in the United States and was approved by the secretary of the Navy on 7 August 1848. It is the national flag but instead of the union with 50 stars it has a blue canton with a foul anchor encircled by 13 stars. Special yacht ensigns exist also in Belgium (civil ensign with the royal crown in the upper hoist), Spain (national flag with a blue royal crown in the centre), France (civil ensign with a white star in the centre of the blue stripe and a blue star on the white stripe) and Poland (civil ensign with a badge in the upper hoist). The Royal Yacht Club of Norway uses the war ensign with the club badge on a white square in the centre of the cross, and the ensign of the Royal Netherlands Yacht Club is the national flag with the badge in the centre.

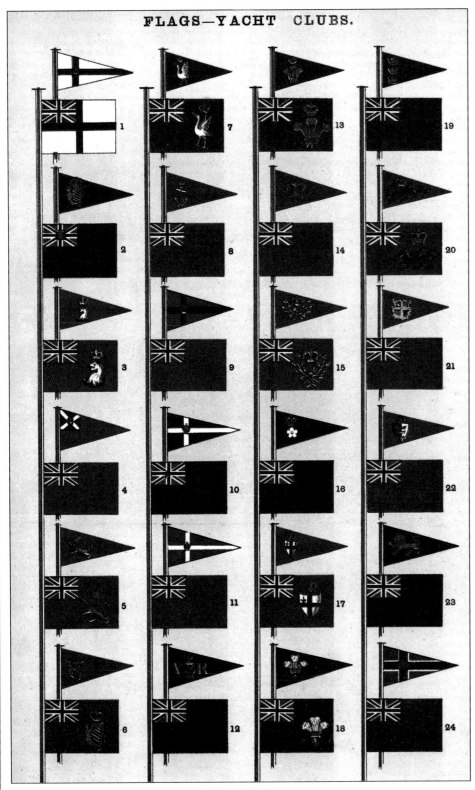

FLAGS—YACHT CLUBS.

Flags and burgees of British yacht clubs at the end of the 19th century.

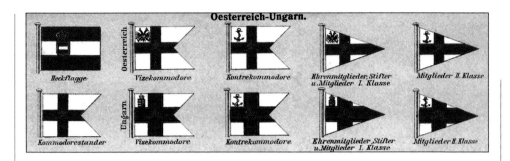

Oesterreich-Ungarn.

Heckflagge — *Vizekommodore* — *Kontrekommodore* — *Ehrenmitglieder, Stifter u.Mitglieder I. Klasse* — *Mitglieder II. Klasse*

Kommodorestander — *Vizekommodore* — *Kontrekommodore* — *Ehrenmitglieder, Stifter u.Mitglieder I. Klasse* — *Mitglieder II. Klasse*

♦ **LEFT**
Flags of yacht clubs officers in Austria and Hungary in 1913. Part of the plate from *Nachtrag III zum Flaggenbuch*, Berlin 1913. (*Top row*) Merchant flag, Austria: vice-commodore; rear commodore; honorary members, founders and 1st class members; 2nd class members; (*Bottom row*) commodore, Hungary: vice-commodore; rear commodore; honorary members, founders and 1st class members; 2nd class members.

In some instances a yacht displays the undefaced war ensign. The first such privilege was granted in Great Britain in 1859 to the Royal Yacht Squadron, and in 1863 the Prussian government entitled members of its Royal House to use the war ensign on their yachts and pleasure vessels. Currently some Italian yacht clubs may also use the war ensign.

The club burgee represents the club of which the yacht's owner is a member. It is usually triangular, in a few instances rectangular or triangular swallow-tailed, and the proportions are 2:3. The burgee of

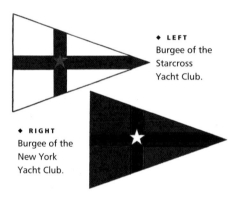

♦ **LEFT**
Burgee of the Starcross Yacht Club.

♦ **RIGHT**
Burgee of the New York Yacht Club.

the Starcross Yacht Club was a canting one, a yellow five-pointed star centred on a blue Cross of St George on a white field. Its design influenced the burgees of several clubs in Great Britain and the United States. A cross and saltire are still today the most popular charges but field partitions are rare; the emblems include crowns, stars, heraldic devices, nautical instruments, species of marine life and initials.

In a few countries officers of yacht clubs have flags, such as those used in the 19th century in Austria-Hungary. Today there are usually four flag officers: commodore, vice-commodore, rear commodore and fleet captain. In some clubs there are also flags for commodores and honorary commodores, as well as for the secretary and treasurer. In at least one instance (Great

Lakes Cruising Club of Chicago) there are distinctive flags for a fleet surgeon and a judge advocate. In the United Kingdom and some Commonwealth countries the flags of club officers are swallow-tailed, otherwise their design is generally the same as the club burgee. The flags of the vice-commodore and rear commodore are distinguished from the commodore's flag by one and two balls respectively in the upper hoist. In the United States the officers' flags have the design of the canton of the yacht ensign; the order of colours is the same as in the Navy.

RANK FLAGS OF YACHT CLUBS IN THE UNITED STATES

Commodore.

Vice-commodore.

Rear commodore.

The private flag represents an individual yacht owner and have their own distinctive style. It is rectangular, only rarely triangular or swallow-tailed. Private flags of yachtsmen are registered to avoid complications that might arise if they were used by more than one person.

In recent decades fun flags have appeared on yachts. They are especially popular in the United States, where they are used to advertise social activities on board such as a party, cocktails or beer. Other fun flags signify "Wife on Board", "19th Hole" or "Jolly Roger".

Fleet captain.

FUN FLAGS

Wife aboard.

Cocktail.

BIBLIOGRAPHY

Much of the data in this book is based on official government publications and flag specifications from the 19th and 20th centuries, preserved in the files of the Flag Design Center, established and managed by the author.

Further valuable information has been extracted from hundreds of articles published in the *Reports* from the International Congresses of Vexillology and in the following vexillological journals:

The Flag Bulletin (Winchester, Massachusetts, U.S.A.); *Das Flaggenkabinett informiert* (Berlin, Germany); *Vexillinfo* (Bruxelles, Belgium); *Vexillologie* (Praha, Czech Republic); *Banderas* (Spain); *Vexilla Italica* (Torino, Italy); *Vexilla Helvetica* (Zollikon, Switzerland); *Vexillologia* (Paris, France); *Vexilla Belgica* (Bruxelles, Belgium); *Raven* (Trenton, U.S.A.); *SAVA Journal* (Pinegowrie, South Africa); *Der Flaggenkurier* (Berlin, Germany); *Flagmaster* (Chester, England) *Znak* (Lviv, Ukraine).

The following are important sources of vexillological knowledge or contain information on particular flags used in this book:

BARRACLOUGH, E.M.C. & CRAMPTON, WILLIAM G., *Flags of the World* (Frederick Warne, London – New York, 1978);

BROWNELL, F.G., *National and Provincial Symbols and flora and fauna emblems of the Republic of South Africa* (Chris van Rensburg Publications (Pty) Ltd, Melville, 1993);

BRUCKNER, A. & B., *Schweizer Fahnenbuch* (Zollikofer & Co. Verlag, St. Gallen, 1942);

CALVO PERÉZ, JOSÉ LUIS & GRÁVALOS GONZÁLEZ, LUIS, *Banderas de España* (Silex, 1983);

CAMPBELL, GORDON & EVANS, I.O., *The Book of Flags* (Oxford University Press, London, 1974);

CANNON, DEVEREAUX D. JR., *The Flags of the Confederacy* (St. Lukes Press and Broadfoot Publishing, Memphis 1988);

COLANGELI, ORONZO, *Simboli e Bandiere nella Storia del Risorgimento Italiano* (Casa Editrice Prof. Riccardo Patron A.S., Bologna, 1965);

CRAMPTON, WILLIAM, *Flags of the World* (Dorset Press, New York, 1990);

DLUGOSZ, JAN, *Banderia Prutenorum* (manuscript, 1448, reprint by PWN, Warszawa, 1958);

FERRO, CARLOS A., *La Bandiera Argentina* (Ministerio de Cultura y Educacion, Buenos Aires, 1970);

Flaggenbuch (Oberkommando der Kriegsmarine, Berlin, 1939);

Flags of the Native Peoples of the United States (Raven, Volumes 3-4, 1996-1997);

Flags of the World (The National Geographic Magazine, Special Edition, 1917);

FURLONG, WILLIAM REA & McCANDLESS, BYRON, *So proudly we hail, the History of the United States Flag* (Smithsonian Institution Press, Washington D.C., 1981);

GALL, FRANZ, *Österreichische Wappenkunde* (Verlag Hermann Böhlaus, Wien – Köln, 1977);

GALLUPINI, GINO, *La Bandiera Tricolore nella Marina Sarda* (Ufficio Storico delle Marina Militare, Roma, 1971);

GALLUPINI, GINO & GAY, FRANCO, *Insegne Bandiere Distinctive e Stemmi della Marina in Italia* (Rivista Maritima, 1992);

GAYRE OF GAYRE & NIGG, ROBERT, *Heraldic Standards and other Ensigns* (Oliver and Boyd, Edinburgh – London, 1959);

GERARD, R., *Flags over South Africa* (Technical College, Pretoria, 1952);

GHISI, E., *Il Tricolore Italiano* 1796-1870 (Milano – Torino – Roma, 1912);

Godlo i barwa Polski Samorzadowej (Instytut Wzornictwa Przemyslowego, Warszawa, 1998);

GORDON, W.J., *Flags of the World, Past and Present, Their Story and Associations* (Frederick Warne & Co., London - New York, 1915);

HAYES-McCOY, G.A., *A History of Irish Flags* (G.K. Hall & Co., Boston, 1979);

HESMER, KARL-HEINZ, *Flaggen und Wappen der Welt* (Bertelsmann Lexikon Verlag, Gütersloh, 1992);

HORSTMANN, HANS, *Vor- und Frühgeschichte des Europäischen Flaggenwesens* (Schünemann Universitätsverlag, Bremen, 1971);

IVANOV, K.A., *Flagi gosudarstv mira* (Transport, Moscow, 1971);

KANNIK, PREBEN, *The Flag Book* (M. Barrows & Company Inc., New York, 1957);

KARTOUS, P., NOVAK, J. & VRTEL, L., *Erby a vlajky miest v Slovenskej republike* (Vydavatelstvo Obzor, Bratislava, 1991);

KIEBOOM, JAQUES VAN DEN, *La connaissance des Pavillons ou Bannieres Que la plúspart des Nations arborent en mer* (La Haye, 1737);

Libro del conocimiento de todos los reinos, tierras y señoríos que son por el mundo (manuscript *c*.1350);

LITTLEJOHN, DAVID, *Foreign Legions of the Third Reich*, vols. 1–4 (R. James Bender Publishing, San Jose, 1987);

LUPANT, MICHEL R., *Drapeaux et Insignes de Gendarmerie et de Police*, Vol. 1, 2 (Centre Belgo-Européen d'Etudes des Drapeaux, Ottignies 1993, 1995);

MEUSS, J.F., *Die Geschichte der Preussichen Flagge* (Mittler & Sohn, Berlin, 1916);

MÜHLEMANN, LOUIS, *Wappen und Fahnen der Schweiz* (Bühler Verlag AG, Lengnau, 1991);

The National Flag of Canada (Department of Canadian Heritage, Ottawa, 1998);

NEUBECKER, OTTFRIED, *Fahnen und Flaggen* (L. Staackmann Verlag, Leipzig, 1939);

OVER, KEITH, *Flags and Standards of the Napoleonic Wars* (Bivouac Books Ltd, London, 1976);

PEDERSEN, CHRISTIAN FOGD, *The International Flag Book in Colour* (Blandford Press, Dorset, 1971);

PERRIN, W.G., *British Flags* (University Press, Cambridge, 1922);

PREBLE, GEO. HENRY, *Origin and History of The American Flag* (Nicholas L. Brown, Philadelphia, 1917);

RABBOW, ARNOLD, *dtv-Lexikon Politischer Symbole* (Deutscher Taschenbuch Verlag GmbH & Co. KG, München, 1970);

RICHARDSON, EDWARD W., *Standards and Colors of the American Revolution* (The University of Pennsylvania Press, 1982);

SCHULTZ, KARL, *Die Deutsche Flagge* (Mittler & Sohn, Berlin, 1928);

SIEGEL, R., *Die Flagge* (Dietrich Reimer (Ernst Vohsen) Verlag, Berlin, 1912);

SMITH, WHITNEY, *Flags Through the Ages and Across the World* (McGraw-Hill Book Co., Maidenhead, 1975);

SMITH, WHITNEY, *The Flagbook of the United States* (William Morrow & Company, Inc., New York, 1975);

STRICKLAND, ADRIAN, *A Look at Malta's Insignia* (Cyan Ltd, Balzan, 1992);

STYRING, JOHN S., *Brown's Flags and Funnels* (Brown, Son & Ferguson, Glasgow, 1971);

Symbols of Canada (Department of Canadian Heritage, Ottawa, 1995);

Wappen und Flaggen der Bundesrepublik Deutschland und ihrer Länder (Bundeszentrale für politische Bildung, Bonn, 1994);

Die Welt im bunten Flaggenbild (Kosmos Sammelbilder, Memmingen, 1950);

WILSON, TIMOTHY, *Flags at Sea* (Her Majesty's Stationery Office, 1986);

WISE, TERENCE, *Military Flags of the World* (Blandford Press, Dorset, 1977);

ZNAMIEROWSKI, ALFRED, *Stworzony do chwaly* (Editions Spotkania, 1995).

INDEX

254